Reconstructing Organization

Dear Martin,

of course this was not possible without you. I found adding anchovies to my Caesar salad gave me all the energy I needed to write this.

All the Best

Damian.

Damian P. O'Doherty

Reconstructing Organization

The Loungification of Society

palgrave
macmillan

Damian P. O'Doherty
Alliance Manchester Business School
University of Manchester
Manchester, UK

ISBN 978-1-137-48920-3 ISBN 978-1-137-48922-7 (eBook)
DOI 10.1057/978-1-137-48922-7

Library of Congress Control Number: 2016956488

Printed on acid-free paper

This Palgrave Macmillan imprint is published by Springer Nature
The registered company is Macmillan Publishers Ltd.
The registered company address is: The Campus, 4 Crinan Street, London, N1 9XW, United Kingdom

Acknowledgements

It is a little over 5 miles from my university office to Manchester airport, but in terms of travel this research not only required the navigation of what can be measured of distance and time but a fundamental change in how one experiences and understands the time, space, and organization of travel. After the work of Marc Augé (1995), it has become somewhat of a cliché to refer to airports as 'non-places', but if you choose – to all intents and purposes – to live in one for a year, as I did, then one might find help and guidance in the stoicism of Epictetus who wrote: 'For you did not come into the world to select unusually fine places', he writes in his Discourses, as reported by Arrian, 'but to live and go about your business in the place where you were born and were enrolled as a citizen' (1989: 2.23). It is certainly those who have been closest to me over the years to whom I owe the greatest gratitude for the completion of this book and for helping me to understand that our future citizenship is with the earth and our dwelling in it – as 'earthlings' or the earthbound' as Bruno Latour has recently called us late moderns – where the true significance of this thesis on loungification is to be found.

Most of all I have to first thank the people who work at Manchester Airport and the Manchester Airports Group, and particularly those who work in Olympic House who opened up their world to me. For 2½ years I was their 'resident anthropologist' or 'terminal man' and without their patience and tolerance I could not have completed this research. My first debt of obligation is to Brad Miller without whom none of this would have been possible. It was his remarkable vision and daring that first allowed me to enter the airport, and his unwavering support and loyalty over the years has got me out of many a nasty scrape, though he couldn't prevent the football tackle that broke and dislocated my right thumb whilst playing football for the airport football team. Unable to write for 6 weeks following this accident, one might suspect foul play, but if I was unable to write I could always rely on the time and patience of those who worked at Olympic House, some of whom may still be a little confused about what all this research meant. I have to thank the former Chief Executive Officer Geoff Muirhead OBE, and the current CEO Charlie Cornish who was able to rescue this research at a time when I was in danger of throwing in the towel. Special note should also be extended to Andy Cliffe who was also instrumental in driving the research forward at this critical time. John Sherrington was a true scholar and inspiring teacher – and managed to summarise my research for me at a time when I was struggling to hold it all together. Mathew Garner was also a tremendous interlocutor and confidant – and if I could keep him supplied with Caesar salad for the rest of his working life I would still be in his debt. Everyone in what was then called 'MAG projects' deserves a mention for their support and indeed in many cases friendship: John Bedson; Dave Gore; Debbie Kelly; Mark Bradley; David "Hannibal" Haimes; Laura Cunnane; Alan Evans; Gemma Garton; Brendan Biggar; Huziafa Patel; Kevin McQue; Jose Perez; Chris Smith; Gavin Taylor; Dave Freeston; Steve Kelly; Gary Knowles; Simon Marriott; Neville Morton; Robert Taylor; and Terry Turner. I also learned a great deal from the Quantity Surveyors who worked at the airport during this time, James Walmsley and John Mayor; both James and John were particularly insightful and generous with their time – though I suspect it was John who tried to make that tackle on the football field. I must also thank Adam Thornton and Sarah Robson of HKR architects who helped me understand Design and Architecture and provided documents and approvals at critical times in the research. In the wider airport, mention should also be made to Bob Molloy. Chapter 7 of this book would not have been possible without Bob, and though now retired I am sure the airport would not work today without his continued absent-presence and inspiration.

Turning to the world of the academy I would like to thank a number of colleagues in the Alliance Manchester Business School, some of whom looked upon my ambition to ethnographically study an airport with a mixture of fascination and revulsion. Without their support, however, I would never have taken this venture. Professor John Hassard should be thanked first and above all. John has managed to hold together a group of Organizational Analysts at Manchester for the past 15 years by virtue of an unstinting commitment to originality, diversity, rigour and creativity. He may not entirely support the position to which this thesis arrives, but without his encouragement to constantly experiment and test what it is possible to think and do in organization studies I doubt I would have had the courage to persist with this airport folly. Amongst that group of Organization Analysts I would like to particularly thank Dr Simon Bailey, Professor Damian Hodgson, Professor Paula Hyde, Professor Leo McCann, and Dr Dean Pierides. Their stimulating conversations, patience and engagements with my work over the years is the kind of daily life-blood that still makes the university such a wonderful place to work.

I also owe a big thanks to Professor Paul Cousins and Professor Martin Walker. Both served time as chair of the School Research Committee during my research for this book, and both were able to find financial support without which I would not have been able to continue. Ethnography demands levels of time commitment that in the current climate may appear expensive and 'inefficient' and so it is a pleasure to work amongst colleagues who have not succumbed to the barbarism and seducements offered by the neoliberal university. The former head of school Professor Mike Luger was also encouraging and supportive and his sartorial advice on black tie corporate events was most welcome. Assistant head of school until 2014, Cathy Cassell was also instrumental in calming the nerves of some senior executives in the airport, and her charm and wit at lunch was perhaps a significant game-changer in keeping the project on track.

Another very important group of people are those colleagues who work in Social Anthropology at the university of Manchester and members of 'Theme 4' at the ESRC Centre for Research in Socio-Cultural Change (CRESC) at Manchester University and the Open University. It was through CRESC funding that I was first able to commit a year of full time study to the ethnography in 2009/2010, a rare privilege in Higher

Education these days. I owe a special debt of gratitude to Professor Penny Harvey, who really made this project happen. It was her enthusiasm and indeed unpaid supervision that helped develop my appreciation of ethnography and what it could be made to do. Penny also read and commented on several chapters in this book, and this work bears the influence of her incisive reading and commentary. Not without a certain mischief, Penny and colleagues at CRESC thought that my funding application would make an interesting 'experiment': what happens to a mid-career business school academic who basically wants to return to the equivalent of laboratory 'bench work'? Needless to say I would not have been able to navigate this intellectual and existential undoing without the support of a number of colleagues and friends in CRESC – Dr Gillian Evans, Dr Gemma John, Dr Hannah Knox (now at University College London), Dr Keir Martin (now at the University of Oslo), Dr Madeleine Reeves, Dr Nick Thoburn, and Professor Albena Yaneva, all of whom have been hugely influential on the development of my thinking over the years. I would also like to thank Professor Karel Williams. A legend to many in the academy, Karel provided everything that could be hoped for in a research centre director and I learned a great deal from him about how to deal with particularly unpleasant sections of our mass media.

I am also fortunate in being part of a broad if dispersed community of researchers who continue to recognise the importance of the social sciences and humanities in business and management studies. First there is an international group of scholars broadly aligned with 'Critical Management Studies'. Of most importance for my work has been the influence of Professor Hugh Willmott. Each line of this thesis is in some ways dealing with his immense contribution and legacy to business and management studies. My former 'DoctorFather' as PhD supervisors are called in Europe, Hugh has been a tremendous inspiration and influence and though I fear this airport research ends up in spaces that will not meet with his approval, this book is in many ways a sustained appreciation and conversation with his work. Others in the community of critical management studies to whom I owe a special debt of gratitude include Professor Theo Vurdubakis of Lancaster University. Theo is without doubt one of the most modest scholars in the academy but his erudition and learning is surely without equal in the Business School. He has been a constant companion during this research and an important influence on its direction; I am not the first to acknowledge his intellectual breadth and depth, and he has been there throughout the time it took to complete this research. Indeed his influence dates back to 2003 when Theo had been a co-enquirer into airports, and this book reflects many, many important conversations I have been fortunate to share with him over the years. Dr Chris Westrup has also provided an enormous amount of time and thought, and as Principal Investigator of an earlier ESRC funded research project [ESRC RES-334-25-0012 'The Role of ICT based applications on business knowledge processes'] Chris was instrumental in making the airport available as a site for empirical research. As a member of this research team, Dr Hannah Knox should also be acknowledged (again), and without whom I might never have made that first crucial interview with airport staff back in 2005.

I have also benefitted immensely from a group of scholars to whose work I have become extremely close in recent years and who have become important readers of my ethnographic work at the airport. Each chapter has been read and commented on extensively by each of these people and I am forever in their debt: Brian Bloomfield, Steve Brown, Peter Case, Bill Cooke, Barbara Czarniawska, Liz McFall, Daniel Neyland, Martin Parker, and Helene Ratner. I would also like to thank Gibson Burrell who is of constant inspiration. His incisive reading of the introduction to this book helped push me to be more careful whilst also being bolder in reach and argument. He remains a true exponent of the principle to always connect! I should also mention at this stage the importance of Bruno Latour and his collaborators working on the on-going AIME project (An Inquiry into Modes of Existence). Sections of this work were read at the Copenhagen workshop 24th–26th February 2014 and I benefitted enormously from the contributions of Bruno Latour, Christoph Leclercq, Donato Ricci, Vincent Lepinay, Pierre-Laurent Boulanger, and Patrice Maniglier. Other members of that workshop included Paul Kockelman, Gustavo Onto, Emil Urhammer, Carsten Wergin, D.T. Cochrane, Niels Albertsen, Oz Gore, Jose Ossandon, Anna Seravalli, and Anders Blok.

Early versions of papers that eventually formed this book were read at a number of seminars and I would like to thank in particular my good friend Christian de Cock at Essex University and his colleagues who attended the reading of chapter 5 in March 2014: Philip Hancock, Sam Warren, Martyna Sliwa, Chris Land, and Steffen Boehm, were notable for their incisive questions and commentary, but whose intellectual company I have benefitted from since the start of my academic career. Carl Rhodes organized a reading of a very early chapter 6 at Leicester University in March 2014 and was most supportive in his response and critique. Steve Linstead at York University invited me to keynote his annual CEGBI/CSWL/WRCEO summer conference at York University in June 2014 where I was able to present an outline of the thesis at a time when I was still struggling with its overall shape and contribution. I would like to thank Professor Marcus Lindhald at the Institutionen för Teknikverenskaper in Uppsala Universitet for inviting me to present 'Olly' in January 2015. I should thank Thomas Lennefors, Rickard Grassmam, David Skold and Nina Fowler, for their help in organizing and contributing to my work over those 2 days in Uppsala.

Many former and existing PhD students of mine should also be mentioned. Without doubt they have been the most generous and severe critics over the years. Above all they have been close *close* readers of my work and I have surely learned more in trying to teach them than they have from I. Early drafts and final chapters were read by Rowland Curtis, Sideeq Mohammed, Daniel King, and Felicity Heathcote-Márcz, and I thank them all for their generosity of spirit and on occasion for putting up with requests for proofreading at 2 am and for help with referencing and various other requests for help with diagrams, drawings and SmartArt.

As is the want of many academics I have tried and tested the patience of my publisher and hence I would like to formally thank and acknowledge the support of Liz Barlow and Maddie Holder at Palgrave-Macmillan who have both done far more than might reasonably expected in ensuring this rather unconventional book achieves publication.

Finally, none of this would have seemed worthwhile without the support of my wonderful family: Hannah, Imogen, Francesca and Beatrice. I started this research as a single man, and on its completion I was married with 3 children. How this happened or how I deserve this will surely remain a mystery.

* A version of chapter 7 was published as 'Feline politics in organization: The nine lives of Olly the cat' in *Organization* vol. 23(3): 407–433.

Contents

List of Figures

1

An Introduction to Loungification

The Business School

How are we being organized today? From the perspective of the social sciences many would point towards things such as 'business', 'finance', 'management' and 'the economy' as the main forces organizing our lives. In recent years, these have become subjects appropriated and in part re-invented by the contemporary business school and displaced from their origins in the social sciences. Such basic questions about organization – *what is it that is organizing us* – however, threaten the boundaries and integrity of these divisions. So broad in ambition, it appears to lack sufficient focus and threatens to return analysis to interminable doubts about those hoary old chestnuts, epistemology and ontology. Most would rather defer questions about these topics to colleagues in departments of philosophy so that normal science might prevail allowing research to continue its onwards and upwards advance towards mastery and complete knowledge.

One candidate answer to the question of how we are being organized might well point to the airport, and if there is a place or 'non-place' (Augé 1995) where the boundaries around modern knowledge suffer from vertigo and jet-lag it is these strange border posts of the nation state. And

D. O'Doherty, *Reconstructing Organization*,
DOI 10.1057/978-1-137-48922-7_1

Fig. 1.1 The Escape Lounge, Manchester Airport Terminal 1

yet we must beware when stepping inside the airport. The airport is a 'Bermuda triangle for concepts' according to the architect Rem Koolhaas, and a place where all manner of bombast and exaggeration finds inspiration. Airports are at the centre of what is called today 'global business' and the much-lauded inter-connected network society of which Castells (1996) has spoken. What some see as the coming age of the 'aerotropolis' (Kasarda and Lindsay 2011) is also being driven by new business focused on these so called mega-project border cities (Taylor 2004) where the boundaries of the nation state dissolve into the bounties of inter-national or post-national commercial opportunity.

Not that the Business School has been of much help in this business growth, the reasons for which are partly constitutive – in the way the British schools have been set-up following the Franks report in 1963 (Wilson 1992), for example, but also in part institutional inertia. The oldest and most respected schools are essentially publicly funded and underwritten by the state. They have become – as many have shown – old and complacent institutions running outmoded teaching programs based on a model of business that was probably not even relevant in the 1960s (Chia 1996; Engwall and Zamagni 1998; Pfeffer and Fong 2002; Mintzberg 2004; Bennis and O'Toole 2005; Knights 2008). Strictly speaking, nor can Business Schools be seen to provide anything of competitive advantage for its students and clients. Hence, they are 'constitutively' and practically useless – for some, the basis of their very charm, or danger.

The business school would have certainly failed to provide the conditions within which the major claims of this book could have been nurtured and developed. These claims require transgression, or a series of transgressions, some of which include the very audacity of proposing to take time out mid-career to return to primary fieldwork, and *ethnographic* fieldwork at that. However, it was on the basis of what eventually became 2½ years full-time ethnographic fieldwork at Manchester Airports Group in the UK, that this study was able to uncover the spread of this thing called 'loungification'.

Whilst ethnography remains an alien species to most in the mainstream of the Business School, even fewer people will have heard of this 'loungification'. In many ways loungification is a business akin to a vast social experiment, but it remains at the time of writing only a 'minor' genre of social change in contrast to the rather more dramatic claims made on behalf of 'McDonaldisation' (Ritzer 1993) or 'Disneyization' (Bryman 2004). The elements out of which loungification is being woven fall below the radar of most business and management studies, and are to be found in relations that are not visible to the dominant epistemological and ontological assumptions and paradigms within which business and management studies is conducted (Burrell and Morgan 1979; Bryman and Bell 2015). Much of the burden of this book is devoted to an explanation of how it is possible to trace this loungification and to take the measure of its organizational implications. As yet though, we do not have the linguistic and conceptual resources nor even the sensibility within which to track the fleeting signs and nascent patterns of organization through which loungification is being forged. Organization Studies perhaps offers the best chance, however, a discipline noted for a greater tolerance and experimentation with ontological and epistemological practice than is typical of subjects promoted by the business school (Hassard and Parker 1993; Czarniawska 2012; Burrell 2013; Adler et al. 2014)

Organization Studies

To learn something of new business, or how innovation works, it seems we have to step outside the curriculum and administration of the Business Schools, and to re-think *organization*. Staffed by people who, it will be said, do not have the stomach or presumably the talents for the demands of the business world, these moribund institutions could not be more irrelevant for the understanding of how business develops nor how business might be developed in ways that will best sustain our collective potentialities and possibilities. If there is an underlying logic that informs 'The Business School' in toto, it would be one that always looks to commodify and recycle last year's trend, to schematise it, and to reduce it into ready-made formulas and equations. In what is essentially a parasitical exercise, the most ambitious schools want the big stories, the blue-chip clients, the FTSE one hundred, and the patronage of the large and prestigious world of corporate giants. This is all *dead* business, however, and its veneration amongst the mass market only serves to generate graduates destined to become its call-centre clerks and administrators. This is a diagnosis towards which many in the mainstream of business and management studies have slowly been moving and there is now a small industry in jeremiads and journal publication bemoaning the state of the business and management studies curriculum (Pfeffer and Fong 2002, 2004; Bennis and O'Toole 2005; Mintzberg 2004; Khurana 2007; Pfeffer 2009; Rubin and Dierdorff 2009).

Ironically, under the patronage of the business school – or *despite* this patronage – Organization Studies as a discipline and practice has proliferated and diversified in recent years (Parker 2000a; Knudsen 2003; Burrell 2003, 2013; March 2007; cf. Pfeffer 1993). And if there is a subject area in the business school that has promoted ethnography it is *Organization Studies* (Ybema et al. 2008; Czarniawska 2012; Garsten and Nyqvist 2013). Indeed, there is a case to be made that the very foundations of this discipline are rooted in anthropological methods given the importance of ethnographic research conducted at Hawthorne and reported in Roethlisberger and Dickson (1939). In addition, major breakthroughs and promising paradigmatic challenges to the understanding of organization are usually accompanied and supported by ethnographic research (e.g. Mayo 1945; Dalton 1959; Burawoy 1979; Latour and Woolgar 1979; Kondo 1990; Rosen 2000; de Rond 2008). What happens first in Organization Studies, we might say, soon happens for the rest of business and management studies. The recent *Oxford Handbook of Management Theorists* (Witzel and Warner 2013), for example, offers some indication of the significance of the problematic of general organization for stimulating 'pay-off' in terms of major breakthroughs in theoretical and practical management.

Organization Studies has also proven to be one of the most daring disciplinary or post-disciplinary subject areas in the Business School and the connections it forges with the social sciences and humanities means that it is constantly innovating and experimenting.[1] One virtue of this intellectual restlessness and curiosity is that it can help generate sensitivity (but also suspicion) to novelty and creativity associated with contemporary business and management, one expression of which is a phenomenon identified in this ethnography as 'loungification'. Of most help in this study are those advances in Organization Studies that have sought to sidestep the most obvious categories and standardised forms in which business and management is represented – strategy, accounting and finance, corporate governance, human resources, marketing, leadership, etc. Instead of looking at organization in the way business and management like to represent its activities, Organization Studies have sought to deploy a whole series of otherwise marginal, tangential, and even apparently aberrant categories of analysis as a way of navigating or traversing business practices. Grappling with the most basic questions, 'what is business?', and 'how is it managed?', these angular cuts through organization help illuminate business practices in often surprising and unsettling ways. For one practitioner of the ludic and irreverent, for example, we can learn more from business and management by approaching it with language of magicians and devils, Dionysiac cults, hirsute wild men, and the bizarre sado-masochistic couplings of man and beast (Burrell 1997)!

Despite this often wild creativity, Organization Studies has not really challenged what is considered by many to be the fundamentals of business and management studies. Instead, the subject has been positioned by many of its most creative exponents as *surplus* or *remainder* to the mainstream. After all, it is neither an occupational specialism nor an expert business management discourse-practice, and this remains either its strength

[1] A sign of weakness for some i.e. Pfeffer (1993), who would rather have Organization Studies replicate the methods of economics so that power can be acquired around the institutionalization of a consensus program.

or weakness. No one in the world of business, for example, is 'Head of organization'. Practitioners in the world of business can speak of strategy, accounting and finance, marketing and human resources, but they rarely operate with an understanding of what this thing called 'organization' is. And those specialists with responsibility for its teaching and research would be equally hard pressed to define or explain it. Despite its multiplicity and 'aporetic' conditions of possibility (O'Doherty 2007), the study of organization has largely been domesticated and neutered – either in the form of 'organization behaviour' that fits the purposes of the dominant paradigm of 'institutional theory' (see Greenwood et al. 2012; cf. Willmott 2015; Quattrone 2015), and thereby deemed functional for MBA teaching, or in a form that is too easily re-presented as a shopping cart of images and metaphors (Morgan 1986). This has left those who prefer the less behaviouralist connotations associated with 'Organization Studies' – usually based in Europe – to proliferate their highly theorised discourse, whether Lacanian, Foucauldian, or Derridean, and to bask in the margins of the Business School (see also Clegg 2006). Here, Organization Studies seems content to enjoy the intellectual superiority of scholarly integrity – familiarity with the current state of Continental European philosophy, for example – whilst leaving business credibility to those who peddle the tired clichés of managerialism (cf. Knights 2008; Reedy and Learmonth 2009).

The Escape Lounge

Despite the strengths of organizations studies, a taste for the eccentric and exotic may not have been sufficient to alert attention to the strange goings-on taking place out in a field in one small part of (an ever decreasing) England – in the civil parish of Ringway, a small and almost forgotten community that lies somewhere in the borderlands of Manchester and Cheshire. However, inside this field a state-of-the-art luxury airport departure lounge called the Escape Lounge was built over a period of 9 months between August 2009 and June 2010. Its effects and repercussions are legion forming part of what this study identifies as a nascent movement in organization called 'loungification'. One dimension of this loungification is that the Escape Lounge becomes a model for a series of lounges branded 'Escape' that have been opening up within the terminals of an expanding Manchester Airports Group. However, beyond the airport, lounges have rapidly been taking over our high streets and even our universities. We are on the cusp, it seems, of 'lounge life'. Yet, at the time of its construction, the Escape Lounge might have appeared to be the most unremarkable of projects. With a modest budget of £1.7 million project spend against an estimated yearly profit of some £500,000 over a 10-year life cycle, it was not the most exciting or audacious business project to have been conceived. Composed of tried and tested business planning scenarios, in which much of the design was based on a derivative concept inspired by the earlier construction of the Heathrow Airport 'Virgin clubhouse lounge', the lounge would not have attracted much interest – and certainly not from those working in the business school.

In many ways, ethnographic preoccupations with the physical site of the lounge and what might happen in and around the immediacy of its locality would typically produce a classic micro-study of its local business, management and construction. However, such an approach risks myopia, particularly as this particular Escape Lounge in terminal 1 at Manchester Airport is only one specific instantiation of what we have been able to discover of 'loungification'. How to explicitly diagnose this loungification phenomenon remains the central burden of this thesis. At this stage one might liken it to a process of enculturation that takes place between and beyond any one formal organization that simultaneously changes the scales in which we normally attribute organizational phenomena: i.e. macro and micro, structure and agent. To detect it requires sensitivity to the peculiar ontological status of loungification, which like some Borgesian conceit refuses to admit, for example, customary distinctions between fact and fiction.

To make headway in this peculiar ontology this study reports on the development of loungification as an experimental concept. With this concept the ethnography sought to learn from the field so that it could replace and re-situate any preoccupation with the specifics of local particular site within a more extended network of materials, relations and practices. Ethnography is typically critiqued for this preoccupation with the 'local' at the expense of the 'global', the 'micro' and not the 'macro' (Burawoy 1985; Buraway et al. 2000). One way of reconnecting the local and global is to recognise how the aesthetic design of the Escape Lounge is only one component in a complex array of causalities and determinations that are clearly not *unique* to the practices of a local management team. Instead 'concept design' and other practices must be understood as part of wider professional bodies of knowledge and discourse-practices. As we follow the various actors at play in the world of business and management, ethnography is soon drawn back to the very place from where this study started – namely the business school, and specifically the Alliance Manchester Business School.

Recent developments in organization analysis have been attracted to the promise of aesthetics and design, which has become popular in what is now widely regarded as a spatial and aesthetic turn in the discipline.[2] Important work by Gabriel (2005) on 'glass palaces', for example, and Dale and Burrell's (2008) project on 'an-aesthetics and architecture', build productively on a long line of research in organizational aesthetics (Frost et al. 1985; Gagliardi 1990; White 1996; Strati 1999; Linstead and Hopfl 2000). To pursue this approach would, however, prove equally misleading. To abstract and isolate the aesthetic form, or one particular instantiation of loungification would commit an error similar to that of 'historicism' in historical study (Foucault 1971a; Latour 2005b). Typically, this form of historical analysis proceeds on the basis of *anachronistic* concepts and categories that reflect a taken-for-granted contemporaneity, the classic error in this method being the study of 'society' in the 'premodern' era.[3] This serves only to retrieve history for the purposes of domestication that supports a prevailing status quo and fails to fully grasp the genealogical method pioneered by Foucault but so often claimed of inspiration in organization studies.

What was distinctive about Foucault was an approach that not only sought to *expose* what remains apriori fragile and contingent in the contemporary[4], but also his commitment to *actively* participate in the test-

---

[2] See also Baldry (1999), Case (1999), Beyes and Steyaert (2012), Burrell and Dale (2008), Calori (2002), Carr and Hancock (2008), Clegg and Kornberger (2006), Czarniawska (2004a, b), Dale and Burrell (2008), Halford and Leonard (2006), Kornberger and Clegg (2004), Knox et al. (2008), van Marrewijk and Yanow (2010), O'Doherty (2008), O'Doherty et al. (2013), Taylor and Spicer (2007), Tyler and Cohen (2010).

[3] Society was a discursive invention of the modern period, either sociological in origin as in many popular accounts (Bauman 1989), or bourgeois, deployed as a way of delimiting the wealth and the otherwise 'divine' jurisdiction of the 'ancien regime' and its sovereignty (see Foucault 2003).

[4] 'Expose' belies a simple representational and realist discourse at odds with the 'activist' politics of Foucault's histories.

ing and possible amplification of that which *might be made* – or might be being made fragile and contingent, and so giving opportunity to the extension of political experiment and its sites of contestation. This *making* contingent in and of the present typically happens through actions, forces and relations that are not immediately or easily evident to the bureaucratic practices of the scholarly disciplines.

'Contingency' has of course has been a perennial problem in the discipline of Organization Studies, defined and re-defined in a number of ways since Hawthorne and the Aston Studies. Recent developments have sought to re-think contingency using the work of Laclau (1990) and Laclau and Mouffe (1985) which promise much to revitalise its political significance. This approach brings with it a highly theorised arsenal of concepts including 'radical contingency', 'hegemony', 'antagonism', 'dislocation', 'constitutive outside', 'floating signifiers', and 'negative ontology' (see Willmott 2005; Bohm 2006; Spicer and Bohm 2007; Al-Amoudi and Willmott 2011; Glynos et al. 2012, 2015; Cederström and Spicer 2014; Lok and Willmott 2014; Thompson and Willmott 2015).[5] Some mastery of Lacan and Derrida is required here to understand the full significance of these concepts, but synthesised in Laclau and Mouffe forms something like an analytical system that its supporters claim provides powerful explanations for how political struggle becomes organized in complex and over-determined ways.

If genealogy can best recover the *contingencies* of the present by engaging in history, how Organization Studies might best contribute to an ontological delimitation of the present remains an open question. The work of Laclau and Mouffe seems promising in this respect. However, central to the work of Foucault, and consistent with the ambitions of the interlocutors associated with what has become known as 'post-structural' continental philosophy (i.e. Deleuze and Guattari, Derrida, Cixous, Irigaray), is a commitment to something that looks like a form of *praxis* but one directed towards the invention and opening up of new lines of political struggle and contestation.[6] The radical *immanence* of this praxis

[5] A full reference list and review of this material can be found in O'Doherty (2015).

[6] Crucially, the analyst does not occupy the position of all-knowing, theoretically abstract sovereign agent (addressed most explicitly by Foucault in his interviews and essays collected in Kritzman (1988).

is, however, often missed by Laclau and Mouffe and their followers, who operate with an intricate and coherent *anterior* theoretical apparatus (or machine) formed on the basis of underlying transcendental moral and political commitments. Once 'applied' this apparatus can quickly enrol and re-inscribe practices and events into utopian and totalising social blueprints. In other words, it misses what is *event-like* in organization, which simultaneously changes and reinvents our conception of *what* is political and what is *possible* politically (cf. Bohm 2006). A question then, and one of perhaps more radical intent, is *how* one might extend and animate 'the political' – or how one might seize a politicisation *latent* in new objects and problematics. 'Distributed' across a range of heterogeneous and apparently *disconnected* practices and materials these objects and problematics might form 'parts' of an hitherto unforeseen and emerging discourse-practice of political change.

Such immanence poses a considerable challenge to Organization Studies. One promising route towards a grasp of this immanence might be advanced by way of an ethnographically informed – or an ethnographically *transformed* – Organization Studies capable of grasping what some have called the 'happening' of organization, or what Schatzki (2006) calls 'organizations as they happen' (see also Knox et al. 2015). The political implications of engaging with this dimension of organization still remain muted, yet from process theory to practice theory[7] the efforts to engage and study organization as (variously) verb, becoming, crisis, uncertainty, event, or happening, are myriad and have attracted some of the most significant theorists of organization.[8] How to forge a distinctively *organization* analysis has, however, proved more difficult. Typically, the most insightful analysis of process and becoming draw heavily, almost derivatively, on concepts devised for more abstracted and philosophical purposes. So, in these contributions we learn a lot about Bergson, or Bateson, Deleuze, Serres, and Whitehead, for example, but what difference *organization* makes is not often so clear.

---

[7] Both deserve generous referencing and a veritable library now exist of studies that exemplify and extend this approach, but authoritative reviews can be found in Feldman and Orlikowski (2011), Nicolini (2012), and Sandelands and Tsoukas (2016).

[8] It is noteworthy that some of the most established and possibly conservative of North American organizational analysts responsible for the positivist and functionalist foundations of the discipline have sought revision in the light of recent interest in contingency, improvisation and the limits of rationality (see March, 2007).

The widely respected practice-based 'turn' does have the merit of focusing on the minutia of habits, rituals, and practices in work organization, as they are constituted through socio-technical materials. Of most significance is the possibility that the practice-based turn attends to a multitude of human and non-human 'agencies' in ways that allow us to study a complex *distribution* of action – what Hutchins (1995) sought to specify in terms of a 'distributed cognition'. Such complexity and distribution means that socio-technical relations observe no teleology or 'higher' logic and can only ever be partially orchestrated to form something that might appear as coherent organization (Law 2004). This offers significant advance in both method and theoretical conception, and yet despite these gains there is still significant myopia in focus carried by an intellectual problematic marred by a restrictive realism. Most research in this genre remains confined to discrete bureaucratic and managerial practices that are understood to take place within a highly conventionalised 'formal' bounded organization. In addition, as some have pointed out, the practice-based turn does not fully grasp the intricacies of reflexivity intrinsic to the ambitions of the turn to practice and to which it only pays lip service (Gad and Jensen 2014).

Is it possible to study the mundane, everyday 'practices' in ways that do not lose sight of what is traditionally called the 'bigger picture' – whether we understand this bigger picture as politics or ontology – or in ways that can situate organization as a multitude of partially orchestrated socio-technical agencies complicit in the making of *ways of being or becoming in the world*? Weick (1985, 1993), for example, has established a managerially relevant and practical mode of studying organization in which organization is understood as a generalised collective 'existential' condition, constituted by the periodic interruption of what he calls 'cosmology episodes'. The imaginative scope of this conception is compelling, despite the restrictive humanism latent in this work. Recent developments in what has been called the 'ontological turn' seem more promising in helping us position the apparently mundane matters of management and work organization within a more expansive attention to *ontological* or for Stengers (2010, 2011) 'cosmopolitical' matters.[9] And in airports,

[9] The concept of a 'cosmopolitical' is patiently derived by Stengers (2010, 2011) in two volumes of detailed exegesis and critique of modern scientific knowledge. In brief, the cosmopolitical is distin-

management might well be considered to be implicated in the *cosmopolitics* of taming the skies and moving heaven and earth to establish an extra-terrestrial infrastructure for business, travel and recreation.

Ontological Politics

The ontological turn is most popularly associated in Organization Studies with the 'ontological politics' of Annemarie Mol (1999, 2002), and it is also used extensively albeit often implicitly in the work of John Law (Law 2004; Law and Benschop 1997), but it now embraces a vast and multifarious range of approaches, sparking controversy and heated debate (see the debates in Holbraad et al. 2014).[10] Sometimes referred to as 'empirical philosophy' by Mol (2002) – or 'empirical metaphysics' – the ontological turn draws on conversation with recent advances in the social studies of science and technology (Haraway 1989; Latour 1993) and a diverse range of work in contemporary anthropology – including Viveiros de Castro (1992), Helen Verran (2001), Marisol de la Cadena (2010, 2015), Mario Blaser (2010) and Eduardo Kohn (2013), all of whom are variously engaged in what is called 'post-representational' and 'post-reflexive' forms of ethnography (Maurer 2005; Riles 2001; Strathern 1988, 1999).[11] Of

guished from the more humanist cosmopolitan by virtue of a broadly constructivist ('instaurational' would be more accurate, following Souriau (1943) – see Latour and Stengers 2016) and post-foundational analytics. Both the 'cosmos' and the 'political' must be grasped as mutually constitutive, neither has priority, there is no social construction, or astrophysical apriori real.

[10] Alcadipani and Hassard (2010) have sought to recommend an ontological politics for Organization Studies, but by virtue of being a meta-theoretical account largely fails to seize the reflexive and constitutive properties associated with the kind of 'enactment' of organization produced by Mol (2002). The 'politics' in ontological politics compels one to reflect far more radically on the analysts' co-implication in the practical 'enactment' of organization. There is a latent realism in Alcadipani and Hassard that obstructs the full fruit promised by the ontological turn in the social sciences. Such considerations are entirely absent, however, in Whittle and Spicer's (2008) efforts to comprehend actor-network theory. Organization Studies carries on as business as usual in both these papers and indeed with a very rudimentary form of representational realism and moral transcendentalism.

[11] Despite the recent flourishing of ethnographic study in management and organization, the most popular and widely read ethnographies in business and management studies remains stuck in a more basic 'realist' disposition (Van Maanen 1988). Notwithstanding gestures towards montage, pastiche and multiple voices that briefly animated ethnographic interest in the wake of the fascination with all things 'postmodern' (Linstead et al. 1996), ethnography in business and management

most significance for the study of loungification is that the ontological turn is more a method, a sensitivity, or *disposition* towards 'fieldwork' than it is a formal or elaborate theoretical apparatus.[12]

The challenge these various developments in the ontological turn pose to ethnography is one that enjoins its practice to embrace a more experimental attitude so that research can work more productively with what is inevitably an interventionary and reflexive constitution of the world it studies. It is one that chimes with recent interest in performativity and non-representational theory that has taken hold widely across the social sciences (Thrift 2009). Experiments in ethnography associated with this turn are all engaged in debates with the political philosophy or 'cosmopolitics' of Bruno Latour (2013) and Isabelle Stengers (2010, 2011), both of whom draw extensively on counter-enlightenment traditions of Western thought. At the risk of simplifying and over-synthesizing what remains diverse and contested, an ontological politics moves beyond relativism and the idea of multiple representations (in which nature is essentialized, but cultures diverse (see also Descola 2013)), and instead draws attention to the ways in which ways of knowing are also ways of enacting realities. It might better be called 'ontologies-in-the-making'. Indeed, in this dimension the ontological and the epistemological disappear: while they may be convenient heuristics or abstractions, in practice – or studying practices reflexively – we find neither in pristine form. Instead both are found to be mutually co-imbricated in the making of worlds. This then becomes a highly political question, *what worlds should we be implicated in* making? Totalising and coherent utopias? Experimental worlds?

studies is still predominantly realist or – when more creative – Geertzian in its influence, and it is still yet to really come to terms with Clifford and Marcus (1986), or the implications and responses that followed in the wake of *Writing Culture*. These have been much more fully developed in anthropology, in particular by those associated with the legacy of Strathern, and the more recent 'ontological turn'.

[12] The paradox here being that this introduction conveys this approach in an abstracted and theoretical way. However, this seems in part a condition of working in business and management studies where writing is expected to be rendered in recognisably transparent and clear ways, telling the reader *what* you are doing, rather than just doing. Far less justification is required of the ethnographic method in anthropology, for example, where practitioners just get on and do it, rather than worry that they have to continually explain themselves at a meta-level. Leave that to our readers and interlocutors, otherwise we end up doing nothing and only claiming to be doing something: 'This paper argues', for example, 'this paper has argued', etc., with nothing in the middle!

Agonistic worlds? Radically democratic? – the franchise of which would include non-humans?

Significantly, the ontological turn extends politics beyond the human to include what some call 'a parliament of things' (Latour 1993), but for which we still have not found ways of listening – if voice be their mode of communication (see Kohn 2013; de la Cadena 2015).[13] This radical extension of politics to the non-human – to animals, forests, mountains, soil, water, etc. – poses a considerable challenge to how we think and proceed with politics in Organization Studies. It is not a question of giving voice, granting 'rights', or even 'finding' voice for these non-human others, so that we might, for example, more reasonably engineer something like sustainability or a more liberal and heterogeneous ecology of being; these often self-righteous liberal-humanist responses only serve to impose an all-too-human blueprint based typically on utopian and totalizing commitments. Rather, the nature of the political challenge the best of this ontological turn poses is to learn to *experiment* with and tap into other modes of consciousness and being that generate hitherto unknown and unanticipatable 'becomings'. There is no 'human' at the centre of this extended ecology; instead we discover complexly multiplied and extended relations of association that break down the unified and bounded entities presumed of things like 'the individual' or 'the human'. In studying these relations analysis must yield to matter in a more disaggregated and vital, more primitive flux.

It is difficult to pre-judge and adjudicate on these becomings because they do not permit classification within the established checkerboard of modern political divisions – left or right, progressive or regressive, emancipatory or incarceral. Moreover, it is difficult to talk about this politics in this schematic and abstracted way – and possibly self-defeating – because the ontological experiments embarked upon in this ethnography remain resolutely *immanentist*. In order to become receptive to the forces and energies available from these experiments research must seek to abandon all apriori moral or other transcendental commitments. To give chance

[13] Kohn develops attention to what he calls the multiple modalities of semiosis. There is, for example, a bio-semiotics (Hoffmeyer 2008), more extensive and generalized than the human mode of symbolic representation. Using Charles Sanders Pierce, Kohn (2013: 9) proposes that 'it is through our partially shared semiotic propensities that multi-species relations are possible'.

to the possibility of new values we must submit to the finest level of 'local' specificity available from any particular site or object of empirical enquiry.[14]

The politics of biosemiotics and post-human ecologies would seem far removed from the local specificities of an airport departure lounge with its highly rationalised and technologized construction and designer customer experience. In one sense, the lounge is a highly artificial and self-enclosed space with little evidence of 'nature'. In fact, one notable feature in the design was the very lack of natural daylight. However, what posed the greatest challenge to the ethnography of this lounge was the possibility that something like a 'vicarious existentialism' or a 'second nature' was at work in a lounge and one imbued with all manner of the most 'fantastic' multi-species and trans-species beings and ecologies. From Wii machines, to footfall analysis, the 'Manchester experience' to 'alpha territory' loungers, the lounge could easily be understood as being populated with an exotica equivalent to that often reserved for the animism of a remote anthropological tribe. The lounge itself seemed to become animate as it took on features of life normally reserved for the human or 'nature'. There may not have been a 'forest' consciousness or thinking (Kohn 2013) evident in the lounge, but there were things like 'talking chairs', 'airport brain' and 'feline politics' that were profoundly unsettling to assumptions of human distinction or autonomy.

The abject nature of this phenomenon means that it is rarely considered to be relevant to the practice of business and management, but in this ethnography we discover a whole series of hitherto neglected items that would appear to be nonetheless essential to management – including walking practices, angular reasoning, scattered attention, and crini-cultural politics – or what we call 'the politics of the "Bob-cut"'. One would be hard pressed to find these in a manual of management training (but see O'Doherty 2016a) but they all form part of an extended repertoire of practices made evident when we make loungification the object of ethnographic attention. The challenge this poses to the ethnog-

[14] It will become clear that 'local' risks being misleading. The ethnography developed for the purposes of this study of loungification does not return to the 'micro' or 'local' at the expense of the 'macro' or 'universal'. Instead it tries to learn from its interlocutors and abandon or sidestep these dualisms.

raphy was to take seriously their contribution to organization without reducing it to tried and tested formulae that could only see evidence of exploitation or subjugation. In isolating some of these practices and objects, the study was encouraged to respond and take seriously their 'actorial' status. By multiplying a far greater range of 'actors' than is normally considered relevant to business and management, the ethnography was motivated by the possibility of tracing a far richer set of relations that might weave together what is normally separated into discrete realms: structure/agency, for example, and the macro and micro. This weaving runs counter and cross-wise to the ways in which formal organization is normally situated – or contextualized – within stratified levels of political economy: government and the economy at one end of the scale, and at the other the domain of a 'micro'. Neither macro, nor micro, loungification demands experiments and explorations in a space of organization that produces a very different understanding of sociological scale and social 'dynamics'. In so doing, we test whether this more ethnographically informed and disciplined isolation of 'aberrant' phenomenon can help advance questions that seek to address the 'taken-for-granted' (Garfinkel 1967) constitutive practices of organization.

In what precise ways, then, can we isolate the 'foundering' of organization that takes place in the seen but unnoticed practices though which organization is both *founded* but also *founders*[15]? The thesis developed over the 6 substantive ethnographic chapters of this study builds towards a treatment of management that is made available for analysis *once the lounge is positioned as a matter of ontological significance*. The Escape Lounge is not just an isolated lounge in the borderlands of Manchester and Cheshire but instead is best seen as something that participates in a wider ongoing reconstruction of social practices and organization involving new objects/subjects and their relations. This is *Reconstructing Organization*. Studies of business and management rarely venture into the ontological status of its organizational practices, and where ontology does get treated it is nor-

[15] Derrida was periodically drawn to the double work available to analysis with the word 'founder' – with 'founders', 'foundering', and 'foundations' forming part of this semantic chain. It is a trope that appears throughout his writing, in his treatment of Hegel, and *Violence and Metaphysics*, for example, but perhaps most succinctly dealt with in his 2002 essay on the 'Force of Law' (Derrida 1992).

mally restricted to the preoccupations associated with existential anxiety. The deployment of this conceptual neologism 'loungification' forms part of the experimental ambition of this research which aspires to advance an adequate treatment of its ontological significance and to trace the evidence for its reconstruction of subjectivities and social practices. It also reflects an effort to *raise* or *extend* the *politics* of its organization.

Politics in Organization Analysis

Politics has been most obviously tackled in Organization Studies through the work of critical management studies, which has sought to develop a far greater theoretical sophistication in the study of management than is typical in the business school (Alvesson and Willmott 1992, 1996; Parker 2002; Alvesson et al. 2009b). The foundational statements of CMS drew on debates in Marxism and particularly the contributions of the 'Frankfurt school' of critical social theory associated with Adorno and Horkheimer, Herbert Marcuse, Erich Fromm and Jurgen Habermas. In more recent years the work of Foucault and Derrida have also been drawn into debate, but this has often been the cause of tension and incoherence. In a much-cited paper Fournier and Grey (2000) respond to this threatened incoherence by suggesting that what galvanizes CMS is a commitment to 'denaturalisation', 'reflexivity', and 'anti-performativity' (cf. Spicer et al. 2009). With these analytical commitments management must be seen as a political agent, not in a restricted sense of the 'politics of organisational life', but as a participant in the production and reproduction of a specifically capitalist mode of economic accumulation. Management is therefore complicit in a much more expansive and conflictual politics occupying a much bigger political stage than the one that is routinely understood in studies of business and management. In the main, politics in relation to management is typically restricted to things like the politics of empire building, or departmental and personality clashes (Mintzberg, 1973).

The real target of critical management studies is the mainstream of business and management education through which management is taught as a rational, technical and a-political exercise modelled on quasi-natural scientific methods of enquiry (French and Grey 1996; Grey 2004). The diminution of people at work to the status of functional elements of behaviouralist analysis, prediction and control, and/or their reduction of their role to that of bearers of economic categories, produces an impoverished and mechanistic interpretation of management and organization. The attention to subjectivity and identity in the core foundational texts of CMS (Knights and Willmott 1989, 1999; Knights 1990; Willmott 1990) provide a major advance and opens up areas of work organization obscured and neglected by both orthodox business and management studies and established traditions of critical sociological studies of work. In its most elaborate formulations, subjectivity is understood to be media and outcome of wider social conditioning such that there is no dualistic opposition between subject and object, or structure and agent. When pushed to explicit reference, CMS scholars will often cite and draw on Giddens (1976, 1979) and adopt the language of 'structuration' in which structure and agent are seen to be mutually constitutive and co-dependent, or 'moments' in a more profound historical dialectic.

CMS is thus able to draw attention to a much broader spectrum of phenomena in organisation than catered for by the over-rationalised reductive and economistic focus of most sociology of work and organisation. However, there is still totalizing representational ambition in CMS, and the deployment of terms such as 'the social context', 'political economy', 'structure', 'society', 'capitalism', and 'exploitation', etc. paint with broad brush strokes and reproduce powerful meta-narratives that are as seductive in their discipline as that against which they are putatively waged. Terms such as 'power' and 'society', for example, are often mobilised as if there were consensus on what they might mean and then applied to or identified with examples or instances thrown up from empirical research. The work of Laclau (1990) and Laclau and Mouffe (1985) has become central to efforts to avoid such representational reductions and its allied ontological simplifications and to develop a politics that is attentive to a more 'constructivist' ontology marked by contingency and undecidability (Willmott 2005; Glynos et al. 2012, 2015). However, despite its rigour this produces what is essentially a vast and abstracted theoretical edifice whose sensitivity to empirical research remains limited.[16] These tendencies mean that empirical research is often

[16] A full critique of the limitations of the 'Essex school' of Laclauian critical discourse analysis is developed at length in O'Doherty (2015).

conducted in ways that neglect methodological rigour. The risk here is that empirical research becomes little more than exercises in the collection of evidence to illustrate the utility and explanatory veracity of these sophisticated and abstracted theoretical concepts.

With its transcendent moral critique and commitments to emancipation and authenticity, the CMS author, moreover, self-identifies as a privileged agent of debunking who can liberate readers and ordinary members of organization from their deluded and alienated condition. In contrast to Foucault and the politics of the 'ontological turn' CMS seems rather conventional and restrictive, if not authoritarian; perhaps it is more accurate to say it remains hampered by the legacy of humanist and utopian thinking.[17] Chapter 2 begins the slow process of reworking critical management studies prompted by the experience of negotiating access to the 'corridors of power' at Manchester Airports Group. Despite the theoretical resources provided by the post-structural turn, promoted most effectively in the business school by critical management studies, I was surprised to find how inhibited my research was by a preoccupation with personalities and the intrigues of domestic career politicking. How might we escape the temptation to critique, to seek blame or culpability, to close the world down into the known and familiar antagonistic politics of 'capital and labour', management and worker, or market versus community, etc.? To grasp loungification we need to find a way of entering practices and relations in management that are to some extent thinkable as *prior* to the separation and consolidation provided by those familiar sociological dualisms.

Organization Studies is still to define how one might take seriously the fact that critique is in many ways reflexively part of the empirical world we are studying. There is a fundamental analytic problem when the categories and divisions of the critical school are also those of our empirical interlocutors.[18] Reflexively questioned, mobilized, and deployed, such discourse would stimulate various forms of action and reaction that would be missed

---

[17] With all this entails for the possibility of barbarism and righteousness.

[18] In many ways this is the starting point for Clifford and Marcus (1986) and the 'reflexive turn' in ethnographic practice. We are still to take this reflexive turn in ethnographies of business and management, let alone all that has followed in the wake of Clifford and Marcus as ethnographic practices have developed and advanced to include the implications of Strathern's (1988) *Gender of the Gift* and the more recent 'ontological turn'.

if we stuck literally to the mapping of the world in these terms – as if they were *not* part of the world we are helping to enact rather than simply studying. Hence, to use concepts at a meta- or etic level that were also those used by members of the discourse-practice in the emic world, seemed problematic, and possibly self-defeating, circular and tautological.

These questions all began to press as I sought to deepen my ethnographic practices at the airport, and in struggling to find ways around this problem I was taken into an increasingly bewildering and uncharted world. It was only once I was able to venture the concept of 'MAG men', for example, that I found myself in a position or *movement-in-organization* that allowed me to pick up the subtlety of relations and associations that were forming networks of 'world-making' I later came to understand in terms of loungification.

Loungification

To follow loungification requires organization analysis to escape the legacy of a sociology of work in which the factory, or the shop floor, a particular bureaucracy, or a formal organization, are retained as the central object of study, and an object, moreover, set within a surrounding context. All of these 'objects' are really better conceived as *projects* bound into complex relations of maintenance and repair (Graham and Thrift 2007). These relations make the object drift 'laterally' so that the object is never quite the same from one day to the next. Loungification strings together a 'lash up' (Latour 1993: 382) made up of a dispersed series of materials, ideas and subjects. In tracing this 'lash-up' loungification also helps adumbrate something like a fragile 'crack' (Ansell-Pearson 1999) or 'line of flight' that runs like a zigzag through the content and boundaries of formal organization. This heterogeneous collection has not been distilled and separated out into structure and agent, but continues to provoke and unsettle these distinctions. Loungification finds organization in a primitive and more vital state, but also one that has not yet stabilized into an actor/net-work.[19] This might appear to resonate with the concept

[19] It is important to retain the double formation implied in actor-network, the hyphen added for effect here (see Latour 1999). It is both *actor*-network and actor<network. One must also recall *net*-work and net-*work*. See Czarniawska (2004a, b) for a similar effort with her proposal to study 'action-nets'.

of structuration, proposed by Giddens as a way of synthesising structure and agent in ways that help us conceive of society as something akin to what he once likened to living in a house that needed to be rebuilt anew every day (Giddens, 1982).

Never having been on a construction site, nor followed its supply lines, Giddens would not have been aware that loungification takes place *outside* what structuration theory delimits in the form of a synthetic mutuality of structure and agent. Seen from within these terms the lounge and the wider process of loungification might be considered a classic *liminal* space – which has been of much interest in contemporary organization studies following a return to Van Geneep (1909) and Victor Turner (1969) (Garsten 1999; Czarniawska and Mazza 2003; Clark and Mangham 2004; Costas 2013; Land et al. 2014; Knox et al. 2015). However, whether we can retain the term 'liminal' when we do not have the bookends of 'structure' and 'agent' would seem to pose a significant problem for contemporary social science. To borrow from Deleuze, the 'ways' in which loungification come into being are multiple and dissipative, leaving only a thin ghost of organization amidst a tremendous amount of noise and failure. If it is *organization*, loungification is that organization which exists in what Ballard (1991) calls 'the next five minutes',[20] i.e. *beyond* the transitory liminal, and into an organization that is out of context and *out of time*.[21]

As a concept 'loungification' is of course limited and time-bound, and one eventually to be thrown away by virtue of the fact that it will not do the (limited) work that it does in this time and this place. It is an improvised and contingent experiment that attempts to trace the contours of a possible emerging organization that could not be traced so long as we stick to established theoretical categories – 'the market', for example, or 'society', 'politics' and 'political economy' in organization studies. Chapter 3 begins to explore the emergence of a space of organization where the customary categories and divisions of both orthodox and critical studies no longer hold. Much is to be learned of management if analysis can learn from those managers who are able to find a way to operate in these inter-

[20] Ballard, J G (1991). *The Next five minutes: literature and history*. BBC for the Open University, London.

[21] Evident in the perennial problem of jet lag and the multiplicity of times in the airport, from vast departure boards displaying arrival and departure times to the rows of multiple clocks in terminal departure halls showing the time at various places.

stices and its aporias. Without clear 'demand' or 'supply', for example, no clearly delineated client or contractor, or no evident boundary between inside and outside of the airport organization, and where temporality and its measures or boundaries fall into disrepute, management is thrown into what is called 'disorderly convulsion'. To operate in this space requires the capacity for 'scattered attention', but this remains a fragile and contingent accomplishment. In chapter 4 the ethnography finds that a capacity to dwell in this scattered attention, akin to a tolerance for a Keatsian 'negative capability', provides the possibility for the emergence of certain creative energies through which highly irregular actions and decisions emerge. I call this 'angularity' and 'disjunctive synthesis'. Structure and agent may well be best considered a heuristic convenience or analytic distillation that puts closure and also a post-hoc *Reason* around the random way in which organizational practices build associations that connect and continually transgress what is customarily referred to as the macro and the micro.

To advance these ambitions the empirical research upon which this thesis develops follows things like a pencil-inscribed tick on a customer survey document as it travels from Manchester to Lac Lemen in Switzerland via European Air Transport Institutions and political parties, marketing agencies, and Pearson correlation techniques. Out of this circulation starts to emerge a strange figure I call 'the lounger'. More surprising perhaps is the fact that in simultaneously making *both* the lounge and lounger, management becomes embroiled in the interstice and aporia of subject and object. There is no *lounger* without a *lounge*, for example. And what comes first? What is cause/effect? The complexity of this problem, distributed across a dispersed series of objects and sites outside the control of any one agent, perhaps explains the quite remarkable feats of imaginative creativity that seem to be stimulated amongst managers working on this project. This *dis*-position of management is one marked by the absence of formula, rule and procedure. At a time when management expertise, capacities and capabilities were also being redefined – in ways that create opportunities for some, and closure for others – we are invited to consider the possibility that the lounge itself enjoys something like an agency status of its own. Here, we find evidence in this chapter that management might be subject itself to a 'becoming lounge', or perhaps even 'thinking like a lounge' (cf. Scott 1998).

In chapter 5 we follow more closely the practices and materials responsible for the construction of this intricate figure – 'the lounger'. It is a figure perhaps easy to caricature or ridicule, but one must resist these temptations and exercise caution in its treatment. Loungers pose problems to organizations; we don't know what to do with them, and we don't know what they are capable of. And, yet, they are coming into being - and by and large in ways unbeknownst to management and organization studies. Some historical precursors are suggestive that we are not the first to alight on this problem. The urban studies fashioned by the Chicago school in the 1920s appear to have happened upon an earlier incarnation of the lounger, notably in the study of hotel lobbies by Norman Hayner (1928). The lounger is 'released from the bonds of constraint', Hayner writes (1928: 792), and so 'tends to act in accordance with his impulses rather than to patterns and ideals of the group'. The 'resulting behaviour', Hayner goes on to note, 'ranges in nature from a mere "good time" to an explosive "blow out"' (ibid.: 795). If correct, the possible growth of loungers would certainly be something that specialists in organization analysis should be alert, particularly if there is business being made here, or potential new threats to the capacity of management to contain an unruly consumer. Whereas the latent Freudianism in Hayner is unfortunate, seeming crude and unpersuasive, the quest to study 'the unmanaged' or 'unmanageable organization', as Yiannis Gabriel (1995) calls it, is a valuable exercise and one that has been a long-standing preoccupation of Organization Studies.

In sum, Loungification poses problems for critical analysis. Is it something to be welcomed? Might it even pose problems to the management of capital accumulation, perhaps rendering management – as we know it – impossible? Is the 'Escape' that appears to be promised in the lounge real, emancipatory, or subjugation? Should we chastise its practitioners for the promotion of frivolity, decadence or narcissism? However, driven by these questions and the commitments they imply would cut short the patience required to ethnographically explore all the materials and their alchemy as they form around this figure of the lounger. We would also be unable to extend politics in organization, to *politicize* the lounger in ways that add to the repertoire of political struggle and possible future organizational imaginaries made thinkable and doable by virtue of the lounge. The existing critical apparatus would re-inscribe 'the lounger' back into the contours and divisions of the existing political chessboard – left/right, good/bad, emancipatory/subjugation. What if the lounger changed the terms of these relations, and made us think again of what might be good or bad, utopian or dystopian?

It is these fleeting signs of new political imaginaries that I want to explore in this book, and learning how to collect them formed an important part of the ethnographic experience that is recounted in this study. What kind of politics is possible from a commitment to *immanence* that eschews ready-made political slogans and formulas informed by abstracted and transcendental values? Chapter 6 explores the possible politics of loungification that might form around what is called 'the crinicultural' (defined in the OED as 'of or relating to the care for the condition or appearance of hair'). Inspired by the appearance of the Bob-cut in the lounge this chapter considers the possibility that established divisions between a realm of political economy and the space usually reserved for the ethnographic – namely the micro – might be problematic. Moreover this is a division that is possibly being reconfigured in ways and manners not normally considered by organization analysis. If the lounger is a project entangled with the lounge, which is entangled with new forms of management and expertise, how do we begin to recognise the agency of the cricicultural, which includes the unruly material properties of hair?!

Hair is not the only surprising (perhaps even shocking, or faintly ludicrous) non-human actor we find gathering around loungification. The final substantive ethnographic chapter recalls the appearance of Olly, the airport cat, who we discover becomes an important political actor in the fate of airport management.[22] A consummate lounger, Olly comes to live

[22] The airport is a site of tremendous animal activity including gulls, buzzards, swifts, kestrels, geese, and pheasant, which are of considerable managerial concern on the airfield because of the danger of 'bird strike'. There are also bats, rats, mice and other vermin which are a constant threat in terminal operations. Airports are also sites for the proliferation of other non-human life forms, including bacteriological diseases and viruses. The ultimate lounger, of course, might be the great crested newt, a community of which occupies the carefully manicured grassy fields on the airfield during their breeding season. During one year this protected species held up the construction of a multi-million pound taxiway development scheme. There is a complex post-human ecology of management here, and one in which the boundaries between the human and animal are brought into question. There are 'bird men' for example, who work on airfield operations, there are people who drive 'animals', and there are 'animal spirits' at play in duty free. To paraphrase Allan Flanders, management is going to have to learn that in order to regain control it is going to have to share it … with workers and other animals. Chapter 7 is hence a case study of this wider field of multi-species organizations that displace the sovereignty of management and might even *re-humanise* the workplace.

'nine lives' at Manchester Airport during the construction of the Escape Lounge and in so doing inflects a certain 'feline politics' to organization. The extended role for the animal and the wider non-human realm has become an important part of what is known as 'multi-species ethnography' (see Kirksey and Helmreich 2010) amongst a number of scholars increasingly preoccupied in recent years with the Anthropocene. Drawing on the influence of Deleuze and Guattari (1987), Haraway (2003, 2008), Derrida (2002), and Agamben (2004), and debates therein, these studies of human-animal relations – and other species-being relations – challenge thought and action to reimagine the limits and possibilities of existing politics. Barring one or two exceptions, this has received scant attention in Organization Studies.

This may be a neglect we can no longer afford to indulge, particularly as the emancipatory project of critical pedagogy is beginning to be questioned in terms of its 'anthropocentric' and 'speciest' foundations (see Corman 2011). Recent papers on post-anthropocentric ethics in Organization Studies (Ezzamel and Willmott 2014) are encouraging in this respect, but can we advance this concern when we give up the reification of 'nature'? Chapter 6 seeks to pose questions about what forms of pedagogy might be developed to engage more fully with the alterity brought about by the presence of animals in organization suggestive of the possibility of *multiple natures* or 'multinaturalism' (Viveiros de Castro 1998; Descola 2013). What can we learn from the animal or human-animal relations in our efforts to make organization? Might the very posing of this question, moreover, be suggestive of a 'becoming lounge' that abandons any possibility of a politics that can remain the exclusive preserve of that which the mere *human* animal can think?

Conclusion

As you approach the entrance of the Escape lounge the doors slide back and with a barely audible pneumatic swish you are invited to step inside a globe of subdued and ambient lighting, perhaps recalling what Sloterdijk (2014) calls the 'great comfort structure' of the air-conditioned interior of contemporary capital. The lounge projects a radiance that glows like a corona within which more focused pools of light and the splash of subtle pastel colours are brought into relief composing a kind of dappled visual harmony of rhyme and contrast. You might see some people tapping quietly away on laptop computers, others lounging in black leather Eames-style recliners, reading newspapers, resting or sleeping, talking in hushed tones to their companions and fellow travellers. There may be a smell of freshly-baked croissants and coffee, the hiss from an espresso machine and the distant clink of crockery suggesting breakfast and the comforts of pampered personal service familiar to customers of the experience economy.

When entering the lounge an untrained lounger might not have seen *Connemara* in the Irish bog oak congealed in the polished frame of the vast reception desk (Robinson 2006). But can we see the cat, which runs wild through the pages of a manual on *Wildlife* discretely placed into the library that forms part of the study? Is that Louise Brooks who steps out from behind the reception desk, the gloss from her Bob-cut hair blinding and mesmerising? We feel suspended, light-headed, perhaps a sign of what some see as contemporary 'life in the air' (Gottdiener 2001). Such experience is not immediately apparent as 'loungification', but the burden of this book is committed to an ethnographic experiment in which we might develop a disposition in which such connections and relations can be grasped and forged for their potential as political agency. To see Organization – and to see the lounge in terms of what Ansell-Pearson (1999) calls the 'crack-up', is not always a laughing matter. Part of this experiment involves the invention of MAG men, scattered attention, disorderly convulsion, angular reasoning, disjunctive synthesis, crinicultural and feline politics.

These conceptual neologisms do not come without a certain authorial embarrassment, but their slow patient distillation provides something that helps us experiment with 'thinking like a lounge' and thereby to attempt to take some measure of the unique features of this loungification. In *Home Rules* (1994) the geographer Denis Wood famously made explicit what were 223 rules that governed the use of the 70 objects of his lounge. For Wood, the lounge is conceived as a microcosm that distils and makes manifest wider social meanings[23]; but what happens if the

[23] Much like Bourdieu's (1973) analysis of the Berber House.

lounge is not simply a passive recipient of wider context and determinism but also an active agent? If thinking like a lounge can make us hear chairs as they talk, as some professional lounge managers appear convinced, what forms of intellectual practice must we develop to harness the materials and energies of this lounge in ways that help make it multiple in its potentialities? Underneath the Escape Lounge, for example, flow the engineered waters of the river Bollin whose transports might well once have led to the fabled *Tuatha De Danaan* (Gregory, 1970). If it is never very clear whether my interlocutors – those emerging as the experts and professionals of loungification – are serious, frivolous, ironic, or agnostic, then something of this undecidability is retained or maintained with the deployment of these concepts. It allows us to ask without judgment 'Who is this lounger to which we have given birth – and what are its organizational conditions and implications?'

2

'MAG Men': Access to the Corridors of Corporate Power

We are riding 'The Animal', speeding across the apron and making turns that cause the vehicle to sway wildly from left to right. We are off to 'Westside', the 'Wild West' as it was known, where we are going to inspect a lounge make-over project in the Airfield Safety Unit building, part of a 'restrooms project' to revitalise and refresh 'MAG culture'. Bleeps are coming from the short wave radio. A red light intermittently flashes on the dashboard. A voice crackles through the radio: *ok, MAG 243, clear to alpha nine* – it's ground control giving an official coded clearance to drive across the taxiway. There are four of us in the car, all senior project managers, one of whom is the group projects executive director. Everyone is talking at once. I gather that in 'Westside' there are other *animals*, people who call themselves 'the dirty', 'the polluted', and 'contaminated'. Suddenly, a huge tail fin looms up, slicing the air diagonally. Less than 100 yards in the distance the body of the aircraft swings into the taxiway; its engines roar, and then whine, the car shaking and rattling. In the rear view mirror I see the airport campus, a 'junk-space' (Koolhaas 2002) of grey concrete cubes, terminal buildings, car parks, kit model hotels, and ashen faceless office slabs – all bobbing and swaying, lurching up and down, planes of rectangular shards shooting

D. O'Doherty, *Reconstructing Organization*,
DOI 10.1057/978-1-137-48922-7_2

into view and swinging like inverted pendulums. Tangles of different coloured lines are painted on the apron – square, circular, ovoid. Some long and thin, narrow strips of white line swooping off to the horizon before arcing back. Some of them mark out safe zones of passage and keep aircraft away from regular service vehicles and other cars. 'Does anyone know what these lines mean?' Martin shouts. 'I reckon whoever painted them has long gone and no one can now remember what some of them are supposed to mean'
Ethnographers Diary, November 18th, 2009

Any casual observer to an airport is likely to be first struck by the hodgepodge of buildings and the multiplicity of lines that define its architectural space. There are perpendicular lines that mark the edge of buildings, lines of cars arriving and departing the terminal, and lines of passengers queuing up for check-in or security. There are also queues of aircraft lined up for take-off, tramway lines demarcating traffic on the taxiways and airfield 'apron'; there are lines that keep you in and lines that keep you out, and there are lines that direct you this way and that. All the time, the precise meaning and jurisdiction of these lines remains, however, ambiguous. But on first encountering this space we might tell ourselves that *somebody* must know. For a body in movement these lines become even more complex as they assume a kind of shape-shifting all of their own. As these lines oscillate and fluctuate their boundaries become unclear as they emerge into one another or become discontinuous, marked by abrupt changes in angle and flow. It is a quite bewildering and disorientating experience (Fig. 2.1).

The story of the Escape Lounge is in many ways, precisely about learning to navigate these lines, but also how (or how best) to participate in their 'enactment' (Mol 2002). This chapter will explore how this complexity of lines becomes no more obvious or transparent to the ethnographer even once inside the organization with access to management committees and the 'off limits' and 'secret' spaces, the 'restricted' and 'critical zones', occluded behind the scenes in an airport. Even after considerable time in the field this complexity does not simplify. As we shall see, these lines proliferate, multiply and weave ever-more complex labyrinthine patterns.

Fig. 2.1 Manchester Airport (Photograph by author)

For many writers, airports are designed precisely to keep people out, or to keep passengers blindly locked into a series of confined and restricted spaces. One has to pass through a series of defensive boundaries and lines of exclusion to navigate access to an airport, but beyond this the ethnographer discovers only deeper and more obscure lines of demarcation and restriction. Once inside the offices and the meeting and committee rooms where the management of the airport plies its trade, one finds a whole series of other lines, and all of them at different but interacting scales: from staff reporting lines on company organograms through to the vertical and horizontal lines of the ubiquitous Microsoft XLS spreadsheet. There are also lines of organizational structure depicted on charts and maps with lines of responsibility that attempt to distinguish the respective areas of managerial expertise.

These maps give some indication of the (contested) lines of jurisdiction between things like 'group' and 'airport', which is of particular interest in this chapter. It is a division that provides a considerable pedagogic challenge for the ethnographer who must learn to 'see' these lines of division with adequate political sensitivity at the same time that the learning exposes the ethnographer to the inevitability of mistakes that demonstrate political naiveté and thereby, paradoxically, inhibiting access to organization. This chapter explores how the ethnography began to slowly unpack the competition and rivalry between different parts of a large organization. Such struggles are widely recognised in organization research (Crozier 1964; Pfeffer 1993; Knights and Murray 1994; Drori and Ellis 2011), and in this respect Manchester Airport is nothing new. One might consider this competition and rivalry to be part of a wider social and political context, which is also necessary to grasp in order adequately understand something like the Escape Lounge project. However, this chapter explores the emergence of a rather different understanding of 'the politics of organization', one that transpires precisely around question of access to the executive and elites of corporate organization and the reflexive dilemmas that this involves. Studying corporate executives also entails problems associated with what Nader (1972) first called 'studying up', i.e. when those you are studying may answer back by virtue of the fact that they often have an equivalent understanding of the same theoretical resources upon which you may be seeking to draw to explain their activities (Riles 2001, 2011; Maurer 2005).[1]

In this chapter we are introduced to the men who occupy senior executive and management positions in Manchester Airport. At first glance these 'Manchester men' seem to offer another illustration of those characters familiar to critical studies of management and organization, the testosterone-fuelled competitive masculine egos that operate in a world

[1] It is surprising that little attention is paid to the negotiation of ethnographic research access in organization studies. Access is usually discussed in terms of personal contacts that occasionally intimate the existence of wider social networks and even the institutional influence of ever closer ties between the university, the business school and the private corporate world (see Hertz and Imber 1995; Thrift 1999; Bryman and Bell 2015). Those few exceptions that have tackled the question in more detail (Bruni 2006; Alcadipani and Hodgson 2009; Whittle et al. 2014) are notable for their preoccupation with a confessional and existential angst that appears to have been stimulated by a series of moral and ethical dilemmas thrown up during the process of research. These papers note that the granting of access is often predicated on an implicit if not explicit *quid pro quo* in which the senior manager who approves the access typically expects information and insight about work practices that would otherwise be obscured or protected. For critical scholars committed to progressive if not radical social change and emancipation, to serve this 'managerialism' at the expense of the worker is a retrograde and politically unacceptable practice. However, this chapter explores how ethnography is made almost impossible when such firm and *a priori* or even transcendental moral absolutism are deployed as ethnography is reduced to the exercise of collecting empirical material to illustrate and extend existing theory.

of corporate greed and intrigue (Jackall 1988; Collinson 1992; Casey 1995). Here we discover organization as defensive, inhibited, paranoid, restrictive, punitive, and disciplinary, confronted with a ruthless world of economic competition and capital accumulation. However, in tackling the on-going problem of access the ethnographer was forced to confront the question as to whether such personalities and accompanying organization was the consequence of a certain mode of reflexive and constitutive practice deployed (often unwittingly) by the ethnographer. As we shall see, I was only able to improve access and advance my understanding of organization at Manchester Airport when I was able to achieve some distance from particular predispositions and value-judgements inherited from an established repertoire of 'critical theory' in business and management studies. This was possible when I came to understand management as 'MAG men', a conceptual neologism inspired by an AMC television network drama 'Mad Men' which aired during the time of this research.

As I came to deploy the concept 'MAG men' personalities and personal rivalries and ambitions receded into the background. This helped me acquire some distance from the superficial immediacy of experience and one mode of reflexive engagement and constitutive *enactment* of organization (Mol 2002; Law 2004). In its place a more open and extended understanding of organization (spatial, temporal, historical, etc.) began to be made available, which as will be explored also required attention to more complex forms of 'politics' than is customary in management and organization studies. As this chapter concludes, 'MAG men' encouraged the research to consider the significance of a range of socio-material objects and practices that rendered management much more contingent and provisional than was possible within a strictly 'critical' frame of reference.

'Terminal Man': Sensational Exposé in Tabloid Headlines

The shit hits the fan. 3 months in and I'm going to be asked to leave, I'm sure of it. My sponsor approaches me. He appears anxious and angry. He tells me that an email has been circulating in which one senior executive

(Andy Thompson), who I have never met, tells another (Robert Grant – who also does not know me, and with whom I have never spoken) that I am not to speak to the media. 'Have I been speaking to the press', my sponsor asks me? I am told that Andy has written that 'he has been led to believe' that a 'Damian O'Donnell' (sic) has emailed Liz McCreedy at the Manchester Evening News to arrange a meeting. The tone and language is interesting; indeed he seems outraged. In spite of the fact that, apparently, I have been told that media contacts must be conducted via his team, Andy asks Robert to *make sure this meeting does not happen.* Liz is not even that interested, as it happens. If any meeting takes place, we need to be in control of it so that we ensure our reputation is properly managed. In no uncertain terms the email tells Rob that I am NOT, repeat NOT, to arrange to speak to the media about MAG without our prior permission which has not been sought or given. I am not even a MAG employee! Can I please be reminded of this obligation?

Andy Thompson has no idea who I am. It seems he has been asking around and discovers there is a Damian O'Donnell working in MADL (Manchester Airports Development Ltd.), a department that had recently been closed down and its members reformed and redistributed into alternative groupings with new titles and acronyms. Robert Grant is executive head of estates, a department that is on the same floor as my desk; but I am working, or so I thought, in 'MAG Projects'. I had once written to Robert some months before getting access to the airport, but my email had been left unanswered. Andy's email eventually gets passed down the line and I am asked for a response. *What* I might possibly have been able to tell the media – and of this, *what* might potentially be the cause of embarrassment was never made clear, nor why I might be so motivated to seek such embarrassment (see also Neyland 2008).

Most confusing was the fact that I had previously attempted to contact the airport press team to establish due procedure, but my emails had been unable to elicit any response. Keen to avoid the naiveties and pitfalls of the clumsy ethnographer, I had been preoccupied with the task of establishing who the people were that I needed to talk to in order to help manage journalists who were increasingly showing interest in my research. I had thought this would have been easy. The most basic introduction to business and management studies introduces students to organisational structure through which authority is established and its attendant processes and regulations mapped out (Boddy 2008; Mullins and Christy 2013). We might therefore expect that there was due process to be observed, jurisdictions, territories and demarcations, reporting lines, spans of control, zones of responsibility, and structures of authority. However, this was far from my experiential reality at the airport and I subsequently discovered I was not alone in seeking definition about organizational structure, reporting lines and due process. No one, it seemed, was very sure to whom I should talk and in what sequence in order to set up a meeting either with the internal press team or outside media interests. Indeed, I discovered that any 'nature' of work and organization (cf. Thompson, 1983) – and any 'reality' of line responsibilities and reporting procedures – depended in large part on who was asking, and how one asked.

The broad turn to reflexivity in ethnography (Clifford and Marcus 1986) and more recent 'post-reflexive' forms of ethnography (Riles 2001, 2011; Maurer 2005) encourage us to be mindful that *how* one talks is an on-going practice and matter of concern in ethnography (Alvesson and Skoldberg 2000; Cunliffe 2003). The way I went about asking for this chart, therefore, had consequences; consequences that in part helped position me in the organization (how senior, to whom one reported, current project, etc.). In turn, information about 'my position' entailed further implications as members of the organization made inferences about which 'process' I would need to be told to observe – or what kind of process needed to be drawn on/invented/conjured.[2]

After considerable effort I was able to locate someone who had a copy of an 'organization chart'. However, when it was printed out and given to me, a document running to 64 pages, I was told to be careful with it and not to rely upon it because there was still considerable on-going 'negotiations' and 'grey zones' on the map with certain positions still to be agreed.

[2] The legitimacy and authority of particular rules and process was always subject to ongoing interpretation bound up with the various ways in which they were drawn upon and enacted. Whether Manchester Airport or Manchester Airports Group was a bureaucracy remains moot, in this regard. There was no central depository of formal documentation, or committee meeting, or records, and little in the way of detailed minutes or a collectively shared understanding of how decisions get made.

Proud of this acquisition I showed it to Rob Fuller, the departmental head where I was currently being housed. He looked astonished. 'Where the hell did you find this … you toe rag!' What was even more surprising was the fact that I was the only person on level 3 to have a copy. Other people showed some interest in this document, but their interest was more casual and matter-of-fact. On occasions it was even treated with humour, as if this document was only of minor relevance and by no means vital or terribly informative (cf. Dalton 1959). On proceeding to look more closely, Rob expressed surprise at the way in which some of the people and some of the lines connecting different people. 'You see here, there's two HR departments. One on level 5 – with Brenda Harding, that's MA HR – and then on this page here … you see? You've got *MAG* HR, under Hilary. They never talk to each other! And then you have 'regional airports', that's a wholly different structure, probably invented just to keep Roy happy'.

'Regions', 'Group', 'Manchester Airport', 'terminals', 'commercial/ operations', 'airfield/airport', 'landside/airside', 'executives/management', 'civil engineering/electrical engineering' … the more time I spent at the airport, the more aware I became of the multiplying divisions, divisions that seemed to proliferate with time. The organization was variously 'cut' one way and then another, but at times it went beyond this multiplicity and began to resemble a palimpsest of co-existing parts and layers – all in 'process', and all defined and understood in different ways, and superimposed one on another. Even with this chart I could not establish coherence and consistency. I resorted to my own desperate attempts to sketch and map the organization, but even the modest task of producing a floor plan of the office in which I worked (Fig. 2.2, below) proved tremendously difficult.

Here sat Rob Fuller, Jenny Riley, Mason Dean, Peter Riley, Robyn Jones, Don Harrington, Martin Garnish, Paul Meadows, and David Plumb. These were the people I was slowly getting to know in projects. And there was of course much to their lives. One was a famous and once semi-professional angler, another project manager managed projects much the same as the way he approached rock climbing, there was another going through a divorce, and one returning from a reputed breakdown. It was tempting to accept various characterisations and self-

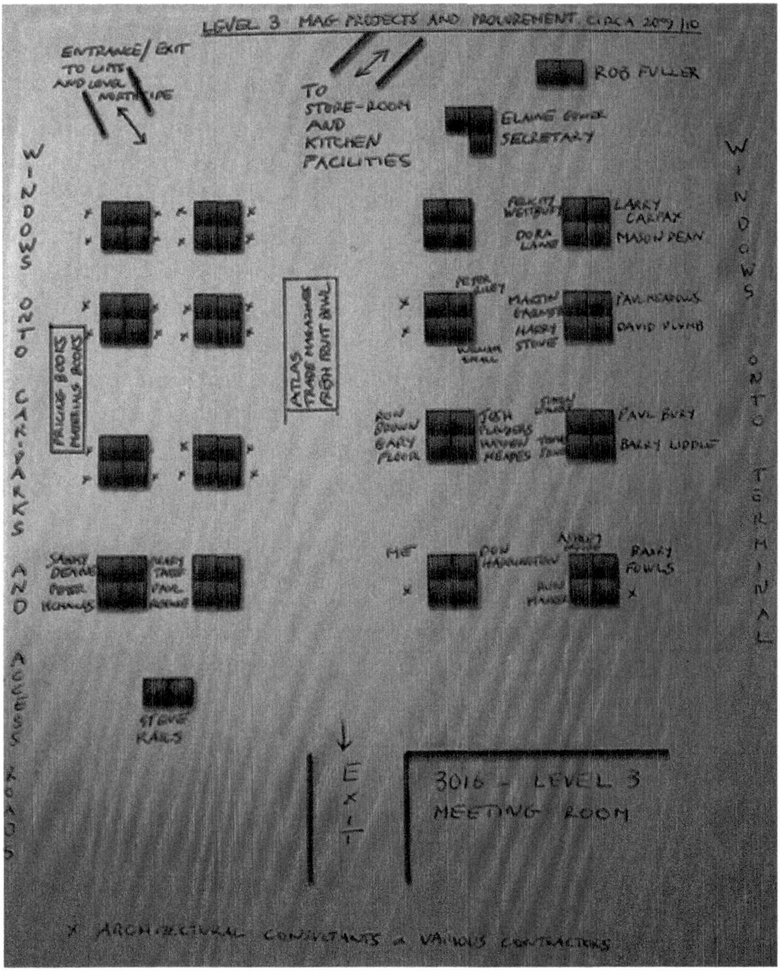

Fig. 2.2 Olympic House, level 3, October 2010 (author's sketch)

identifications in which the usual cast of characters appear in ethnography: a joker and a clown, there was the disenfranchised, the young and ambitious, the old and cynical, all forming a gamut of personalities and inter-personal dynamics.

The traditions tell us that no ethnography can proceed without entering into the personal lives of those that become participants in the ethnography. But as this ethnography developed it became more and more difficult to produce the kind of pen-portraits of characters that Collinson (1992) or Casey (1995) were able to achieve in their ethnographic studies. Much like the furniture and the allocation of offices and space, people were constantly changing – getting older, getting married or divorced, some becoming cynical, others more optimistic about the future. No sooner had I established the diagram above, for example, than an announcement was made to inform the group that desk arrangements were changing. As furniture and relations changed, people seemed to change.

Whilst Rob was able to draw additional lines on my map indicating the presence of 'group' and that of the 'airport', I also came to realise that most of the people on level 3 were actually consultants or 'contractors', which meant they were not strictly employees arranged in simple lines of hierarchy and subordination. But this would also change over time with people slipping from one category to the next. This meant that getting a fix on anyone, or anything, proved elusive and frustrating. A little over a year after this drawing a major refurbishment of the building commenced and we were rehoused for 3 months to another building on the airport campus. How to navigate such a complex and fluid world poses a considerable challenge to an ethnographer, and this perhaps explains why despite my inherited theoretical 'training' (O'Doherty 2009), I sought reassurance in the organizational chart – as if it was there where I might understand how to navigate the world.[3]

Whilst showing Rob the organizational chart, I was surprised that he did not appear to know the structure of his organization, or at least did not think the chart that helpful in learning how to work organization. As I reflected, I realised how little I understood the structure of my own organization. On further analysis, I began to see that Rob was in fact exercising greater ethnographic skill than I, treating the document as but one artefact in a complex stream of information and data within which one might establish relative positions and relationships. For Rob, this was an artefact of ethnographic interest and its status was unreliable.

---

[3] I came to see this as a question of power and how power operates. In one sense the whole of this ethnography is devoted to that question.

It began to dawn on me that these charts were not going to be of much help in working out my failure to secure access or why I had been positioned in the way I had, and to all intents and purposes excluded. I was both naïve in my failure to grasp that I had become mobilised in and by the politics of the Manchester Airport, but also that my actions (or inactions) were triggering and amplifying latent political struggle (or the possibility of political struggle) between different factions or potential factions in the organization. I had taken the furore around the media exposure far too personally and I was also somewhat juvenile in expecting clear instructions and clarity of policy and process that would allow one to know how to make one's way in an organization. The neat lines and boxes offered simplicity and reassurance and with no place on the map for the ethnographer it appeared to offer an objectivity rendered absolute by an apparent sovereign and total bird's eye view of the organization.

At the time, I rationalised the difficulties I was experiencing in securing 'access' in terms that I characterised as the pathologies of management and bureaucracy, which seemed particularly acute in an airport. If only I had been given this chart earlier or had not had to contend with hothead fools such as Andy Thompson, I would be able to make much better progress in my research. Yet, in the discussion with Rob I began to suspect that my difficulties of access might have nothing to with a lack of knowledge about process or an inability to obtain clear maps of the organization. In fact I was being identified as part of Rob's department, and therefore positioned as 'projects' – a group function. On the other hand, those who were involved in the management of the terminal where the Escape lounge was being constructed were 'the airport', i.e. Manchester Airport.

These subtleties and complexities were obscure to me because at that time, and for reasons that remain opaque, I was preoccupied with correcting perceived injustices and wrongs by challenging authority deemed responsible for such injustice whilst also granting myself the right to expose what I understood to be hypocrisy (Alvesson and Willmott 1996).[4] Without an easily recognisable culprit to hold accountable for injustice

[4] A legacy of training and enculturation in Marxist Industrial Relations, Labour Process Theory, and Critical Management Studies, a full reference list for which – running to of over 500 source texts from Marx to Madonna – can be found in O'Doherty (2002).

and inequality I was predisposed to the assumption that the perpetrators must be located in the inaccessible heights of bureaucracy. The chart seemed to offer a route to power, and this predisposition also meant I was quick to seize on evidence of political rivalries and jealousies that might suggest that the order of things was not quite so secure or impervious to change as I had imagined. At the same time my training in critical management studies had left me all too-knowing in explaining how this state of affairs had come about, and in tandem with supplementary theories of a more psychoanalytical and existential nature (i.e. Klein 1959; or Laing 1967), ready-made explanations could quickly be mustered to explain the invidious position in which I found myself. Such analytical work was going to get me into more trouble, as we shall see in the next section.

An *Open Forum*? Communication and Its Discontents in Organization

Opening up my email one morning I came across an announcement inviting me to the next 'Manchester Airport Forum'. Progress! – after weeks of being cooped up and getting nowhere. Despite acquiring an 'access all areas' security pass, which allowed me to the enter the warren of backstage corridors, offices, and passages that are found behind the walls of an airport, I was still meeting few people and struggling to secure invites to even the most minor of meetings. With this announcement of an 'Open Forum' there seemed the promise of a breakthrough. The email explained that these forums are an opportunity for MA colleagues to meet the senior team, to hear about the current business performance, and to ask any questions. 'You do not need to book a place – just simply show up'. Perfect, I thought, reflecting on the likelihood of a debating chamber, in the round, with people from all various different sections of the airport thrashing out their differences.

Arriving at the interview room on the 5th floor I found only two people present both of whom, it transpired, were from engineering. This was not what I was expecting. I recalled being told '[D]on't whatever you do, try and speak to anyone in engineering. You hear me? You understand?' My excitement was only tempered by a sense of trepidation as two senior members of the airport management team arrived a couple of minutes later, one from Group customer services and another from Human Resources (Airport HR). On entering the room, neither of the managers acknowledged my presence, despite knowing them and having been introduced on previous occasions. People introduce themselves, and then heads turn towards me. Silence. I explain my role and ask if anyone had objections if I kept some notes. Following this, one of the senior managers tells those in the meeting that 'we'll be a bit more practiced next time' and that Robin is present because there will be some 'information updating on customer experience'.

Rather than a 'forum' it seemed to me at the time that both managers had conceived of the meeting as an opportunity to *impart* information. However, before either could begin, one of the engineers spoke up to tell us that he is here because he wants to ask some questions for *and on behalf of* engineering. Basically, he says, he wants to talk about the 'lack of morale' and mentions 'the review' which happened about 18months ago and the impact of restructuring. As we are talking another man enters. He looks flustered and is carrying paperwork. He introduces himself as Ron – and says he is one of the 'TUPE'd gang'. 'It would have been helpful', he goes on, 'if it had said Olympic House on the invitation'. The invitation had said 'interview room, level 5', but it was true that there were many buildings with a level 5, and it may not have been obvious that the meeting was due to take place in Olympic House. It seemed I was not alone in struggling to follow charts and maps and due process in organization. Following the entrance of Ron I was then party to several hours of often-bitter complaint and grievances, including accusations of under-manning, lack of team-leadership, the absence of operational management, and the frustrations and chaos of day-to-day work practices. It's all 'broken-promises' the engineer concludes.

By this stage both senior managers had become extremely uncomfortable, no doubt exacerbated by the fact that I was sat there as a good ethnographer dutifully taking notes throughout the meeting. In an apparent effort to recover some loss of order the manager from HR intervenes and in an effort to summarise what she had heard announced 'The problem is basically, then, one of *closed-loop communication*'. I winced at the use of this phrase. As if culled from a PowerPoint slide announcing the latest managerial fashion (ten Bos 2000), it seemed to completely miss its target. It did however seem to encapsulate what appeared to be a gulf in experience and understanding between management in Olympic House and staff in terminal operations. At the same time I noted that if the problem was indeed one of 'closed-loop communication' then this *Open Forum* might be the start of a solution to the problems being articulated by the engineers. However, it seemed to me that the closed-loop communication was being identified as a problem 'they' – *the engineers* – were suffering. I was struck by the apparent irony of this statement and by the fact that there appeared to be no acknowledgement or self-awareness amongst management that they might also be caught up in their own self-referential discourse and agendas. As the frustration in the room built, the HR manager asked in a tone of some exasperation 'What keeps you working at this place?' 'The lads, I suppose', the engineer replies, 'you know ... the crack'.[5]

Finally, I had uncovered the hidden and secret truth. Evidence of silo thinking, conflictual relations between management and staff, accusations of bullying and ineptitude, and suggestions of a vast inequality in experience and fortune: precisely all those things for which a critically attuned scholar looks. I wondered if what I was hearing was as bad as it could get. Perhaps these were clues to 'skeletons in the closet' that might explain the reticence and nervousness amongst many to my research – which had been characterised by one manager as 'a cultural audit' of the organization. After all, Manchester Airport had been the subject of periodic industrial relations disruption, which had attracted some academic commentary and analysis (see Darlington 1995). In more recent years a well-publicised strike amongst security staff at terminal 3 had also made the press.

As we were leaving the meeting, I apologised to the two senior managers and said that I understood that there was a lot of sensitive information shared during the meeting but that consistent with the ethical agreements and confidentiality commitments under which my research was bound I

[5] As the introduction made clear, I too was later to become interested in 'the crack', not perhaps unrelated to the one that we might imagine is being referred to here.

could be trusted to observe anonymity and discretion. In this context I thought the persistent suspicions about my research could be explained by virtue of the fact that I was beginning to crack 'the code' (see Wieder, 1974). Only later was I to realise that it was probably more to do with a critical management studies and my own ineptitude as an ethnographer. This was before ontology began to *crack*.

Reprimand: Hauled Up in Front of the Senior Management Team

'Damian, I need to see you, urgently'. So read a text message that was awaiting me at 6.30 am the following morning. My sponsor was now being subject to more than just teasing by senior colleagues at hosting 'an ethnographer'; his judgement and reputation was now being called into question. I needed to report to the weekly Manchester Airport Senior Management Team Meeting and to explain my activities and research. I was not given a date when I was to present to the SMT, but was told it was imminent.

I was becoming increasingly anxious and even paranoid. Following the Open Forum, the senior manager from customer services had completely ignored me, averting his eyes as we shared a lift in Olympic House. A few days later, we shared a lift again. The doors closed on us but it wasn't until they opened again that I found the courage to speak out. I asked him if he would be happy to talk with me, that I thought I could learn a lot from him, and would be keen to avoid making the kind of mistakes I appeared to be making in the organization. He almost recoiled in surprise as I spoke. Visibly shaken he replied that of course he would be more than happy to speak to me. Once I returned to my desk I quickly wrote an email. A couple of weeks later, after having received no reply, we met again in the lift. Silence, once again. This was now getting embarrassing, but I could do little but remind him of the email. He repeated that he was happy to sit down and talk. Somewhat relieved – I quickly replied that I would be in touch. However, my emails were sent in vain and I was forced to wait until the SMT at which I would present my research.

Following this presentation, which was greeted with smiles and cheery bonhomie, and with very little in the way of what I would have understood as critical or even searching questions, I thought I had finally convinced the senior management team. The doors would now open for me. I was intrigued that the manager from customer services was quick to articulate concerns that my research was problematic. 'It might raise expectations', he explained. Naïvely, I responded that raising expectations might be a good thing and was in many ways consistent with current management ambitions for organisational change. Developing my response I sought to emphasise the seriousness of these concerns, pointing out that they resonated with profound questions of methodological and epistemological import. Across the social sciences scholarship is currently preoccupied with such questions and, I argued, it was not long before even the more conservative mainstream of business and management studies would become informed by such concerns. I noted that for a long time now considerable dissatisfaction with the MBA and the mainstream business curriculum has been made public (i.e. Bennis and O'Toole 2005; Pfeffer and Fong 2002, 2004; Pfeffer 2009; Knights 2008). Most suggestions for reform, however, conceived the problems in narrow and restricted 'technical' ways and offered little robust way out of some of these problems. In these circumstances it is possible, I speculated, that ethnography might have a great deal to contribute (Van Maanen 2011; Watson 2011).

I was then asked about what my research would add of *commercial value* to the organization, and in a mischievous tone the manager from HR asked me for a solution that would resolve current HR problems in the organisation: 'So, *come on*, what would you do about this organization?'. My response sought to build upon the previous methodological point to argue that the ethnographic method would generate insights inaccessible to other methods. These could be harnessed, I suggested, in ways that might help develop the organization from – using the terms I had acquired from members of the airport – a 'conservative' and 'inhibited' culture, to one characterised more by 'openness' and 'self-critical awareness'. Heads had nodded, more smiles. This was going really well, I thought. But again, I must have been misreading what was really being spoken because a couple of hours later Rob Fuller called me to ask how the meeting had been. He was compelled to correct me on hearing my enthusiasm and positive experience. It had in fact not gone down too well. Not at all well. '*There were* some good things', he went on, 'but you made one or two comments that really scared the team'.

To say I was dumbfounded was the proverbial understatement. 'Come on, think', Rob went on, 'you know what you said; it's obvious'. Finally he told me what I had said. I was utterly devastated to realise that when asked to comment on what was good about the organization I had mentioned the laudable efforts the senior management team were making to become more approachable to staff. As an example of this I noted the appearance of members of the senior management team at Joe's cafe and how one of the waitresses had later commented how much delight and confidence it had given her to be listened to and talked to by Ken Devonshire. Apparently, Ken was outraged at this observation, and concerned that it would reflect badly to 'the shareholders'. I was shocked – and sought further clarification from Rob. 'Look Damian, people at the top spend a lot of time away from home, they travel a lot and they don't see a lot of their families', he tried to explain … The penny finally dropped. It seemed that my observation could be construed as critical, focusing on what might be perceived as inappropriate liaisons with staff, which as Rob explained 'could easily look like time wasting … having all day to sit around chatting at Joe's cafe'. How did I think this might play out amongst shareholders?

I was astonished at this possible interpretation. 'Stick to level 3 Damian', I was told. 'You're just not very corporate, are you?' After having cut my hair down to a more corporate length, and wearing the best pin stripe suit my wardrobe could muster, I felt a little disappointed. How much more corporate could I be? A little while later I was told I could no longer speak to James Foreman working in customer relations for Howard. James had been told to tell me that in future if I wish to speak with him I should go through Rob, who would then speak with Howard. 'Howard likes to know what is going on', James told me. Of course, I couldn't get an interview with Howard, and I was confined to level 3. James was only a 30 second walk away from my desk but in order to speak to him I now needed to make a requisition that would travel up two levels of seniority in the projects team, and then across to a member of the organization roughly equivalent in status and rank to that of Rob, and then down to James. I felt restricted and inhibited, and so much of what I thought would help explain how an airport operated seemed to be taking place behind doors closed to me (Law 1994). However, it was precisely these exclusion mechanisms that provided insight into my own culpability in reproducing such suspicions and exclusions.

Hunkered down in level 3 I was able to gather evidence of what people were calling 'silo thinking', and variously a 'blame culture' or 'culture of fear'.[6] Rob produced an essay for the MBA he was studying in which he talked about the difficulties involved in changing an organization with a conservative culture to one that was more innovative and creative. In this essay he recounted how the airport was once run by the various city councillors and the local authority, but now was becoming more 'commercially focused'. The executive board was restructured in ways that cut down on the number of local council representatives and a number of non-executive directors with private sector experience were appointed. I collected other evidence from documents that cited the existence of what one member of the projects team called a 'CYA mentality'.[7] As I pursued this path I became increasingly drawn into a world of suspicion, paranoia, and gossip, and began to hold my own in conversations about who was in favour and who might have fallen out of favour.

Learning the Art of Bare-Knuckle Fighting: On the Edge of Transformation

Thursday February 17, 2011

I ran into Mason Dean outside room 3 on floor 6 where Bernard Burns [The CEO] was hosting his monthly open-invitation 'coffee with the Executive Committee'. There was a huddle of people crammed into

[6] I had still not made sufficient progress in *practically* working with and managing the constitutive and reflexive factors that help explain the production of this evidence. Whilst capable of producing a theoretically sophisticated and informed account of the various strands of reflexivity in the social sciences (Ashmore 1989), of its 'constitutive' nature in ethnography (Clifford and Marcus 1986), and later developments that fine-tuned this insight as performativity (Mackenzie 2006, 2007; Callon 1998, 2009) and 'enactment' (Mol 2002), I was still *practically* immature in terms of reflexivity.

[7] Cover your ass.

the corridor, pillars and posts blocking clear lines of sight. Mason had just come out of a budget meeting with all the managing directors and senior finance directors from across the group. Through the window of the room I could see Bernard and Rob Fuller, Harry and others. The room slowly started to empty and I heard Rob in his broad Essex twang. 'All-right mate, how's it going?' He's joking, joshing, and bantering with some of the 'ops staff': airfield, engineering, car parking, etc. some of whom were looking a little uncomfortable as they waited in line outside the room for the start of the 'Coffee with EXCO'. Like Hamlet, Rob seemed able to move comfortably across all kinds of class and status boundaries, his strong working class Essex accent standing out from the more demure English middle class tones of other managers.

Mason then exited the room and saw me. He approached aggressively and interrogatively, his eyes piercing into mine, but at the same time I couldn't help detecting a degree of consternation and confusion. Indeed, there may have been in this complex mix of visual cues, an element in which he looked a little sheepish. '*What* are *you* doing!?', he asked combatively, but also in a mixture of genuine enquiry, anxiety and incredulity. I casually respond, trying to affect a tone of indifference, as if to ignore his tone of interrogative anxiety. I feel myself as if pinned against the pillar. We are slightly out of sight from the main huddle and with my back against the wall. I change tack and with a degree of self-righteousness and mock incredulity I toss off a reply: 'I'm going to see Bernie. At this 'Coffee with EXCO' event … I asked if I could go and they said yes'.

It was important I said 'Bernie', not 'Bernard'. 'Well, *don't* ask any questions. OK!?' he shouted, 'He *doesn't know you're here* …'. As Mason was saying this I saw Rob come out of the room and we caught each other's eye … 'Rob, Rob …', I gesticulated, cutting across Mason and moving towards Rob, who was looking around and inviting conversation. 'Mr Fuller, to you' he said, joking, to which I replied in mock subservience and obsequiousness 'Sorry Mr Fuller, *Mr* Fuller'. Faces turn from the huddle and look towards us. 'Stop!' he laughed, "I'm joking". I became aware that we were surrounded by an audience, all of whom seemed to be enjoying this burlesque. I looked around at one point, but Mason seemed to have disappeared and was no longer standing by the pillar in which we had first run into each other. 'Did you get my text messages?' I asked, 'yes,

yes, I got them'. 'Both?', 'Yes, both of them'. 'Well, the second one comes with a price tag!' I pitched this as a market trader, invested with a tone of humour, which I quickly followed up with 'So don't *nick* it', as if arguing about the price per pound of the last few mushrooms left on a market stall at 4.00 pm. 'Right, right', he laughed walking off with a crowd of managers as I took my turn to enter the room where coffee with the chief executive was just about to start...
(Diary 3, p. 56)

Tense and nervous, portentous even. There is a lot going on in this excerpt, with evidence of Machiavellian scheming, but really too much to treat adequately in one chapter. On first reading one might suspect Mason is preoccupied with authority and due process: Who has authorised my presence on level 6 of Olympic House? Who knows I am there? Has my presence been 'signed off', in the parlance of middle management! As recorded here we might hear in Mason's voice a mixture of incredulity and anxiety: what can I possibly be doing so close, at least physically, to the newly appointed chief executive officer? The complex drama being played out in this episode reveals much more, including the skilful practices of the ethnographer who, whilst chancing his arm, seeks to find the right balance and tone between self-righteousness and humility that takes seriously the challenge of Mason. Another person, in another role, with another relation with Mason, might have simply smiled and walked off, ignorant of or dismissing what appeared to me to be requests to account for myself. In my effort to secure access to this meeting with the CEO I gambled a response that resembled a careful and minor shift of position in a barely disguised boxing match of parry and counter-parry, bluff and counter-bluff.

For many the conduct of the ethnographer detailed in this excerpt will reflect a certain degree of acquired political acumen, calculation and skill, strangely *enacting* the accusations of 'instrumentalism' and 'cynicism' often directed at 'neo-liberal' capitalism by the critical school (Alvesson, 2013). Like Mason Dean, but unbeknownst to me at the time, I seemed to have become a fairly accomplished pugilist, a practice not normally associated with the skills of business or management (but see Murphy 2005; cf. Jackall 1988). Shouting, sparring, jousting, degradation rituals, and finger pointing, together with the more subtle arts of interruption, cutting across conversations, conversational exit strategies, and the cold shoulder, had all become second nature, none of which I could have been prepared for by reading the MBA curricula and reading lists.

Note here how the pugilist carefully chooses the patronym 'Bernie', for example, which seems to have been deployed to affect a certain familiarity with the chief executive officer and in order to invite suspicions that I was on personal terms, or that I had at least had some contact with him before. There was tactical advantage to this, but it was unclear whether my assumption of familiarity was based upon a casual and citational use of 'Bernie', or whether I was signalling membership of an exclusive and privileged group of people close to the CEO, or indeed, whether I was speaking on the basis of a personal relationship. That was a risk the pugilist took – in effect to gamble that Mason was not himself close to the new CEO. If it was the case that I knew or had some relation with Bernie, this would pose some threat to Mason, in part because he did not know about it – and indeed he openly risks allowing himself *to be known as not knowing* in his reply: 'He doesn't know you're here' – but also because I might have provided information about the projects team to Bernie. Clearly, my response to Mason implies that Bernie does know of my presence. This seemed to have the desired effect. I had responded, it sounded legitimate, and the counter response was easy to recognise as bluster.

Following the meeting with Bernie I am assigned to 'shadow' the group strategy director and an email is sent announcing my involvement in Transformation 2011.[8] The doors had been opened! I swaggered back to level 3 and enjoyed taking the long walk down to Mason's desk in front

[8] Many reasons might help explain this turnaround in fortune. As a new CEO Bernie may have identified with my struggles to establish trust and secure access to knowledge and work practices. Or, I may have been a potentially useful ally. On the other hand he may have been intrigued by the promise that the rather unusual anthropological sensibility and methodology might produce insight into organizational inertia, inhibition and the fear of change that might prove helpful in designing and implementing his plans for 'transformation'. Or, I was being 'played', precisely because my presence was disruptive and unsettling, to which Bernie could learn. Equally compelling is the possibility that I was not only learning the pugilist arts necessary for survival in the corridors of power, but was also beginning to exercise more subtlety in how to manage inter-personal organizational relations. At this time I was also beginning to see in the day-to-day ethnography how personality was a relatively minor item in understanding where new ideas, discourse and practices in the management of organization had their origin. As the chapter explores later, the development of the concept of 'MAG men' was of immeasurable assistance in developing greater reflexivity and changing the terms within which I was subject to the vortex of 'political' squabbling.

of all the project managers. 'Right, I'm in charge now' I fantasised saying to Mason 'you can move your things as soon as you're ready' – thrilled with an adrenaline surge that seemed to relieve me of the experience of so much bullying and humiliation. However, at this very moment I also felt at my most uncomfortable. What had become of me? The complexity of layers, of subtle ruse and feint, gesture and bargaining that was going on in a matter of a few seconds outside the CEO's office, seemed infinite in its capacity to unfold meaning and implication– and all in ways that do not reflect well on the ethnographer.

To unravel some of this, note how the appearance of Rob Fuller provides the ethnographer with a resource upon which he could draw in order to exit from the conversation with Mason. In this episode I wager that Mason can't complain about that. Rob is more senior, and it might be expected that Rob would be accustomed to a certain degree of deference. But at the same time it is a slap in the face! Rob is younger than Mason, and has rapidly been promoted, and not without a certain amount of commentary and gossip amongst peers and colleagues, including speculation that he had been unduly favoured by a father figure in the executive board. In moving towards Rob I exaggerate my movements and voice, but only slightly, and within the terms of this burlesque 'theatre of organization' (Mangham and Overington 1987) my exaggeration is modest and calibrated, stretching the parameters of acceptability only a little beyond their customary terms. However, this caution aside, my actions are more than sufficient to display my comfort and ease at operating at these levels in the hierarchy, whilst also dismissing Mason. In addition, the performance is *staged* so as not to openly show deference to Fuller, but at the same time deploys irony as a resource. Deference *is* being done, but by *not* being done, which it does by drawing attention to itself and commenting (at an even more meta-level of commentary) on this *being-done-whilst-drawing-attention-to-itself*. It is a dizzying and quite remarkable collective orchestration and achievement.

I was also being played by masculinity. It suddenly struck me, though blindingly obvious, that so much of these 'managerial' practices in which I was now engaged were so stereotypically male. And it was exhausting, demanding constant vigilance and attention. Over dinner with one of my trusted colleagues in the airport I began to explore and confide some of this. I found myself turning to the popular television drama 'Mad Men' to help explain. As we shall see the analytical work stimulated by the concept of 'MAG men' began to open up more fruitful lines of enquiry that helped make my research more receptive to what was introduced in chapter 1 as 'loungification'. Helping to achieve a greater degree of reflexivity, MAG men helped draw connections and relations across a more generous socio-material register in organization. It also provided conditions in which more compelling explanation for actions and decisions hitherto excluded by a preoccupation with personality and the all-too-human politics of personal competition and rivalry.

'MAD Men'?

On one level 'MAD Men' tells the story of the rise of the advertising profession in the 1960s. Set in a fictional advertising agency located on Madison Avenue in Manhattan, the show mobilises a series of social and historical associations that weave together the major public events of the 1960s with the more intimate relations and experiences of individuals working in and around the advertising industry. It can be seen as highly stylised and schmaltzy, offering little more than a nostalgic retro-rendering makeover of the 1960s. However, it has attracted considerable and much serious academic commentary and analysis that ranges across philosophy (Carveth and South 2010), psychoanalysis (Stoddart 2011), and the humanities and social sciences more broadly. Tackling issues of power, identity, sexual politics and gender roles, visual aesthetics, and 'cultural memory and the American dream' (Edgerton 2011), the show has offered considerable inspiration to the academy.

The plot revolves around Don Draper. He is the brilliantly creative advertising executive at the Sterling-Cooper advertising agency, but he is also a haunted and in some ways traumatised character leading a double life – if not multiple lives. Early in the show we discover Don Draper is really Richard 'Dick' Whitman. Embarrassed by the confines of his humble rural background, and born to a prostitute who dies during his birth, Whitman seizes an opportunity to escape his life when his colleague Lieutenant Don Draper is killed in action during the Korean

War. Taking the 'dog tags' and identity papers from Draper's dying body, Whitman returns to the United States and assumes the identity of his alter ego. Periodically, however, he is reminded of his previous identity, easily triggered, for example, by objects and events that surround Don as he goes about the task of 'selling dreams' in his day-to-day work at Sterling-Cooper.

Much of the plot revolves around this tension between Don's hidden past and the role he is performing at Sterling Cooper. Most fascinating, however, is the way MAD Men explores more generally how corporate organization compels, on one level, emotional sacrifice, but also a certain *re-emotionalisation*. The corporate world is a complex hall of mirrors involving multiple layers of displacement and projection such that there is no easy distinction between real self and role. Much of the tension in the series hinges on the fact that the viewer expects that certain episodes in the narrative and drama will demand an emotional response from the respective characters in the plot. However, via complex processes of translation (or transference) emotion is avoided by being displaced, but also *translated* and invested into the objects and images conjured in the television adverts. These relations and translations go beyond any simple reification or alienation.

In many episodes there is a *double telling* of the narrative (see also Meek 2015). What is going on or being avoided (or denied) by Don Draper and his colleagues in what we take to be their ostensible real life gets told and worked out through that kind of 'dream logic' at play in the various adverting campaigns. These fantasy worlds of scripted plots staged amidst a cornucopia of products, goods, and services, seem on one level to promise harmony and resolution to the trials and tribulations of the everyday. Of course, this promise proves illusory. However, this is more than simple displacement and avoidance. Emotions become more complicated, self evolves and develops, objects become animate, and adverts become folded back and confused with 'real life'.

As I explain to my colleague over dinner, a closer analysis would suggest that the two worlds are not mirrors, a real world and a fantasy world, but strange *variations* of each other, slightly out of kilter, in which causality and effects can be seen to flow in both directions. What might be relied upon as real – as these two worlds are constantly brought into collision, and then separated – is forever deferred and suspended. On the one hand it seems that advertising, as depicted in the show, is not simply *alienation*, but instead provides something equivalent to a theatre stage, providing props and other resources with which to work-through and work out issues that trouble and preoccupy corporate executives. On the other, this fantasy world at times becomes more real. It takes on a life of its own that shape and create effects that rebound back in the putative real-world lives of the characters. There is something alive here that is beyond the human, something non-human. The product acts back on the producer but in ever-more elaborate and convoluted circulations of effects such that it soon becomes impossible to clearly delineate 'product' from 'producer': both remain unfinished and entangled.[9]

As I outlined the plot and these associations, the wife of my colleague showing ever greater interest suddenly opened her eyes wide to announce, '*That's it.* Your study is about '*MAG* men'! That's the title of your book'. As time went on, the coining of this concept increasingly allowed an object to be made of the world I was studying and one that allowed the ethnographer to take some distance from the machinations of day-to-day managerial conduct. As we shall see it also opened up the possibility for another way of relating to the field site, one less parasitical or abstracted in the terms of high academic theory.[10]

Unlike paranoid-psychotic dynamics, subjugation, or colonisation, the concept of 'MAD men' is not freighted with pejorative associations in

[9] One might also be reminded of the artificial and constructed nature of the televisions series itself (cf. Meek 2015). 'Mad Men' is not simply a *product* of our times, it is also a factor shaping what some will still want to keep stable in the form of an outer 'contextual' reality. Inspiring the design and sale of products ranging from retro 1960s Brook Brothers suits to versions of Ken and Barbie dolls and a line of Mad Men nail polish, for example, the influence of the show runs, ironically, through merchandising and advertising to the very shaping of presidential speeches, notably in Barack Obama's state of nation address in 2014 as reported in the Washington Post (March 27, 2015). The show is, in other words, a political intervention.

[10] This kind of creation of concepts was, moreover, a tactic I had learned from the field. Popular culture was often drawn upon formally and informally by managers of the airport and features of it deployed to help members make sense of their world. In 2009 the HR team, for example, developed an approach to performance management using data analytics called 'talent management' as various schemes such as employee 'star of the month' and other awards ceremonies became a regular feature of management practice. The TV 'game show' format, for example was harnessed for training and development workshops, and talking heads video diaries began to be used for internal communications projects.

which the academic claims to know best. It also remains local, contingent, and particular, providing assistance that helped develop the ethnography rather than facilitate the judgement of a particular set of practices as conceived according to universalist theoretical ambition and transcendental morals. At the same time it invited new ways of understanding how historical conditions of possibility for actions and decisions were immanent to practices and not something structural or layered into the outer ring of the organization as context. In the series the viewer is often witness to the ways in which the products of the advertising world (goods and services, images and ideals) come to feedback into the lives of the MAD men and their wider communities. Moreover, MAD men actively shape their 'contexts' with their promotion of new products, services and lifestyles, at the same time as they rely on their market research departments to tell them something about this world – as if the data could report on something that was independent of their practical activities and interventions.

As I explored the possibilities opened up by the conjugation of MAD and MAG men,[11] I came to see that the (often paradoxical) loops that twisted the realm of fantasised television adverts with the real life of characters helped explain my own activities as an ethnographer. As I became ever more seduced by the explanation that a conservative and inhibited culture was responsible for my lack of access I was drawn further into a world of personality and gossip 'politics'. And it was this enrolment that was precisely generative of the very same paranoid and psychotic logics that I hitherto been projecting as taking place around me as an observable organizational reality. With the help of 'MAD men', I was no longer certain that these kind of dynamics were an essential or apriori characteristic of the airport. I began to see that this was a *possible* relationship with the world around me, and one which constituted – and at the very least sustained – a particular way of being-in-the-world as ethnographer. The possibility that it was *relationality* that was sustaining the sense of competitive, masculine egos, rather than the responsibility of people like 'Rob Fuller' or 'Mason Dean', helped *de-personalise* the politics.

[11] Not quite as elegant as the acoustically silent 'a' of difference (Derrida 1982), but productive of similar work.

In its place the concept encouraged the analysis to explore the possibility that something more *systemic* or *relational* might explain activities and practices that would otherwise be attributed to personality. In Don's character in *Mad Men*, for example, the viewer is often invited to consider how his apparent flaws and contradictions reflect a man struggling to work out what it was to be a man in early 1960s New York. His relationship with his wife is interesting in this respect, as both are shown to be struggling with role models and stereotypes that circulate in popular media providing 'resources' but also 'traps' in which the respective partners might work out what is expected of the 'good wife' and the 'bread-winning' husband. We the viewer are offered the pleasure of seeing the limited capacity of the characters in Mad Men to frame their relationships in the contingencies of historical ontology (Hacking 2002), but this stimulates an awareness of one's own limited grasp of history in the here and now.

In this respect, the scheming, Machiavellian person we see outside room 3 on floor 6 is the ethnographer on the cusp of becoming (unknowingly) one version of a 'MAG man'. However, once I had achieved the possibility of naming it thus, I was able to better see the complicity of my own constitutive participation and then to acquire some of the more reflexive qualities of my interlocutors – to which I had otherwise been blind. In some circumstances, for example, what I had thought was the identity of Mason Dean proved entirely erroneous. Indeed, towards the end of the research, I became far more empathetic of his struggles. He was, in part, the version of 'MAG man' with I had become familiar, but in other respects it was possible to relate to him in other ways, as victim for example – the once-bullied bully – something other MAG men appeared to be able to do, and hence why so many colleagues were able to avoid being drawn into a restricted and antagonistic relation with him.

MAG men also helps draw relations and associations beyond the putative boundaries of the corporate organization in ways that allow for a more expansive understanding of what this study of the airport increasingly comes to understand as 'extended organization'. Often referred to as a 'private club' or 'its own little world', management at Olympic House were vulnerable to insularity and parochialism, typified in a presentation by one of the capital programme managers who in posing the fascinating rhetorical question as to '*where* the money comes from' for capital expenditure, concluded with the answer that it is 'internal funds ploughed back into the business' (Diary 5, p. 25). This closing of boundaries restricted the opportunity for members of organization to think more broadly and more systemically. 'MAG men', by contrast, provides a reference that encourages re-contextualisation(s), or better an awareness of the contingency of context that encourages research to explore organization in other ways. At the same time the concept attributes and acknowledges a shared collectivity, but one that does not definitively or authoritatively claim to know 'the real world' in the terms of a fixed and determining context. In the world of 'MAD Men' contextualisation was not given but was shown as the outcome of relations and practices that could not be separated into the realm of 'market' and 'business'. Could MAG men seize the more relational properties of their practices as managers? And in ways that rendered the environment or context more contingent and provisional? Might this also encourage them to grasp the more *ontological* significance of their work? Or, were they in fact always, already doing this? These were the questions that formed during this stage of the research, and whilst doubtless still naïve, encouraged me to think in terms which led me to approach and treat my interlocutors very differently.

These modest analytical achievements proved of vital importance in developing an understanding of what was at stake in the Escape Lounge where it became ever more clear that MAG men were not a 'microcosm' of some world-at-large, nor a 'causal outcome' of prevailing norms, gender, class, or otherwise, nor a 'reflection' of wider social and political forces. Instead, thinking with 'MAG men' gave access to a whole set of new features of organization to which I had been formerly excluded – *but to which I had to all intents and purposes excluded myself.* I was soon able to contemplate the possibility that the management office was akin to a television studio or a film-set made up of a multitude of 'props'. These props are not simply objects of manipulation or use by subjects; they also *enable* and *facilitate* management. As one reflects on the 'properties' of these objects and materials it becomes clear that they are *more* than simple expressions or *mediators* of human purpose.

The conversation with Mason Dean outside Bernie's office on level 6 could now be seen not just as the sparring of two male egos, nor simply a collective *social* achievement, but as a 'collective' performance made possible by a range of materials, objects and artefacts (walls, pillars, clothing) that could be interpreted as helping to frame and motivate the behaviour of the protagonists.[12] The warren of walls and corridors, divider screens, could all be seen as helping to encourage a divisive and defensive mentality. The organization was, then, speaking to me in a number of ways – but for which I had hitherto been unable to listen. Moreover, to make analytical room for all these material and artefactual things helped to demythologise the presumed power of deep structural or existential theories of organizational behaviour that might otherwise be vested with too much power, legitimacy and authority (Latour 2005a). Performances such as the one between Mason and I are accomplished then, by both human and non-human actors that, as Malafouris (2013) develops in her thesis, help 'shape the mind'. In brief, the performance cannot be simply attributed to an 'I' abstract or devoid of materiality.

MAG men also allows us to put together (or rebuild) a whole series of features of organization normally held in disparate and separate domains: representation and reality, structure/agent, subject/object, even fact/fiction. If we can displace our attention from the person sat behind the desk, for example, we might begin to see a veritable drama taking place. All manner of parliamentary politics and agencies of the state are at play on the desk. Look again. Amidst the pile of papers, the A1 folded architectural drawings, the mobile phone and iPad, the screen upon which Microsoft Office is running, there are also three books neatly stacked by the window that might otherwise not compel much interest: *Blue Ocean Strategy* by Kim and Mauborgne (2005), *Emotional Intelligence* by Daniel Goleman (1995), and *The Tao of Leadership* (Heider 1985). These are fashionable books that have captured the imagination of many studying MBAs in recent years. When Rob talks about 'collaborative working', 'company spirit', and 'managerial flow', we can better situate his thinking and actions as a relay within a network of influences that could be traced out from his desk through long lines of association bring-

[12] We will see in later chapters how architects invest considerable time in thinking through the way buildings might motivate particular behaviours and moods. Indeed, buildings themselves become invested with the status of personality.

ing together universities and business schools, publishers, news media, management consultants, popular culture and what Thrift (1999) and others have identified as the 'global supply chain' of ideas and concepts. Moreover, they are made possible by long chains of concatenated materials and practices, all of them rather humble and mundane: reading lists, spreadsheets, PowerPoint slides, buyer catalogues, software programs and their algorithms, and even Google thesaurus.

A different sense of contingency is achieved with this conception of organization and one that encourages us to see that level 3 of Olympic House is not quite as confined or self-referential as an ethnographer might imagine. Indeed, it gives access to the whole world. Or, rather it has as much claim to *be* the whole world as any other site to which an ethnographer might go and explore. Preoccupied with the relatively superficial politics of personality, it was I who had become myopic and fixated on moments that reified features of organization within the closed confines of Olympic House. Look again at Rob's desk. You see that document carrying the logo of the Department for Transport? It is an official report on runway maintenance. Here, the very 'state' is co-present, right in front of our eyes. A focus on these documents allows us to follow the report back to its putative authors. But if we could ethnographically trace these authors we would inevitably only find another desk much like the one Rob occupies. 'The state' suddenly did not appear quite such a behemoth, something that exists in the remote heights of those in power, but instead becomes a more distributed and fragile thing, accomplished through the on-going repetition of a multitude of actions, materials, practices and routines around which people are assembled and mobilised (Foucault 2008, 2009; see Mitchell 1991; Carroll 2006; Passoth and Rowland 2010). I began to acquire a much greater sense of the relational qualities of things that students of organization typically divide into macro and micro. A minor change in the composition of particulate matter making up airfield asphalt concrete, for example, might necessitate new regulations on things like 'take off distance available' (TODA) and 'take off runway available' (TORA), for example, but this also changes the composition of 'the state', and the relative balance of power between its different elements as new expertise and new interests groups are slowly formed.

From high to low, from the heights of 'the state' to a mundane office desk found on level 3 of Olympic House, MAG men are distributed across chains of association and connection that provide the conditions of possibility in which managerial work is performed. Access to the heights of power was therefore illusory, in part because it was the conception 'heights of power', which is misleading. In fact rich empirical data was all around me, but had been ignored because I had been labouring under what Foucault (1980) would identify as a 'sovereign' and 'hierarchical' understanding of power. The lines of association that weave these things together but which we continually separate in the terms of macro and micro, the state and civil society, structure and agent, etc. are more sinuous and complicated than the boxes and orthogonal lines that striate an organizational chart. To follow these lines, however, requires more flexibility from the researcher and more sensitivity to the human and 'non-human' complexion of politics in organization.

Conclusion

Access to organizations demands something more than technical or methodological prescription and application. As this chapter has shown the experience of navigating one's way into organization motivates research to confront questions of a more political and ontological import. One should perhaps not be surprised by this, given the fact that we are in an airport. In the 1930s Corbusier was quick to point out that air-travel and the airport is nothing if not a (non)place that stimulates dreams and the possibility of other realities that transgress borders of propriety and self-identity (Corbusier 1935). The sense of danger and threat, of a security that borders a profound insecurity, is never far from the experience of management in these places.

It is an experience available to the ethnographer that invites all manner of critical and psychoanalytical discourse. If management existed as jousting and preening male egos, however, this chapter has proposed that there was something more systemic that better explained it than individual personalities and their proclivities. Jousting and preening male egos was also something to which I was implicated by virtue of my own (limited) reflexive and constitutive practices. We have seen how the struggle to escape this existential tautology demanded conceptual but also practical displacement that helped wean the ethnographer off the fascination with individuals and the gossip and intrigue of corporate politics. So much so in fact that once I stopped participating I began to wonder if it had been a figment of my own imagination (cf. Wieder 1974).

Here I began to *realise* MAG men. I say *realise* because I was then – and now – in part helping to bring them into realisation by circulating new terms of questioning and engagement with my interlocutors at the airport. The ethnographer is often asked to account for his line of questioning, and I began circulating the term 'MAG men' as a possible resource for the crafting and explanation of certain actions and behaviours in which I too had participated. Hence, MAG men do not come fully armed with behaviours, tastes and attitudes; they are an intervention and an enquiry that might throw into relief otherwise obscure features of organization. As such, it proved productive and gave access to dimensions of organization otherwise occluded to me, especially the complex web of entanglements into which the familiar world of objects and subjects, the social and technical etc., cast by the dualisms of organization and management studies, began to dissolve as organization was rendered in a more vital and unsteady state.

This chapter has also noted that MAG men were more astute and skilled ethnographers than the one who was putatively studying them. They were also more attuned to objects and relations into which they were entangled, which I could not see because of my preoccupation with the machinations of rivalries and (micro) politicking. I recalled an episode in which Rob Fuller and I had both been present in an office in the Voyager building. 'Can you feel that rumble', he asks me? 'This is where PlutoArc were based, the old architects', he goes on to explain, 'in these very offices'. Once it had been brought to my attention I too noticed that there was a very tangible – albeit very slight – vibration and an ambient low-level hum. Turning one's attention to this hum and vibration led to a condition in which it became difficult to distinguish inside from out, so much so that the source of the rumble seemed to be one's very own bones.[13] 'Some buildings are happy and others are sad', his colleague explains. He tells me that one can even tell the *mood* of the management responsible for construction from the way a building works or doesn't work, the way it fits together, the finish, etc. In the case of PlutoArc, they were actually fired for the quality of work they were producing on a major project for the airport. On looking at their final design for the new terminal retail scheme the CEO famously declared that the space looked like the hospital ward where he had recently had a vasectomy. His (female) strategy director immediately added, 'and where I had mine done too!' Apparently intimidated and nervous, over cautious, there was no originality and vibrancy or vitality in the design. But was it the building or the individuals who occupied it who were responsible for the drawings and the design?

Increasingly reflexive and self-critical, becoming ever more self-conscious and aware, this chapter has shown that MAG men like Rob had a capacity to mediate and bring into action and being a far greater range of materials and phenomena than I had been capable. This complexity will be missed if we persist with the deployment of ready-made analytical categories that position his agency dialectically or otherwise within a duality of contending structure and agent. Sophisticated theories of existential anxiety seeking to break down the dualisms of sociological theory in management studies only exacerbates this foreclosure as we become preoccupied with collecting evidence that shows how people like Rob might have become fixated on confirming self-identity (Collinson 1992). Such an imperious and synthetic organizational vision does not attend with sufficient respect to the empirical. In the next chapter we find ways of attending in detail to the intricacy of materials and artefacts that make up this empirical, the humble spreadsheets, paperwork and documentary practices that go into the making of a lounge.

[13] Not mine alone, but those of the designers and managers who helped construct and then inhabit the space, '...by incorporating living labour with their dead substance, the capitalist at the same time converts value, i.e., past, materialised, and dead labour into capital, into value big with value, a live monster that is fruitful and multiplies' (Marx 1954: 189).

3

The Management of Escape: Scattered Attention and Disorderly Convulsion

Introduction

If access to the airport and its organization was facilitated by the discovery of 'MAG men', the precise nature of this 'access' has also signalled the possible beginnings of a departure from inherited modern organization theory. That this discovery was made in an airport may not be surprising given the fact that these organizations were largely the invention of a 20th century whereas we still inhabit, in the main, the terms of 19th century social science within which to try to understand it. This is made worse by virtue of the fact that in many ways, the airport reaches *beyond* the 20th century and stands on the cusp of flight into dimensions of being for which we still do not have an adequate language (Bachelard 1988; Pascoe 2001; Koolhaas 2002). For Le Corbusier, the airport leads into a condition where 'Everything Escapes Me', as he famously wrote, which means that we 'no longer possess an instrument which gives dimension, which makes form finite, complete, entire' (Corbusier 1935: 122). In more than a literal sense, flight means we no longer have our 'feet on the earth' with our 'eyes five feet or so above the ground' (ibid.). Given this, one might ask to what kind of 'flight' must one subject organization theory if it is to

D. O'Doherty, *Reconstructing Organization*,
DOI 10.1057/978-1-137-48922-7_3

'catch up' with what is happening on the borders of our nation states, in these places we call airports?

Central to this emerging condition of 'airport life' is what this study has named 'loungification'. Can we identify an explanation for this loungification? A compelling argument might be made to the effect that it represents a reaction or accommodation to the stresses and pressures of contemporary life and work, characterised by what some commentators see as 'work intensity, long-hours cultures and the normalizing of extreme work behaviours and cultures' (Granter et al. 2015: 443). As one industry spokesperson said during the course of this ethnography, airport lounges offer 'escape' from 'the hell' that has become the terminal. Caution should be exercised, however, with such simple causation. Let us ask first, *how* do these escapes get built? How are they managed? Surely that most sober of modern administrative sciences – management – must still have its feet on the earth and its eyes 'five feet of so' above the ground? However, is it possible for management to manage such 21st century projects when trained to understand its practice in 19th or 20th century terms? Must it also risk taking leave of these assumptions when working with loungification?

In making loungification the centre of our analysis, we become drawn into a vast range of materials and methods, practices and techniques involved in its construction and any adequate survey or synthesis of this heterogeneity demands skills and practices that exceed the mono-disciplinary functions of management. Management must be a good material scientist, a bureaucrat, a studious observer of people, a politician, and even a social worker, to manage projects of such complexity. In this chapter we find that in trying to follow the practices associated with loungification ethnography must be prepared to transgress the offices of bureaucratic organization and to reach further afield into often disparate and disconnected sites (Marcus 1995; Coleman and Von Hellerman 2012).[1] Like the project managers we follow in this chapter

[1] Often confused with comparative ethnographic study, multi-sited ethnography remains on the fringes of management and organization studies, despite the pioneering work of Czarniawska (2004a). In this respect Prasad (2013) and Ekman (2014) are promising and perhaps suggestive of an emerging interest in the value of such methodology. See also Yanow (2009) and Garsten and Nyqvist (2013).

the ethnographer must also learn to circumvent the carve up of organization into those typified divisions that postulate things like organization and environment, or demand and supply, inside and outside, or even cause and effect. In tracking the movements and relations across the putative boundaries of modern organization we are also made aware of a different *distribution* of things that make up organization. These occupy what might be thought of as a first approximation as *liminal* or *hybrid* spaces in organization.[2] So, whereas management is typically understood as an agent of action, responsibility, and decision, this chapter discovers a tension between the *dispersal* of management into a granular detail of objects, matters and techniques, and periodic efforts to collect this dispersal into synthesis and order. As this chapter shows, both movements – and their attempted reconciliation – can promote paralysis.

One form of collection was the assumption, claim, and assertion, of control. It was not unusual to hear that the Escape lounge project, for example, was the brainchild of one senior manager, or that the airport *belonged* to the leader of the city council. This glorification of the power and centrality of ownership and senior exective management in organization is shared by both mainstream and critical studies of management. But it is misleading. This chapter is the first of three chapters that draws heavily on the ethnographic study during which we move progressively away from this conception of management. The analysis will show that management is a contested outcome of *loungification*, as much as it is a prime-mover or initiator. In many ways management is a project in search of itself, as remarked in other ethnographies (Dalton 1959; Watson 1994), but in this chapter we find that it is not a project in either a technical or *existential* sense. Such quests for explanatory closure are entangled with practices that implicate an array of associated materials and technologies that all pull and push in a multitude of directions during the progress of a project. These materials and technologies are only ever partially under the control or comprehension of management.

---

[2] Ultimately these terms are misleading and imply a position *between* two relatively well-defined dualisms. We need a language that captures the active work performed in this 'between' and which works to change things like structure and agency, or object and subject. Giddens meta-concept 'structuration' has appealed to many but this remains too grandiose and synthetic for the kind of processes uncovered here in this study of loungification.

This chapter follows the various office technologies and materials[3] that come to bear on the Escape Lounge project and as they transpire and coalesce in the working practices of one manifestation of 'MAG men' – namely the character we call 'Robyn' – the project manager assigned to the lounge. As the project progresses Robyn finds himself immersed in ever-greater entanglements of process and matter – which include GANTT charts and 'best-practice' methods enshrined in the PRINCE-2 project methodology, standard construction product pricing books, and the specificities of the legal contracts (the Joint Council Tribunal's 'Design and Build Contract') used to regulate construction and its management. We might call this a multiplicity of 'market devices' (Callon et al. 2007) and this chapter shows how they snowball during a project. This snowballing demands of the project manager (and the ethnographer) an ever-greater capacity to suspend any simple ontological assumption about organization so that projects can be allowed to dwell in ambiguity and uncertainty. Without this tolerance for incertitude, a number of tautologies and aporias are made present. The demands of formal 'paperwork', for example, means that the slightest 'error' – the failure to dot an I or cross a T – might substantially cripple progress or even completion of a project. As project managers become ever more immersed in the gap between the words and things of these market devices, they have to contend with the possibility that some things – in the specifics of this project to build Escape, for example, a seemingly simple air-handling unit – seem to both *work* and *not work* at the same time!

Watching how Robyn works I learn to fashion the concept 'scattered attention' that helps show how one can overcome these proliferations and threatened paralyses whilst also retaining a grasp of the co-presence of a bewildering accumulation of matters. The practice of scattered attention also brings into association things that are normally kept distinct and sepa-

[3] Perhaps on the cusp of its disappearance or transformation, there have been some signs of an emerging interest in the apparently mundane objects, materials and technologies associated with the modern office. These include the typewriter, the memo (Yates 1989), records, record keeping, the filing cabinet and more recently email, the XLS spreadsheet, and the PowerPoint slide (see Yates 1989; Yates and Orlikowski 2007). These objects and tools have been shown to be far from marginal or irrelevant, but are in fact constitutive of wider organizational effects. Indeed, without the humble paperclip it is possible the modern office would not have been viable in the form to which we have become accustomed (Petroski 1992).

rate in business and management studies. However, scattered attention is always at risk from what we discover to be 'disorderly convulsions'. This is a concept that Deleuze (1992) originally coined to explore the affects stimulated by the techniques of German expressionist cinema. With its dynamic form of montage, the cinema of Pabst, Murnau and Lang brought together that which was normally separated in cinema – foreground and background, for example. But these cinematic constructions also helped fuse that which is normally kept separate in terms of animate and inanimate, the natural and artificial, the organic and inorganic, etc. Even that which appears dead and that which seems alive becomes con-fused and uncertain. The re-working of 'disorderly convulsion' in this chapter helps gives access to – and an understanding of – an extraordinary denouement experienced during the project. In this moment, the most basic spatial and temporal coordinates of organization seemed to come 'out of joint' (Derrida 1994). During this episode, neither Robyn nor the ethnographer possessed an instrument to give dimension, to make form finite, complete, or entire. Linearity constantly gives way to a more labyrinthine tangle of lines.

Is it any wonder we might aspire after the comforts of a lounge?

27th May 2010, Escape Lounge Site Visit. 10.20 am

Tony, the site foreman, proceeds to pull up a sheet of corrugated plastic sheet floor-protection. We are being invited to look at what appears to be a most strange configuration of marble floor tiles, made up of 5 or 6 irregular fragments of varying size and angle. They form a complex tesselated pattern at the intersection of two broad pathways of more regular and orthogonal floor tiling, one row running vertical and the other horizontal. These pathways will eventually form the two major walkways through which lounge customers will eventually traverse the space. Projecting a large central cross on the floor plate, these two pathways appear to anchor or structure the lounge. At the pivot of its intersection Tony appears to be reading our faces, explaining that 'the lads' have had to improvise with the tiling because there is an apparent 'discrepancy' between the drawings and what was 'practical', he says, given the actual dimensions of the space.

Working in the Tramlines

The various project managers gathered around the mosaic of tiles are wielding clipboards and various paper documents: GANNT charts, process maps, architectural drawings, floor plans etc. This tangle of lines that form across the arrangement of tiles stands in marked contrast to the apparent clarity and definition of the lines represented in the spreadsheets and site report pro forma, lines that are curiously reproduced in the pin stripes on the suits worn by the men from the commercial team.

Most obvious to any casual observer is the prevalence of the Excel spreadsheet. Only the Power-point slide can perhaps lay claim to more ubiquity – and with debatable consequences for the health and sustainability of organization (Tufte 2003; Adams 2006; Yates and Orlikowski 2007; cf. Stark and Paravel 2008; Kaplan 2011). The spreadsheet is everywhere in MAG projects: it sits on portable iPads, iPhones, and desktop computer screens; they can be found lying around on desks, piled up on old-fashioned paper 'in-trays' and 'outboxes', projected onto whiteboards and visual display units, and can be seen routinely circulating hand-to-hand in meetings. The Excel spreadsheet seems to be the quintessence and blueprint for all these documentary practices of the managers working on the Escape Lounge. They give the impression that people work in straight lines and square boxes. Indeed, strict record keeping, linearity and order is assumed and enforced by the strict adherence to PRINCE-2 methodology which project managers at the time were under increasing pressure to deploy to help manage projects in the airport.

It is documents such as these that allow us to be more specific *where* we are in the project and *what* we are doing during this site visit. By attending to the tramlines that position and fix the work of the project teams we achieve a certain measure of clarity and precision. Using the summary and schematic GANTT chart devised as an overview for the project for example, we occupy the horizontal row number 40 (see image 2 below) titled 'On Site'. We are, therefore, about halfway through the 50 days allocated for this phase, hence we are located in the cell highlighted in the image below (Fig. 3.1).

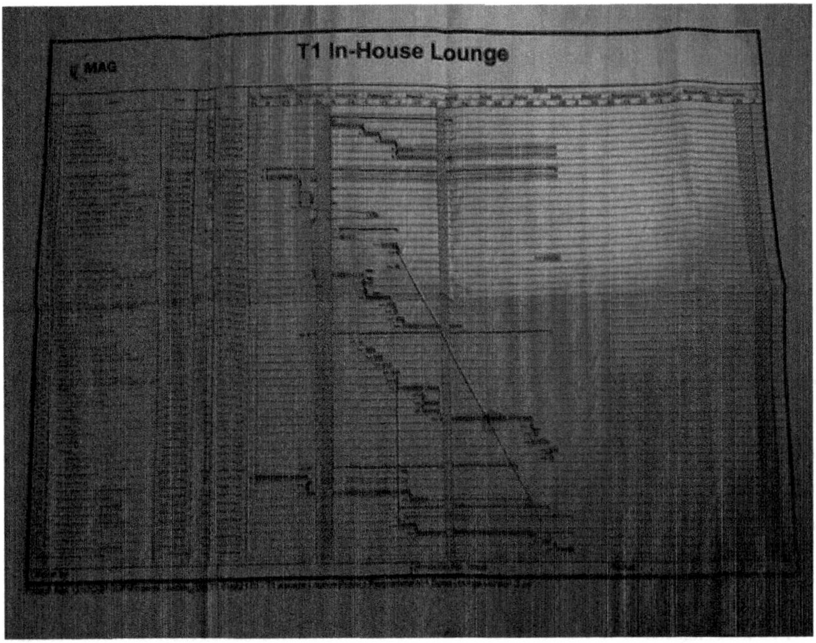

Fig. 3.1 The GANTT chart

There are more detailed charts that accompany the work of the project manager; the full GANTT chart, for example, runs to 486 sequenced processes, all subdividing into ancillary and supporting templates and 'process maps'. According to the summary 'process map' recently devised by the Project Management team we can be located precisely in the 'Reporting cycle and Delivery Phase', which follows 'Start on Site' and precedes 'Operational Readiness'. The 'Delivery phase' subdivides into three main activities for the project manager: (a) Meetings, Reporting and Communication, (b) Gateway Process, and (c) Change Control Process. Akin to an 'archive fever' (Derrida 1996a), each of these again subdivides into more sub-categories and sub-processes of activities, the conduct of which is detailed in various meta-guidance documents, all presented in the form of elaborate boxes, lines and sequences and made available on the projects intranet and online information systems. On this 27th May site visit, the lead project manager for the airport, Robyn, is compiling data that will eventually be recorded in a variety of documents, including project meeting notes, the risk register, an issues log, highlight reports, the schedule of outstanding defects, payment certificates, and sectional completion, all of which have pro-forma and guidance notes to assist in their completion.

Early in the project, for example, Robyn has to work on a draft 'project brief'. On first glance this brief provides straight lines and simple boxes to tick. Indeed, the Escape Lounge made its first appearance in the form of a Draft Project Brief V0.01 template (Fig. 3.2).

The purpose of this document, it tells us, is 'to provide a full and firm foundation for the initiation of the project'. Further instruction follows to inform the user/reader that this 'Project Brief will go into the PID when fully completed'. Now, one obviously needs to know a lot about project management and PRINCE-2 methodology to make much sense of this and to have some grasp of how it has been compiled and the purposes it ostensibly serves (Garfinkel 1967). One might reasonably ask: 'What is 'fully completed''? Or, 'What is a PID'? As always we cannot abstract or isolate a part and assume it has meaning and definitional integrity. However, nor can we assume that this is even something like a *part*. A part needs a whole, but the ethnographer is never able to find the whole into which these 'parts' of the PRINCE-2 documentation could be inserted. And there is a more complex hermeneutics than part/whole going on here as well.

Consider the PID, the 'project initiation document'. In some ways this acts like a *master file* collecting and storing a series of what become sub-documents, such as the project brief, but also the business case, team structure documentation, role descriptions, quality management strategy, configuration management strategy, and risk management strategy (OGC 2009: 254–255). How to correctly compile and use a PID, however, can be an object of considerable discussion and analysis. The sheer volume of secondary literature designed to guide the project manager through the various documentary practices of PRINCE-2 methodology is itself bewildering and disorientating (Charvat 2003; Newton 2006; Bentley 2009; and their respective reading lists for a selection). Without the completion and approval of the project brief, however, we cannot begin to make a lounge, nor can we begin to initiate the processes that will produce the documentation that appears in the PID. However, it

DRAFT PROJECT BRIEF V0.01

Project Ref:	**PDR 2179**
Project Name:	**Manchester Airport Executive Lounge, T1.**
Distribution:	
Date:	**18.03.09**
Author:	
Acceptance Signature:	
Purpose of this document:	**To provide a full and firm foundation for the initiation of the project. The Project Brief will go into the PID, when fully completed. The Project Brief is a key document in its own right. It is the basis of the PID, which gives the direction and scope of the project.**

Background

As part of the Terminal allocation strategy it is proposed to develop Terminal 1 as the Full Service Long and Short haul Terminal. This has identified the need to increase the number CIP/ Executive Lounges within the Terminal. As result of the existing Terminal 1 retail and security development and the proposed short term T3 security expansion the existing Meridian landside catering facilities were made redundant.

Phase 1 of the development consisted of extensive refurbishment of communal areas and the creation of 'developer' shell and core space for Emirates to fit out at the front of the fallow area.

Future phases within the building are currently open for discussion with tenants.

Project Objectives

The objective of the project is to increase our commercial rental income through the provision of a Manchester Airport "Spec" Lounge on this level. (To a standard that does not overshadow Emirates but does not detract from the communal areas – but above the other terminal lounges).

The lounge should have an open plan feel but incorporate the following general areas or be zoned in the following way –

Seating area for self service buffet style food (as per T2 Escape Lounge)
Small Reception / Entrance Zone with admin area
Comfortable seating area

Fig. 3.2 RAPAMAG, draft project brief

seems we also need to know quite a lot about how to build a lounge and how organization works *before* we are able to complete the initiation document. Have we not then already engaged in the *initiation* of the project? Indeed, it might seem reasonable to suppose that we have somehow begun *prior* to the completion of the paperwork.

The documentation offers a recording *after the fact*, yet it is also supposed to provide a guide as to how to proceed in time and sequence. We therefore seem to enter a complex and treacherous temporality in organization, somehow both *in time* and *out of time*. This is what Derrida (1994) might call 'time out of joint'. For the PID we need a project scope, an outline business case, an indicative design and architectural space drawings, for example. All of this requires expertise that can only be sourced from specialist outside contractors (in this case an architect), which involves considerable work of organization and also, signficantly, payment. Before any payment is made, however, the project manager will need to obtain some capital expenditure approval. However, at this stage we don't even have a project brief. In the approved process, a brief *follows* a 'mandate'. Now, it is logically difficult if not formally impossible to 'sign off' a mandate without some outline of what it is that one is being asked to grant a mandate! The hermeneutic circles of Gadamer and Heidegger might seem to pale into rudimentary exercises of style compared to some of the hermeneutic work our project manager is doing here.

While all this is going on project managers working at the airport are encouraged to keep track of their projects by reference to a summary 'process overview' (Fig. 3.3):

However, if one tries to follow the sequence and logic implied in this process template, it would appear as though one has to complete a project mandate *before* opening the project files! One has to complete the future, before returning to the past and retaking one's place in the presumed continuity of a forward moving linear sequence. Such fantastical 'logic' and time travel appears *non-human*. Even in the context of an airport this seems incredulous and something that risks a kind of jetlag all of its own. However, there are many practical solutions to the apparently circular and tautological logic of formal PRINCE-2 style methodology: one might rely on favours for architectural drawings, for example, in which the

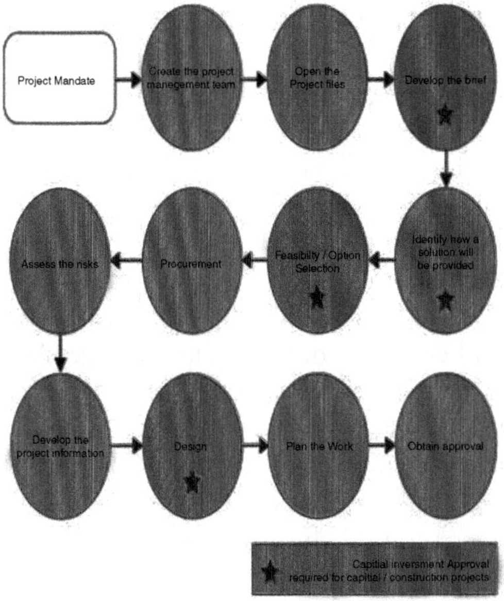

Fig. 3.3 Process overview (RAPAMAG handbook, 2006: 11)

architect might be encouraged to think that this favour might help their chance of selection during a tendering process. Alternatively, the architect might be involved in another project for which there may be contingency allowing a more generous payment for ongoing work that will cover (or cross-subsidise) the costs associated with the new Escape project. Here the lines of organization are becoming ever more complicated.

In practical terms the simple lines and linear sequencing of published project management methodology and approved ways of working can only be achieved if the project manager has been able to trace out and work through the lineaments of a more complex series of tangled and non-linear lines. Indeed, as the project gained momentum Robyn increasingly found himself embroiled in multiple lines of association that could be extended *out* to the farthest reaches of what is routinely called the apparatus of the nation state, and *inwards* to the more intimate sense of gender and identity, only some of which we are able to tackle in this chapter.

Re-assembling the Organization

As we follow the circulation of these documents, it becomes evident that more and more parts of the airport become present, or make their presence felt through the paperwork. We need to know something about the relations between what members call 'group' and 'airport', for example, in order to make much sense of what is going on when Robyn fills out his Draft Project Brief (see Fig. 3.1 above); indeed we need to know something of this airport/group relation in order to begin to understand the emergence and evolution of the Escape Lounge. As indicated in the project brief, in the section demarcated 'Background', the need for an Escape Lounge is explained in terms of 'terminal allocation strategy'. The precise details of this 'strategy' and how this might translate into practical day-to-day operations and decisions are a little hazy – not least amongst those participants responsible for the lounge. Indeed, this 'strategy' gets slowly marginalized or at least placed in the *background* as the project proceeds and later iterations of the brief are published.

Far more documentary space is subsequently devoted to explaining the objectives of the project as one that aims 'to increase commercial rental income through the provision of a Manchester Airport 'Spec' lounge ...'. For the airport's commercial team, passengers are customers – or potential customers – and terminal 1 provides the most lucrative space in which to construct the Escape Lounge. What might make sense in terms of a strictly operational point of view, for the airline and the airport, might not make sense for the commercial team (see Mol 2002). At the time of the launch of the Escape Lounge the commercial team is largely dominated by Manchester Airport commercial, but the Lounge is also being branded as a *group-wide facility* with the intention that the product would be rolled out at other airports in the group. Manchester Airport is strictly a regional airport, at least from the vantage point of 'group', but it retains considerable privilege and dominance, partly because of its size. Hence it is not included in the organizational charts that represent the 'regional airports division'. This tension between MA and Group becomes evident as we follow the progress of the project, particularly as we learn to devote attention to the detail and apparent mundanity of paperwork, which plays an important and interesting role in these wider struggles.

At one meeting for example, the project team is joined by Jenny, a senior manager from one of the other airports in the group. The fact that she is from another airport appears significant when the senior marketing manager for the group announces that 'It's important to see ESCAPE as a *sub-brand* of the MAG *commercial brand*' and 'the concept needs to be consistent across MAG because this is *a MAG product*, not an MA product'. Jenny, however, seems unfamiliar with what is being called the 'MAG commercial brand' and what this entails in terms of projects, process, or strategy. 'I haven't seen the research from the focus group' she says. Recall that the title 'Escape' has not been mentioned in the early documentation. Indeed the initial work and drive for the project came from 'product services' which according to the rough organogram quickly sketched for me by the product services manager was a sub-function of '*Manchester Airport* Commercial Development'. To complicate matters further, the product services manager confesses to me 'I'm not committed to the ESCAPE lounge brand … this is a historical legacy arising from a lounge in terminal 2, which is basically a few dry nuts and biscuits. The name is the product of a quick and dirty marketing campaign which is past its shelf life'. He goes on to tell me that 'the brand is not strong enough' and 'we don't want the name'.

Over time, however, the product services manager, or more senior figures in Manchester Airport commercial development, either change their minds, or the *group* marketing and branding team (possibly with the support of the group strategy team) manoeuvre in ways to *insist* upon the brand 'Escape'. It is also possible that the MA commercial team increasingly began to ally themselves with the ambitions of those identified as 'Group Commercial' strategy – there will be increasing roles made available at group, for example, particularly if the Escape Lounge becomes a group product.

In sum, in attending closely to the 'project brief' we can see how documentation becomes a site through which a number of different parts of the organization are being assembled and made, and a site where different parts of an airport are seeking/negotiating role and influence. At the moment, we can see from the document that we have an airport specific *operations* function, and a *commercial* team. In turn, the commercial team is divided between airport and group. During the evolution of the Escape project, members of 'group' increasingly assumed the role of custodians, and by hook or by crook the project is soon colloquially referred to as the 'Escape Lounge project'. With this nomenclature and its uptake around the organization it seems there has been a shift in the balance of power between various groups and departments in the airport. Indeed, the lounge can be understood as a vehicle through which power was sought and mobilised, negotiated and 'settled' (cf. Hull, 2012). In addition to struggles between airport, group, commercial and operations, another dimension of this struggle for power – in what seems to be a version of 'war by other means' – is a generational struggle between the young and old members of the projects management team.

The Rise of Project Management

Our project manager on Escape finds himself in a *crossfire* of these multiple intersecting lines of force. Robyn is a young member of the projects team, one of the graduate intakes but with about 6 years of experience in projects. In these terms we can see that the insistence on documentation, process and transparency provided a discourse that allowed younger and newer members of the MAG projects team to break into the older network, displacing more established individuals and groups embedded in its former incarnation 'MADL' (Manchester Airport Developments Ltd), a group with apparently limited company status in which as one former member said 'we ran the books, charged PMs [project managers] out at £70 per hour and then added 10 %' – the director, by all accounts, known as 'Mr. 10 %'.

Robyn might also be considered a bit-part player in the ambitions of the projects management department, ambitions that found expression through the actions of the recently appointed young executive director of projects, Rob Fuller, for whom 'process', 'procedure' and 'accountability' offered a resource that could support the future growth of project management. In line with this new commitment to process and 'professional practice' project management at the airport increasingly began to account for its activities within the terms of the PRINCE-2 project management methodology, adapted and applied in the form of a RAPAMAG process (Running a Project at Manchester Airport Group).[4]

Project management was clearly in the ascendency, in part *because of the lounge*, the 'sexy project' as it was referred, but also because of this commitment and display to process and procedure.[5] Of course, what explains the lounge cannot be satisfactorily answered by looking inside the discrete organization of Manchester Airport. There were wider forces at play including the commercialization of airports, and the fashion for passenger lounges. These were forces, however, that could be harnessed and given further expression and extension through the promotion of the projects management department, with potential career gains for many of the key players associated with Escape.

The lounge then acts as much as a *resource* for negotiation in the shifting balance of power in the airport – and in the wider professions and knowledge expertise – as it is an *outcome* of established power and resource. We can also say that, in part, the lounge gives rise to *new* 'interests' and 'ambitions'. It would be a mistake to see the lounge as simply a passive object of various occupational or managerial ambitions who act as subjects or agents of its construction. Project Management is partly an *outcome* as much as it is an *agent* of lounge construction. Part of this 'outcome' is realized in the fact that project managers learn new skills and acquire new design expertise as the commissioning and construction of the lounge proceeds. What project management can offer as expertise, then, does not come *prior* to the lounge, in part because the lounge is not something that is *known* prior to the process of its design and construction. More strictly, as recent advances in architectural theory confirm, what is known about a project, something like the lounge, for example, emerges as a series of potentialities or 'virtualities' that are only partially

[4] During the period 2009–2010, Rob insisted that every departmental project complete the PRINCE-2 training program, one that I was also able to complete and qualify during the ethnography becoming credentialised as a 'foundation' project manager.

[5] Members of the project team have moved on to other lounge projects in the airport and in the wider industry. Some have been promoted to senior project manager roles and one member of the team became managing director of one of the group's airports.

brought into being, or articulated, during the process of its design and construction (see also Yaneva 2009).

As was implied earlier, what is *known* about the lounge is critically dependent on the documents and templates (in the digital and online form) that are used to represent the lounge. 'Where' the design is in terms of schedule and time boundaries, for example, or budget or quality, can only be known through the medium of paperwork (see also Hull 2012). And here there is another 'virtuality' at work. We have seen earlier how documents and paperwork become entangled with other documents and paperwork in an infinite deferral of meaning. The project brief can only be made sense of in relation to a series of *interlinked* documents that are referenced and implied in the project brief (the PID, CAPEX, Mandate, etc.).

This relationality lends a processual 'liveliness' to paperwork. However, attending closely to working practices also shows how the paperwork becomes a more *active player* in the construction of the lounge. Indeed, it can come to take on a life of its own. In fact, paperwork takes on properties more commonly assumed to reside exclusively with human agents. Paperwork, for example, gives instruction and seeks to discipline its user. Consider the section 'Purpose of the document', which includes the following instruction: 'To provide a full and firm foundation for the initiation of the project. The Project Brief will go into the PID, when fully completed ...'. One must submit to and observe the requirements of the paperwork, and much of the time Robyn can be found in front of his desktop screen filling out seemingly endless amounts of paperwork. Tracking the movement of these documents also reveals that there is often no reader. This marks more than a simple *deferral* of authorship. Without author and without reader, the paperwork becomes increasingly self-referential, and perhaps even parasitical (see Serres 1982) in its assumption of an autonomous life (Dery 1998).

Getting entangled with 'papereality' (Dery, ibid.) implicates management in a series of infinite regresses. This provides stimulus and resource to management, but also potential paralysis. As the production of paperwork proliferates and multiplies it generates ever more work for monitoring and control, which therefore demands ever more managerial resources, and also calls for more systematic project planning. The establishment of a 'project management office' (PMO), for example, is often deemed the *sine qua non* of professionalized project management (see Hill 2014; Dai and Wells 2004). Here the paperwork becomes an *ally* of managerial ambition and political struggle. However, it is also a potentially treacherous and unreliable ally. If documents are vehicles through which project management can *extend* its presence in organization, in this multiplication more and more complexity comes to bear on the documents. We can show this by exploring the role of the 'project management team structure' documentation.

Team Structure Documentation

Early in a project, RAPAMAG methodology recommends that the project manager agree a team structure, a 'chart showing who will be involved in the project' (OGC 2009: 255) and a summary of the 'role descriptions', which in the language of RAPAMAG is amalgamated into a 'Roles and Responsibilities Report' that 'the Project Manager prepares and submits to the Project Board for approval'. Typically these roles are understood in the following terms: 'corporate' or 'programme management', an 'executive', a 'senior user', a 'senior supplier', a 'team manager', 'project assurance', and 'project support' (Fig. 3.4).

There is so much going on here that it is difficult to retain all the elements in play, or to establish a sense of priority, scale or directionality. Once again, we see here a complicated set of lines, indicative of a *double movement*: straight lines and boxes – with linkages and clear boundaries; but then there are also broken lines, some that deviate and zigzag, at times appearing to cross-over otherwise neatly bounded spaces. The lack of directional arrows here is worth noting. Paralysis by the over-accumulation of linearity is here supplemented by a form of paralysis engendered by a palimpsest of lines deviating and leading in multiple and ambiguous directions (see Callon and Law 2005). The role of the project manager might be textually unambiguous with respect to the *authorship* of the Project Brief. However, in terms of their position within the

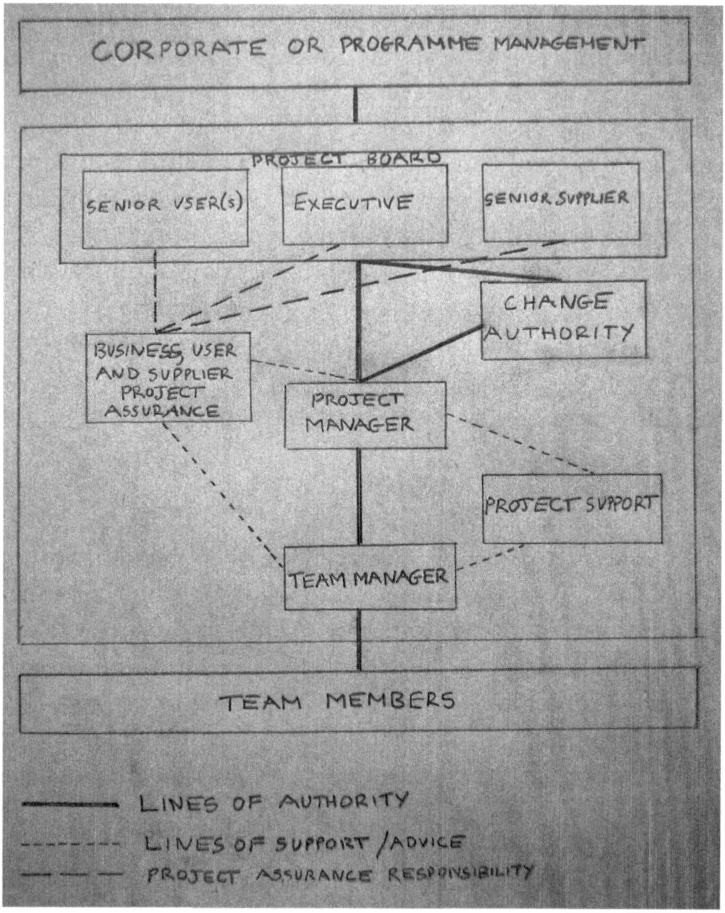

Fig. 3.4 Typical project management team structure (author's sketch)

project management team structure, the role appears more ambiguous. So much so that one is liable to get a little lost. Let us take this slowly….

The role of the project manager is defined as that of a 'producer' who is 'responsible for the product's production' (OGC 2009: 129). One might think that the product is the lounge. However, in the professional discourse of the project manager a 'product' is an 'input or output, whether tangible or intangible, that can be described in advance, created and tested' (OGC 2009: 308). This now gets even more complicated. There are in fact *two types* of products according to the principles of PRINCE-2 – 'management products' and 'specialist products'. We are not yet at the bottom. A further sub-definition breaks up specialist products into a series of *mini-products*, examples of which include 'an advertising campaign, a car park ticketing system, foundations for a building, a new business process' (OGC, ibid.: 313), all suggestive of the possibility that it is specialist products 'all the way down' (cf. Geertz 1973).

To cut through some of this complexity it is helpful to return to some basic assumptions about economic relations and processes at work in a market. If the role of the project manager is to produce products (PRINCE-2 style paperwork), one of which is the production of a brief that lays out what it is the client wants, then what the client wants would be understood as 'demand', in the terms of an economist. The PM is responsible for this 'demand'. The main 'supplier' would appear at this stage to be the architects, at least pre-construction – or pre-appointment of a construction firm. In the language of standard economics, there must always be someone who does the demanding, and another who provides the supply, with a price emerging in relation to the relative balance between demand and supply (Samuelson and Nordhaus 1998: 447–468). It is the role of the architects to take the brief and from it develop a design that can then form part of what is known as a *tender package*, which will be published 'in the market' and circulated amongst interested contractors. Recall, the brief provides what is called the 'firm foundation', i.e. this is what *the customer* wants: a Manchester 'Spec' Lounge, or later an 'Escape Lounge'. The brief tells us that the airport wants 'more of a 'wow' factor', a 'high quality but not over-stated entrance', a 'neutral, cool feel' and be 'classy and timeless', and perhaps above all else to 'increase our commercial income'.

If we are to follow these processes to discover what is supplied, we need to know something about how the architects *make sense* of these requirements. In the next section we follow the processes of translation associated with this sense-making where we uncover additional ambiguity and a further proliferation of roles.

Architects and 'the Brief'

In their presentation to the Project Board on the 26th November the architecture team are responding to the brief. Images of jet aircraft vapour trails and ceiling fins are being projected using PowerPoint; there are fashion magazine pictures of young men and women drinking cocktails in fashionable city centre bars; we are told that 'incorporated lighting helps to create emphasis and a 'wow' factor on arrival'; there are dens and snugs, study spaces and 'the attic' – a place that 'truly reflects the Escape Brand – to be different and fun … in a grown up manner!' It is fast and flash, a multi-media show in which we see how the architects have translated and imagined the brief in architectural terms: materials, spatial properties, style, interior design, 'look and feel', etc. The grey flannel suits and pin-stripe suits of those from the airport contrasts with the swirling patterns of paisley open shirts and multi-coloured scarfs sported by members of the architecture and design team.

Once again we encounter here a movement of circularity and aporia. The architects' design, for example, makes a number of assumptions about things like customer profile, the size of the space, and the numbers of customers that will be expected to use the space in any one hour. None of this information is provided in the brief. At the same time the manager from 'product development' is still preoccupied with the development of 7 different 'business case' scenarios based on a number of different projections and assumptions dependent on space, cost, size. We have a project that seems to have started, without a firm business case, which prompts one to ask: what comes first? The design, or the business case? In fact, both are mutually constructed. The business case is dependent on the design, but this can only be developed with confidence if the architects know the customer profile or the client market, which form part of the business case. Here is another vicious circle. To build a business case *one needs to know the product*, but to invest in the development of a product one also needs to have an architectural design, for which one needs a business case, a paradoxical and vicious circle that has yet to be fully explored in the literature on the making of markets and the 'captation' of publics or the making of consumers (Miller and Rose 1997; Trentmann 2006; Cochoy 2007; Callon et al. 2007; Zwick and Denegri

2009; Muniesa and Trebuchet-Breitwiller 2010; Ariztia 2015). Breaching the logic of this circularity entails risk and a preparedness to submit to this risk, but the difficulty arises as to *where* this risk might lie, or *to whom* this risk might be attributed?

These circularities and aporias become more evident when we drill down into the brief and follow its assembly and organizational biography, or what we might call the 'social life' of the brief (Appadurai 1986; Brown and Duguid 2002; Savage 2013). In the following extract from an early design team meeting, the architects articulate very clearly the phrase "*your* A4 brief". Studied retrospectively, the progress of this meeting is notable for the subtlety of negotiation and ruse as the phrase "*your* A4 brief" becomes ever more explicit and definitive. Earlier, one of the junior architects had commented – more in passing than directly – that 'we need more of a steer on exactly what you want in the offer'. There was just a *hint* of frustration, but of course, any trace of frustration is carefully modulated and I extract this quote from a complex and skilful conversation involving all manner of shadow play and negotiation. The intricacy of these negotiations is bewildering, particularly as we listen to how it is being conducted between more senior members of the project board.

Let us briefly explore some extracts from these exchanges to illustrate this complexity and the care with which it needs managing:

Senior Architect: 'well, *your A4 brief* contains the information about what the lounge is going to do, which has now been signed off ... what we need to do is use our 'fluffy stuff' and your brief together'

Project Manager: 'Yes, so we need *a map* to close it down'
(Emphasis added)

Twice the architect uses the term '*your* (A4) brief', which is really an assumption because the details of the A4 brief have not been collectively debated or agreed amongst the client team (the airport). The ownership of the existing brief remains unclear, but its content also operates much like the 'brackets' that Riles (2001) has studied in the writing of United Nations documentation. In our case, the lack of definition and closure permits agreement to proceed whilst deferring any potential disagreement to a future committee meeting. No one challenges the architect that the A4 brief does *not* do these things (i.e. contains the information about what the lounge is going to do). This lack of clarification might allow the architect to make the assumption that silence is approval, and that the A4 brief does in fact do these things. This would have the tactical advantage of allowing the architect to declare that their presentation responds adequately to the brief. Any perceived lack of clarity or definition in the presentation can then be attributed to a lack of clarity in the brief – or '*your* brief' (i.e. the airport project managers' brief, or the 'client team' (see Alvesson et al. 2009a; Sturdy and Wright 2011)). By assuming the brief tells us what the lounge is going to do – *but only in the most general of terms* – then the lack of specificity or technical precision in the outline designs can be explained by the fact that the architects can only work on the basis of the brief that they have been given. We might then see that this interjection on behalf of the architect forms part of a tactical set of speculations; in effect, he is asking whether the brief is doing the job that the client wants it to do.

As the conversation develops, one of the directors for commercial development at the airport confides, late into the meeting, 'look, we need your ideas to help develop the brief'. He goes on to say that 'We need to be sure it [the lounge] works for all our demographics'. Yet, the architects have already noted that the airport has not provided any clear or comprehensive and reliable statistical data on airport passenger profiles. As we will explore in more detail in chapter 5, one might well ask how can there be data for a category that doesn't yet exist, namely the lounger? In fact, as the project develops the architects are asked to do some of this analytics, but as they confess in a later meeting, getting hold of this information is extremely difficult.

For our purposes here, what is important to extract and draw out from this meeting is the uncertainty and the evolving and changing role definitions that increasingly confuse and transgress the separation of demand and supply. At this stage, the architect is in one respect the *supplier* of products and services in the form of a design that responds to the brief, which takes up the role of demand. However, they are also deeply implicated in helping the airport to forge what it is the airport thinks it wants from the Escape Lounge. Demand and supply, or buyer and seller, appear too imprecise in situations where the lines of division are complex, multiple and mutable. We are still in a crossfire of roles and responsibilities, with no clear demand, or supply, and no price. *Everything seems to be in movement.*

Scattered Attention

At the centre of all this movement we find Robyn. He is being pulled one-way and then another. There appear to be no points of fixity around him, a problem exacerbated but also in part created by the kind of charts and maps and process documentation provided by PRINCE-2. To acquire some understanding of the position of our project manager it is more helpful to conceive of him as inhabiting a centre-point amidst a series of radiating *forces*. Not only do these forces *extend* in space and time linking up people and objects in relations beyond the boundaries of formal organization, but they also provide the resource for a different kind of temporal and spatial definition. In order to find where one might be one must learn to grasp location not as fixed or linear in sequence, as promised in the formal documentation, but as *movement.*[6]

Attending more closely to the fact that everything is in movement we begin to see that Robyn must draw ever more complex lines in order to translate and make coherent all the things that begin to 'come out of the woodwork', which was how one project manager characterized the typical progress of a project. Let us follow Robyn on an average working day from when he arrives in the office and opens his email to the point at which he leaves the office. In doing this one finds that he spends quite a lot of time *walking*. Perhaps this is unique to a site based project manager, and in particular the demands made on projects by virtue of his workspace being an airport. Along complex and sinuous pathways Robyn walks, forming lines across the airport campus sometimes 2–3 miles in length.

[6] I experimented with variations of Csikszentmihalyi's (1990) concept of 'flow', which appeared promising in the attempt to map and develop the required disposition that could find ways of resolving the apparent paradox of simultaneous position and movement. Gleick (1987) was also suggestive. However, apart from one unpublished thesis (Miller 2012) that came out of this work, there was little uptake of 'flow' more widely within MAG projects, where more resources were being invested in methods akin to PRINCE.

This involves the use of corridors and subterranean passages off-limits to airport passengers and behind the scenes of the carefully designed spaces through which the passenger is moved.

Following Robyn is instructive. The lines he draws are complex and labyrinthine. Often surprising turns are taken; at times he goes underground, and on other occasions has to double back on himself as he burrows through the interlinked array of terminal spaces with its shifting lines of boundary-making and division.[7] Not only is Robyn navigating a series of different roles and gatekeepers as he makes his way through the airport, he is also being brought into contact with the multiplicity of sites and materials that must be mobilized and integrated in order to achieve the building of the lounge. One day we find ourselves high up on a rooftop of the terminal where we meet an engineer who shows us the air-handling unit that the project plans to make use of for the lounge air-conditioning system. On paper, the air-handling unit worked. It has a full service record and is currently in use, *and* with spare capacity. However, as the engineer points at the unit he tells us 'You think it's there, but it's not. Look'. He then opens up the doors of the cabinet. I am invited to peer inside where I see a tangle of tubes, wires and belts – a bit like a PRINCE-2 diagram. A missing belt means that the air-handling unit will not work; the air-handling unit is therefore to all intents and purposes *not there* – or at least it might as well *not* be there. However, it is never simply a matter of acquiring a new belt. *Knowing* this takes considerable expertise to diagnose. Knowing *who* has the expertise can also be a problem. What we are looking at on the roof of the terminal is not an air-handling unit. It is simply a metal case, or shell. Moreover, it is one that both works and doesn't work. As it turns out, another project manager explains, whether it works or not really 'depends on whom you talk to'.

According to the latest engineering survey, the air-handling unit works. Or at least it did on the last inspection. However, since that inspection the belt might have over-stretched, slipped off, snapped, or shorn its tread. In this case, the air-handling unit still works – it is a *component* that is not

[7] This is what Rem Koolhaas (2002: 177) calls the 'junkspace' of airports marked by permanent reconstruction, 'a quasi-panoptical universe in which all contents rearrange themselves in split seconds around the dizzy eye of the beholder'.

working. Therefore if the air-handling unit does not appear to work, one simply needs to replace the belt, which a good project manager should have made a cost allowance for when buying the unit, or when proposing to make (increased) use of it on a new project. However, there was no costing allowance for engineering maintenance in the Escape Lounge business case. As is typical of projects at the airport, these are considered *fixed assets* and therefore maintained by an engineering department. The engineers, of course, complain constantly about the adequacy of their budget, especially when the energy infrastructure of the airport is being used more intensively with each new project. For engineers, who do not have a replacement budget, one has to simply replace the fan belt to make the unit work.

The problem becomes one of *establishing* a case that one has to replace the belt to keep the air-handling unit working. Pirsig (1974) famously draws attention to the inter-relation of parts in a complex system showing that the part that keeps breaking could be a downstream problem caused by something *upstream* – or deeper in the 'gubbins' of the equipment. As Pirsig shows, problems cannot be isolated into any part. Instead, problems are better thought of as that which occurs or lies *between* any identifiable part – and, importantly, in the relation *between* the user and the equipment. The existing engineering services brief seems to betray no ambiguity where those responsible for installation and maintenance are given clear instruction: 'the fan and motor' for example 'shall be capable of dealing with an excess pressure development of 15 % above the required total pressure at the design volume whilst still being within the normal fan operating range and without causing problems of regenerated noise'. But how long should it be capable of dealing with an excess pressure development? How can this be reliably measured?

As we investigate the problem further we are led to wonder whether the belt that keeps breaking is a symptom of some other problem, perhaps electrical, a problem with the filters, or the heat exchanger coils? Or is it a 'social problem' – a leitmotif or resource out of which a wider organizational malaise might be ventured? As any project proceeds, more and more stakeholders, and more and more of what Latour (2004) might call 'matters of concern', appear. At the same time objects become unreliable and even lack objectivity. *Things come crawling out of the woodwork*, as we have already noted. Objects may be both present and absent, both work and not work, and extend out into a bewildering array of sub-components and sub-contracts, each with its own slightly different territorial configuration of responsibility and liability. Each sub-component of a technological black-box comes allied with technical expertise, representation, and spokespeople. All this adds to the general sense of confusion with respect to lines of authority and procedure. As these proverbial things come out of the woodwork, they do so in an unpredictable fashion as projects become immersed in an excess of details all proliferating and opening up relations and extensions of responsibility. They do so in such a way that before very long the cause of a mis-timing belt becomes the history of engineering decline and its neglect and underinvestment in British industry (e.g. Weiner 1981). In these ways project managers become further engrossed in 'movement' *beyond* organization, and a 'movement' that is more complex than the linear or dialectical. This demands a capacity for multi-disciplinary work in which project managers have to cross a tangled series of lines, a task that stretches the resources of even the most experienced.

How does Robyn extract and connect all this heterogeneity, how does he hold it all together? In some respects, it is an active process of sense-making. However, this sensemaking does not proceed simply in the form of abstracted cognitive processes or through participation in the human relations of a 'collective mind' of 'heedful interrelating' – long identified, for example, in the work of Weick (see Weick and Roberts 1993). We have seen how, in part, sensemaking occurs through *mediation*. Objects are 'collected', for example, though translation and representation in the gridiron of horizontal rows and vertical columns that pre-fix *spreadsheets.* It is into these forms that Robyn places and translates a bewildering complexity – in a process of managing that Cooper (1992) calls an economy of *abbreviation* and representation (Cooper 1992). At the same time Robyn also sees and enacts the world through the tools of his trade. As we attend more closely to this we discover that over time something like a 'scattered attention' was being deployed, either consciously or unconsciously.

The art critic Anton Ehrenzweig (1967) identified the capacity for 'distracted attention' to be essential for those wanting to make sense of abstract modern art, whose patterns and organization only revealed themselves to a viewer who was able to see beyond the surface or beyond the immediately recognizable details that appeared in the picture.[8] This was particularly important in making sense of the abstract expressionism of Jackson Pollock whose paintings appear chaotic, but for which a deeper more complex organization inheres. Ehrenzweig urges the viewer not to focus and attach to images in a way that tries to hold the painting still. Instead, one has to grasp the 'movement' in the picture (Fig. 3.5).

In recent years the loops and lines and swirls in *Autumn Rhythm* have become an important reference in both popular management texts (Peters 1994: 182) and in more scholarly work in management and organization studies (Hatch and Yanow 2008). Indeed, in trying to make sense of the airport the director for strategy once sketched a map for me that we both agreed looked rather like a typical Pollock canvas. To see with scattered attention requires one to avoid seeking to identify or project *familiar* (representational) objects into the painting, and to resist the temptation to focus and define what might appear foreground and to become attached to the stability this attention might achieve. Instead one has to somehow allow one's attention to become *scattered* by the movement of the paint. Here, there are no elements, or parts, or wholes. The

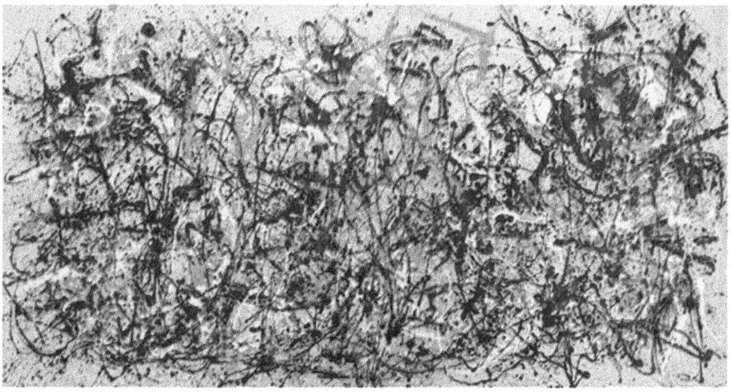

Fig. 3.5 *Autumn Rhythm* number 30 by Jackson Pollock, 1950 (Photograph © Kristina Nazarevskaia for galleryIntell reprinted with permission)

[8] Or, more accurately, to retrieve or return to a sense of the surface where patterns will reveal themselves. Instead of looking *deeper* into the picture in an effort to recover something that is being *represented* according to the traditions of verisimilitude or the realism of Husserl's 'natural attitude', modern art demands the viewer give up on their habitual cognitive and perceptual dispositions.

same applies in construction projects. What might appear an 'elemental' object or component in the construction of the lounge, a rooftop air handling unit, for example, rapidly dissolves into extended chains of parts held together through maintenance contracts and the regular surveys and inspections carried out by engineering services. It is not a reliable component, but part of a temporal flow. This is a vital skill for project managers.

Movements and 'the Market': Pricing the Project

We have seen how the project brief is a palimpsest of authors or part-authors, and also something that resembles a peace-treaty behind which, as Foucault might have noted in his critique of the sovereign theory of power, 'the forgotten past of real struggles' can still be read, and where 'battle cries' might still be heard 'beneath the formulas of right' presented in legal codes and legislation (Foucault 2003: 56). We are also beginning to see how the brief is a *moving* document, subject to elaboration, iteration and revision. As the brief evolves, however, roles and clearly demarcated divisions become increasingly difficult to establish as the 'supplier' becomes part of the demand and the producer becomes client – who in turn also takes on the role of customer. It is perhaps not going too far to suggest that the supplier helps invents the product the customer wants or demands. 'It is not the job of the customer to know what it is they actually want' and variations on this have been attributed to Steve Jobs, but as he did say on record 'by the time you get it built, they'll want something new' (Jobs 1989). Without the brief, no product specification could follow, and without product specification, no accurate price. If the brief achieves definition – at best, over time – but at worst condemned to the status of a ceremonial document produced for the purposes of impression management around which consensus remains tense and fragile. But what happens if – for that little definition we have been able to establish – we cannot find a price?

It is commonly assumed that it is 'the market' that produces the price for products through the reconciliation of aggregate supply and demand.

Following the lines radiating around Robyn, however, I began to spend more time with the quantity surveyors who were busy measuring and pricing outline designs produced by the architect. On the desk of the client QS sits a thick bound red volume called the 'SPON's Architects and Builders price book' (Langdon 2007) and through it I enter a world of remarkable complexity. It is the closest thing I have been able to find of tangible evidence of 'the market' during the progress of the Escape lounge project (Muniesa 2007; Callon et al. 2007; Çaliskan 2010).[9] Nearly a thousand pages in length the book is a collection of what one might be expected to pay for anything that goes into the construction of a building, from architects and surveyors fees, to masonry, timber, cladding, windows, doors, and stairs (the categories match onto standard National Building Specification classifications of construction products). Wesley is a young QS working on the Escape Lounge and during this stage of the project I would invariably find him bent over A1 architectural drawings.

On this particular day Wesley is using what appears to be an old ruler and pencil to measure an area of flooring. 'There is an item listed here in the Contractor's Proposals', he tells me, 'for '100 thick floor screed on insulation', with a measure of the metre squared'. He goes on to explain, 'Now, you can price that (parts and labour) as one, or break it down into screed and insulation, on a 75:25 ratio, for example'. Category M10, page 288 of the 132nd edition of SPON's lists in small 8-point font a number of different types of screed, including 'cement and sand (1:3) screeds; steel trowelled' and 'fine concrete (1:4–5) levelling screeds; steel trowelled' (Langdon 2007: 288). The price listed for 100 mm think cement and sand screed is £16.79 a square metre, but with the caveat that this is 'one coat; level and to falls not exceeding 15 degrees from horizontal; to concrete base; [and] over 300 mm' (ibid.). In addition, this is a 'build up price' behind which is lies a spreadsheet for each of the 10,000 odd items listed in SPON's, which gives a breakdown into parts and materials at a greater level of detail, but where further hidden calculations and assumptions are made.

---

[9] SPON's is also online and available as a CD format, and accompanies the work of the QS, but in complex and not always consistent ways.

The data gathering exercise that goes into SPONS is an enormous project in itself, with over 1700 field agents seeking data by ringing up various suppliers, manufacturers and contractors to ask for the price of certain materials. However, the quote that is eventually proposed also depends crucially on *who* is asking, and *why*, and for *how much*. As is common with standardized instruments of valuation (Muniesa 2007; Fourcade 2011; Helgesson and Kjellberg 2013), SPON's makes a series of assumptions. It assumes, for example, a project value of £3million, and it is also based on outer London prices; as it states 'regional variations for certain inner London boroughs can be up to 14 % higher while prices in the Northern regions can be as much as 10 % lower' (Langdon 2007: 711). Furthermore, there are at least 4 prices at a timber merchant for the same piece of wood which depends on factors such as the medium of payment, cash or credit, on a monthly account, or yearly account, a premium customer service account, etc. Often the QS will simply call up a local supplier instead of referring to SPON's; this is considered quicker and more accurate, in part because of seasonal and other local supply variations such as the existence of what are referred to as local 'hot spots' (ibid.) that can apparently suddenly flare up according to SPONs. Needless to say the costs involved in producing this data are also not included (or it is said they are not) in the price estimates.

It is also important to note that the contractor's QS, working on the contractors proposals for the Escape Lounge, is duplicating the measuring and pricing that has already been done by the client QS in the preparation of the tender documentation package. Of course, this might push up the price of trade goods as they have to incorporate increasing transaction costs – all those search and information costs, sometimes referred to as shoe leather costs in now standard economic theory – which adds further uncertainty and contingency to the printed price. How prices are 'agreed' or even identified is never as simple as deferring to SPON's, but instead involves a complex tangle of professional and social relations. A contractor might even underprice their proposals to 'win the work', a kind of 'loss leader' in order to win a toe hold on a lucrative client such as the airport. Technically this is considered bad practice and the client QS is legislatively bound to identify those practices which might put the client at risk, particularly if quoted prices jeopardise the business viability of the contractor. However, it always happens, and remains a constant risk, which can only be managed with the support of more complicated relations than the simple exchange of tender documents and contractor's proposals.

Hence, the price of the Escape Lounge involves a series of complex and treacherous negotiations. This require such a degree of intricate knowledge of pricing practices that to a large extent the project can only advance through the trust that can be established by means of shared professional networks. It also depends upon an immensely subtle 'give-and-take' based on the awareness of a range of additional 'data' that allows one to detect whether liberties are being taken – and liberties as opposed to say genuine mistakes.

We have only been able to scratch the surface here in exploring pricing (and the pricing of prices), but we are already a long way from the neat intersecting lines of demand and supply curves taught in business schools and economics departments (Çaliskan 2010). There is no going to 'the market', but instead rulers and pencils, mobile phones, spreadsheets, price books, algorithms, and the ceaseless back and forth of paperwork that enacts trials and speculations in a quest to seek relative advantage and (fair) divisions (Muniesa 2014). Design innovation is always introducing new materials and custodial expertise dividing and re-dividing groups and relations, forming part of ongoing incremental changes in the balance of power between a 'big client' such as the airport and the small local contractor; there is no simple or stable power relation that divides capital and labour, or big player/small player. Instead there are ceaseless incremental changes in materials and knowledge embroiled in ongoing reconfigurations of relations in production, all of which are tangled up in the movement of prices.

With our brief enquiry into SPONs we have seen that a price might be attributed to 'the market' but at the same time we have seen that it is a more plastic object of negotiation than standard economics presumes. It might even disappear into an abyssal self-referential loop of production as we follow the work of the price makers (pricing their work) selling the price book back to those people who have provided the data in the first place. For the project manager this amplifies the uncertainties and confusions that attend day-to-day project realities. Trying to fix everything is clearly impossible and at the centre of this maelstrom the project manager must retain a capacity to simultaneously *focus and de-focus* on these kinds of relations and details. On the hand one he must concretise details in things like spreadsheets and employers' proposals, but on the other he needs to let go of the detail and allow objects or prices to dissolve in the extended processes of their production. With this facility for something like Keats' 'negative capability' one can allow 'the detail' to be disassembled into an ever finer grain of amplification ('drilling down' as members often say). In this way one might take cognizance of the metamorphoses of matter as it becomes disaggregated into flows that – like those paintings by Pollock – might suggest the possibility of alternative patterns and configurations at another level of perception or organizational engagement.

The JCT 'Design and Build' Contract

If man is a figure drawn in sand, as famously declared by Foucault (1971b), then for our project manager it is important to be able to distinguish whether this is 'pit sand' or 'soft washed', 'sharp' or 'ballast'. Furthermore, for the project manager to be able to draw a line in the proverbial sand they need to be able to work out what is critical and what superfluous in the construction of the lounge, at least if they are going to effectively police the different occupational specialisms as they seek agreement on requirements, specifications and price. The project manager needs to be able to temporarily hold together this threatened riot of materials, objects, practices and processes. The lines they draw are therefore necessarily complex and angular ones, marked by sudden deviations and abrupt changes of angle. Robyn is soon to be exposed as a figure drawn in sand himself as he tries to retain 'scattered attention' as the project moves towards a formal contract.

The complexity of these bewildering dilemmas came to a point of crisis for the project in March 2010. Operating under the terms of the JCT 'Design and Build' contract the client architect is supposed to take the design up to a point at which a tender package can be published so that a contractor can establish a price and a full 'contract sum analysis' that 'reconciles' the employers requirements and the contractors proposals (Chappell 2003). There needs to be sufficient detail so that the contractor is able to offer a fairly reliable price, but at the same time, under the provision of the JCT Design and Build contract, the full detail of the final design is entrusted to the contractor, or their architect. Yet, whilst the outline design and its 'intentions' are sacrosanct when developing the detailed design, the 'intentions' are never fully realised except in the detailed design – which might variously conform or not to the outline. In fact, under the provisions of the JCT Design and Build contract, it is never very clear how one might establish a clear line of difference between an *outline design* and a *detailed design*.

We need to pay very special attention to these kinds of boundaries and the gaps that open up and close down around them during the life-span of a project, for it is here that we can detect an accumulation of pressure that suspends the reliability of the elemental realities out of which the Escape Lounge is presumed to emerge. Something threatens to *escape* at this level of detail, a level of detailing that gives access to a protean and volatile matter into which action and thinking become indistinguishable. Listen to the senior Quantity Surveyor talking to the appointed contractors following the tender and selection process; this is a pre-start meeting and dated the 12th March 2010:

Client QS:	'The airport wants to issue the full contract. There are drawings now in existence that supersede the tender docs'
Contractor QS:	'What about the contract sum analysis? Are we at that stage now? Or, have there been subsequent revisions?'
Client QS:	'It's a dynamic process'
Contractor QS:	'The danger is that we never get there ... [inaudible] ... So, you'll issue something ... today? ... OK'.
Client QS:	"It's that 5 letter word, 'Trust'.
Project Manager:	'....Who's paying for RTH [the architects]?'
Client QS:	'Look, it's a funny grey period we're in...'
Architect:	'So, that change goes to Beastons [the contractor]?'
Client QS:	'We need the full contractor's proposals'

To explain what is going on here, or even to understand what is explainable and what is deliberately unexplainable, takes a considerable amount of skill. To leave things in a state of abeyance or confusion is not a strategy pursued by any one individual, but rather appears to emerge from no *one*, in what remains a collectively deferred and emergent phenomenon.

As the various parties dance their way around the provisions of the JCT design and build contract, the terms of the JCT are also finding further explication, interpretation and agreement. It is not as though the terms of the JCT contract are all fully known and fully shared between the participants, nor is the relative valency or propensity for litigious actions amongst the respective parties mutually known. All of this is being worked out and interpreted at the same time that it is being enacted collectively, which means that something unknown is emerging out of all the pushes and pulls, prompts, speculations and counter-speculations *between* the various parties – client, contractor, the architect, etc. And the project manager is also trying to work this out, whilst negotiating how much scope for manoeuvre they have, or how much 'grey zone' they want. A project is often understood to take on a life of its own, and typical is the comments of one project manager who made the confession that during the project 'the project manager is the one who does nothing; but without them, nothing gets done'.

Crucial to what is going on in this conversation between client QS and contractor QS for our understanding of organization is the background play of a whole series of legally recognised definitions and classifications, to which the various parties make allusions and subtle hints. The terms 'contractors proposals', 'contract sum analyses', 'full contract', 'issue', 'subsequent revisions', and 'practical completion' are all being toyed with.[10] At what point does a 'revision' to a drawing become a 'change' that requires a formal 'change control'? This all depends on 'time' – or an agreement about where each of the respective parties is in terms of time as it is formalized in legally defined contract stages. Notice that the client QS is asking for the *full* contractor's proposals. The appearance of this word 'full' signals to the literate aficionados. The widely accepted and de facto understanding of the terms of the JCT contract would insist that there can be no such thing; in other words, at this stage, there cannot be anything but '*full* proposals'! This meeting takes place *after* the tender selection process and after the 'appointment'

[10] On the evolution of the term 'practical completion' and its meanings, for example, see J. Jarvis and Sons v Westminter Corp (1978); HW Neville Ltd. v William Press (1981); Mariner International Hotels v Atlas (2007).

of the contractors, although in strict legal terms there is no signed contract exchange at this stage (March 10th). Yet, to all intents and purposes, the contractors are on site, attending meetings, and – depending on how one interprets it – *engaged in work on the project.* However, whilst full contractor's proposals have been issued, any casual inspection of what might be happening on the ground are likely to be deceptive. Have they started *work*, for example? Or are they still preoccupied with what is called 'preliminaries'?[11]

It would seem that the contractors have been 'appointed' but under what is known as a 'letter of intent', a device usually used when the design is not yet fully outlined to the satisfaction of the client. Recall from the exchange above that the client QS at one stage announces that 'The airport *wants* to issue the full contract'. In the background lies a question, namely: who is *responsible* for a possible interpretation that there *has been a failure* to issue the full contract? At least it seems that this is being alluded to, and various tactically motivated suggestions are being exchanged between the parties in a highly elaborate and concealed form. In principle, changes to *outline* design *can* follow once the client has taken receipt of the contractor's proposals and even after 'appointment'. This occurs typically where the pressure of program means that compromises might have been made to the specificity and detail of the outline design in order to get a contractor in on time so that the project has a realistic chance of completing in time for the planned opening. The contractor may be variously sympathetic or not to such a claim, but such 'sympathy' is likely to depend on how they perceive their relative position of power vis-à-vis the client. So, they can be working on 'prelims' and site 'set up' whilst adjustments to 'minor details' in the formally issued employers requirement and drawings that form part of the contract sum analysis. Of course, this leaves open the boundary between 'minor' and something more *major* – the full implications of a design change might only transpire much later in the project. It also reminds us that the question of *when* an outline design becomes a detailed design is formally impossible to answer. In this project, the architects later reflected that they had taken

[11] Here is another distinction that would be oblivious to anything short of the kind of detailing available to the 'thick description' of ethnography (Geertz 1973).

this design up 'to about 50 %, i.e. a lot of the design intent, and performance requirements, but not the specific details'.

Whether a price has been agreed for the construction of the Escape Lounge is also moot, not only by virtue of the ambiguities inherent to SPONs, but also because the contractor's proposals have to be 'signed off' by the client. In the inevitable delay of this somewhat ceremonial 'sign off', 'late' changes to client design – i.e. after the issue of a letter of intent – can still be considered *revisions to design*. This is a point of some subtlety but it allows changes to be made in a way that avoids formal 'change controls'. This is important because if the client issues these change controls then it is they who pay and bear liability (including design and defaults liability). However, to avoid formal change control requires consent, or at least a mutually agreed 'blind eye' and preparedness to continue with the advantages offered by 'team working', much prized in construction following the publication of the Latham report (1994) and the Egan report (1998). Change control requests issued by the client would allow the contractor to make additional charges, usually at an additional 'over-extra' mark-up because of the inconvenience of such a late change.

An added complexity is the fact that it is only the architect who can make changes to drawings and detailing. However, the client architect is strictly – on the 10th March – the *contractor's* architect! Under the terms of legal contract it is not uncommon for the architects who have worked the design up to outline design for the client are subsequently taken on by the contractor, a facility that is called in the world of JCT contracts 'novation'. The architects have been 'novated' over to the contractor; but again the detail is in the timing. They may also be working on different projects for the client and indeed, during this time, the architects occupied a set of desks in the project management team offices at the airport because of the number of projects in which they were engaged at the time. At what point the architect formally and de facto *stops* working for the client and *begins* working for the contractor is in practice ambiguous. In practical terms of course, they are always working for the client, but under different specificities of contract law; of course, this means it is inevitable that the lines get confused.

We are quite obviously in a funny, 'grey period', as one project manager explained. To those not quite as proficient and subtle in their handling of this JCT contract, it would appear that there has been a *retrospective* issuing of employers requirements (and the outline design that accompanies them); we might infer that the airport is requesting that these changes be considered mere matters of detail which the contractor is being asked to agree *are* minor and therefore something that does not necessitate the formality, administration and cost of formal change controls. In practice though, the architect is issuing *themselves* revision drawings, whilst formally novated over to the contractor. Who is paying for whom, and for what, necessarily becomes very confused. It is also possible that the architect might consider the additional work over and above what had been specified in the terms of their original appointment with the airport, and therefore might be expected to request additional payment. On the other hand, this additional work might make the subsequent work required when they have been novated over to the contractor easier – if payment terms have been agreed, the architect might take the view that the work is being paid for anyway.

For all the straight lines and sequential planning processes and paperwork, we seem to be always, at least potentially, in a state of complete uncertainty, overwhelmed by something equivalent to that mosaic of tiles we saw in Fig. 3.1 where a crossfire of lines of force, voids, and grey zones, seem to whirl into a formlessness as what is considered foreground and background, detail and context, the relevant and irrelevant, become increasingly difficult to prise apart. For some it becomes too much. Two days after the pre-start meeting, the lead project manager comes running up to a colleague; visibly shaking, he is shouting and in a flood of tears, his voice a tremulous and staccato oscillation: '*I don't know what reality is anymore* ... the QS's on the Escape Lounge are not talking to each other. Ron Deputy was *talking in Swahili* on Tuesday. It's a mess. The furniture needs to be ordered last week!'

A capacity for 'scattered attention' has been stretched beyond the limit as our project manager appears to retreat back to an expectation that time must proceed logically and in linear sequence, with roles clearly defined and nested inside an organization in which everyone knows what he or she wants. Robyn seems to have succumbed to that 'disorderly convulsion' that Deleuze (1992) tells us is always risked when drawing out the lineaments of a 'northern gothic line' – a sculptural or architectural line that zigzags between things made uncertain by virtue of the line and the movement it introduces. Deleuze (1992: 49–55) shows how this gothic line is made to work – or 'realised' – in German expressionist cinema, but this northern gothic line seems to be also present at Manchester Airport. In these films, Deleuze notes the prevalence of diagonals and cross-diagonals as lines cut across the horizontal and vertical delineations of the screen, mapping out a series of interconnections that produce 'acute angles and sharp triangles'. These complex tapestries of light and shadow are marked by sudden interruptions and changes of direction that reflect for Deleuze 'moments of intensity' that signal a change in the order of things and which cannot find complete articulation within current forms.[12]

Conclusion

In this chapter we have been able to follow some of the practices involved in the construction of the Escape Lounge that show how management is rapidly immersed in a minutia of artefacts, matters, and tools of the trade, all of which need assembling and combining in flexible and innovative and often unprecedented ways. Central to this is the work of documents and paperwork. In following some of these paper trails we have discovered its capacity for proliferation, which we have found can lead to overload and paralysis. Paperwork is also deployed tactically as part of the struggle and contestation for resources amongst management. In addition, documents provide a point of assembly around which different parts of the airport find expression and where boundaries and definitions are tested and various territories extended and withdrawn. Paperwork also has a tendency to become parasitical and self-referential – a 'pape-reality' as Dery (1998) nicely calls it. In these ways paperwork becomes self-acting and constitutive, and therefore a dangerous ally for the project

[12] Following Bergson, Deleuze (1988) calls this the emergence of 'movement' and tangible evidence of the intrusion of an 'open whole' in Bergson's terms, which simultaneously changes the 'part' and the 'whole'.

manager. Paperwork seems to de-centre and displace management and subvert any pretension it might harbour about autonomy or sovereignty. Paperwork can chase you home at night. 'It keeps me awake' one manager confesses, whilst another tells me that he 'wakes up in the middle of the night to make a list of all the things I haven't done'. There are paper realities, paper-dreams, but also expressionist-like nightmares of being engulfed by paper. This is a dark side of organization not yet fully explored within studies of 'writing organization' (Rhodes 2001), particularly those attending to 'grammatocentric' practices (Hoskin 1995) and the paper practices and worlds of paper through which organization is constituted.

In tracing the connections across these many dimensions of paperwork we too have been forced to draw our own gothic line whilst trying to retain some linearity and coherence in providing a metanarrative or 'story' of organizational theory to contain all this material. In deploying the concepts 'scattered attention' and 'disorderly convulsions' this chapter has been able to weave together a heterogeneity of elements that are in play and liable to 'come out of the woodwork' during the progress of a project. There are inevitably gaps and silences that open up in the interconnections of these lines – the allusions, silences, the nods and winks, the grey zones, etc. – which have been shown to provide a source of tremendous potency and vitality. Drawing from their lacunae generates opportunities for power and control. Yet, accompanying this potency, the project manager was (dis)placed as a possible centre in this tangle of lines. As the project manager receded or became dispersed, objects became wild, documents began to talk – and talk to themselves in an apparent parody of human schizophrenia. Meanwhile fan belts disappear and re-appear, things work and don't work, prices multiply, briefs become profuse, and ceramic tiles fragment. Projects even lose sight of 'the' client, who at times also disappears as the project team struggles to keep a clear hold of who is working for whom.

Given this it is perhaps not surprising that some on the project seem to have arrived at a state of confusion and panic. The spatial and temporal confusion evident in the peculiar grammatical tense of Robyn's final sentence seems to arise because of the collision of two sets of expectations – the neat, linear sequencing of PRINCE-2, and the more complicated tangle of lines in which things can apparently happen *after* the event, where revisions are made seemingly *prior* to the original brief, where things both work and don't work, and where nothing is what it seems. In this grey zone, matters appear to be getting out of hand, much like the crazy paving laid out in the Escape Lounge which appears to have cracked under the pressure of too many orthogonal lines converging on one point. It seems that Robyn is no longer able to hold in tension the swirling elements that form something like an 'Autumn Rhythm'.

During the Escape Lounge project management was forced to consider a series of materials for which they had little prior expertise: drive belts on air-handling units, for example, the porosity and performance quality of Irish bog oak, contemporary design principles, popular fashions and tastes as mediated through magazines and professional trade journals, the ambiguities in contract case law, price books, epoxy grout, customer surveys, the ambitions of an emergent corporate group, the thermal properties of ceramic tiles, internal rates of return on capital expenditure, and engineering maintenance regimes (cf. Mitchell 2002: 27–29; Barry 2013). We have been able to explore only some of this bewildering complexity in this chapter.

In sum, the project arrives in a situation in which it becomes evident that our customary categories of supply and demand can no longer hold. Roles and boundaries become confused up to the point at which the familiar divisions and categories of management and organization are brought into a certain crisis: indeed, the very principles upon which 'markets' and 'business' have been understood – structured by the interactions of producers, consumers, and prices – begins to dissolve. Such confusion and ontological dissolutions gives rise to matters that are akin to that 'humus of uncomposed matter' of which Cooper (2006) speaks. Efforts to establish possible patterns of organization in these conditions brings into play a kind of movement *that is beyond or outside* organization – at least as we have customarily conceived it. No producer or consumer, no manager/managed, no client and contractor, we are left with complex negotiations and trials of strength marked by gesture, feint and speculation.

As Deleuze explains, monstrous forms emerge out of the tessellated patterns that mark the gothic line of German expressionist cinema.

Deleuze invites us to look again at those famous expressionistic cinematic images in which the candelabra and the tree branches (Lang) become indistinguishable, which creates uncertainty about that which is animate or inanimate, dead or alive. Most memorably expressed perhaps in the cinematic images of the *Cabinet of Dr. Caligari* the northern gothic line appears in the scene where the shadows of a house appear to pursue a man running along a street. 'A wall which is alive is dreadful' Deleuze writes, 'but utensils, furniture, houses and their roofs also lean, crowd around, lie in wait or pounce' (ibid.: 51). In this chapter we have seen how the allied technologies and paperwork of management seemed to come alive in ways that haunt the imaginary of the various parties that were brought together by the project. At various points we have been able to follow some of the proliferating lines that radiate and converge around discrete moments during the project, lines that bring into relation a multiple and mutable set of objects and subjects.

In business and management studies little attention has been paid to the relations that pertain between the detailed technical/material features of work and those who are designated its managers, either amongst those who celebrate the sovereign heroism of management, or those who critique the presumed power and autonomy of management (but see Law 1994). No doubt a reaction in part to the fear of committing technological determinism, there is little appetite in management studies for the kind of phenomena we have been exploring in this chapter, particularly in cases where paperwork and process appears to take on a life of its own. As the following chapters unfold we discover how other ostensibly inanimate matters increasingly assume autonomy, including the rise of talking chairs and families of furniture, so-called 'wow factors', and loungers who take on the guise of virtual data-doubles or doppelgängers (see also Knox et al. 2010). Here things appear to *lunge*, rather than lounge: they 'lean, crowd around, lie in wait or pounce' – a condition to which many project managers working on loungification will concur.

4

Becoming Lounge: Angularity and Disjunctive Synthesis

Introduction

Less than three weeks before 'handover' and the lounge remains a construction site. So close to the opening day, and we are still without a lounge. Some people are talking about 'practical completion', but this seems a long way off. Taped off with official health and safety access restrictions notices, hard hats bobbing in pools of white light cast by powerful illumination tripods, engulfed in clouds of dust motes, the lounge is far from comfortable. One can hear the high-pitched scream of circular saws and smell the omnipresent odour of plaster and sawdust. The lounge appears chaotic and confusing. It is difficult to tell if it is being *constructed* or *deconstructed* and seems to exist in a strange spatial and temporal limbo, a 'grey zone'. Nerves amongst managers and contractors are getting stretched ....

It seems remarkable that we are only three weeks from the opening of the lounge. The ethnographer, however, cannot be sure whether the nervousness expressed by the supervisors and project managers is appropriate or reasonable given the apparent circumstances. Is this chaos normal at this stage in construction? Securing a reliable answer to this question

D. O'Doherty, *Reconstructing Organization*,
DOI 10.1057/978-1-137-48922-7_4

proves extremely difficult. Such ontological certainties are precluded given the calculative and competitive brinkmanship amongst contractors and clients in UK construction projects, a feature of UK construction repeatedly documented in the specialist literatures (Latham 1994; Egan 1998). Close ethnographic attention to materials and practices can show that these circumstances conspire to create conditions in which the respective parties are only ever a hair's breadth away from what chapter 3 conceptualised as 'disorderly convulsion'.

Such conceptualisation has proved necessary in the effort to master some of the features of organization that get opened up and enacted once we begin to follow the intricate and detailed practices of managers involved in the design of the lounge. We have been introduced to 'MAG men', for example, which find expression in various characters and personalities associated with the management of the airport. And it is these MAG men who become present in practices associated with 'scattered attention' and 'disorderly convulsion'. However, whether these features of organization have been able to grasp something *unique* to this particular project is unclear; they could all be characteristic of construction projects in general. To extract and then establish what it is that is *specific* to the organization of the lounge takes considerable perseverance and patience, but it is towards this ambition that we have been using the placeholder concept 'loungification'.

In this chapter the ethnography is forced once again to innovate conceptually as we doggedly stick to the apparently mundane everyday practices of management: walking, talking, emailing, paperwork, PowerPoint's, reporting, etc. With this obsessive commitment to the trivial detail or routine 'technical' practices of management in action, ethnography is encouraged to explore patterns and associations that are not readily apparent when analysis imports and applies 'ready-made' categories and theoretical formulae. Previous chapters have argued that the application of borrowed or ready-made formulas and templates is typical of ethnographic study in management and organization and in providing the ontological security of a known context restricts and confines an appreciation of process, movement and action in organization. The practice of conceptual borrowing and application typically grants access only to the most stabilised and reified 'furniture' of organizational life.

The critical school largely accepts the mainstream syllabus of management education as an accurate depiction of what management actually does or attempts to do in practice but inspired by the possibilities of an alternative social and political ideal critical studies develop more critical and far-reaching assessments of the causes and consequences of management (Alvesson and Willmott 1992, 1996; 2003). However, instead of devoting attention to that which is *already stabilized* as management practice and activity, which risks reproducing the prevailing 'disciplinary' coherence of management, this chapter seeks to cultivate a greater openness and sensitivity to that which established theory *does not yet know* about management and organization. It does this by tracking a range of apparent marginalia and trivia in management practice thrown up when developing loungification as a mode of ethnographic enquiry. In this chapter we isolate the prevalence of walking practices, meetings, presentations, and PowerPoint slides. By recovering a capacity for wonder and astonishment at these practices, and resisting the temptation to precipitously explain away these features of organization, the ethnography invests considerably more attention to their study than would be normal. This allows the possibility for connections and relations to surface that might not appear readily apparent to more summary analytical treatment.

In this chapter we discover that what allows us to isolate and then juxtapose such a diversity of practices is the emergence of silences, gaps, interruptions, digressions and deviations. There is a kind of analogical or isomorphic 'patterning' of silence across a range of apparently disconnected managerial practices – a patterning which is made available to analysis by virtue of the deployment of a unique concept: 'angular reasoning'. These gaps, silences, interruptions, etc. call out to be filled or repaired, and into these 'gaps' or silences floods a whole series of shards and fragments of organizational matter. Existing in a more unstable state these fragments provide the materials out of which connections and meaning-making is made possible through angular reasoning. Such meaning, insofar as it is achieved, follows the juxtaposition and synthesis of fragments that sometimes produce the most incredulous phenomena, which might be likened to the 'disjunctive synthesis' proposed by Deleuze (1990: 46–7, 68–9, 176–179; see also Deleuze and Guattari

1983, 1987).[1] This chapter introduces the 'gritty virgin', for example, and the 'talking chair', which are two such incredulous characters that come to play an important role during this phase of the project. Moreover, with these concepts analysis can begin to follow *movements* that cut across the divisions and hierarchies of paramount organization, and to range across different managerial and expert discourse-practices.

Angular reasoning is in some ways a response to those organizational silences that were present in the meetings and practices studied in chapter 3. This chapter examines with more focus that which becomes present organizationally by virtue of *not* being said or apparently *not known*. Finding ways of including this non-said helps uncover a patterning in organization that is normally occluded, emerging as it does out of the silences and interstitial borders of organization. Much of the work on organizational silence, however, tends to be preoccupied with a human-centred analysis of organization in which the individual manager or managers are responsible for the tactical deployment of silence (see Feldman 1988; Noon and Delbridge 1993; Fletcher and Watson 2007; Costas and Grey 2014). The analysis of the work of management involved in the Escape Lounge, however, finds that there is no *one* responsible for these gaps, and therefore no obvious agency or intentionality to explain silence.

In these conditions of work, management is far from being the all-seeing, all-knowing agents of capital. Instead it becomes something more improvisational, which whilst a resource of considerable importance is almost – ironically – *unmanageable*, and possibly un-trainable. It appears quite capricious, subject to the pull and whim of a range of objects, forces and persuasions. In these ways analysis begins to detect the way this half-formed object, the Escape Lounge, begins to *act back* on its management, evidence of which might be found in particular management innovations

---

[1] The disjunctive synthesis appears in many places in Delueze's oeuvre, but it is most specifically addressed in *Difference and Repetition* and *Anti-Oedipus*. To schematize: out of the infinite connections that can be produced across a primitive unformed matter, a selection is made that comes to form relations across the categories and binaries that we come to know through mundane reason (Pollner 1987) as subject and object. This is disjunctive synthesis and it proceeds by way of a fusion, joining and merging of a dispersal of molecular elements. Through this process more molar aggregates are formed. A conjunctive synthesis, by contrasts, *binds* subject to object and puts an end to the infinite rearrangements of the disjunctive synthesis. The lounge has not yet achieved a conjunctive synthesis.

and practices emerging at the time of the lounge project. We will begin with the Monday morning walking ritual. This helps us to identify a form of silence that we explore in terms of the 'powers of the superficial' in organization. Complex patterns of organization are then discovered that bring together a disparate set of practices: meetings, practices of 'imaginization', and an emerging design discourse and expertise invested in the lounge. Following this pattern-making one is asked to hear the particular language and agency of 'talking chairs'. This provides a first glimpse of the way the lounge might be coming to take on a life of its own and the possibility that we might all be *becoming-lounge*. As we shall see, this contemporary form of animism is one that appears to have dawned on some airport management experts who as we shall see are left reeling from the experience of loungification and the possibilities this seems to entail for organization.

Lounge Managers: Management by Walking Around

A group of six figures are gathered in the reception at Olympic House; it is Monday morning, 10 am, and there's a palpable stir in the air; familiar acts of deference and tribute are displayed, mixed with usual jocularity and self-effacing stories, competitive joust and mock-degradation. It is the airport senior management team and they are about to exit the building and take a tour of the property and estate. There seems to be some kind of understanding amongst the managers that the tour is a motivational exercise. In part the objective is to see and to be seen, which forms part of a wide-ranging response to accusations that management in Olympic House is divorced from what happens 'on the ground'. Like dignitaries or celebrities, management on this tour have occasion to meet and greet, to acknowledge the presence of various people; there is laughter, handshakes, and eye-contact. Notable also is the constant interruption of mobile phone messages and calls. Somewhat equivalent to the ancient practice of 'beating the bounds', this 'parade' (cf. Mangham and Overington 1987) has become a weekly event at the airport, and one in which the managers are joined by guests or visitors who have been selected to help with the inspection and assessment of particular features of the building fabric, the passenger services, and customer experiences.

It is of course entirely plausible to see this event as a simple exercise in information gathering and data collection, management – as they say – by *walking around* (MBWA) originating from Hewlett-Packard (Mears 2009: 51), and as popularised in best-selling management practitioner texts such as Peters and Waterman (1982: 15, 137). However, to those not educated in the discourse of managerial training, what might be remarkable is the homogeneity of the six – all white, middle aged, middle class, four men, two women. In particular it is the relaxed casualness involved in this performance of 'making group' that may strike those not hidebound by disciplinary normalization and who may therefore remain ignorant of current fashions in management exercise that might instruct us how to read this event. There has been no business-case testing of the value of this walkabout, the presumed benefits doubtless classified in the realm of the intangible. Like the concurrent 'back-to-the-floor' initiative,[2] positive effects were difficult to quantify or measure. It begins to make more sense, however, when we consider such activities as a response to a prevailing conception amongst some senior executives that management was 'out of touch'. Hidebound within 'silos' this being 'out of touch' also meant that 'joined-up' thinking at the airport was impossible.

It is important to remind ourselves that this equation of (a) being 'out of touch', and (b) its response – a weekly 'walkabout' – is not obvious. As we have said there has been no dedicated business case devoted to its design or to test its value. This juxtaposition of 'out of touch' and 'the walkabout' has therefore an element of the fantastic about it, the product

[2] This exercise involves top managers taking a day out of their busy schedule to spend it with someone working in more 'hands-on' operational areas, airfield and safety operations, for example, the fire-brigade, or terminal services. There was also an open invitation monthly 'coffee with the executive' (EXCO) initiative and the weekly publication of a day in the 'diary of EXCO' made available on the staff intranet. As I got to know the managers, it should have been no surprise that they shared ambivalence about the value of trying to cultivate a sense of intimacy and informality. About the coffee mornings, one of the EXCO members tells me, 'I hate doing it ... I only have to do it three times a year. There are 8 of us [on EXCO], once every two weeks, so that's every 16 weeks, every 4 months you have to do one'. Clearly, such activities were in actual fact difficult, and the exercise demanded a consummate and accomplished performance of conviviality and relaxed casualness.

of what this chapter proposes as 'angularity' in the connecting of two things together.

A more critical management studies would typically lose patience with the ethnographic challenge posed here and would rapidly classify this weekly parade as either the narcissistic vanity of otherwise insecure managers, or an element in the engineering of culture (Willmott 1993a; Casey 1995; Parker 2000a; Alvesson 2002). However, there are significant features of the walkabout that are not at first sight immediately apparent but which do bear insight for organization. To pursue these, however, we need to extract and focus on particular qualities that stand out when placed relationally and in juxtaposition with other features of organization that might otherwise appear disconnected. For the appropriately tuned and attentive ethnographer an emergent but otherwise occluded 'pattern' might then be discerned.

Consider the particular rhythm and gait, the bodily disposition of the walker. It is a particular form of walking that might best be described as a 'lounge' – after a certain fashion of walking. Guldi (2012) traces the fascinating history of the origins of the phrase 'lounge' to the London of the 1780s where it was used to describe a form of walking entertained by the circle around the Prince Regent. In his introduction to the republication of Pierce Egan's 'Tom and Jerry', the contemporary comic masterpiece of Regency society, John Hotten (in Egan et al. 1869) notes that he had read somewhere that 'the Prince's *lounge* was a peculiar manner of walking which the young bucks imitated' (cited in Guldi, ibid.: 129; emphasis added). We learn, however, that lounge might be a little too imprecise to characterise the way his characters walk. 'Mark the variety of lounge in which the young men indulge, now a *stroll,* then a *look in*, then a *ramble*, and presently a *strut'* (Egan et al. 1869: 7).

Whilst Egan's book is preoccupied with the variety of 'lounges', what was distinctive about the lounge in general was the intention 'to stroll slowly with apparent observant awareness, indicating an attitude of cosmopolitan availability to conversation' (Guldi 2012: 129). Guldi goes on to note that the lounge of the Royal Family in Hyde Park was described by one contemporary German observer as 'slowly' ambling and 'converg[ing] with many persons of all classes' (ibid.: 129–130). This unprecedented activity stimulated the neologism 'lounge' that whilst known to have been appropriated from the French, remains a word of obscure origin (<*Lungis*, <*Longīnus*).[3]

Such associations proved helpful in the effort to make sense of the Manchester Airport walk, which I began to understand in the terms of a fantastic display of *the lounge*. Doubtless one risks introducing what will appear to be an historically anachronistic use of the term lounge – as we now tend to restrict our understanding of lounge to those designated spaces of public or private relaxation (hotels, railway stations, airports, domestic homes, etc.). However, it is significant for this study that the term lounge was first coined to describe something not concerned with public space or the domestic interior, but a bodily activity, namely a particular form of walking, i.e. something that is in *action* or *movement*. Significantly it was also a form of walking that had never been seen before in public.

Despite these suggestive possibilities, it was more easily explained and variously disposed of by members of both the management team and non-managerial terminal workers as an effort to 'get in touch' with the hands-on operations of an airport or an exercise designed to generate motivation. Such explanations are well-known in management and organization studies, even if not enough attention has been paid to the contradictions, inconsistencies and multiplicities at play in the relation between those seeking to manage and those positioned as 'managed' by such activities. However, after two years of ethnographic labour it was the sheer *repetition* of the Monday morning ritual that posed the greatest challenge, making this lounge increasingly difficult to observe, and almost excruciating. Further reflection prompted the insight that the walking exercise seemed to provide a vehicle through which people could express *both* commitment to the ideals of senior management[4] *and* scathing, or cynical and ironic views about such practices (Fleming and

[3] It is significant for the development of this thesis that 'lounge' retains an etymology that includes associations with threat and suspicion: 'Longinus' being the 'apocryphal name of the centurion who pierced Jesus with a spear' (OED) – and *lungis,* a word used to describe both a 'long, slim, awkward fellow; a lout', and a 'person who is long in doing anything; a laggard, a lingerer'. When one recalls that *lounge* is also never far from *lunge*, these etymological studies are suggestive of something worth pursuing ethnographically and to grant this apparently trivial practice of 'lounge management' further consideration.

[4] I.e. that it was noble of management to mix it with workers on 'the shopfloor'.

Spicer 2003).[5] However, this much is also well-known in contemporary academic debate. More interesting features of this lounge only began to reveal themselves as the ethnography pursued – with an obstinacy bordering on obsession – what still remained irritating about this highly ritualized Monday morning exercise.

It was then that I began to deepen my appreciation of what I call the *powers of the superficial.* I began to see that what was most beguiling was the *combination* of drama *and* superficiality. To hold these two things together without reaching after impatient resolution or synthesis allowed me to see parallels with the ambitions management harboured for the kind of experience being designed and constructed for customers of the Escape Lounge. Any *successful* juxtaposition or synthesis of 'drama' and 'non-event' would however cancel out any relational tension between these apparently contrary features of organization. Hence, the nature of this juxtaposition was 'silence' (see Fletcher and Watson 2007), and one that resisted synthesis or resolution. This was not the silence of a hidden truth, but what appeared to be a *silence in the face of the unknown.* Despite all the pomp and ceremony, nothing much was said during these walkabouts– at least anything of any seriousness or gravity, or even relevance. Given that ethnic, racial and class differences were so pronounced in the airport, this silence was perhaps the only way that cordiality, or at least common currency, could be maintained.[6] Any spontaneous requests for information about future strategy or policies, even when gesturing towards informed criticism or scepticism, were addressed by adding little more than what was available in other forms of communication or announcements. Delivered in an even-handed tone and often supplemented with a plaintive expression, managers seemed to find ways of expressing how uncomfortable and difficult such *inappropriate* questions had made them feel.

The emphasis on informality is seen by some as 'instrumental in the social construction of innovative, organic work organizations' (Morand 1995: 831) and forms part of a popular managerial turn to introduce

[5] It has become quite a sport in organization analysis of recent years to take enjoyment – or is it perhaps 'jouissance' – in the apparently strange practices of contemporary service economies marked by what Cederstrom and Spicer (2015) call the 'health bazaar' and 'the happiness doctrine'.

[6] Conviviality was often discovered in the resort to sport and popular television.

fun, games and spontaneity into the workplace, particularly in those organizations characterised as conservative, inhibited, and excessively bureaucratic. This is a trend in management practice that has attracted considerable academic attention (Rodrigues and Collinson 1995; Sosteric 1996; Westwood and Rhodes 2007). Something more than informality, however, was happening here; one might be tempted to call it *inauthentic* if one had a clear idea of what authentic might mean (cf. Fleming, 2009). But this would also miss the point. In fact, the relaxed casualness was better seen as the product of a highly contrived and studied performance, and one that formed part of an *organization-by-profound-superficiality*. It was, moreover, a ritual in which it appeared equally possible that the actors had *forgotten* they were acting. Theatre has been well documented in organization analysis since Mangham and Overington's (1987) seminal text, but if are tempted to draw the conclusion that everything in organization is performance then we have to contend with the spectre of a certain relativism and the fear of infinite regress.[7]

Whilst this broadly 'existential' analysis could be pursued, it became obvious that the ethnographer and his presence was hugely instrumental in bringing these preoccupations into being amongst members of the organization. Whilst possibly latent within the organization, and quickly – and in some cases *easily* triggered – such ethnographic practices nonetheless encouraged a premature and too easy or rapid exercise of sense-making. Analysis is thereby taken away from what is perhaps more fruitful here, namely the very ease with which the ethnographer participates in the enactment of certain forms of organization *in ways that forget the arbitrary and contingent quality of the production and selection of data.* To allow the deployment of any one analytical preference – an existential/emancipatory commitment in this example – is to preclude or occlude possible others – including those ones being brought into being by those I am studying. However, in avoiding this short cut, does the ethnographer not make an equally arbitrary abstraction in his attention to all those signs that might be gathered in ways that form an attention to *posture* and *comportment*? Possibly, but the point here is that this selection does

[7] It is from here that we might find one source for the ubiquity of paranoid tendencies amongst the MAG men, as dealt with in earlier chapters, but it also might help explain questions about *how* one is to live and work when confronted with such an undecidability around issues of truth, trust and authenticity.

not permit quite such an easy domestication of 'evidence' into prevailing theoretical metanarratives. Avoiding these readymade explanations, the ethnographer makes a whole series of otherwise occluded connections to tell a story of the Monday morning lounge.

It was possible for example that the walk was not just a symbolic performance. However, there was stronger evidence available to suggest that management was being *constituted* by the lounge; the Escape lounge was in other words *acting back*, and acting-back *prior* to – or in anticipation of – its own materialized existence. This helped sensitise analyses to the possibility that human actors are not the only actors at work in the airport, a finding that would be doubtless the cause of some mirth amongst many airport managers if not most academic studies of management and organization. Such apparently fantastical speculations are perhaps evidence of the ethnographers' own angular reasoning, but in taking such risks ethnography has the opportunity to enrich its relation to members of organization. In this case it was the turning point in beginning to forge this concept of 'angular reasoning' that allowed the ethnography to become more sensitive to practices of sense-making shared by the ethnographer and indigenous members of organization.

As explored later in this chapter, members of the lounge team also sought to connect and achieve coherence by forms of narrative and other modes of representation composed of their own arbitrary collections of 'data'. If the accompanying silence associated with the Monday morning lounge was central to what we have called its profound superficiality, in the next section we explore the so-called 'BRATA' technique, which was introduced to help overcome another silence at work in organization: namely answers or insight into what this thing we call the 'Escape Lounge' is in terms of design or customer 'offer'.

BRATA

Hosted in the informal surroundings of the colloquially known 'Brown Paper Room' in Olympic House, the project team has been presented with a workbook and tasked to imagine the lounge in terms of 'BRATA' – '**B**enefits, **R**ole, **A**ttribute, **T**erritory, and **A**ttitude'. BRATA is the acronymized title of a tool introduced to the project team by the client architects designed to unlock what were perceived to be inhibitions that were preventing a full realisation of the lounge. Unveiled during one meeting – as if it was some kind of fashion accessory itself, an item of loungewear perhaps – this 'tool' promised to 'inspire creative thinking towards the potential internal environment and how this works hand in hand with brand direction'. BRATA asks managers to consider what it is they want the lounge *to do*? What are our hopes and ambitions for the lounge? We have seen in the previous chapter the silences and gaps of the client brief, and the careful negotiations around those silences; this tool was designed specifically to invigorate conversation.

Looking not dissimilar to those management loungers who take their constitutional Monday morning parade, the workbook is full of pictures of young, white cosmopolitan people variously lounging in hotels, airports and railway stations. They also look remarkably like the people who are gathered in the room to work on the BRATA exercise (cf. Wittel 2001). The workbook accompanies a PowerPoint presentation packed full of colour images depicting city centre hotels and lounges. There are many photographs of people holding glasses of wine, for example, smiling, laughing, huddled in groups, some are sat around in leather chairs sharing coffee and others share food in domestic settings. Similar posters had been appearing around the city of Manchester at the same time advertising "concept living" and "the way we live now". To the casual observer these could be the same people yet again. One set of photographs represents people at the Radisson Edwardian hotel who we are told are groups of loungers 'celebrating individuality', 'blending tradition with technology', and 'celebrating quality'. The existing 'Bollin lounge' at the airport is also featured in the presentation. This offers yet a different set of attributes and attitudes, including 'exceptional reliability', 'dedicated employees', 'understanding the customer's needs', 'integrated services', 'adding value', and 'commitment to customer service'. All of this is further explained as 'Collaboration', and 'Commitment to become genuine partners with customers' (original punctuation). It is unclear however, if these are the *features of the various lounges* we are being asked to consider, or whether these are characteristics of *the people* who occupy the lounge.

The client team are then invited to free associate on the basis of the categories of Benefit, Role, Attribute, etc. 'Benefit' is explained as those things the product is likely to realise for the consumer, and these might be tangible or intangible. It could be 'status' or a 'fun experience', for example. The 'role' of the lounge is a little more complex, which the accompanying documentation helps to explain by elaborating a more detailed question: 'what is the purpose of the Escape Lounge's existence in a very competitive market. How does this relate to the guests [sic] world?'. 'This is especially relevant' the workbook tells us 'if you wish for your guest to feel that they buy into the concept and a part of the life style (e.g. iPod)'. No one appears to have any difficulties in deciphering the text, despite its apparent grammatical challenges. Robyn might have had to imagine temporality in ways that went beyond the crude Aristotelian assumption of sequence and linearity, as we saw in the last chapter, but here we discover that an over-attachment to grammar risks becoming an obstacle to the imaginization (Morgan 1993) necessary to the task of bringing the lounge into existence. One might be reminded of Nietzsche's injunction in the *Twilight of the Idols* that 'we are not rid of God because we still have faith in grammar' (III: 5).

Working out the 'attribute' of the lounge poses more problems to the team. What is an *attribute*? We are told this refers to 'the clearly identifiable *signature* or *character* of the Escape Lounge' (emphasis added). The lounge is going to be 'a club house' someone from the commercial team responds. They elaborate a little by explaining that by this they mean 'an energised feel … but in a northern way', a 'chilled, relaxed space'. 'Somewhere where you would be happy wearing jeans …' the commercial development manager adds, …'*but not holey jeans*'. After a round of free association 'Territory' is addressed, which is meant to indicate 'where the Escape Lounge will live'. So, for example 'Alfa Romeo' offers 'Italian flare and excitement at an affordable price'. As these questions are being asked and responses become a little more forthcoming, one of the architects makes a series of interjections that seem designed to urge the team on and to encourage them to make more bold associations: 'We need to get the right feel, the right vibe', he say's. 'If Carlsberg did an airport lounge' someone then adds, 'it would probably be the best airport lounge in the world'. This is greeted with nods of approval as the group begins to achieve a sense of momentum. However, this momentum is one marked by digressions, deflations and awkward silences that require constant management and coaching. With energies beginning to flag towards the end, we are asked to address 'attitude': what is the 'brand's attitude thought [sic?] you want the consumer to join into[?]' As an example we are offered Nike, whose attitude is apparently summarized with their tag-line 'just do it'. Many heads nod when someone suggests that the lounge 'is all about the vibe and the city', 'but not Bez,[8] all mong'd out on the wall', another quickly adds. A member of the commercial team adds that Thomas Cook will be about 10 % of the lounge, but also Jet2, and 'City breaks'. 'So it's fun, but not tacky fun', one of the architects responds/requests; a 'jeans and blazer crowd' one of the design team proposes. 'But what about the 'trendy, designer, Ted Baker suit, type'? We also need to think about 'Lufthansa business man', the head of the commercial team concludes.

At the conclusion of the meeting the architects leave the meeting to work on the 'physical interpretation' with a commitment to return to present their results in two weeks' time. They do not appear fazed by this welter of material and ideas generated by BRATA. However, *how* the architects might form a coherent interpretation of what the lounge will look like in terms of architecture and design would appear to require a tremendous effort of synthesis and integration. Their eventual presentation is dramatic and colourful, packaged together with the strap line 'so this is our Culture & this is how we do it' emblazoned across the PowerPoint slides (Fig. 4.1).

There is now a 'concept' for the lounge, we are told, which is explained using a number of textual and visual supports. 'There are several key spatial elements and *devices* with an Escape Lounge', the report concludes (emphasis added, cf. Callon et al. 2007; McFall 2009; Marres and Lezaun 2011), but above all 'The Escape Lounge should not be fussy, cluttered or irrational, nor should it be too hard or soulless'. The accompanying workbook describes the proposal as 'a bold response and confident visual

[8] A somewhat notorious character, dancer and otherwise spirit-guide for the 1980s Manchester band *The Happy Mondays*. According to Professor Steve Brown, he may well be the crown prince of angular reasoning (personal correspondence).

Fig. 4.1 'So this is our culture & this is how we do it'

aesthetic', and outlines a series of zones for the lounge, namely 'a reception', 'the deli/bar', a 'den' ('akin to a members club or smart hotel lounge area'), 'the study', and 'the attic'. The attic, for example, is described as a 'fun space for both adults and children! This facility truly reflects the Escape brand – to be different and fun … in a grown up manner'. This is where 'there are more vivid colours and graphics displayed to subtly portray a chilled out and fun space' and where eventually a Wii play station and a 'giant' Scalextric racing-track will be installed. A 'vapour trail' theme is also picked out for us by the design team, which we are told will inform the shape and look of the feature walls and ceiling; this is important because it 'is supposed to contrast with 'daily life in a box''.

How have these solutions been conceived by the architect team from the data they have collected from the brief, the BRATA exercise and other interactions with the project management team? The work of Yaneva (2005) is helpful in making sense of some of this. Her work explores the way in which the medium and matter in which architects and designers work help inform solutions that would otherwise not be possible. Tools such as the 'modelscope', for example, used by the design team at Rem Koolhaas's OMA practice, stimulates an alternative form of cognition and draws out capacities for thought (and being) that would otherwise not be available. The 'modelscope' is a *visualiser* that allows architects to 'enter' the space of a miniature model of the building and in effect 'miniaturises' the architect and like in 'Gulliver's travels' allows the design team to 'enter' the space and *experience* it (Yaneva, ibid.: 876). In a more recent paper, Yaneva extends her analysis to consider such tools as part of an 'artistically created primal matter' that 'stimulates the haptic imagination, astonishes its creators ... and helps architects fix unfamiliar ideas, gain new knowledge about the building-to-come, and formulate new alternatives and "options"' (Latour and Yaneva 2008: 84).

Whilst airport managers were accustomed to the rather more sober matters of numerical calculation and bureaucratic reports, and were often challenged by these invitations to 'imaginization', BRATA was significant because it helped stimulate new knowledge and insight into the lounge. Once disparaged in some parts of the organization as the 'fuckwits from retail' (Diary 2: 72), lounge managers were finding ways of making the airport over in a way that challenged the prior dominance of engineering and operations. New objects of imaginization like BRATA acted as 'vehicles' that helped forge a distinctive domain of expertise and specialism, opening up and 'enacting' the airport in unprecedented ways, providing opportunities for colleagues formerly attached to older discourse-practices to adopt the newer more rarefied and design intensive practices of those associated with retail and commercial development. However, participants required a capacity or at least a tolerance for this new discourse. The objects that it mobilised were often perceived as 'intangible' or 'conceptual', a 'soft discourse' that contrasted with the 'hard discourse' of engineering or finance. 'Vapour trails', 'brand', 'attitude', 'energised feels', 'WOW! factors', 'mood tones', 'colour palettes', and 'experiential differentiation' became the key organising motifs that held the commercial and design team together. Like the emergence of those superficial objects of organization and socialization that Lury and Marres (2015) have explored in new digital media, BRATA helped generate and socialize a new discourse that stimulate, orientate and organize the activities of organizational members.

Nor could this discourse be dissuaded from its extension by any anxiety that the concepts had not been subjected to rigorous scrutiny or cross-examination. There was nothing that resembled what members of design and construction teams would sometimes refer to as a 'drill down', for example, that might seek to establish anything more definitive about what terms like a 'WOW! factor', an 'energised feel', or a 'Manchester experience' might mean. Neither was there any apparent cynicism amongst members. What we might say is that – at best – there was a judicious investment of silence amongst certain members. This silence allowed the project to proceed. No doubt it takes a certain suspension of belief to operate with this discourse, but as we have seen in the previous chapter, so-called hard engineering objects – an air-handling unit, for example – have just as much epistemological dispute and ontological relativism as the most rarefied concept in aesthetics. In the next section we explore in more detail the emergence of what we call 'angular reasoning' that seems to characterize the thinking and practice of those who are able to operate in these conditions of 'profound superficiality' where belief is suspended in the ontological reliability of management practices. The management meeting, and the 'meeting practices' of those enrolled become important sites in which this angular reasoning and what has been called the 'disjunctive synthesis' are brought to life.

Way Finding Through Airport Meetings: Angular Reasoning and the 'Gritty Virgin'

An emerging new design expertise was enrolling a diverse range of managers from across the organization – helped in part by the successful enrolment of the chief executive whose participation was elicited and made visible through careful management and the deployment of various media and communication. A snowball effect seemed to take place, generated by the fact that the Escape project was one in a stream of projects that had been the cause of a significant (re)calculation of position and role by a number of managers within the airport. 'That was the trendy project to be on', one project manager commented, and fearing they had missed out on the 'winds of change' (the well-publicized strategy initiative) went on to say, ironically: 'I was left with the kitchen and restroom refurbishment project!' Those who had a *capacity to lounge*, and who could somehow permit the extension of their bodies and minds into a set of new materials and practices, found themselves joining an emerging collective mind-set. Proceeding in ways similar to an 'elective affinity' those able to participate in such practices were able to acquire greater approval, and over time, respect and authority.

In order to participate members of this elective affinity group needed some proficiency in this practice of 'angular' reasoning. To participate in angular reasoning members had to be able to follow patterns of conversation and debate that were often marked by digressions and sudden – apparently non-logical – leaps of imagination. Matters that might appear incongruous were often juxtaposed and a kind of 'cut and paste[9]' mentality prevailed – whether in the way in which reports were written or spreadsheets compiled. Reports, minutes of meetings, and the very nature of conversation seemed to have been constructed in this way such that any joints or cuts – much like the tiling we explored in the last chapter – are not seen (or do not appear to intrude so much that they become the cause of comment and possible dispute). To follow the actors, human and non-human, one is often required to follow what appear to be conversational word-salads that take strange detours in space and time. Consider the following excerpt from a verbatim record kept of a business executives meeting, which conveys some sense of this movement and angularity:

> '... Emirates are at the upper end, and ServissAir at the lower end, a range of 1750 to 2500 per metre [...people talking over each other] We started with the Malmaison concept, Don notes, then we have moved towards

---

[9] The classic management report soon disintegrates on close inspection and begins to resemble a montage of fragments and bits and pieces. Reports are rarely 'written' in the sense that a professional writer might understand. Instead, there are multiple authors, and final copy approved through complex negotiations. When we recall that no one reads a full report, we can conclude that a report is neither written nor read. That the pattern of 'cut and paste' might have become a 'culture' is argued by some (Lessig 2004), and the new digital and media technologies would certainly allow one to make this case by extending Kittler's thesis (1999).

Virgin lounge with less density and the fact that we need more space. 2150 is right for the look and feel of this lounge. Based on a re-fit after 10 years. What about carpets and floors [someone]? Don replies 'we're going for hardfloors and paneling on the walls'. 'We have to tick that customer aspiration', Harry replies...'

There is some inevitable editing here – to keep track of who is speaking, for example – but essentially this excerpt forms part of a record of a brief conversation between five people and is quoted *in extenso* here to convey what was typical of meetings held during the design of the Escape Lounge. Note how much ground is covered – from airlines, to concepts such as 'look and feel', to price per square metre, to the properties of different construction materials. The interpretive demands are legion. In just the small phrase '2150 is right for the look and feel of this lounge. Based on a re-fit after ten years', one needs to employ an incredible amount of deciphering and contextualization. Indeed, to get a flavour of this, consider a more literal rendering of this phrase: 'toowonfifty is right f'the *lookandfeel* of th'lounge … based onarefit after ten years'. Short of a full breakdown in the style of conversation analysis (Sacks 1992), this excerpt conveys some sense of the interpretative demands placed on the members of the meeting. Translating as I have done to offer a more organized rendition still requires a lot of knowledge to understand what is being said, let alone to question or validate it. There is no SPONs book price entry for 'look and feel', for example, and what the norms are for a refit and its timing are also, apparently, not up for debate.

It is also not always clear *who* is speaking[10] – which can serve as an advantage to participants and often used as a *resource*. In addition, I have had to filter out and disaggregate simultaneous talking, in ways that might not be how someone else might edit the conversation. One might also assume that there is a shared context that makes it easier for participants to establish understanding. This is true, to some extent – but only partially. Not everything here is indexical, in Garfinkel's (1967) sense. Shared meaning is an emergent and never-complete process, one in

[10] Hence my efforts to insert brackets with names in an attempt to keep track of who said what, when, in what sequence, etc.

which 'context' is always speculated, contested, negotiated, constructed, and re-presented in various ways. Indeed, allowing and even encouraging potential misunderstanding and ambiguity is often deliberate in an effort to encourage 'agreement' to emerge, operating somewhat like the 'etcetera clause' noted by ethnomethodological studies of conversation rules (Bittner 1965; Garfinkel, 1967). Hence, for these lay practitioners of ethnomethodology, context is never complete.

In part, this lack of context explains the novelty of the lounge. Built out of a unique set of associations the lounge is the outcome of a process that both blends together various occupational and managerial disciplines whilst also pushing this expertise into new and unforeseen directions and futures. Questions of a high conceptual order are posed during the project, for example, that would test the philosophical sophistication of many academic specialists: 'Where did the lounge *come from*?', for example. Such questions require a capacity to identify origins, which as we have seen inevitably leads to confusion and diplomatically negotiated dispute. Perhaps one should not be surprised that management tackle issues in their day-to-day equivalent to the problems posed to modern thought that Foucault (1971a) explores in his essay on Nietzsche. Indeed, the origins of something like a lounge pose even more problems than 'modern thought', which was not such an explicit object of preoccupation amongst members of the lounge team. Yet, such questions of the 'origins of the lounge' are increasingly being treated as legitimate and taken seriously amongst the airport management. We have already seen how members of management might be asked '*where*' is the lounge 'going?', or '*How* is it feeling?' Such questions have a strange anthropomorphic quality to them that sometimes stimulate the most fantastic of answers. In answering questions concerning its origins, for example, members would often cast around in the realm of something like a mysterious spirit – it is something 'in the air', one might say, a zeitgeist, a spirit of the times, or 'the winds of change' as the concurrent strategy initiative claimed through its communication posters and promotional media.[11] And, would they be wrong?

[11] This included a desktop screensaver that was hosted on everyone's computer screen during the time of the Escape Lounge project.

In addition to these fantastic speculations, what I want to focus on here is the *patterning* of these conversations and exercises evident in this phase of the design and construction of the lounge. Like those tiles we explored in chapter 3, conversation would appear to proceed in a 'tesselated' manner, made up of bits and pieces of philosophy and social theory as members variously sought sense and meaning. Consider the following diary extract:

> Peter is telling Paula that Russell has been commissioned to do some research 'and he tells me he's not sure what an ESCAPE lounge is and so he's not clear what kind of things he can provide'. '"Is it business or family", he's asking'. 'They are both completely different and have different needs'. Peter is meeting with Russell today at 12.30 to discuss this. 'I haven't seen this research' [Francis from Bournemouth, on the intercom]. But there's a similar profiles ....yes ...'. They agree that there is a similar market at Bournemouth and Manchester and so in terms of branding and identity there are 'synergies and consistencies'. Both airports have similar carriers and a family market. Thomas Cook is very important. 'We also need to remember the importance of suitable zoning, in order to get both business and family in the space'. 'An area in the lounge will be very family friendly'. What about catering? 'The catering has been factored in' (Peter). 'Outside caterers will be more creative'. 'As yet there are still no definite costings'. We've been given a £4 figure from Autogrill. Joseph then asks 'is the idea is to sell direct to customers or to airlines?' ...

Direct quotation, intertextuality, citations, inferences, free indirect discourse, first person and third person attribution, irony, etc.: we cannot begin to definitively enumerate the discursive and rhetorical resources at play in this tiny excerpt from one project team meeting. What I principally want to draw attention to for now is the multi-tracking, the sudden changes of direction, the combination of abstraction and concrete detail and the *angular* digressions of association and meaning making. It is an angularity that also demands an ability for something we might call *multi-channel* thinking. By virtue of this multi-tracking things often lose their discrete boundaries and well-defined content and began to blur and miscegenate. Whilst members were required to exercise a capacity for definition and 'drill down' – demanding a capacity to recall a multitude of detailed *parts* that make up the project – they simultaneously had to seek a synthesis that could posit a 'whole'. During any project, managers have to be continually alert to the possibility that any one discrete part might suddenly loom up to demand focus and attention, often way out of proportion or what might have been considered proportionate or reasonable to the 'whole' of the project. The analytical dualism that posits a whole and its parts, seems inadequate to the task of identifying the kinds of patterns of association and movements of thought taking place in such management meetings. These conversations seem to speak of a pattern that is more 'rhizomic' in its movement (Chia 1999) – a movement-pattern, or 'angular reasoning' – and one that typically involves the confusion of the most disparate elements.

Yet, all kind of speculations, extrapolations, footnotes, digressions, and leaps of the imagination form part of this multi-tracking and all are required in order to progress a project (cf. Yaneva 2005). Listen to this exchange between various participants of a meeting. One of the architectural design team is talking about chairs. They couch their question in the form of a proposal as they look for support and/or confirmation from the commercial team about the number and type of chair.

> I've proposed leather – but it's more hard wearing. We have proposed 12 for the lounge, but if you think there is a need for more …' [Architect]. 'The Wii game consoles, how will this effect the space planning? Are they too close together? Will the players interfere with each other? You need space for a Wii game' [James, Commercial Team]. 'I hadn't thought of that' [Architect]. 'Dixons in T2 will be able to give information about the play area for game consoles. I've spoken to Don H and he says that the different consoles work on sensor frequencies so that they don't interfere' [Project Manager]. '… uhm … Item 2 is a dining table, an oak veneer which matches with other details' [Architect].

Note how the 'question' that appears early on this excerpt ('but if you think there is a need for more …[?]') does not elicit a response, despite apparently having been solicited. One might imagine that it was deliberately being ignored as one of the commercial managers immediately talks over this line of enquiry and begins to discuss game consoles. However we might interpret this, it is tempting to claim that such excerpts do not give sufficient context, and so any angularity, apparent digression, or leap of analytic reason, is merely the outcome of a failure to grasp the wider circumstances within which our escape lounge project team are operating. We can speculate that indigenous members of the organization will have a much greater understanding of what is being said. We might be confidant that different parts of the organization will inevitably be pushing different agendas, and that members enjoy different levels of experience and longevity. It is also a relatively unremarkable fact that the various participants of a management meeting will arrive with different depths and qualities of knowledge concerning items on an agenda. Some people are up to speed, others are 'in the loop', others 'out of the loop', etc. In sum, to make sense, we need the histories, the characters, and an understanding of the wider organization. However, it is precisely this lack of context and detail that poses problems (and resource) *for those participating*. Or, rather, one can never be finished with the quest for definition about these matters. There is no context, stable or reliable other than that which can be achieved through the on-going work of meetings, minutes, circulating reports, and website communications.

What is ever *really* going on, or *actually* happening in a meeting, remains one of the great enigmas in the management profession (Schwartzman 1989; Sayed et al. 1997; Rogelberg et al. 2007). With our newfound attention to the possible patterning revealed by gaps and silences and angular reasoning, however, we can see how conversation proceeds in ways similar to that of the northern or gothic line we discussed in the previous chapter, marked by sudden turns, detours and digressions, interruptions and jumps. Management meetings are tremendous social accomplishments (Garfinkel 1967; Boden 1994) informed by techniques of considerable subtlety. Moreover, close observation reveals that agendas and conversation are not restricted to the space and time of any one particular meeting and it is not only those present at a meeting who are evoked and represented. Many different interests and groups are made present in meetings, hence we can say the meeting *intermediates* these difference interests, but it also *actively mediates*, sending out messages and information, minutes and reports that seek to make a difference in how organization operates. Meetings are vital arenas in which people at the airport were able to work out who had the ear of who, and what the current thinking was about things like strategy. They had, in a sense, a life of their own as part of an ongoing stream of practices and actions.

The Disjunctive Synthesis

Following the actors and practices involved in the design and construction of the Escape Lounge has brought things together that are normally positioned at different scales of organization. Instead of macro or micro, we can now follow an intermediate realm, characterized by noise and randomness and where things *thingify* (so to speak) by way of an association that resembles something this chapter has been calling 'angular' reasoning. This is a metastable dimension of organization in which we can never be sure how real or serious something is, whether something 'has legs' – in the parlance of airport project managers, or whether someone has instead 'set a hare running'. We have seen how the Escape project has sent reverberations through so many different parts of an organization, evidence of which can be followed by tracing the connections that bring together snatches of conversation in a meeting with what are normally considered the more stable realms of wider organizational, social or political context.

Given this it should come as little surprise that there are different and inconsistent understandings of many things, including – most significantly for the thesis of loungification – 'the consumer' for the lounge. At the airport, entrenched divisions between engineering and new marketing expertise meant there were radically different ways in which airport users were understood and constructed. Simultaneously 'passenger', 'customer', and 'citizen', these different figures provide centres of calculation around which different airports are made possible. Indeed, different airports co-exist and inhere with one another in what is ostensibly the same space and time (Knox et al. 2008). It is perhaps these differences and the challenge they pose to coherence and integration, which is a feature of all organization but starkly evident in an airport, and one that helps explain the production of what appear to be *oxymoronic* or *portmanteau* phrasings allowing actors some degree of 'smoothing' or the reconciliation of differences. These (apparent) reconciliations are precisely what Deleuze (1990) meant by the 'disjunctive synthesis'. In our case the disjunctive synthesis operates as diplomatic bridge-building practices and tactical discursive manoeuvring within organization characterized by ceaseless agonistic battle for power and control amongst different management expertise.

Even within the specialist discourse-practice devoted to the consumer, inconsistent understandings would emerge. These differences would proliferate as the project sought to work on what it is the customer of the lounge was deemed to 'need' or 'want' and inevitably these differences would require mediation and compromise. In terms of space, there were equally fascinating problems of definition. We often think of ourselves as being-in-space, for example – being enveloped by space, or somehow being contained by space. Hence, space is outside us. Heidegger (1962) did much to disabuse western thinking of many of these simplistic spatial presumptions, but during the Escape Lounge project angular reasoning would reveal possibilities of spatial configuration unimaginable even to Heidegger. The client team would often talk of the existence of a 'me-space', for example, which appears to be something akin to a *hybrid* term – somewhere between the subjective and objective. At the same time that customers were thought to want this 'me-space' they also were thought to want 'us-space'. Customers apparently needed both a *collective* experience, and an *individualized* one.

The lounge was also understood to offer both a calm *and* buzz atmosphere, there was talk of a certain 'cool-warmth', and of an experience that is somehow both designed (or managed) and spontaneous. The title of the project itself – Escape *Lounge* – suggests something of a disjunctive synthesis. Designers also struggled to make space work for both adults and children; at times the space becomes adult and on other occasions it becomes a children's space. In addition to the aesthetics and functions of space, some of the team also sought to realize what was called a 'Manchester *flavour*' in the design of the lounge. Might a city or the associations conjured around a city be likened to a gustatory taste? But perhaps the most revealing description of the lounge is the one the head of projects coined in response to discussions that sought to imagine a lounge that would reflect a 'clubhouse feel' (after the new Virgin Clubhouse in Heathrow), but also a more 'Northern spirit' characterized as 'wholesome grit and honesty'. To one or two trusted colleagues, Rob Fuller discretely suggested the title 'Gritty Virgin'.

Like the formal circular logic and infinite regress of the Prince-2 project management process, at least when one seeks to understood such things in the expectation of formal logic, the kind of project work taking place in meetings around the Escape Lounge created the conditions in which meaning always appeared to be on the brink of collapsing (cf. Jarzabkowski and Seidl 2008). One might also venture the possibility that it was perhaps the growing sense of this absurdity which partly explains the energy with which members would seek to conjoin the disjunctive and incongruous in ways that were not always to be taken seriously. In this respect, 'Gritty Virgin' strikes one as both genius and mischievous in this respect, and even perhaps a comment on the BRATA exercise itself.

This simultaneous proliferation and 'bonding' of paradoxes and oxymorons suggests a double movement: angular reasoning and a 'disjunctive synthesis'. Akin to those tessellated tiles we examined in chapter 3, these disjunctive syntheses are suggestive that something more organizationally significant is going on than simply a means through which collective agreement is established 'for all practical purposes' – as Garfinkel (1967: 9) would say. Indeed, we might want to argue that far from being a curiosity, or in some ways atypical, the whole of organization studies is replete with oxymoronic concepts and phrases (Lewis 2000; Smith and Lewis 2011) – including the popular 'simultaneous loose-tight properties of organisational culture' (Peters and Waterman 1982) and the more recent 'exploitation and exploration' in organisational enterprise (Andriopoulos and Lewis 2009). On yet another epistemic scale, with its inherited landscape of structure and agent, environment and organization, the objective and subjective, the macro and the micro, etc. such oxymorons might be inherent to the very social science upon which modern management and organization studies has sought to ground itself.

Talking Chairs: Lounge Alive!

It is very difficult to establish without ambiguity whether the lounge is an *outcome* of different occupational interest groups, with their incongruities and 'tessellations' projected into the physical structure of the lounge, or whether the lounge *acts* in part as an agent of 'tessellation' in its own right. As each mode of expertise seeks to advance and innovate on the back of the lounge project, one is obliged to consider a reversal in our customary assumptions of causality. This reversal is made more complex by the possibility that humans are not the only agents of construction and articulation. In this final section, the chapter seeks to exploit the resources available in angular reasoning in order to consider the transgression of another apparent silence in organization, one in which the voice of the non-human is made to speak.

During one meeting of the Escape Lounge project team, it is possible to begin to hear this non-human voice in the form of chairs talking. Listen to Melanie as she tries to explain how furniture might be best selected and deployed in the lounge. Members of this meeting have been provided with an 'Image Guide Revision B', which Melanie refers to in this excerpt.[12]

> 'Item 5 is the circular coffee table. You can see that the three legs splay out. *That language* would work in the lounge. Item 6 is the "love chair" with button colours on grey background, which relates by contrast to the grey buttons on colour backgrounds … It's a case of "mixing and matching" … The price of the F07 lounge chair is £2500 – £3000, but we only need 6 or 7 to make an "impact statement" …' (emphasis added)

We are being invited to look at the furniture and listen to the way it 'speaks'. It seems to be the 'splay of the three legs' through which voice is heard, but only because it resonates or helps resonate with other features of the lounge. In and of itself it has no language. The language seems to be *between* and in *movement*, and one that requires the active participation of a trained designer. Hence, it is not the words per se to which our attention should be drawn, but rather the *movement* and the nature of this movement – angular, erratic, jumpy, digressive, etc. – which we should now be able to isolate and 'catch in flight' with our concept 'angular reasoning'. Similarly, with our attention attuned we might begin to see/respond to the contrast or symmetry of materials that compose the

[12] On the front page of the Image Guide we are also given additional instruction as to how one might make sense of the content, which is 'to be read in conjunction with ABC FF&E List for quantities, and ABC Drawing 03050_10_203 for locations on plan'.

co-called 'love chair', the vibrant colour buttons, for example, set against a grey background, or a sequence of grey buttons embedded in a contrasting colour background. What is significant is the fact that the contrast lies *between* the various items – and it appears to be this *relational* mixing and matching that is considered appealing to lounge users.

But as language struggles to name something that is in movement (contrast, relation, etc.) there is also movement in the form of a *translation* across the human and non-human. Presumed 'human' properties (talking, language) are either *projected* onto the inanimate, or the human ear has somehow become sensitized to another mode of articulation or semiosis (cf. Kohn 2013). Ethnography itself is not immune to this 'movement' either. Diaries and various other artefacts and inscription devices are struggling with the very same problems when making sense and writing descriptions as those the ethnography is putatively studying.[13] For example, one might ethnographically relate how members of the project take a leisurely 'walk' through the design catalogues, or lean back in their chairs through which they are made receptive and attentive. There is economy and convenience here, but it is one that relies on reifications and other 'fantastical' assumptions and effects (Czarniawska 1998).

These simple visual 'rhymes' and movements between the human and non-human become progressively more complex as we begin to consider an increasing range of design features. Materials, tactility, acoustic properties, the frame of the architectural space, and the movement of customers through the lounge, all are bound in relation to each other and in relation to the typified use made of the space by loungers. In some respects, the language accompanying these discussions reflects what has long been recognized as the distinctive expertise of designers (see Schön 1983). Some analysts have also sought to examine this language in terms of a particular shared *grammatical* and *conversational* structure amongst design experts (Dong 2008). However, what is less widely understood is that designers seem to infer a great deal from *what it is that the objects themselves speak.*

[13] This is a problem that has become somewhat institutionalized in anthropology since at least the 1986 publication of *Writing Culture* (Clifford and Marcus 1986), and various resolutions and advances have been made to the way in which the discipline conducts and writes ethnography (for a summary, see Marcus 2007). This is a debate that has largely by-passed management and organization studies (but see Neyland (2008) and Czarniawska (2012)).

Attuned to the peculiar strain of neologisms and the portmanteau-like qualities of language practices amongst project members allows one to consider the possibility that objects might have some autonomy, or some language of their own. So it is to them, then, rather than the authority of any singular human master (i.e. Schön 1983) to which we might have to learn to listen in order to understand lounges:

> 'There is a language that communicates' Designer B continues 'but there is only so much flexibility. Some chairs overlap … the carpets pick up what's going on elsewhere in the room. I chose the chaise longue and two high back-chairs' she notes. 'What about a chair that positions the sitter at the same height as the chaise longue?', one of the commercial team adds. 'Yes, so a matching family', Designer B concludes.

The arrangement of chairs in the models and mock-ups portray chair positioned in the lounge at various angles to one another, a pattern that seems to rhyme with the nature of angular reasoning exercised by the design team. There are often surprises, however, and furniture will do things that cannot be anticipated. This potency and capacity of a chair to take on a life of its own has been recognised by few, but the renegade architect and sculptor Frederick Kiesler (1890–1965) was one such visionary. A curious and marginal figure for much of his professional career (Phillips 2010), Kiesler made his own disjunctive intellectual synthesis informed by contemporary theories of physiology, movement and dance (see Mensendieck 1954). In his drawings and writings he explains how he sought to harness a wider flow of 'cosmic' energies in the design of furniture. Kiesler wanted to get in touch with the human-chair couplet in ways that would help him understand how to nourish and stimulate the body so that it might reconnect with a more vital or cosmic flow. In this expansive open-endedness, the body, chair and the cosmos would blend in a mutual becoming. This invocation of energies and its concentration rendered the human body-chair couplet a kind of machine for transport and travel.

Kiesler also warned of the dangers of this coupling. In seeking a critical edge between forces of degeneration and regeneration there would always remain a certain *unpredictable* capacity for agency vested in the chair: 'If I use the chair … I accumulate its energy and add it to mine',

Kiesler wrote (cited in Phillips, ibid.: 103). We have seen how through their efforts to tackle movement the Escape Lounge design team appear to cultivate a similar relationship to the animate qualities of furniture. Pointing at a couple of chairs in the design catalogue Melanie tells us how one piece 'works' whilst another one 'doesn't'. Another piece 'speaks to me' she says, or 'makes a statement', but another one doesn't. One has to train and cultivate an expanded capacity for listening (Nancy 2007) to hear this speaking, for if furniture speaks we can be sure it must speak with a certain 'non-human' quality. Like Wittgenstein's lion, we might say that if the chair could speak we would not be able to understand it. Instead we must presumably harness and translate, work with it, *give* to it, etc. in various combinations of agility and reception.

Such practices might begin to stimulate awareness of an extended human/non-human 'ecology' of practices and relations taking place in the lounge. Later in the same meeting, the lead designer turns to 'Item 9', a Naughtone Clyde compact armchair upholstered in Bute Tweed fabric. Drawing our attention to the contrasting colour button detail, she describes this item as being in 'the same family'. It recalls to mind an episode earlier in the research when the receptionist was talking to me about 'back in the day' when the airport was often described as 'all family', an observation that was commonly made and repeated throughout my time at Manchester Airport. Increasingly, however, it seems the term 'family' is now being used to address *non-human* features – furnishings and colours, lounges, and spaces within lounges. This might be suggestive of a new kind of *vicarious* existentialism in which objects are invested with those properties that were once used to describe relations amongst staff at the airport. Different colours, different accents, upright or crooked, reliable or trustworthy, the lounge furniture appears to take on qualities once reserved for the human. The Foscarini lighting collection, for example, is considered to 'express strong ideas with a special character of their own' and the design team have chosen their 'Twiggy' standing lamp because it 'oozes elegance and sophistication'.[14] We are also told the Twiggy lamp 'has a terrific "presence" in our room and casts a light that is sufficient for tasks and reading'. If '[e]ach epoch … dreams the next' as Benjamin

[14] See http://www.ylighting.com/fos-twiggy.html

wrote (1978: 162; paraphrasing Michelet), then perhaps it is possible that the object world also helps revive and animate that which has been lost in a previous epoch.

What of the dangers of the human-chair couplet that Kiesler spoke? If we listen carefully, we will hear the design team tread carefully: recall they only 'propose' certain items of furniture; 'I've *proposed* leather' Melanie tells us, and 'We have *proposed* twelve for the lounge'. An object seems to require a proposition; it would seem that one should not be so crude as to make assumptions about the behaviour or response of the chair! In one obvious sense, of course, this acknowledges that final approval is granted to the commercial team of the airport. The design consultant is merely in a position to *propose*, it is for the client to make the decision. In this case, we are tackling what is simply a version of diplomacy and business politesse (O'Doherty 2016a). However, at the same time it is possible the propositional tenor reflects a certain anxiety about how things will turn out. What might happen if there is an accumulation of energy between human users and furniture that becomes unstable and dangerous?[15] There may be some cautious calculation going on here with respect to who might take ownership and responsibility for this decision. We have addressed some of these points in the previous chapter, but it seems prudent at this stage to consider what the chair wants.

Typically, we might baulk at the suggestion that chairs have wants or needs. Surely, this reflects anthropomorphism at its most facile. However, what if the *quid est* we are examining here *is* a process of projection and anthropomorphism (cf. Latour 1996)? Is one to doubt the experts for whom there are '50 chairs that *changed* the world' (Design Museum 2009; emphasis added)? In an important study of modern French furniture Auslander (1996: 19) takes this a little further in her observation that chairs *share* an existential equality with humans: '*I have been made* by that chair', Auslander writes, 'and I have made that chair' (emphasis added; cf. Scarry 1985). So it is perhaps not too far-fetched to consider how each item of furniture might relate and get on with each other: a case

[15] In chapters 4 and 5 we pick up some of the dangers brought to life by the lounge including over-drinking, inappropriate clothing, lewd and lascivious behaviour, stealing, the peculiar properties of airport-brain, and the 'compulsive lounger'.

of my family and other animals, perhaps. This is a possibility of which the design team seems cognisant as it seeks to accommodate the forces being conjured here, a difficulty made evident in the word 'proposal'. What will happen in the lounge, and what might happen to the lounger, therefore, cannot be entirely predicted, and their behaviour might be difficult to manage or control. The lounge takes on the guise of a veritable laboratory experiment in which we negotiate the emergence and co-emergence of life with apparently inanimate matters ....

If the chapter began by exploring the role of silence in organization, we might now be struck with sheer astonishment that the non-human is capable of speech, even if we cannot entirely understand what is being said. This astonishment seems to be shared by airport analyst Martin Moodie who gets carried away by the demands of angular reasoning as he tries to explain the experience of entering the airport terminal.[16] His shock is palpable in his hand-held camera report of the new 'commercial offer' in Manchester Airport as he takes his viewers on an angular walk through the terminal to explore the new 'zones' of 'reassurance' and 'desire'. In this report we listen to Moodie as he tries to find a language to describe the various objects and features of this new airport experience. He seems to positively reel from shock as he continues to repeat the exclamation '*Look* at that!...', '*And just look* at that!'. The camera visibly shakes as he invites us to share his shock or excitement, describing for us 'the most chic and elegant currency exchange offer that I've seen in many a long day'. It puts you 'in a holiday mood straight away' he concludes.

A few moments later, we hear him almost stutter in exasperation: '*Look* at that! Lovely lightning, and a *lovely* overhanging canopy ... and the PID [passenger information display] screen up there, there's *loads* of them'. As he describes how good it is to see the 'Sock Shop making a come-back', one begins to realise how the airport not only talks to him, but it is also apparently *alive* – for some 'people' at least. Down and out, back against the ropes, the Sock Shop seems to be taking on the characteristics of a prize-fighter. He is back in the ring, a contender once again. At times it is as if Moodie is describing models on a cat-walk, and his stuttering and aphasia certainly recalls the experience many recount after meeting a celebrity. His

---

[16] http://www.moodiereport.com/document.php?c_id=0&doc_id=21156

whole body seems exercised and animated by the experience of the retail offer of 'World Duty Free' which is described as having been brought to life with the strategy of 'contentainment' (another portmanteau, or disjunctive synthesis), which is a version of 'experiential marketing' that promises to get customers to 'sense, feel, think, act [and] relate' (Schmitt 2000).

As the tour continues, the language strains even further. '*Just take a look at this* … we'll just pan around; over in the distance there you can see SSPs Cafe Rittazza … looking *really* good, possibly the best execution of the brand concept that SSP has done'. He is supposed to be reporting, managing the experience, but he appears almost intoxicated, overcome with emotion. 'Just above it … *that* …', he then pauses in his breathless commentary, and struggles for the appropriate words '… *white* …*wave-like* effect. Affectionately known here … as 'the wasp's net'. And it really softens the area, doesn't it?' A wasps' net that softens the area? Once again we have here the juxtaposition of incongruity, a reaching after the inexplicable, a tessellated juxtaposition, marked by silences and voids. The effects of loungification are far from docility or passivity. But here the human voice is possibly being crowded out by the clamour of animate matters (Bennett 2010).

Do we have the language to describe these new spaces and these new experiences? In the background to the Moodie report one begins to hear a song. It is Credence Clearwater Revival's 'Bad moon rising' which in its quasi-biblical Old Testament lyrical tone sings of hurricanes and lightning, conjuring a palpable sense of impending doom.

Conclusion

In this chapter peculiar patterns and forms in organization began to appear as the ethnography suspended its desire for precipitous descriptive and explanatory conclusion. These patterns were first made possible by attending to the silence marking what was called here a 'profound superficiality' evident in the performance and exercise of particular management rituals such as the Monday morning walkabout. With this concept analysis became more sensitive and responsive to connections and relations across a diverse range of practices in organization. These connections were suggestive of a possible 'pattern propagation' (see Kohn 2013: 20; 186–190) that formed across and between established divisions of discourse and expertise in the management disciplines. More complex and enduring patterns in organization exist outside the functional and bureaucratic forms to which management is typically trained in the business school (Thrift 1999). Yet, this is not to say that management is not forced to confront more complex organization as it steps out of the pages of the mainstream manuals of best-practice.

Eschewing established concepts and theories, ethnography is encouraged to dwell longer with the practices and socio-material conditions of indigenous members of organization where it may be given chance to isolate and extract that which remains immanent, *in potentia,* inchoate and novel (Cooper 1998, 2007). The stabilised entities that form around our 'natural attitude' (Pollner 1987) begin to dissolve and disperse into more processual or primal matter. This is a claim often made in organization studies, but typically only on the basis of derivative philosophical and theoretical speculation (Chia 1996; Tsouskas 2005; Hernes 2008), and this philosophy is often less convincing when applied to empirical enquiry – though airport studies have provided an impetus to redress this problem (Knox et al. 2008, 2015). As stable matter and form begins to *un-form* members of the lounge management team were discovered to be preoccupied with their own forms of pattern making as they sought to make connections across disparate phenomena. This requires a capacity for what has been called here 'angular reasoning'. Stitching together ostensibly incommensurate parts or fragments of phenomena allowed some kind of shared meaning or collective understanding to emerge, at least in so far as a certain silence be taken as a sign of agreement. This stitching together was characterized as disjunctive synthesis which often brings into being the most incredible phenomena in organization, something with a status we might liken to that of 'concept-beings': wow factors, Manchester flavours, gritty virgins, and the wasps nest, but even 'loungers' might qualify, and the very 'Escape Lounge' is a portmanteau itself, made up of movement and stasis. Despite their apparent obscurity these concept-beings have significance and organizational consequence in the Escape Lounge project and this chapter has sought to explore some of them in preparation for a fuller itemization and cataloguing of contemporary 'loungification' in organization (cf. Wood and Beck 1994).

At this moment in the project, management is grappling with the fact that it has no object or subject, no lounge or lounger, no product or consumer. Stuck in this middle and bereft of a well-defined object to manage, (lounge) management can itself quickly lose definition, purpose and direction. Indeed, this chapter suggests that management is often in danger of being *taken over* by those projects it is trying to objectify and bring into being. This chapter has shown that management is at risk of becoming progressively more subsumed and entangled in the lounge, subsumed to the point at which their voice is partially drowned out as one is invited to *hear the lounge speaking* in ways that suggest management is not in control of its object.

It is as if we have to imagine that 'the lounge' has begun to assume agency–like properties of its own that help shape and (de)form the practices and self-definition of management. Not in some reductive and technologically deterministic way so long criticised from a variety of perspectives in sociological studies of technology (MacKenzie and Wajcman 1985; Woolgar 1991; Pickering 1995; recent reviews in Bijker et al. 2012; Grint and Woolgar 2013). Rather, this 'agency' is better thought as more collective or distributed, and one that works by way of extending unforeseen capacities and potentialities. In this space of organizing, producer and product remain ill-defined but co-joined, dispersed in an array of contingent parts through which the mutual construction of subject and object formation take place. The lounge makes itself present through the particular gait or stride pattern of a group of managers engaged in the Monday morning 'constitutional', but also comes into being through the emergence of concept-beings or the stuttering exasperation of managers as they seek to find a language appropriate to the lounge coming into being. Latour would call these 'hybrids' or 'quasi-objects' (Latour 1993). We can begin to register their organizational significance if we can become attuned to the work of the portmanteau language and oxymoronic phrasings that emerge as managers struggle to deal with phenomena that inhere in dimensions of organization where the customary dualisms of social scientific enquiry have little purchase.

As the lounge is slowly being brought to life by managers – part aspiration and part fantasy – managers are themselves being brought into being through the very same materials and practices directed towards the creation of the lounge. Quickly mobilised by the seemingly most fantastic of ideas, as triggered by tools of imaginization such as BRATA, management is asked to consider the possibility that with talking chairs the lounge seems to take on a life of its own.[17] But there are also signs of an emerging language of mutual respect and cooperation. In this extended ecology of practices management cannot be confident that it enjoys a privileged position of sovereignty or control as there appears to be no telling how objects and artefacts assembled in the lounge might react to their surroundings and new relations.

Inside the lounge, energies are being stoked-up and accumulated as things are coming together in their own way. This chapter has followed practices through which the lounge is becoming vested with attitude and attribute, with taste and style. The buzz of the chainsaw and the clouds of dust motes seen and heard three weeks before the opening of the lounge might cast a portentous shadow over the future. We have been able to identify some of these things through the work achieved by angular reasoning, but we have had to sacrifice a more extended study of a whole range of other matters in the lounge – including virtual tennis players, air conditioning systems, chemicals, lacquers and polishes: all of which remains metastable matter. Only a matter of weeks from the planned ceremonial opening, there are some who might be worrying whether anyone will turn up to use the lounge. Moreover, *who* will turn up? This is another source of anxiety amongst the lounge management team and in the next chapter we are going to carefully follow the slow emergence of a remarkable new type of consumer, that person who will come to occupy the space as a 'lounger'.

---

[17] Even the most conservative and functionalist of approaches to the study of project management acknowledge that the 'project takes on a life of its own' (Meredith and Mantel 2011: 182). These authors go on to elaborate some of the features of this peculiar anthropomorphism, suggesting that over time 'A disease known as *projectitis* develops. A strong "we-they" divisiveness grows, distorting the relationships between project team members and their counterparts in the parent organization. Friendly rivalry may become bitter competition, and political infighting between projects is common'. How much of this is attributable to the alien-like qualities of the ostensible *object* of the project is not discussed, but we can hear the authors straining with some incredulity at the affront to functionalist rationality to which this alienation seems responsible.

5

'The Lounger': Re-assembling the Airport Customer

It is eleven o'clock in the morning, August 15th 2010. A typical mid-summer, late morning at the airport. The early rush has departed and a more leisurely atmosphere now prevails in the lounge. Bathed in light and dulcified by song, one senses the lounge is relaxed, but animate and alive. You might see a couple of passengers drinking champagne, one of whom is reclining in an Eames lounger, reading a newspaper; another couple have just entered the reception area and are being booked into the lounge; uniformed lounge staff circulate discretely and in silence, picking up glasses, collecting books and newspapers, putting them back on the shelves, polishing the tables. There is a song playing softly on the PA, the words of which envelope the lounge: *Sailing on a trip to your heart, sailing every secret little part, Sailing to the sky that is free, fireworks exploding across the sea, the clocks on the wall set free. …* Paula, one of the receptionists at the Escape Lounge, 'loves' this song, 'Sailing' by the soft funk band *Land, Air and Blaze.* She is humming along to the song before she welcomes a newly arrived couple and invites them to take up seats available in the 'quiet area'. The 'muzak' is not intrusive, but provides a notable background presence, a kind of aural wallpaper that 'soundtracks' the lounge. The song is not random or happenstance, something that just happens to

D. O'Doherty, *Reconstructing Organization*,
DOI 10.1057/978-1-137-48922-7_5

be playing on a radio, but forms part of a carefully curated musical selection, each track themed to flight and travel, and designed to 'put people in the mood' for the adventure of holiday and sun.

One of the lounge hostesses approaches me. Her name is Edie. 'It's a different world in here, isn't it [?]' she tells me (or asks) as I take up my seat for the day. I have begun to spend days in the lounge. Today I am next to the television area – or what is known in the formal design literature as 'the snug'. Edie has just graduated from a personal grooming training program provided for lounge staff and she moves gracefully, attentively and with a studied deference. She can 'fetch you drinks', she explains, or 'offer advice' on the menu. 'You know, we have a Wii game in 'the attic', and free Internet access in the study? … What time does your flight board, Sir?'

We seem to have stepped onto the stage of an elaborate theatrical game of fantasy and seduction, part of that 'experience economy' that has been extended and developed since Pine and Gilmore (1999) to include 'augmented realities and digital hyperconnectivities' (Boswijk et al. 2012). This would make easy material for the well-established literatures in critical management and labour process studies that have addressed the rise of 'emotional labour' (Hochschild 1983) and 'aesthetic labour' (Warhurst et al. 2000). Routinely associated with companies like Disney, Apple, and Google, the design of experience has become synonymous with what some have previously called the 'aestheticisation of everyday life' (Featherstone 1991) or the 'Disneyization of Society' (Bryman 2004). Behind the surface of this apparent fantasy world we are told there lies a panoptic world of surveillance and disciplinary technologies that alienate and subjugate workers from more authentic subjectivity and identity (Burrell and Dale 2003; Hancock and Taylor 2007).

With this in mind the ethnographer might be tempted to collect data that evidenced the complex strategies of resistance and accommodation. There is the play of cynicism, humour, and irony, for example, which could be supported perhaps with theoretical explanations that draw on Lacan. Those who have done so argue that this amounts to a 'false misidentification' where any 'cynical distance is just one way to blind ourselves to the structuring power of ideological fantasy: even if we do not take things seriously, even if we keep an ironical distance, we are still doing them' (Zizek 1989: 32; quoted in Fleming 2010: 175; Fleming and Spicer 2002: 73; Fleming and Spicer 2003: 163; Fleming and Spicer 2005: 187). This would certainly provide a powerful and compelling explanation elevating the academic to a position equivalent to the seer who sees through the inauthentic and alienated.

In making progress ethnographically this study of the Escape Lounge has been learning the value of caution and suspicion in the use of these kinds of abstracted theoretical metanarratives. Instead of deploying the heavy apparatus of theory we have been drawn to the day-to-day practices of members of organization in ways that acknowledge and take seriously their reflexivity. Critical studies rarely acknowledge that those they accuse of 'false misidentification', for example, might also have read the zeitgeist pop philosophy of Slavoj Zizek, or that the power of an academic explanation is secured through an equivalent ideological fantasy into which the social scientist is implicated. In resisting the temptations of powerful theory, this chapter advances this ethnography in ways that attempt to track more closely the immense complexity and difficulty associated with constructing a subject (a traveller, a consumer, or 'lounger') for the lounge. We will become entangled with the intricate detail of a heterogeneous set of practices and materials implicated in the on-going assembly of a consumer for the lounge. This includes customer sampling practices, questionnaire design, airport quality surveys, benchmarking exercises, awards ceremonies, customer service training modules, industry conferences, fashion magazines, newspaper columnists, consultation documents, and geo-demographic profiling and clustering techniques.

Behind every square inch of constructed space in the Escape Lounge lies a vast and extended network of people and materials. This includes expertise in materials science, structural engineering, and architectural design, but also more recognizably managerial expertise in capital expenditure plans, business models, and cost-benefit calculations. Models and calculations of customer profiling are also required to build the lounge; in addition 'footfall analysis' is conducted, staff personal grooming exercises designed, there is image training, and attempts to manipulate social media trending. All this forms part of an intricate array of knowledge practices and expertise invested in the lounge. Just to maintain the very physical fabric and presence of the lounge, for example, requires ongoing survey, feedback, and analysis that involves constant repairs and retuning – from the maintenance contracts for the air conditioning unit, to the recalibrations of the colour codes invested in the aesthetic design. Hence, there is no singular management of the lounge.

We have also noted that loungification can only be 'found' in bits and pieces that circulate across a diverse series of sites and practices and all at different 'scales' of organization. This includes Gannt charts and project briefs to fashion magazines and popular television programmes. In this chapter we follow traces of 'the lounger' that are suggestive of the emergence of a new subject position in management and organization. In so doing the ethnography makes further progress in tracing the emergence of a possible new specialism in lounge management expertise. This quest takes take us to a data processing centre in Leeds, to an office in the pretty little town of Gland on the shores of Lac Lemen in Switzerland, to the work of the Airport Council International (ACI) and the International Air Transport Association (IATA), and on to Whitehall in the UK, the Civil Aviation Authority, and the Department for Transport. Traces are also found at another scale – in the apparently mundane and 'micro' that hardly register in most management and organization studies: paperwork involved in the administration, distribution and collection of airport passenger surveys. We find enrolled into this paperwork 'Pearson' statistical coefficients, but also PowerPoint slides, popular magazine articles, awards ceremonies, mannequins and fashion models.

What allows us to hold all these things together and to trace emergent patterns of organization is the deployment of this concept *loungification.* It is a concept that helps tune our attention to things in process, which are extended complexly in space and time, and in multiple bits and pieces – the weaving together of which into relatively stabilized or coherent 'wholes' happens without any prime mover or identifiable causal agent. As we follow these traces we find they are mobilized and tied up in a set of complex political struggles within and across formal organization where new groupings emerge and old coalitions fall into abeyance. At the same time, these struggles connect management to the ceaseless negotiation of borders and boundaries across different organizations. Our focus in this chapter is specifically on the partial stabilization of 'the customer' or 'consumer' who we find emerges as an outcome of this complexity –

and in many ways a fantastical creature that is only partially known and under the control of formal management. There is some specificity to this customer, however, and one that seems to be accomplished by the deployment of the term 'lounger'.

The role of the consumer has attracted growing interest in organization studies since the pioneering work of Gabriel and Lang (1995) and du Gay (1996)[1] and the work of those interested in the workplace implications of organizations being restructured to achieve greater customer-service orientation (Sturdy 1998; Hodgson 2002; Korczynski 2003).[2] What distinguishes more recent interest in the consumer is the fact that the old sociological commitment to the sphere of production or the workplace is no longer privileged. In this chapter we find a space of organizing that comes prior to the dualism of producer and consumer and at some remove from prevailing constructivist or realist assumptions concerning the ontology of organization (Burrell and Morgan 1979; Donaldson 1985; Willmott 1993a; Chia 1996; Reed 1997; Ackroyd and Fleetwood 2004; Fleetwood 2005; O'Doherty 2009). Maintained and reproduced by the familiar categories of 'manager', 'worker' or 'customer', we find these classifications too blunt and insensitive to the movements and processes that make up loungification.

This ethnography of the lounge has already discovered that 'management' does not exist in the form of a well-defined entity, and in this chapter we discover similar things about the consumer. Better conceived as an unseemly amalgam shaped by the immense struggle involved in the development of a product or service – to which customers might become attached – we find 'the customer' does not exist in any ontologically reliable way. Instead, it is always being made and re-made, and more often than not in ways that would be considered *failures* rather than success. Without an object (a lounge), without a subject (a lounger), as we have previously noted, management finds itself in a most invidious position,

[1] See the burgeoning work in the mainstream management and organization journals including Rosenthal and Peccei (2007) and Nayak and Beckett (2008), and the recent special issue of *Organization* which includes important papers by Arnould and Cayla (2015), Cova et al. (2015), and Fontenelle (2015).

[2] The organizational implications of the rise of the customer was also extensively researched in the critical study of call centres and total quality management, much of which sought to extend labour process theory and analysis (Taylor and Bain 1999; Sturdy et al. 2001; Callaghan and Thompson 2002).

and one that simultaneously demands an on-going self-(re)invention of management as well. To help advance our ethnography of this difficult dimension of organization-in-action we draw once again on recent work in economic sociology that has addressed the role of market devices, intermediaries, and new market professionals in the 'making-up' of the consumer (Callon 1998; Araujo 2007; Cochoy 2007, 2008; Araujo et al. 2010). Here we find ongoing trials and experimentations that bring into association and configurations different relations of people, materials and practices that circulate across (whilst also transgressing) established dualisms in organization studies. Attending to this level of practical detail, and allowing a more extended space and time for this organization-in-action, multiplies the number of actors – human and non-human – relevant to the achievement of organization.

The Airport Services Quality Initiative

It is 5.30 am and I am handing out Airport Service Quality (ASQ) questionnaires to passengers who are milling around the shops and restaurants in the departure terminal. I have two black 'Bic' biro pens, a clipboard and a stack of paper questionnaires. I am told the terminal has no isolated or clearly demarcated departure gates around which passengers gather. The relevance of this becomes clear when the ASQ supervisor, Mary, explains to me that this makes the task of distribution and collection difficult because you can waste a lot of time going up to people who are travelling on an airline or destination that are not part of the sample plan for the day. The people to whom we need to distribute the questionnaires could be anywhere in the space, at the shops, or the adjoining cafes and restaurants. Mary is contracted for 4 hours of work this morning and so she must focus her efforts efficiently in order to collect the requisite number of completed questionnaires. She asks me to help in the distribution and collection. 'You're not supposed to speak to the passengers and you definitely cannot fill out the form for them, even if they ask you'. However, they do need some guidance and instruction, she explains, but it's not clear at what point one is likely to stray from 'guidance and instruction' into forms of assistance that might actually influence and therefore 'pollute' the data we are trying to collect.

I approach one elderly individual who is happy to fill out the form – Mary tells me to expect some brusque responses from passengers, particularly those who are tired and jet-lagged. 'Am I going to need my glasses to read this?', I am asked. 'Will it take long?' He asks me where I am from. On hearing that I live in Manchester he tells me that his wife used to live in Manchester, during the war, when she actually worked at Manchester Airport with the air squadron based there. She's dead now, though. And today, he is off to their old holiday home. He still goes, but tells me that it has been 3 years since he and his wife went together. I am asked if I like Manchester. I become a little nervous. Mary is busy circulating and collecting completed questionnaires, but fearing the consequences of appearing rude I cannot find the correct choice of words to politely make my departure. Despite this, it is a fascinating conversation, and I learn a great deal about the airport through the eyes of this one elderly gentleman. However, it takes considerable effort to get him to focus on the questionnaire as I try to point him towards question 1. This question asks for the airline with whom he is travelling, the flight number, the departure gate, and departure time. He has to shuffle through his papers to retrieve the ticketing information, which he then slowly transcribes into the relevant section of the form.

The questionnaire is basically composed of 34 'key performance indicators' arranged in the form of a tabular Likert scale tick-box exercise that evaluates each KPI on a range from excellent to poor. These include things like ground transportation to/from the airport (A), availability of parking facilities (B), value for money of parking facilities (C), the courtesy and helpfulness of inspection (I) and airport staff (R), and the quality of the shopping facilities (V). On one level such exercises might be interpreted as evidence of the disciplinary and 'surveillance society' (Lyon 2001) to which a broad body of work ranging from studies of 'the mystery shopper' (Ball 2010), financial accountancy (Hoskin and Macve 1986; Robson 1992), the electronic panopticon of call-centre technologies (Bain and Taylor 2000), and techniques of personnel management – including career management (Grey 1994), and performance and appraisal (Townley 1994), have contributed. However, whilst such techniques and technologies put pressure on management and workers to deliver greater service quality, they also help *constitute* airport experience in ways that help passengers think of themselves *as* customers, and more specifically *customers of airports*. Through such techniques, a customer of the airport is being made, then, at the same time that the airport is being made-over as a service provider. However, the devil, as always, is in the detail….

From the brief ethnographic excerpts detailed here one can begin to sense how much arbitrary and contingent material finds its way into surveys and data. Yet, the translations and aggregations are important and consequential. To forge a subject and object of airport consumption is a long, fraught and bewilderingly complex process, and one that is never complete, bearing with it untold consequences and outcomes. The ethnography shows that it takes considerable skill simply to fill out the ASQ form – and not all those surveyed are skilled or equally skilful. Those surveyed, for example, are required to distinguish airport staff from airline staff, inspection, check-in, and security. There are many different employees with whom a passenger will routinely come into contact, even within the limited confines of the terminal. These include UK Borders Agency, the airline, their check-in and handling agents, and the airport itself – who may employ security staff directly, or a third-party specialist security company. Whilst a contested and often tense and antagonistic affair between different bodies within the airport, responsibility for passport control and its staffing remains with formal state institutions. There are also employees of retailers and baggage handlers, who will work for different employers. Indeed, it is quite possible that you may never come across a direct employee of the airport during your passage through the terminal. How much control the airport can exercise over certain criteria on the ASQ survey is therefore moot.

With the benefit of greater familiarity it is possible that passengers will become more 'skilled' at identifying the different responsibilities and demarcations amongst uniformed and non-uniformed staff in an airport. However, all this suggests that there can be no simple locus of responsibility around which we can study the work involved in the making of a specifically *airport* customer. At any one time an individual in an airport is a passenger, a nation state citizen, a security threat, a shopper and perhaps – increasingly – this new category: 'airport customer' (cf. Knox et al. 2008).

DKMA, ACI, IATA: The Corridors of Power

To understand how this questionnaire is made to work we must trace it as it travels through airport terminals in Manchester to a data-processing centre in Leeds and on to the offices of a company called DKMA. In following this trail one might expect a moment during which we 'change scale' (Latour 2005a), so to speak, when we step from the micro and approach something closer to 'the macro' – institutions, structures, and political economy that regulates and shapes commercial enterprise and something we call 'economy' (but see Mitchell 2008). However, as we shall see, nothing like this happens. We simply enter different offices, with jurisdictions and decision making responsibilities that are equally unclear, and constantly changing and subject to contestation. The personnel are also constantly coming and going. On the back of new knowledge expertise some are in the ascendency, while others are falling out of fashion, new agendas are forming, as older interests get redefined. There are 'restructurings', divestments, institutional mergers and acquisitions, and a constant transgression of borders and 'revolving doors' as commercial experts become regulators, or political advisees, for example, only later to take up positions back in the commercial sector. We will find there is no context, but something more like shifting coalitions and landslides as formal divisions of institutions are removed and staff reassigned, and sometimes around all this change can be found the results of a humble questionnaire....

Head-officed in the picturesque Swiss rural hamlet of Gland, nestled on the banks of Lac Lemen, DKMA might be considered the authors of the ASQ. In tracing these circulations, however, we discover that the questionnaire does far more work than we might imagine and cannot simply be thought of as something that allows Mary to collect data so that airports can be benchmarked in terms of quality. We discover, for example, that it takes considerable time and effort for the questionnaire to stabilize in the form of a reliable object that can be routinely handled by Mary and airport customers. Each interaction with a passenger requires a re-construction of the questionnaire as things have to be explained and assumptions made so that the questions can be answered. At another level, the ASQ survey remains contested, for some it forms part of a fully-fledged business proposition, even an entrepreneurial venture, possibly a speculation or financial investment (e.g. DKMA). It is, however, for others, an object of dubious proprietorial status (ACI). There are also some for whom it remains an experiment – of doubtful methodological standing – with possibly deleterious consequences for the airport. Senior executives responsible for security or airfield operations, for example, had little time for the ASQ at MAG. Despite their suspicions and protestations it eventually formed part of a wider strategy of airport service quality management at Manchester Airport (at least for a while), advanced by an emerging team of 'commercial management', some of whom work every day on ASQ, and might be considered to be partly working for DKMA.

Yet DKMA is little more than one small open-planned office on Rue de Riant Coteau in the little Swiss town of Gland. The office is sparsely furnished with one or two desks, divided into a few smaller discrete spaces by grey fabric office partition screens. Only 2 or 3 computers are visible. It is in many ways an example of the ubiquity of 'non-place' (Augé 1995), and one might hardly suspect that it serves as an obligatory point of passage in a grand apparatus responsible for loungification. Their website explains that the ASQ survey is 'owned and directed by Airports Council International' and that 'DKMA provides market research, analysis and information solutions exclusively for the airport industry'. Evidently the ASQ survey forms only one part of their business interests – they offer a range of consultancy service packages involving varying degrees of collaboration and involvement.

On an astonishingly clear day with bright blue skies and hardly a breeze in the air I meet with Derek Klinsman in the head office of DKMA in Gland, Switzerland. The sky bears no trace of aircraft vapour trails and there is no roar from jet engines so familiar to the 'residents' of an airport. Derek is trying to explain to me the origins of the ASQ survey. Before long we have covered an incredibly complex tapestry of organizations and institutions that speaks of a tangled and messy political terrain – and one that involves most of the various bodies and organizations associated with the airport industry. The drawing I make looks a lot like Pollock's *Autumn Rhythm*. Marked by memory lapses and a lack of accessible or shareable (commercially sensitive) documentation, Derek constantly reminds me that what he is saying is also – of course – *only* from *his point of view.*[3] It is however, a point of view consistent with many others voiced in the corridors of airport management and in casual conversations amongst delegates at industry conferences and trade events.

IATA is one organization that Derek helps me draw, delineated with a square box in my sketch. The International Air Transport Association is an institution that positions itself as a representative of the interests of airports *and* airlines. Some in the industry argue, however, that they are essentially a trade association for the airlines. Airport Council International (ACI), on the other hand, represents the airports. Where IATA charge a fee to airlines for membership of the association, the ACI charge airports. Derek explains that in the early 2000s membership of IATA was dropping and as a consequence fee revenue was declining. To respond, the association sought to find new ways of generating commercial revenue. 10–15 years ago many began to see that airports were more stable and viable as a long-term business opportunity. Subject to state led marketization, national airlines, on the other hand, were becoming more volatile (Doganis 2005). Drawn into complex mergers and acquisition following the reduction of state aid, airlines were increasingly exposed to the possibility of commercial insolvency and were becoming much more financially risky. However, because IATA was a trade association for the airlines, airports were not inclined to see how IATA might best serve their commercial futures. Yet it was within IATA that the first signs of an international benchmarked customer service program was being delivered. In what follows we shall see that this involved close collaboration with the ACI during the development of what eventually became known as the ASQ.

According to some, the first idea for an international benchmarked customer service programme was formulated in the market research department at IATA. In fact, it was more than likely somewhere *between* those offices in IATA and offices of those with similar responsibilities in the ACI where one might source the original idea. In looking for an origin in this way is of course a treacherous exercise and can rapidly trigger all kinds of anxieties about 'muckraking' involving disputed stories about

[3] The litigious paranoia is one that extends to the construction of this book, an issue I will take up in a later publication.

ownership and territory. It is striking that when Derek talks about these issues, he talks in terms of 'signs'. Signs, of course, are untrustworthy and often unreliable, and they demand vigilance and interpretation. The 'first signs' of a benchmarked customer service program were found 'in' IATA, but they were perhaps only 'signs' of what later became hugely successful in the form of the Airport Services Quality programme. They are, hence, signs only *retrospectively*. Looking for unambiguous authorship ultimately proves frustrating; on occasion an individual might *claim* to be the originator, but at other times the same individual would describe the survey as 'something that was in the air', an old statistical technique, or basic customer research. It seems that the attribution and calculation of ownership depended on who it was that doing the asking, and for what purposes.

What precisely is *original* in the idea also reveals a history of confusion. Typically any definition of this originality is left in abeyance. Prior to the ASQ, for example, many airports ran their own customer satisfaction surveys, and in the UK periodic passenger surveys and enquiries into service quality were conducted by state institutions such as the CAA (Civil Aviation Authority) and the DfT (Department for Transport). Some consensus might be built around the idea that the data gathered by IATA on customer service was underdeveloped, or considered poor. This prompted some to seek greater collaboration with members of the ACI to develop a more detailed questionnaire and to extend membership of the survey.

We tread on delicate territory in seeking to answer the question as to why there was this turn to the ACI and the founding of DKMA. There are many candidate answers. Some members of IATA might not have seen the value of investing further resources into the promotion of a survey of value principally to airports. An internal 'strategic review' ordered in 2011 by incoming CEO Tony Tyler is certainly suggestive of complex internal politics in IATA (though no more complicated than in others) with one line of division apparent between the commercial side of the organization (human capital, corporate planning and finance) and internal functional departments such as training. According to some analysts and commentators, and again not unlike most large organizations, IATA is subject to ongoing 'internal wrangling'. For at least one commentator they have 'resolutely failed to add value for the quickest growing part of aviation, the low cost business' (cited in the online trade magazine loadstar.co.uk). Seeking to sell its own advertising space, of course, and speaking on behalf of the supply chain industry, IATA makes a convenient target for *loadstar* editorials, and so caution must be exercised in our analysis. 'It's a legacy organization for legacy carriers', *Loadstar* concludes in their 23rd September 2011 blog. With 67 offices and over 1500 staff, IATA might be considered a slow and unwieldy organization. This would certainly provide one rationale why some might feel the need to speed things up by working on the borders and margins where things are not so encumbered with bureaucratic procedure and policy. Perhaps this helps explain the turn to ACI and the opening of an inter-institutional space.

A change of personnel in the market research department at IATA meant new skills were being developed which perhaps also contributed to the conditions in which a new survey could be devised under a 'joint venture' with ACI. However, we should expect no formal record of a 'joint venture', let alone archived records of negotiations, analysis or 'experiments' wherein which we could pinpoint the birth of the 'ASQ'. This would, after all, be commercially sensitive. Indeed, there is no need for any formal agreement to establish a joint venture. Working out who within the respective organizations would be responsible for devising and then approving such a joint venture might also raise questions about formal governance 'structures' and processes. And then we would be led to ask whether any joint venture would represent the interests of IATA? And, would this be all of IATA, or only certain parts[4]? These are questions that members of the respective organizations are capable of and likely to be asking as well.[5] For an ethnographer to ask such questions would, however, likely stoke up suspicions that the ethnographer was interested in questions of legality or internal corporate governance. Where things are inevitably complex and emergent, held together by expertise to which

[4] Here our ethnography arrives at the insight that organizations are fragile agreements within ongoing disputes and contestations about strategy and direction that involves competition for power and resource alongside quests for *how* power operates (does *someone* have it, is it legally defined, vested in impersonal norms and cultural assumptions, socially embedded or codified (structured) in wider political institutions and governance?) But we discover this to be something to which members of organization are also preoccupied. These are not simply academic questions.

[5] Go in search of a questionnaire and you end up in the ontological quicksands of organization!

one remains an outsider, the ethnographer might then become a potential *threat* to the various relations within and across both organizations. Such 'relations' remain immensely complicated, but essentially the modus operandi of most large organizations.

We are in strange and difficult waters here where cause-effect, push-pull, and precise definition are impossible to establish. Sometime around the late 1990s Derek leaves IATA and following the founding of DKMA, ACI contract directly for the management and delivery of the ASQ data. DKMA is 'I suppose, *licensed* by the ACI', Derek concludes. Over the next few years, members of DKMA attend trade conferences and sell the benefits of benchmarking to various airports through which the construction of performance measures and league tables begins to enrol more and more airport personnel. What also needs to be considered when explaining this enrolment of new experts in customer service and quality is the extent to which DKMA had particular skills or training that made them good *salesmen* of the ASQ. This is likely to be something that did not exist *prior* to the emergence of ASQ and therefore their status or otherwise as good salesmen cannot serve as a robust prime mover or explanation.

As recent advances in practice based studies of organization analysis show – DKMA staff likely *learned by doing* – in what is called in some literatures 'practical-coping' (Chia and Holt 2006), something which is itself achieved through extended patterns of 'interconnected activities' that includes 'non-human' actors (see Nicolini 2012). In part this involves travelling to airports, drawing on personal relations to engineer meetings with those managers in airports who have or might be in a position to develop an explicit commercial focus, attending trade shows, and presenting at conferences. The art of charm and persuasion is evident in a lot of these activities (O'Doherty 2016a). According to one presentation package, the survey can help airports 'understand strengths and weaknesses of delivered services' and 'identify areas of improvement and optimise investments'. But there needs to be a receptive audience for this version of an airport and its activities, and potential champions of the *passenger-as-a-customer* of airport services employed within airports. Who or what makes an audience, and who or what makes the audience 'receptive' to the idea of an airport customer, from which the lounger might eventually be constructed?

In tracing the rise to power of the ASQ it is helpful to ask *how* the agents deemed responsible for it went about doing some of this.[6] However, we have seen that in asking this question it becomes impossible to establish any clear line of authorship. Rather than individuals, it seems the explanation lies in a *collection* of people, and a network[7] of materials and impersonal resources (including biros and paper, Pearson correlations, airports, government policies, email, PowerPoint slides, etc.).

Such ethnographic detail is invaluable when studying how airports are being made objects of consumption and customer interest, but we should not lose sight of the fact that the construction of a consumer for airports is an astonishing achievement – and one that is only ever partially achieved. It is one that involves schisms and fractures in existing institutions and their formal governance structures, and such a blurring of all our categories and analytical resources that something like a generalized ontological dissolution rapidly looms. The process is one in which *all the various elements* are co-constituted and co-emergent: airport, customer, product, and manager.[8] If everything – customer, manager, product, etc. – is co-dependent and mutually emergent, then we cannot explain the emergence of the consumer (or the lounger) as the product of management, or the specific branch of management we might be seeing emerge here, namely customer service managers. In order to track the coming into being of the airport customer, the ethnographer has to suspend and break down these familiar categories of organization analysis. The ethnographer is then left with bits and pieces that flow in flux, coming together and falling apart. Something is found that is being held steady, and around which this network might be explained, but that is a novel concept – the 'airport customer', out of which eventually will come the airport 'lounger'.

The central paradox – in what will strike many as a remarkable *tautological* construction – can be identified as one where the ASQ can only sell

[6] What other potential candidates for consuming management time might there have been? What was taking up *less* management time to make room for all this attention to the ASQ?

[7] Or to better capture the dynamism of this process we should use the term *networking*, but we risk overloading the text with more grammatical contortions in the effort to capture or analytically *move* with *movements*.

[8] That airports and their management consider themselves in *competition* with each other *for* customers is likewise an incredible turn of events. How far this understanding reaches 'down' and 'through' the various layers of management and operations of an airport remains moot.

its services and gain legitimacy by appealing to the idea that customers *are already there* – at the same time that, by virtue of these very same activities, the ASQ remains centrally implicated in their construction. A whole series of new people, materials and practices have to be mobilized and allied in order to bring this state of affairs into reality. By following closely the people and materials involved in the ASQ one can begin to see how this mobilization happens across the boundaries and in the interstices of established formal institutions. Most of the 'expertise' gets defined, designated, employed and developed by formal institutions, but this only happens *after* the invention of the new product or management specialism.

To follow the *processes* responsible for innovation requires a multi-sited ethnography (Marcus 1995) sensitive to relational work in which established analytical categories in organization studies do not hold. Ethnography remains a minor interest for those studying innovation and as a discipline innovation studies has largely failed to develop adequate ethnographic methods that would take them into this complexity.[9] Without well-defined subjects and objects it is immensely difficult to study this inchoate organization and in following the work involved in the construction of the lounger, analysis must develop a sensitivity to the *co-emergence* of a bewildering and heterogeneous range of human and non-human actors. Specialist consultants in questionnaire design, dedicated airport customer quality managers, and the administrators and analysts reading and presenting the findings – all of these elements must be simultaneously in play. This is complex because there is no prime mover and each of the elements remains complexly (and tautologically) inter-dependent on the existence of each other.

This kind of complexity is typically ignored in both critical studies of airports and more functionalist analysis where the rise of more commercial orientated management is often attributed to simplified and blunt 'strategies' such as 'state-led privatization' (see for example Francis et al. 2002; Freathy

[9] Exceptions would include Dopson's (2005) work on Elias and 'figurational sociology', which comes close theoretically, and Nicolini (2010, 2012) continues to develop an interesting version of practice-based studies influenced by socio-materiality. However, both remain restricted to an interest in what I would call *managerialised* organization which falls short of an interest in wider ontological politics. In an important paper Hoholm and Araujo (2011) come closest to developing a form of ethnography adequate to the kind of complexity involved in innovation, but it is important to note that all these studies come from outside the discipline of innovation studies.

2004; Graham 2013). Such reified and abstracted summaries also lose sight of the tremendous energy and effort associated with a range of practical managerial activities that are not confined within neat and nested structures of causality. In tracing some of the ancillary and supplementary processes involved in making the ASQ survey work, the ethnographer has to navigate an extensive network of offices. This chapter has only begun to scratch the surface of what is a bewildering diversity of practices that seem to sub-tend the object we are tracing – from algorithms to continuous methodological fine-tuning, but also annual awards ceremonies, trade conferences and presentations. And in turn, all of this is wrapped up in the politics of intellectual property rights and other territorial disputes around legitimacy and responsibility. Nor does this proceed without suspicion and contestation from other areas of an airport organization – for whom it is airlines, demographics and route development that brings passengers to an airport, not the ASQ.

Conferences, Awards Ceremonies and PowerPoint: Making Customers for the Airport

There isn't a month that goes by when Derek from DKMA is not attending some conference or other devoted to the airport and aviation industry. Like the academic circuit, the conference is a vital source of information and exchange that helps build and develop community whilst also providing a site in which important new practices and ideas emerge. New lines of tension and division also emerge and are worked upon by participants in relation to the ebb and flow of network and alliance building where new authorities are emerging and older ones receding (see also Lomnitz 1983; Collins 2004: 449–453; Gonzalez-Santos and Dimond 2015). In 2014 there were 29 conferences organized by the Airports Council International alone, all of which might claim Derek's attention, ranging in topic from an annual economics and finance conference to the set-piece World Annual General Assembly held May 26–28 in Seoul, Korea. The ACI is only one professional or trade association amongst hundreds in the industry, each with its own calendar of conferences and trade fairs. One important commercial conference is the annual Passenger Terminal Expo with over 180 exhibitors, 4500 attendees, and in excess of 1350 speakers and conference participants. DKMA are regular attendees and speakers at events of this kind, which give them a chance to showcase the work of the ASQ and to meet potential clients from the worldwide airport industry. Typically a presentation would include such statements as 'We help airports and airlines grow their revenue by placing the passenger at the centre of their business. Our speciality is creating business information and management frameworks to improve performance'.

One important PowerPoint slide that began to circulate at these conferences was what was called a 'prioritisation chart' that claimed to be able to show how airports could identify those areas of terminal service where one could improve customer service. Based on rather simple surveying and statistical techniques, what this chart does essentially is to superimpose two different datasets on a 2 x 2 box. In preparing this chart, each of the KPIs on the ASQ questionnaire is isolated and measured to ascertain its relative importance to 'overall satisfaction' at the airport (on the x axis), and the 'satisfaction gap' between the ratings of this factor at one airport in comparison to the average satisfaction level amongst competing airports. Question 8 of the ASQ survey asks those surveyed to list in rank order (1–3) which of the 30 or so service items 'are most important to you at this airport'. From this the ASQ can then isolate those factors that make the most difference to improving overall satisfaction from various different starting points and, making use of basic Pearson correlations, establish what we might call the 'elasticity' of the various factors. This then allows DKMA to distribute the KPIs into one of the four quadrants (Fig. 5.1).

Those identified as 'primary concerns', for example, are those situations where there is a high correlation with satisfaction but currently below average performance. Those situations where the airport might wish to review its level of commitment include those where they are achieving above average performance in aspects of terminal facilities and operations that are only of relatively minor importance in terms of their contribution to overall satisfaction.

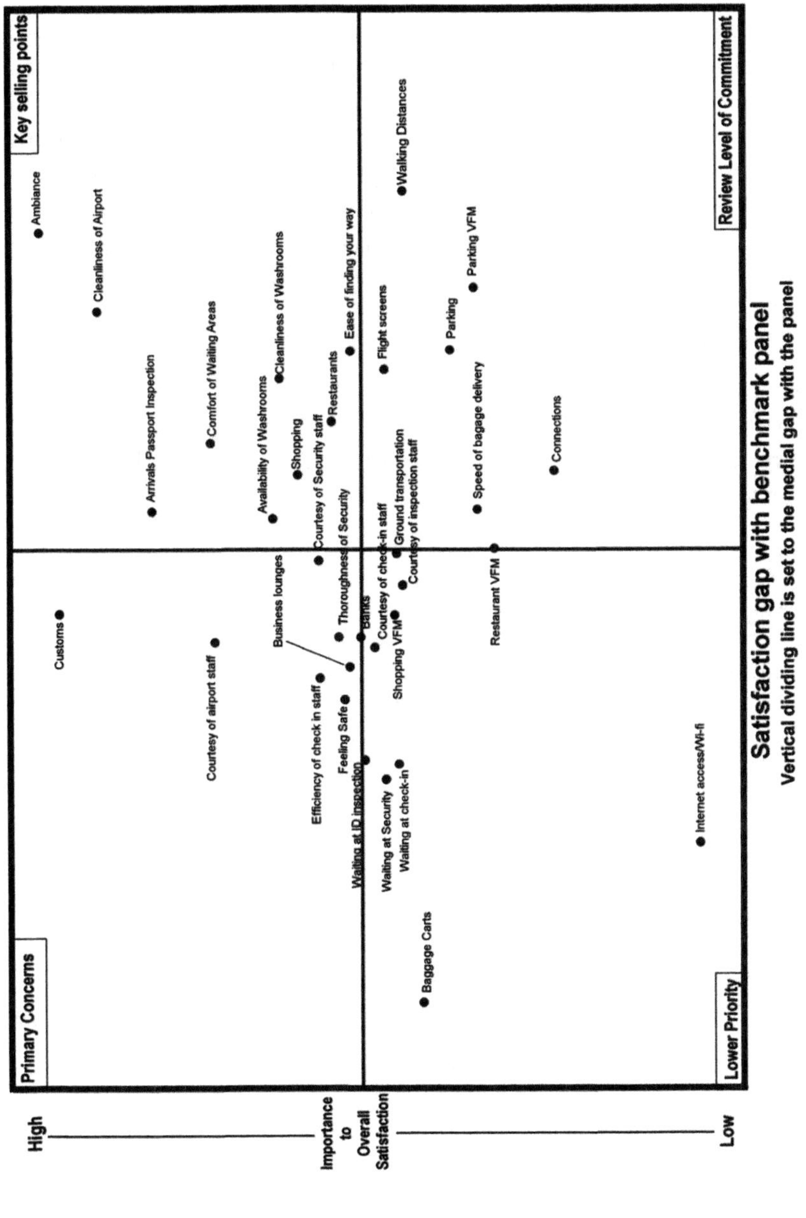

Fig. 5.1 Airport customer service prioritisation analysis

However, the capacity for improvement also depends on your starting point – that is, whether you are a high scoring airport or low scoring. If you are scoring low within the league table, one can acquire immediate and considerable improvements by focusing attention on items such as 'value for money' or 'IT facilities'. One acquires a more than average step change in overall satisfaction levels from an investment in these two items than one would by architecturally re-designing the terminal, or indeed by investing in new baggage handling equipment. This 'factor' of course, is not seen by airport customers, but could feed through to things like flight delays or baggage damage, neither of which are measured in the survey, though if one is a frequent user of the airport with persistent problems with flight delays, for example, the experience might feed back into the mark awarded in the ASQ survey section that asks about 'overall satisfaction with the airport'.

Derek talks to me about how these findings help generate a PowerPoint similar to this (Fig. 5.2):

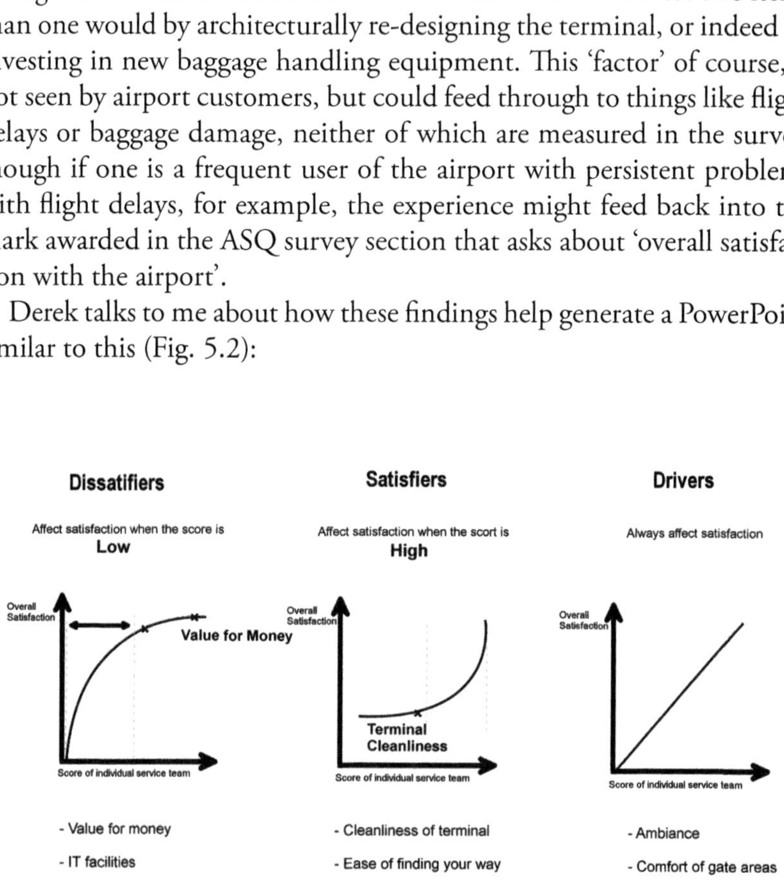

Fig. 5.2 Drivers, satisfiers and dissatisfiers

This shows that some factors – defined as 'drivers' – will always drive commensurate improvements in overall satisfaction. Other factors reap only diminishing returns after a certain level of satisfaction has been achieved. One can never, however, exhaust the payoff provided by investment in 'the drivers'. From the data collected 'ambience' and 'comfort at gates' seem to be the 'drivers' for which customers, apparently, remain insatiable.

A slide similar to this begins to circulate through the conference circuit and I acquire four copies during the ethnography – one from staff at Manchester Airport, one from the 2010 Passenger Terminal Expo in Brussels, one from staff at the DKMA offices, and one from another industry conference website (see also Halpern and Graham 2013: 131–33). We can see how such diagrams help make and legitimate 'the customer', and more specifically a customer *of an airport*. In so doing 'the airport' itself is being (re)made an identifiable object and space for interventions of this kind with the presentation of data appearing to show how well-targeted investment in facilities are determined by the specific circumstances of each particular airport. From this data and its presentation we are offered evidence to show two things simultaneously, (a) how the target – an airport – is *manipulable*, and (b) that *there is* a customer for these kinds of features of an airport. In effect the data are being collected about people in an airport who are deemed to be customers – not, say, *passengers* of an airline – and in the very completion of the questionnaire, individuals are of course being, in part, *trained* to think of the airport in new and highly particular ways. Through the very processes of data collection and aggregation what might appear to be an entirely arbitrary or even possibly specious break-down of something holistic like experience into various categories and distinctions (ambiance, shopping facilities, thoroughness of the security inspection, etc.) helps creates items of experience that become increasingly normalized. Moreover, these categories and distinctions begin to take on active agency-like properties of their own.[10] In turn, the language of 'drivers', 'satisfiers' and 'dissatisfiers' becomes increasingly normalized as it helps establish new experts of airport customer service managers, a discourse-practice that is also beginning to spread through the ranks of more established management and occupational specialisms employed in airports.[11]

---

[10] In Manchester a project concurrent with the Escape Lounge called 'back to basics' helps circulate and socialize the importance of these products and services that speak of new experiences in an airport.

[11] By contrast senior members of terminal operations at Manchester Airport harboured greater suspicion of these new fads and fashions in management thinking. As one of the design team told me "Initially Roger [from Terminal Ops] was in there with Gary [lead designer] with an attitude of 'I've got the UK borders

For airport managers responsible for customer satisfaction, these charts, data, and graphic artefacts are key documents that provide resources for persuasion and the mobilization of support. They find their way into monthly presentations to senior management at Manchester Airport and are cited in project briefs and other internal documentation that circulates during the making of the Escape Lounge. Meanwhile, on the back of such data, DKMA have been able to build a whole series of consultancy packages, which they then in turn market to airports. One of their services, 'ASQ performance', for example provides an additional level of analysis that in their vernacular 'drills down' further into the data whilst deploying 'actual measures of the service delivered' in each airport. DKMA have also developed an 'ASQ assurance' certification scheme that involves what they call on-site verification audits, an 'ASQ Retail' module that focuses on the benchmarking of quality standards achieved in retail services, and 'ASQ management' which offers a broad range of consultancy services that helps train airport management in the implementation of 'best-practice'.

In many ways these developments are consistent with those practices that have been identified as part of the 'audit society' (Power 1997), much analysed in the public and former public sector in UK and Europe. For some, these methods cast a rigid and mechanistic, and ultimately self-defeating form of performance management in organizations. However, in focusing on one particular element we have been able to discover a far more complex picture behind what might otherwise appear to be a vast panoptic incarceration. Explored ethnographically, each connection – in what is a vast socio-technical network required to operate something like the ASQ – illuminates considerably more contingency and uncertainty than would otherwise be available to organizational analysis. On the back of this fine gossamer or capillary set of connections business have been built (DKMA), capital investment funds secured (the ASQ formed part of the CAPEX application in the early days of the Escape Lounge project), terminals redesigned, new roles created for management in airports, and discerning customers of airport services skilful in the use of the ASQ categories have begun to emerge. However, we should remain alert to the fact that each connection, from the application of Pearson coefficients to the production of data analytics, and to Mary who is collecting the data

behind me'". In this context of territorial claims it was difficult – as members of the design team ironically suggested – 'to introduce the idea of 'pink fur' as a design option!'. However, 'Now, every 6 weeks, I get an email from Roger asking for advice about changing a light here or adding vinyl to a unit there'.

from our airport terminal, involves *endless translations* and a vast amount of effort that cannot be relaxed at any point in the circuit.

It is surprising that little is said of this in the mainstream management textbooks devoted to airport management (see Doganis 1992; Young and Wells 2011; Graham 2013). Without this network there is *no customer* of an airport. There might be customers of retail outlets, or customers of airlines – though they still tend to be known as passengers – but customers *of an airport* is of more recent historical significance. We should not underestimate the complexity and difficulty of this construction. At the very least, an airport proves intransigent as an 'object' of construction or intervention. And 'the airport' is itself a misnomer and better conceived as many organizations in one, or rather 'more than one, but less than many' (Mol 2002; Knox et al. 2008). The making of customers for an airport faces additional difficulties by virtue of the fact that the 'reach' airport management has in an airport is difficult to establish. Where the specific responsibilities of 'the airport' start and finish, in comparison to those of an airline, a third party contractor, or a state agency (Borders Agency, for example), remains opaque. It is then little wonder that the ASQ might confuse many 'customers' who might be surprised that it is not the airport who is responsible for their missing luggage or for the fact that a flight has been cancelled. And such boundary questions are not the confusion of the ignorant; they remain opaque to most working in an airport where the boundaries are contested and emergent.

To understand something of the complexity involved in the construction of the customer one must consider the scale of the network through which this customer for airports is forged. Consider the annual awards ceremony for airport staff working on the ASQ. It might be said that this provides a resource that serves both motivational and legitimating functions for the emerging discourse-practice of customer services management in airports. It also helps circulate categories and classifications through which customer service and quality is known. The ceremony offers rewards for the 'best airport' in 5 categories – ranked by size (passenger numbers); for the 'best airport by region' (6 awards); 'best improved airport', again by region; and 'best small airport' (6 awards). Each conference has an active promotion, recruitment and media campaign that draws on different aspects of business school curricula and teaching (Thrift 1999). In addition to social media techniques designed to attract attention to the work of these ceremonies/conferences, those in attendance are also treated in ways that encourage them to act as champions for the ASQ back at the own respective airports.[12] An award, however, carries little significance unless it receives recognition by industry colleagues and airport customers, hence awards are publicized in various media and promotional artwork that includes poster campaigns, which participating airports can use to inform passengers of their successes. Airport passengers are accustomed these days to vast advertising billboards announcing things like 'XYZ airport – proud winners of the ABC award for 'best improved regional airport''.[13]

That a considerable amount of lobbying work takes place here between members of DKMA and participating airports is not without significance in explaining this sustained popularity. As one participant explained, a minor change on the wording of a question can have a massive impact. If we change the words from "restaurant/eating facilities" to "restaurant/eating concept", for example, customers can be cued and attention trained in ways that will potentially reward the more design conscious airport. 'Intense lobbying can take place', Derek confirms, and representatives from participating airports attempt to lobby for word changes in ways that will more accurately reflect their most recent renovation/investment plans. So, whilst the questionnaire undoubtedly helps to constitute the identity of the 'airport customer', and in ways that are potentially subjugating as the critical discourse would argue, we are also forced to acknowledge the extended and fragile, contested nature of its organization. It is perhaps most accurate to conclude that the ASQ survey operates more

---

[12] There was some discussion amongst certain senior executives at MAG as to who would make the ideal candidate for the promotion of the ASQ in the airport. Could Adrian act in a sufficiently *promotional* way for the ASQ? Was he much of an entrepreneur or champion? Whether Adrian was hedging his bets on the long-term viability of ASQ at Manchester Airports Group, on the other hand, was an equally plausible explanation for his apparent lack of passion or drive. Investing too heavily in the practice of ASQ might make one vulnerable in the future if the airport decides to track its performance in different ways, or if the ASQ comes to an end replaced by an alternative system.

[13] The ethnography also picked up evidence in some quarters of ennui with what was perceived as an 'awards culture', but this does not appear to have tempered any enthusiasm amongst others, at least if we take one measure of this to be the attendance at these conferences and associated ceremonies. Participating membership in the ASQ continued to grow during the period 2009–2014.

like a pivot around which gather representatives of existing organizations in the industry who are simultaneously involved in internal changes to their own organizations (i.e. internal airport management structures) and the construction of new organizations (i.e. the community of ASQ users) in order to make the survey work.

Customer Training

As Mary and I carry the completed questionnaires back through the terminal we make our way into a labyrinth of internal corridors and courtyards that open up between the terminal buildings. On the way we pass various staff restrooms and a number of administrative staff offices. Uniforms sometimes offer clues as to who is working for who, ranging from Special Branch (police services), outside construction contractors, the UK Border Agency staff, representatives of the CAA (who regularly conduct their own surveys of passengers), airport cleaning contractors, and staff working for third party retailers, etc.

In one office we see posters announcing a new UK Borders Agency 'customer charter' on which a series of promises and pledges are announced. Such artefacts prove to play an important role in this making up of airport customers, but they also provide a resource for its study. This poster and its contents can only be understood if one can trace the trails and documentation that lead back to the UKBA. In following these trails we do not find a singular institution or author of customer service. Instead one finds an organization in some turmoil as efforts are made to makeover the UKBA in the image of 'the customer'. The promotion of the customer under the auspices of the UKBA follows a whole series of official government criticisms of immigration services, including John Reid's now infamous statement that the immigration directorate in the home office was not 'fit for purpose' (Hansard, HC Deb 15 May 2006, vol. 593, col. 701). From this it would seem that airport customers are not only shoppers, passengers or lounge users. They are also people seeking entry or exit from the UK.

To ethnographically follow the emergence of this 'customer', a customer specifically of border agencies, entails getting embroiled in other fractious and contested histories. One begins to see the poster as an outcome of a long and complicated series of official state enquiries, cabinet office reports, suspensions and resignations, reorganizations and restructurings. The rise of "the customer" within UKBA, but also in other state bodies such as the CAA and DfT, forms part of a series of highly politicized efforts to address what are sometimes deemed embarrassing 'episodes' in the airports and aviation industry. These include popular and periodic – but of course highly mediated 'outrages' – things like security queues, 'travel chaos', and immigration controls at airports. Appeals to 'the customer' often provide the means through which governments help leverage change or at least appear to be addressing the problem. Whilst obviously not some state-led top-down project of subjugation achieved through the mobilisation of power/knowledge discourse, the changing institutions and landscape in which the state seeks presence and articulation can be understood as one which is slowly being reconfigured around 'the customer' (see Miller and Rose 2008: 114–141). An 'overdetermined' set of motivations and tactics will inevitably be identified in explaining the appeal of "the customer", but preoccupations with the customer and 'customer experience' have become a conspicuous feature of official rationalisation for enquiries and restructurings into existing state bodies (Department for Transport 2008; Civil Aviation Authority 2009). New powers and positions have been forged on the back of this and it is within these conditions – beyond and outside the boundaries of airport management, or any one specific regulatory body – that allows us to make more adequate sense of the rise of a customer for airports.

This shows once again that as we follow the ethnographic traces of the customer we are led outside the putative boundaries of any one 'organization' and into a series of projects and working practices that are supported only because of the provision of resources (financial and otherwise) provided by allied and supplementary organizations. Following the threads that lead to these adjunct organizations takes us to spaces often distant and seemingly tangential to the day-to-day practices of airport management. One might be tempted to reach after a metaphor of 'laminate' or 'layers of laminate' to explain what it is that is organizing and holding together a series of materials, discourses and practices. Yes, this is too static a metaphor. The airport is a space where other organizations meet and negotiate territory, but also a space in movement itself. What is base, what is laminate, is never clear. The standard hierarchical bureaucratic form that we assume exists internal to well-bounded and discrete organization is itself immersed in this process flow of materials and practices that find their animus and energy in relations and networks that extend far out in space and time.

Human Resource Training

One of these supplementary organizations is the profession of human resource management, which has also been championing the discourse of the customer in recent years, creating new roles for CIPD members (Chartered Institute for Personnel and Development) and accredited HR experts, sponsoring new publications, revising training curricula, and venturing into the development of new online learning toolkits (see Cook 2008; cf. Sturdy et al. 2001; Skålén 2009). The influence of emerging HR customer expertise is evident in the Manchester Airports Group including initiatives developed by the newly found 'Group Customer Services' team. A program of customer training days was developed that all airport staff were obliged to attend. At one of those meetings the assembled staff were told that whether one is a fire officer, working on airfield maintenance, or employed as a security guard, we 'all have an important role to play in the delivery of customer experience'. Let me take you inside one of these meetings.

'Welcome to cultural awareness', Deena, the trainer tells us, as she formally introduces the objectives of the day. 'Do I need my glasses for this?' one of the security officers asks as he pops his head around the corner, a little late but nonetheless apparently keen to participate. The room is arranged in a 'horseshoe' of desks, with the trainer at the centre operating a laptop on which a PowerPoint presentation is being run. Participants have been issued with the usual accoutrements of business meetings and branded pens and paper pads sit neatly in front of us on our desks. Members are invited to introduce themselves. Following this we are asked how many languages we know how to greet people. Amidst all the paraphernalia associated with the popular management of training, the ice-breakers, the 'what are we looking to get out of this workshop', the break-outs and instant feedback evaluation forms, the Certificates of Achievement, etc., I am struck by the way in which the much discredited work of Geert Hofstede's (1991) seems to have come alive in this room. For most of the morning we are engaged in talk about 'language, beliefs, behaviours, different parts of our country – kilts for example!' (an interjection prompting some laughter amongst participants). One exercise involves a team competition in which we have to identify as many different countries as we can from a PowerPoint slide depicting the flags of the world. As the training proceeds, we are periodically asked how we might apply the knowledge we are acquiring on the workshop to improve customer experience. At one point a member of the security staff talks about the 'stags and hens.' This seems to be a problematic passenger 'type.' However, it would appear that if you have 'banter with them' they are put at their ease. Just because they are 'hens' it doesn't mean they don't deserve good treatment, someone adds. Naively I was expecting the stereotypes and clichés of this form of cultural awareness to become the subject of critique and irony. Not so, or at least not directly or immediately.

What was perhaps more remarkable was how much time was permitted to the rituals of joshing and banter, all of which involved considerable digression and tale-telling, an indulgence that appeared very necessary – in part, one might suspect, because of the over-familiar stereotypes and anodyne figures of 'the customer' being circulated as part of the training. I began to realize that this was perhaps what Bill meant when he said that 'banter' with customers was a way of putting them at ease. The assumption seemed to be that if we treated customers as we treat ourselves, they too will be happy. However, after the formal close of the training, Bill and Deena remain in the room. They know each other well, and with over 40 years of service between them they appear to share a considerable amount of trust and informality. These conditions appeared to prompt a different kind of story.

Bill asks despairingly about the uniforms, which appears to be an ongoing problem. Deena sympathises. It seems the uniforms make the staff feel like they are from 'Morrisons' Bill explains.[14] Staff in other airports look more official, according to Bill, with a 'Search Division' logo

[14] A low cost, convenience food supermarket in the UK.

emblazoned on the uniforms. The conversation moves seamlessly from the scruffy fleeces, cardigans and old jumpers that people like Bill wear, to the abuse to which they are subject. Pilloried and hectored by passengers, in which every delay and queue is the fault of whoever happens to be on duty on the security line, there is evidence of what Granter et al. (2015) call 'extreme work' where as one security guard reports 'everyday, it wears you down. There's only so much of it you can take ... and you start to take it home...'.

This exchange between Deena and Bill produced a very different version of 'the customer' and 'customer service', and perhaps speaks of a set of relations and working habits that are a lot more complex and difficult than what was catered for in the official training. Theoretical explanations of panoptics and subjugation seemed far too neat an abstraction to capture what was again complex and over-determined, and in part reflexively constituted through certain types of questions and prompts, artefacts, spatial configurations, furniture and other arrangements. If the customer was being forged through things like the ASQ survey, then another version of the customer was being created and circulated here.

My own role in this was not negligible. As is widely known in the traditions of ethnographic research, trust takes time to establish. As I began to become a more familiar piece of furniture in the airport and therefore better able to mirror the actions and behaviour of my interlocutors (though without any obvious conscious intentionality), I was able to participate in a more complex and diverse set of practices, which enacted very different understandings of the airport. It was notable, for example, that this version of the customer and the customer service relation was first elaborated *outside* the formal time boundaries of the training event. Whether this lent 'the customer' any greater degree of truth and authenticity, however, must remain largely undecidable; but there were certainly implicit rules through which the degradation of 'the customer' or 'management' was performed. The way in which the question of uniforms was deployed, and the way this was linked to wider security concerns, and indeed wider social implications, was a skilful accomplishment.

In other words, it took time to become an acceptable critic of 'the management'. On the other hand, it would make an easy critique of management to proclaim their complicity in the production of new 'hegemonic' subject positions ('customers' and 'customer service agents'). Moreover, it was not clear that much coherence was achieved around such identities and positions, which seemed at best only partially and superficially realized. Even within the terms of the training program, for example, the figure of 'the customer' that seemed to circulate in the room was a shadowy and ill-defined one, and one that was attended to with little interrogation, question or dedicated attention by participants. The appropriate and desired way in which the trainer wanted security staff to relate to people passing through security as 'customers' was also largely unclear and lacking in detail. So, the figure that was being brought into being is perhaps better described as nebulous and multiple. At times, this figure seemed to lurk in the terminal hall robed in a patchwork quilt – a figure partly made up of fantasy and nightmare. The discourse of 'customer' and 'the customer service agent' could at best only be considered a narrow enfilade carved out from this much greater multiplicity and vagrant potentiality.

Devising the Escape 'Lounger'

This problem of defining the consumer was further explored in the efforts of the Escape Lounge commercial team who were confronted with the difficulties of simultaneously working out *both* the product and the consumer for the lounge. This 'working out' often assumed that the consumer existed, which led to the assumption that all management needed to do was find a suitable way to access 'the consumer' (surveys, focus groups, etc.) and then an appropriate method to transparently re-present their characteristics and needs. In other words, the assumptions of positivist social science seemed to prevail, in which managers deferred to a reified and naturalistic conception of the world of consumption and production.

Yet, the customer remained a shadowy figure at Manchester Airports Group – and positivism soon reached its limits. Data was poor and the airport did not have a tradition of market research that could be drawn upon to develop a picture of who it was that used the airport. Even posing the question about 'the demographics' of airport users, for example, was difficult, in part because it would only occur to *specialists* in market research. Demographics is not something that slips off the tongue of many and without a legacy of consumer orientated commercial management where would these people come from to raise its question? And who would be championing their appointment, at the possible expense of resources for other parts of the airport? Once the question had been deemed legitimated – and then formulated – working out what appears even the most basic question, i.e. how long do customers spend 'airside', proved hugely problematic, creating all kinds of interminable wrangling about measurement and classification.

The precise time it takes for passengers to get through 'security' was productive of the most complex and perplexing epistemological dilemmas, for example, and included perhaps the most basic: *what* or *where* is the 'start' of a queue? At what points do we measure the start time and finish of a queue? Indeed, posing and pursuing such questions ethnographically threatened to unravel the intricate set of relations and translations that hold an airport together as a system.[15] Attempts to measure security processing produced difficulties around occupational boundaries and territories, for example. Might inefficiencies caused by airline check-in be generating the peaks and troughs in 'arrival patterns' that would then in turn be the cause of downstream processing problems in the security hall? And what are the boundaries of the security hall when the complex spatial construction of airports often precludes the drawing of any clean or neat operational divisions? These tautologies and aporias get partially worked out in practice, of course, but not without considerable struggle and contestation that was only productive of further dilemmas, some of which become evident during the work involved in the construction of an escape lounger.

[15] Legend was told that the whole of the terminal was designed on the number '234'. To work out how many new X-ray backscatter security scanners the airport needed a numerical figure was needed of how many people one scanner could process an hour. Then by dividing the peak number of passengers in the security hall by 234 the number of scanners needed could be calculated so that the airport did not infringe service level agreements with airlines. According to many, the figure 234 was largely plucked out of the air. Pursuing this ethnographically led to a shadowy world involving airports, technology developers, US and European security technology legislation, security hall procedures, terminal space planners, and stochastic modelling of queuing complete with Poisson distributions, non-linear 'feedback', and 'reflected Brownian motion' (see Gross et al. 2008).

During one meeting, Harry, the senior executive responsible for the lounge project declares 'We need to know who are the dinkies and when they travel'. Colleagues are worried that Harry may be getting frustrated. He has forced an interruption and cut across the conversation as he tries to, as he says, 'nail down the specifics'. We need the 'nitty gritty', and much more 'data crunch'. 'We can't get away from the fact that the airport is 80% departing leisure passenger'[16] he continues, '*that* is the kind of airport we are. The lion's share of our business is family/leisure and that we are trying to develop a product that has a sense of being '*designed just for you*''.

If the rise of the airport customer is a fraught and contested one, involving an immense network of agencies and a host of intricate material artefacts, then Harry is confronted with an enormous challenge. On the one hand he is trying to establish or prompt his colleagues into finding out the likely users of the lounge, but also what kind of lounge they might want. 'Dinkies' presumably refers to the category 'dual income, no kids' (Van Gils and Kraaykamp 2008), and in this first attempt at categorization a certain image of the kind of people who will be able to afford what management is anticipating they will charge for entry to the lounge.[17] Yet, the category lacks a degree of precision, and even if a numerical measure of the number of Dinkies in the terminal at any one time could be identified, whether they are likely to want to lounge, and/or how they might want to lounge, remains undetermined. To all intents and purposes, 'Dinkies' are not known in the airport. Quite simply *they do not exist* and remain mixed up with other latent and only partially delineated and explicated categories.[18]

In response to these problems the project team has called on the services of the customer insight manager, who has been working on the ASQ survey for the past 2 years. He has recently begun to pro-

---

[16] A shared transgression was frequently indulged amongst Olympic House management in the term 'buckets and spades', used to describe passengers. That I was able to hear the use of this term was some indication of my growing nativity in the airport.

[17] Even price is contingent at this point. Members of the project team are here struggling as practical sociologists.

[18] Notice that Harry also refers to the 'departing leisure passenger', and 'the family/leisure business'.

mote the use of the Mosaic geodemographic consumer classification tool devised, in part, by British sociologist Richard Webber and now marketed and developed with the global information services group Experian (Harris et al. 2005). Drawing on census data and other commercial and non-commercial databases Mosaic applies a form of cluster analysis to derive a spatial distribution – based on postcodes – of patterns of consumption, habits and lifestyle. It organizes these patterns into 11 distinctive demographic 'groups', which then break down into 61 more finely grained patterns at the level of what it calls 'types' (see Burrows and Gane 2006; Savage and Burrows 2007; Webber 2009). 'Alpha Territory' are one such group, for example, and make up around 10% of the population. The types of people in this group are identified as the 'global power brokers', 'voices of authority', 'business class' and 'serious money'. With this data, characters such as 'Piers and Imogen' depicted in elaborate lifestyle imagery begin to circulate in the airport. In the Experian text 'Piers and Imogen' are described as people who are:

> 'likely to purchase bespoke luxury items such as expensive brands of jewellery, cars, kitchens and furniture. They are most likely to pay for private education and healthcare, and to employ staff to clean their homes, tutor their children, and maintain their gardens. If not found on their own private yacht, then they are most likely to be seen in the business or first class cabins of airlines, to holiday in their own foreign property and to enjoy the service of exclusive hotels and restaurants'. (Experian, 2009:9)

Representing a far bigger proportion of Manchester airport's catchment area than Piers and Imogen, however, are those identified as 'suburban mindsets' – people like Surinder and Bina:

> 'The most common feature of these people is their industriousness. Whilst some Suburban Mindsets have modest incomes, very few people are without a job, suffer long-term sickness or claim benefit. People in this group value their independence, rely on their own judgment, rather than social or community attitudes, and do not necessarily get involved with their local community... Much of this group's personal wealth is tied up in their property, of which they are justly proud and many of them are likely to rely

> on their own skills rather than those of local tradesmen to maintain their homes and gardens... Suburban Mindset people have unpretentious tastes and are among the most likely to purchase mainstream brands and to shop at nationally known retail chains. They are responsive to advertising that illustrates value for money as well as endorsements from satisfied users'. (Experian 2009: 11)

According to some data circulating in the airport, this is an important category representing a base volume of 644,347 individuals within a 90 minute drive of the airport and constituting 12.4% of the overall demographic.[19] Subsequent calculations provide the basis to establish the so-called 'mid-market customer' that is estimated amounts to 21% of the catchment area. In contrast to this mid-market category, commercial management begin to consider another hybrid figure that represents 24% of 'the market' made up of what they call 'upmarket couples and families' and covering a range of mosaic types including 'business class', 'serious money', 'mid-career climbers', 'footloose managers' and 'soccer Dads and Mums'.[20] 'Graham and Caroline' begin to circulate in documents as representative of this market and are described as people who consider themselves to have 'expensive tastes and are happy to pay more for quality goods. They are interested in the arts and other cultures and prefer to take holidays off the beaten track. Family orientated they enjoy entertaining at home or pottering round the garden' (Diary 1). In designing the lounge, management is trying to forge a product that will appear to both these types of 'market' and by zoning the lounge they attempt to cover all the bases and accommodate everyone.

Drawing on an internal survey of terminal users commissioned by management, the lounge design team further identify three 'mindsets', mindsets which aggregate and cut across the mosaic types to form different patterns and distributions; these are the 'time to relax' passengers, 'harried and hassled', and 'airports are boring' types. The architects then show how the zoning of the lounge will appeal to all three types detailing specific design features that will likely stimulate and arouse various

[19] Figures cited during key project presentations.

[20] Data from Manchester airport passenger surveys and commissioned research conducted by media advertising consultants Carat, reported in meetings and drawn on by the project architects.

desires. Escape 'calms and services' those 'harried and hassled', for example, by features such as 'The welcome' which offers, as described in the form of a bullet point list: 'calming straight away. Luggage taken care of. Warm, friendly greeting. A quick tour of the lounge to set you at ease' (Diary 1). The deli and bar area is designed as a place to 'get away from the crowds and sit with your family and wait to be served'. For those who are 'bored with the airport', the deli/bar area is being designed in a slightly different way where it will be 'not just the place to collect your food – but a place for entertainment in itself' (ibid).

Performing the Lounger: The Return of the Unruly and the Unknown

The aesthetic design and zoning of the lounge was one way in which management attempted to maximize and accommodate a diversity of possible customer types into the lounge. However, it was striking how aesthetic differences – at times displaying marked tension in the material form of the lounge – became evident as it became describable ethnographically. Prejudices about underlying differences in social classification and taste, and the un-reflexive deployment of familiar sociological modes of classification, acted as a resource to *enable* description and distinction. In this way things could be made to stand out, casting into relief a foreground against an undifferentiated background. In the play of this penumbra (Mehan and Wood 1975; Pollner 1987; cf. Strathern 1991), light and shadow are mutually constitutive in ways that facilitate powerful analytical diagnosis. Imagine entering this lounge. Do you see the pastel coloured original art works, specially commissioned for the lounge? Take a read of the menu, which offers a range of culinary delights from the comforts of 'a soft boiled egg with toasted soldiers for breakfast to an open sandwich or toasted focaccia'. Everything might be read as a carefully calibrated judgment or discipline, designed for the purposes of stimulating aspirational values or assuaging the snobberies of various social strata.

To further acquire definition of tastes and aspirations a series of focus groups was commissioned during the early days of the Escape Lounge. The results, however, proved ambiguous and disappointing to those responsible for the management of the lounge. 'The problem with the people who attend the focus groups is that they do not really think outside the box', the customer insight manager explains to the design team in one of their early meetings. In other words potential customers are an unreliable guide to what they might want or what the airport might be best advised to develop as a new or innovative product.[21] We have encountered some evidence of what transpires here as uncertainty, in the multiplicity of different types of lounger that have been circulating in various documents and PowerPoint slides, for example, in management meetings, and in marketing and other promotional literature. Hence, getting to 'know' the market prior to the launch of a product would appear to pose intractable problems. At least it does if the ambition is to secure certainty and definition in advance of making a decision. Uncertainty, therefore, has to be assumed and simultaneously denied, despite the proliferation of potentially disastrous and unforeseen consequences that might follow decisions taken in its midst. A number of different loungers, for example, come into being after the opening of the lounge – some of whom, as we shall see, are troubling and quite unexpected.

Listen to Emma, the lounge manager as she recalls and dramatizes a recent episode in the lounge shortly after the opening. She is telling me about a young girl who enters the lounge in a 'mixed group' (in age and gender, it would seem) of about 10–12 people. On being told about the free bar the young girl responds 'Oh great! We can get legless'. As Emma goes on to say 'There was eleven of them and they were wearing football shirts ... and *she* looked about twelve!' One of the other lounge hostesses tells me that 'Somebody left a copy of *Nuts* yesterday. *We removed it* [hushed voice]. It wasn't really appropriate, not the kind of thing we want to have around here as it doesn't create the right impression. We don't like to see tabloids being left around the place, but some of the passengers tell us they want *The Mirror*!' (a UK 'redtop', or tabloid newspaper).

There is a lot going on here, but without mobilizing the heavy hand of critical theory we might note at a minimum that lounge behaviour is often unpredictable and does not always transpire in ways that management would desire or welcome. Clearly 'The Mirror' was deemed inap-

[21] Again, evidence of what we might perhaps call an 'intra-criticality'.

propriate reading matter for the version of the Escape Lounger that the local staff and management had expected. Emma goes on to tell me that 'sometimes it's all about crowd control', and that many of the loungers are '*Holiday Extras*', by which she means that the lounge is sold through third party agents who market the virtues of the lounge in ways that emphasize things like the free drinks. Many loungers apparently calculate that they only need four drinks before they have more than recouped their ticket price.

Theft also seems to be a problem. 'You wouldn't believe it Damian … we had 6 salt cellars stolen last week, spoons, soaps, and several of our Royal Moulton hand dispensers'. Down on the shopfloor it would seem a different truth about the lounger is in evidence, one that might appear to promise a story of recalcitrance and resistance, the insubordination of the 'unmanageable consumer' (Gabriel and Lang 2006) beloved in critical studies. An Escape Lounge dress code is soon published on the website following the opening of the lounge instructing loungers that whilst their comfort is of 'paramount priority …. we do request that while visiting the EL [sic] you wear smart casual or business attire. We also have a no baseball cap or football shirts policy'. Following this, a legal contract of terms and conditions is published that sets out more fully where responsibilities lie between the airport and the lounger. The contract stipulates a whole set of behavioural expectations and obligation such as 'Any Guest whose behaviour falls below a reasonable standard will be removed from the Lounge', and that the airport 'reserve the right to refuse entry to any person, at any time, for any reason deemed appropriate by us, including (but not exclusively): capacity limitations, intoxication or any conduct that we consider would offend or disturb other Guests.'

Another version of the lounger is being enacted here, one who is not yet trained to conduct themselves in a lounge appropriate manner. If the railway in the 19th century brought with it new modes of comportment, vision and behaviour – amounting to a very different kind of (travelling) human subject (Schivelbusch 1980) – then there is evidence of similar fears and anxieties about what might have been unleashed with the development of (let us call it) an *airport lounge culture*. In Krakauer's (1925/1999) study of 'The hotel lobby' this fear finds some precedence where the effects of the lounge are so powerful that the lounger becomes 'detached from everyday life' in which 'aimless lounging … vanish[es] into an undetermined void'. Similarly, as Hayner's (1928) thesis makes clear in 'Hotel Life', lounges provides a space for the birth of the modern lounger who 'released from the bonds of constraint' gives free licence to a range of behaviours including 'parties, fighting and destruction'.

This fear of anomie and destruction perhaps plays on the minds of those responsible for the management of the lounge. 'You have to learn to read people', Ella working on reception tells me one day. Couples and families are intermittently arriving at the desk; they often look lost and a little disorientated; but an important part of the 'welcome' service is the tour of the facilities in which the lounge hostess explains to loungers the various features in the lounge and the protocols concerning how one makes use of them. Lounging apparently does not come easy, and many need help and training. 'You have to try and work out where to place someone', Ella explains. Some are quite obvious, single travellers in suits, carrying a laptop, for example. You will take them to the study. Others, with young children are taken down to the other end of the lounge where there are televisions and games machines. With up to 200 people in the space during peak times, the lounge is often described as a pressure-cooker, as if waiting to blow. What local staff call 'policing the boundaries' has become an issue, and a 'No children' handwritten note appears on the desk where the laptops are placed, supplemented one day with a more formally printed 'polite notice' that reads 'dedicated business/adult laptops'. Downloading pornography has also become a little embarrassing in some of the airline lounges and such preoccupations help explain how the lounge management team have become alert and vigilant to possible abuses of the facilities.

Taking the opportunity to lounge, so to speak, and thereby avoiding the impatient mobilisation of classificatory schema and analytical explanation, I began to understand and relate to these comments and observations not so much as representations of reality, but as complex and *performative*, embroiled and entangled in the constitutive making of 'the lounger'. There were many examples of staff reacting to claims that Manchester Airport was guilty of a certain snobbery, for example – of 'rising above its station' as one colleague confided – which tended to stimulate forms of counter-action that on occasion paradoxically produced precisely the kind of behaviour that might be deemed uncouth or obnoxious.[22]

But first let us consider what is happening when the lounge manager shows me a copy of a brochure promoting the exclusive Chewton Glen hotel and spa as the 'kind of thing we should be doing here', and tells me the airport should employ the FT columnist Tyler Brûlé as a marketing consultant to help promote the lounge. As I am talking with the lounge manager a middle-aged couple enter into the lounge. He is wearing a Manchester City football shirt with 'Tevez' written on the back, and sports a shaven 'Mohican' hairstyle. A blue ink tattoo is visible on her back, displaying the name 'Rob'. I wonder how the staff might treat this couple, and how the couple might react to this treatment. Might they qualify as loungers? As I reflect on these questions I am overwhelmed by the presence in the lounge of what I see now as instructional literature, recalling those manuals of etiquette published during the railway boom and designed to help shape and inform appropriate behaviour for anxious new subjects occupying these new spaces of travel and recreation (see Curtin 1987; see also Miller and Rose 1997; Araujo 2007; Cochoy 2008). Today, it seems, these manuals find expression in coffee table magazines that litter the Escape Lounge – *Country Life International*, *Motorsports*, and *Ascent* for example, the cover of which reads 'the ultimate guide to what to see where to go and where to stay'. Another headline in *Ascent* reads 'Fine Dining inside the world's most exclusive restaurants' and elsewhere on the cover we are invited to turn to page 18 where we can read its regular column 'dress code'.

A copy of *QP magazine* is also to hand, described as 'the UK's leading luxury watch magazine', with the current issue (no. 43) leading with articles about 'London's vintage connections, astronomical time, [and] the Portuguese'. The cover also announces 'Maurice Lacroix's Decentrique OFF BEAT' and 'IWC – Portuguese fleet' (which turns out to be 'a fleet' of watches manufactured by the Swiss luxury watchmakers). Subversion,

---

[22] In a later chapter we will meet Olly the cat who as perhaps the supreme lounger at the airport was offered board and lodging on the front steps of the corporate head office. Pampered and promoted, Olly became something like a cult or totemic head of the airport. Some executives were concerned that in stimulating such lavish displays of intimacy and affection, the behaviour of staff was not consistent with an appropriate corporate image.

irony, appropriation, mix-and-match, and re-appropriation no longer seem to offer resistance or an alternative to the disciplinary contours of this kind of literature – which might also be considered examples of what Callon et al. (2007) call 'market devices' – but instead all seem wrapped up in complex modes of identity and display. Alongside these quite aspirational literatures there is also a profusion of tabloid newspapers with headlines and stories attending to questions such as 'Should Coleen dump Rooney' (*The Sun*), and on the cover of 'Hello' magazine the headline reads 'Cheryl The Smile Hiding Divorce Drama' and 'presenting new baby Flora Russ and Sally Lindsay Introduce the family they have built against the odds'.

The lounger appears to be multiple and in part contradictory, unruly, unknown, and largely unfinished, and around which various management practices converge, some acquiring a new lease of life – but in a new terra incognito or what has been defined in recent organization studies as the 'white space' in organization where customary roles and identifications are not yet formed or defined (O'Doherty et al. 2013). Who or what the lounger is, and what it is they might want, largely remains unknown – even, it would seem, to the loungers themselves. 72% of terminal passengers surveyed at Manchester Airport, for example, could not tell the interviewer whether they had ever used one of the lounges at the airport, even after having been shown a series of images (Carat 2011). A further 58% didn't know which lounge they would consider using (ibid). As one member of a lounge focus group noted in a survey commissioned and presented to lounge managers, 'Because you read that list out [of the Escape Lounge offer], we knew what we were looking at, but if you just saw that [the DVD] without that explanation, I don't think it would impress you'.

This was consistent with my own interactions with loungers with whom I found it extraordinarily difficult to get very far in conversation, particularly when broaching questions of aesthetics or design, ambiance or style. 'It's all right, I suppose. Quite nice, really', seemed to be the best I could muster and the most popular response. Without the categories (and definitions) of a structured survey, and bereft of the cultivated or specialist discourse of the design experts, these loungers retained qualities reminiscent of the *tabula rasa*, or blank canvas. Hence, 'the lounger' remains a contingent and unstable outcome of a multitude of factors, only some of which we have followed in this chapter dispersed as they are across an extended – and always extending – space and time of organization.

Conclusion

We have dealt with a complex set of practices and relations in our quest to track the origins of 'the lounger'. 'The lounger' does not originate with airport management and in tracing the lines of association relevant to its construction we have had to tackle the shadowy and apriori figure of 'the consumer'. This has led us to a disparate set of spaces, from the high to the low – high 'political' institutions based in the capitals of Europe (ACI, IATA) to the 'low' practices of routinized data collection exercised by people like Mary roving the departure gates of airport terminals at 5.30 am. Routinely reified and naturalized in critical accounts of management and organization, we have discovered how difficult it is to establish and normalize a character such as the 'consumer'. What appears is in many ways a far more fantastical and chimerical figure than we might have imagined, one haunted by a strange retinue of data-doubles and doppelgangers: 'Alpha territory' people with 'time to relax mindsets', 'mid-market customers' and 'buckets and spades'.

In following the practices associated with the construction of the lounge and the lounger we have been led into a circuitous network of relations that cross-cut and bifurcate those relations routinely assumed to be the principal ones in the conduct of organization – i.e. those structured within the hierarchical orderings of bounded and bureaucratic organizations. What compelled these journeys across the sites of various formal organizations was the myopic fixation on what at first might appear rather insignificant and minor, mundane, or even tangential features of management and organization: the questionnaire paperwork, PowerPoint slides, the routine practices of industry practitioners – conferences, presentations, training days, meetings, etc. Something like 'the customer' emerges out of these materials and the practices in which they are deployed. The chapter found that this customer is perhaps best thought of as an ongoing 'project' of coordination and alignment that demands ever more management and innovation in practice and definition. This carries forward into the actual opening and use of the lounge where we found that people lounged in very different ways, some of whom were deemed to need *help* in how to lounge appropriately.

We have also discovered that nothing new emerges without the fracturing and splintering of a number of established institutions – what is normally referred to as 'the context' that regulates industry and political economy. Following the experiments and trials involved in the construction and invention of 'the customer' provides insight into the ongoing destabilizations and reconfigurations in organization that are *simultaneously* changing both structure *and* agent, or the context *and* foreground of organizational activity. Management is deeply implicated in these processes and practices, yet it is also partly an outcome through which new skills and expertise are being developed. Management is not a sovereign agent of change or invention but rather a 'downstream' outcome of forces that can only be inferred from studying something that we might liken to an extended *relationality and processuality of emergence* that takes places across vast expanses of organizational space and time (Jones et al. 2004). This chapter helps show how this emergence is an eminently practical and empirical problem but one that is nonetheless amenable to forms of organizational research that stick to the *immanent* whilst avoiding the temptation of reaching out after established and heavy-weight theoretical terminology.

There are as yet few offices of lounge management at work in organization at the moment, no job card or craft practice, and little in the way of professional association, organization or institution. If lounge management exists, it does so as a series of bit parts and fragments of knowledge, objects and artefacts being cut and paste in new ways, and only slowly crystallizing into possible distinction. Algorithms, Pearson correlations, geodemographic analysis, survey data, fashion magazines, architecture and design, prevailing social aspirations, snobbery and judgment, all of these things are being woven together in ways giving rise to the lounger and perhaps a coming lounge society. Yet, a certain inflection or swerve in the assembly of an algorithm might change everything. As we have seen, things 'small scale' can rapidly snowball to effect change at what is recognized to be 'large scale'. At the same time we have as yet little in the way of language, concepts and sensibilities with which to take the measure of this coming lounge society. Nevertheless, a new politics of the lounge might be imperative. In the next chapter we turn to a more explicit consideration of politics where some of the effects of this becoming lounge turn out to be highly volatile and unpredictable.

Meanwhile, *Land, Air and Blaze* will still be playing in the Escape Lounge, an irony one might think in conditions of global warming and climate change in which airports might be encouraging as much blaze of land and air as they are encouraging ever more lounging. *Sailing on a trip to your heart, sailing every secret little part, Sailing to the sky that is free, fireworks exploding across the sea, the clocks on the wall set free….*

6

Extending Politics in Organization Studies: The Bob Cut and 'Criniculturalʼ Politics

What are the politics of an airport lounge? Whilst the prospect of a new politics of the lounger was introduced in the last chapter, it is rare for management and organization studies to ask 'What is Politics'? It is a question, we might say, that is avoided by the mainstream journals. However, it is a question so obvious and basic that one might argue that it is at the very least *implicit* in everything studied about organization. Whilst it may be implicit, politics – even amongst the self-identified 'politically motivated' – remains inhibited and increasingly programmatic if not dogmatic in its diagnoses and analyses. Hence, the doubtless shock caused when mention is made of a *politics of the lounger.*

Despite a recent interest in 'event' and a return to forms of 'praxis', organization studies has struggled to *inspire* politics. When translating Derrida on the 'political event' (Bohm 2006), for example, the lessons drawn are often a strange mix of o'er reaching theoretical ambition and naval-gazing. This is a type of instructional literature which often find recourse to despair and the perennial question: 'what's wrong with critical management studies' (Grey 2005; Parker 2013). In part this frustration might be explained by a failure to explore the question: *what* is the

D. O'Doherty, *Reconstructing Organization*,
DOI 10.1057/978-1-137-48922-7_6

organization of politics, or what is the possibility for political *experience* when thinking organizationally?

This chapter begins to ask what are the *politics of loungification*? If you were to have entered the Escape Lounge in late summer 2010 wondering about the current state of politics you might have picked up one of the newspapers on display in 'The Study', or made use of the free desktop and Wi-Fi access. Here you can browse the BBC website, where if you wanted to appraise yourself of recent issues pertaining to politics you would have likely sought out the politics section. In August 2010 you would have read how a sharp rise in immigration is going to 'add pressure on David Cameron',[1] and how flood schemes have been abandoned because the Department for Environment 'has to find savings as part of the government's cost cutting strategy'.[2] You may have been drawn to a story that tells the reader that Philip Hammond, the UK minister for transport, is determined to find money for more and bigger transport schemes. Alternatively, your attention might have been arrested by the intriguing headline announced in an FT blog 'What did Cameron do with the cash down the sofa?'.[3]

On the other hand, if you were to have looked up from your newspaper to consider the scene unfolding around you in the lounge, you would doubtless have seen a couple of people playing on a Scalextric track off in the distance and heard their shouts of excitement and groans of disappointment. Or you may have caught a glimpse of the high-definition wall-mounted television screen showing an episode of '60 Minute Makeover' where someone's domestic lounge is being transformed from 'tired 1970s' to 'contemporary' and 'chic'. Imagine yourself in this space. To your left someone is ferrying drinks back and forth from the bar area, the sound of a Cappuccino steamer is periodically hissing, and the smell of fresh bakery makes you think it's time for breakfast. You may have caught the eye of one of the lounge waitresses, her glossy black Bob cut hair framing her face in a way that reminds you of a film poster you once saw: Was it Tarantino? Or Louise Brooks?

---

[1] Financial Times, August 26, 2010.

[2] 'A hundred days of the 'greenest-ever' government', http://www.bbc.co.uk/news/science-environment-10981853 (last accessed 12.9.15).

[3] http://blogs.ft.com/westminster/2010/10/21/ (last accessed 11.9.15).

Following Strathern (1999), the recollection of these episodes might be understood as an 'ethnographic moment'. In writing this it seems I was struck by a spectrum of colours and lights that flickered and sparkled – expecting these impressions to recede into the background or to be dismissed as a mere superficiality, or triviality, a surface appearance, a prelude to the serious business of political enquiry. But it is intoxicating. At times the light in the lounge will wash the room in pastel amber or produce a kind of moonlight haze. Pockets of burnished orange and vermillion red colour the carpets and soft seating areas, but elsewhere lines of white light splinter in fragments and crystals. If you look closely, this light casts complex knots and tessellations across the grouting of the highly polished floor tiles. I learned to see that the cadmium green divider-screens in the bistro adds what the designers call 'statement' and 'definition'. Stunned by the light, one may very well seek retreat to the pages of the *Financial Times* and a return to 'politics', or at least a politics that most of us are familiar: London, Westminster, ministerial intrigue, departmental budget cuts, gossip and scandals. Yet, with this syllabus and its focus on the bureaucracy and formal institutions of parliamentary process it is perhaps little wonder that cynicism and despair have become for many the defining feature of politics in contemporary society and refuge sought in the apparent soporific qualities of an aesthetic (Sloterdijk 1988). Disengagement and apathy, to a more fundamental rejection of institutional politics, particularly amongst the young (Furlong and Cartmel 2012), have led some to talk about a crisis of democracy (Farthing 2010) and, in the context of a rise of global corporate power, even the 'end of politics' (Boggs 2000).

These diagnoses of the political are all too familiar to organizations studies. As a derivative sub-discipline within social science, its practitioners know a lot about political theory, political science, and political economy. The disciplinary influence of these social sciences means that organization studies operates, at least implicitly if not always explicitly, with an understanding of the 'political' that vests great fortune in the notion of a 'political context' – sometimes referred to as 'the bigger picture', the political 'environment', or the political 'structure' (Clegg et al. 1996; Baum 2002; Tsoukas and Knudsen 2003; Cunliffe 2008; Adler 2009; Bailey and Clegg 2008; Hatch 2012). In this vein most textbooks define 'politics' as an environmental factor, a background condition, the place in which laws and legislation gets passed, and where public policies and industrial strategies get formulated – all of which is understood by organizational analysts to be filtered through layers of intermediaries to impact *on* organization. For organization studies, there is also a politics of class, a political economy, a politics of gender, of identity, a politics of discrimination, exclusion and social responsibility, etc.; there is now a green politics, ecological politics, business politics, and managerial politics. There is also Marxist politics and more liberal politics; there is the politics of more 'conservative' persuasions (du Gay 2000), a post-structural politics (Willmott 2005), and a recent turn to 'corporeal politics' (Pettinen 2007; see also Pullen and Rhodes 2014; Dale and Latham 2015; Kenny and Fotaki 2015). Yet, despite this proliferation few have been able to follow the *formation* of politics pertaining to *specific* objects or spaces available in *particular* sites of organization.

Periodically, political theory returns to organization studies with an interest in what might be called the 'politics of aesthetics' – whether through Adorno, Benjamin and Lukács (Jameson 1990) – or in recent years by reference to a more radical counter-enlightenment tradition of thought where Deleuze or Rancière have become popular (e.g. Linstead and Thanem 2007; Huault et al. 2014). But can the discipline of organization studies begin to recognise and treat politically what might otherwise be considered a most trivial and superficial phenomena, namely this Bob cut hairstyle of the lounge hostess? Not to be found in the *Financial Times*, to be sure, where 'politics' is confined to the sub-editorial pages of the 'Politics and Policy' section. Any withdrawal to the politics in a newspaper proves misleading in this respect and fails to engage with the politics that is present in the here-and-now of the lounge. To see this politics though – or to see this *as* politics – requires the cultivation of a mode of enquiry and the creation and deployment of an associated lexicon of lounge concepts. With this approach we discover that politics is not restricted to a fixed agenda of issues or delimited to the activities of those institutions presided over by the specialists of political science. In this chapter, for example, we discover a possible 'politics of the Bob cut'. It is a politics enmeshed in a heterogeneous range of materials: popular magazines, city council economic development strategies, furniture and design catalogues, project briefs, architectural colour charts, light analysis, games designers, food presentation, cappuccinos, and 'makeover' TV. These are the principal characters at work in the lounge, some of which we have explored in previous chapters. In this chapter these characters take on a different inflection as we learn to see how they gravitate around the 'Bob cut', which takes up a privileged position as point of translation and mediation and a re-articulation of 'the political'. Attending to the Bob we can explore some of the inchoate and formative processes of *making politics* that remains difficult to grasp in the established repertoires of organization analysis. This difficulty arises because this politics takes place processually and relationally – and in ways that extend and re-define *what* is political. If we can learn to engage these movements we will discover often surprising coalitions of forces as they find expression in apparently benign things that become charged with controversy and political vitality.

This stunning rendition of Louise Brooks might be identified as one such surprising 'coalition of forces'. Easily dismissed or all too rapidly explained away within existing theoretical discourse, this chapter treats the Bob as a possible fleeting sign of a nascent 'crinicultural politics' at work in organization. Much like the curve and the apparent lack of baseline foundation of the Bob cut – most popularly associated with the work of Vidal Sassoon (Malcolmson 2013) – this chapter seeks to work in the absence of naturalised or reified foundations of 'the social' or 'the political'. In order to respond to the politics of the loungification we cannot assume a fixed *context* and *content* of political matters in organization.[4]

Taking materialism seriously, in this chapter I pose the question: what political *difference* does the Bob cut make? One is unable to identify this difference if we subordinate analysis (difference) to the *identity* provided by the established lexicon of political analysis positioned within the fixed ends of a relational dualism. With these resources the Bob cut would be quickly dispatched as a symbol of subjugation to patriarchal power, for example, or a reflection of pretension and class aspiration. This twin framing of context and content typically provides the basis upon which analyses 'observe' politics in organization, a politics often thought of in

[4] Like the gravity-defying *suspension* achieved by Sassoon with his 'wedge' cut Bob, recent developments in organization studies have shown that analysis must learn to study organizations in a world characterised by a 'post-foundational' ontology (Al Almoudi and Willmott 2011; Cederstrom and Spicer 2014). In contrast to Sassoon, however, it is the work of Laclau and Mouffe that is deemed essential to the advance of political theorising in organization studies. In O'Doherty (2015) I lay out a more fully theoretical critique of this work.

terms of *dynamics* or occasionally, in more sophisticated variants, as a *dialectics* that drive towards the reconciliation of social scientific dualisms. However, to treat something like the politics of the Bob cut in ways that can approach its *differential* and *potential*, demands we find ways of weaving together the arts and lifestyle section of the newspaper, with the pages dedicated to fashion, technology, business strategy, culture and economics, and global news. It is in the movement across these categories that politics can be found in the making, and we postulate that important 'politics' is currently being made around things like 'the Bob'. In this way the chapter gradually takes it leave from the politics of organization analysis available within critical management studies and begins to find ways of engaging more productively with what has been called 'ontological politics' (Mol 1999; Law 2004; Alcidipani and Hassard 2010).

The chapter then explores the ways in which hair and its styling is variously mobilised by nascent management groups-in-formation associated with the Escape Lounge that is revealing of another dimension of this 'crinicultural' politics. Hair is not, however, a simple object under the control of a subject; instead, analysis is compelled to move beyond the idea that hair is a symbol or object of representation and manipulation to consider the ways in which it becomes unruly and *agency-like* in its activities. One version of the lounger being enacted here is what we might have to call 'hair-lounge people', a conceptual neologism that helps us hold together what would normally be separated out into active and passive, subject and object, etc. As a concept it encourages analysis to focus on one of the dimensions in which human actors are positioned and distributed through the multiplicity of their material and technological prostheses in the Escape Lounge. It also helps render us more sensitive to forces of organization that are temporal and processual, defined by circulation and movement and on-going construction, maintenance and repair. By sticking somewhat obstinately to the strands of association that form around the Bob cut we are able to tease out some of these movements and forces that weave together the 'high' offices of state functionaries with mundane artefacts that populate what is typically designated as the 'low' sites of organization: micro interactions characterised as more ephemeral and episodic in nature. As we shall see Margaret Thatcher and David Cameron, considered by many to occupy the apex of power in politics, emerge as more modest political figures, but nonetheless participants in this 'flattened' ontology made available for analysis by taking seriously a crinicultural politics of organization.

Emotional and Aesthetic Labour?

'It's important, though, isn't it ... how you dress for work ...(?)' Edie tells me. Edie is one of the lounge hostesses recently employed by the airport. In our conversation it is not clear if I am being *instructed* or *invited* to respond to a question. We are sat talking in the Escape Lounge a couple of months after its inaugural opening in the summer 2010. Edie is telling me about the recent 'grooming training' she attended, during which fashion consultants and hair designers sought to help the newly appointed lounge staff think about the way visual impressions are important in creating the right experience for the loungers. Her strictly defined high-glossed jet-black Bob style hair design helps make Edie standout, an effect that seems to gain added allure by a capacity to deploy pop-cultural knowledge. The customer is perhaps made to feel clever if they can see the reference to Louise Brooks or Uma Thurman in Tarantino's *Pulp-Fiction*. As we speak, the PA system is playing soft lounge music. She smiles, but almost imperceptibly, and her eyes look right through me. Perhaps we are being invited to dance. This is the Escape Lounge, after all, and we have been encouraged to think that anything is possible once 'duty-free' in an airport.

Specialists in the study of 'emotional labour' who follow in the wake of Hochschild's seminal work (Hochschild 1983; Bolton 2000; Bolton and Boyd 2003; Brook 2009; Korczynski 2003; Williams 2003), and those broader critical studies of 'aesthetic labour' (Hancock and Tyler 2007; Nickson and Korczynski 2009; Warhurst et al. 2000; Witz et al. 2003),[5] would have little trouble explaining the politics at work in the play of sexual allure, innuendo and promise. The cultivation of the

[5] This opens up another library of work, much of which has been championed in the pages of the journal *Work, Employment and Society*. For recent reviews and debates by two leading UK researchers in the field, see the exchange between Bolton (2009) and Brook (2009).

female body and the commodification of private emotions in customer service work also attract considerable critical attention from feminists and exponents of critical studies of work (Tyler and Hancock 2001; McRobbie 2004; Skeggs 2005; Williams 2003; Wolkowitz 2006; Barry 2007). Marked by a strong moral foundation, this work makes short shrift of what is at stake politically in the way sense is made of the lounge and the experiences that can be articulated on its basis. McRobbie's (2004) study of the popular television make-over program *What Not To Wear*, for example, shows how women are subjected to class forms of prejudice, and indeed violence, in how they are made to understand and present their bodies.

In these terms Edie would be cast as gendered victim of subjugation and inauthenticity, her clothing a symbol of bourgeois and male exploitation, and her customers, or clients, either victims or perpetrators of similar oppressions and subjugations themselves. And no doubt certain forms of ethnographic practice could provide evidence to substantiate these politics of the good and the bad. Yet, how are we made to find these things attractive or seductive? What explains the desire and attachments? One might turn to the influence of popular media and literature, of which there is no shortage in the Escape Lounge. One journal in particular catches my eye: 'ASCENT'.

As I pick this magazine up I look around the room and I see many people flicking through similar magazines. Most were scanning the text and images, before reaching down to pick up others. ASCENT magazine describes itself on the front cover as 'the ultimate guide to what to see where to go and where to stay'. The front cover also carries a picture of the then England national soccer team manager Fabio Capello which accompanies the headline 'The Godfather of English soccer on his world cup dreams'. On page 28 there is a regular feature with the title 'dress code'. Another headline reads 'FINE dining inside the world's most exclusive restaurants'. Elsewhere in the magazine we read 'The Price of Paradise – A guide to buying your own dream island' and of Carlos Slim Helu, apparently 'the world's richest man'.

It is certainly possible that these magazines were instructing or disciplining people in how to wear their hair, and how to read and appreciate bodily decoration. Other magazines available to loungers could be interpreted as providing a resource through which to develop the appropriate lounge skills. Picking up the June 26/27 2010 edition of the Weekend Financial Times, for example, I meet the columnist Tyler Brûlé. 'I've decided to offer a few summer pointers to get the disorganised thinking about where to go' he writes in his column 'The Fast Lane', and 'how to get there and what to wear once they've settled in'. In the July 3/4th edition of the paper Brûlé talks about the importance of 'ranking' the guests of hotels: 'Its[sic] controversial territory to start ranking hotels by the quality of the guests' he writes, 'If I did it, it would be seen as ageist, sexist, racist, anti-silicone, anti-botox, homophobic and toddler intolerant'. Curiously, guests are described in the column as 'ingredients' in which 'getting the right amount of spice, sweetness, colour and texture into the mix is essential'.

Infused with a language of aspiration, snobbery and judgment these textual and imagistic worlds in the media become difficult to distinguish from the putative world they are supposedly representing. Who is mirroring or modelling who, what is cause and what is effect, becomes increasingly unclear, a phenomenon captured well in the airport terminal photographs of Martha Rosler (1998). In one of these photographs, for example, we see a group of passengers pulling branded suitcases in front of vast advertising hoardings depicting airline passengers pulling suitcases... There are similar recursive loops at work in the lounge and they make it appear like an elaborate machine of circulating images and discourse in which people are partly, as Tyler Brûlé argues, 'ingredients'. Critical Management Studies is highly attuned to how these apparently local and personal issues, reading a magazine, or the way one is encouraged to wear one's hair, reflect the infiltration or colonization of the lifeworld by the system. Whether 'society' or 'neo-liberal capitalism', 'the system' is immanent to its micro instantiation and (re)production. Hence, the slogan: the personal is political.

At the same time this is a politics that tempts one to judge and condemn (see Fleming 2012; Cederström and Spicer 2015). Despite claims to practice reflexivity, the critical school tends towards the same judgmental practices that we see being encouraged in these lifestyle magazines. Existing critical politics in business and management studies tends to be impatient, precipitously reaching after the usual suspects and ready-made explanatory 'bad guys' – management, capital, government, etc.[6] In this way its practitioners separate out those who are guilty perpetrators of false-needs or existential identity fetish/attachments and those who are the innocent victims (in need of enlightenment and emancipation).

Such analysis forestalls any enquiry that might seek to extend the description of how such 'images and ideals' in popular media have been achieved or constructed. To motivate such description we might ask: where do the photographers, the writers and the editors of these magazines get their ideas? Inviting 'mere description' in response to these questions would appear to produce an irritating level of detail for many within the critical school – for whom description must be handmaiden to theory. Empirical description is deemed either raw material that is better explained at another level of theoretical abstraction and economy, or a practice only made possible by apriori theoretical commitments that help orientate and isolate relevant details from what is otherwise feared to be 'buzzing, blooming confusion'.

In an effort to avoid these ready-to-hand concepts and to suspend the reassurance that comes with the deployment of such grand sounding concepts as 'neo-liberalism', 'capitalism', or 'society' – deemed to act behind the backs of the actors – I decided to focus my attention on the immediacy of the Bob cut. Instead of providing a resource upon which to extrapolate the workings of an already known 'political economy', I wondered if this focus might shift our perception of what is foreground and background, relevant or irrelevant, part and whole, or that which pertains to mere 'text' within a more encompassing 'con- text' (see also Cooper and Fox 1990). These oppositions help carve up the world into the familiar 'empirical' domain of discrete entities and bounded objects (Chia 1996) in ways that seem to reduce our appreciation of contingency.

[6] Much recent agonizing within critical management studies is evidence of a certain disquiet concerning the political relevance and efficacy of their practice (see Grey 2005; Brewis and Wray-Bliss 2008; Bell and King 2010; Parker 2010, 2013; Rowlinson and Hassard 2011). The cantankerous exchange that has opened up about the coherence and/or possibilities of a 'critical performativity' (Spicer et al. 2009; Alvesson and Spicer 2012; Gond et al. 2015; Fleming and Banerjee 2016; Cabantous et al. 2016; Spicer et al. 2016) is also suggestive of an anxiety that proliferates as metacommentary rather than experimental political practices. The main obstacle to politics in the critical school remains the moral and normative commitments that remove the possibility of decision and event (Derrida 1996b; Beardsworth 1996).

By elevating the Bob cut to the centre of my analysis might we bring into focus a more elaborate configuration of connections and relations that help explain the binding of lounge with lounger? Might such a strategy help extend or multiply the points of vulnerability and contingency in such configurations and thereby help *politicise* a far greater range of phenomenon? Hence, following the Bob cut might take us into a more 'relational ontology' as pioneered in various ways by Bateson (1972), Strathern (1988), Law (2004), Latour (2005a), and more recently Kohn (2013). In relational ontology things are not structured or reified in ways that restrict politics to the usual levers of pressure and resistance (as it will inevitably be portrayed). A relational ontology both makes room for the 'the Bob' as a potential political actor and opens up the question how precisely 'the Bob' has come to be and function.

In order to follow the Bob it was important to avoid the theoretically ready-made language and concepts and attempt to simply describe. What to describe then? Well, perhaps the making of the 'what' – in this case 'The Bob'. What is the Bob trying to 'achieve'? Given the longevity of its 'fashion' we can only presume it has been successful; but what accounts for this success? To follow and describe this 'making' demands we think far beyond the space and time of the lounge where Edie is working her customers. Let us briefly consider first the histories of the Bob.

The Origins of the Bob

The Bob cut finds one origin story back at the turn of the 20th century in Paris. Here we enter another lounge – the studio lounge of the celebrated hairdresser Antoine, widely attributed to be the inventor of the Bob. He was certainly not shy in making retrospective claims to be the originator, an achievement he attributes to the time he spent restyling the actress Eve Levelliere in 1910 (Cox and Widdows 2005; McMurtrie 2010). One might equally make claims, however, that it is Joan of Arc or Cleopatra who are the originators and role models. If we are still hung up on originality we should also recognise medieval military technologies, specifically the metal spear. The skin and bone piercing qualities of the metal tipped spear – or rather of the *spear-soldier couplet* – made it necessary to design protective chainmail body armour and headwear whose casque like shape became the 'model' for Joan of Arc's haircut.

These 'metal women' are clearly made of strong stuff, and in drawing this line of association from Cleopatra and Joan of Arc to Edie in the Escape Lounge, we are reminded that the Bob cut should not be dismissed as mere frivolity or the mere symbolic expression of male power and gender inequality. The cut has more agential capacity than this. For Vidal Saason – perhaps the most famous exponent of the Bob in recent decades – it was the inspiration of Bauhaus architecture that led him to experiment with a 'Bauhaus hairstyle'. But if Antoine was the originator this might suggest Bauhaus architecture followed the fashion first established in hairstyling and which might have encouraged the architects to explore the possibility of suspension and uplift available in the material properties of steel and concrete. The elevations and daring cantilevers previously unimaginable in architecture are mirrored in those lifts and angles achieved in the hair designs of Sassoon and as popularised by people like Mary Quant.

McMurtrie's work (2010) helps us decipher the originality of the Bob by showing that the achievement of the cut depends on the integration of two 'systems' of hairstyling that had previously been considered incommensurable, indeed paradigmatically incommensurable: namely strength and freedom. Strength is a system of hairstyling that seeks to make hair appear solid. This is achieved either by means of a 'blunt' cut, i.e. exclusively with scissors; or by using a combination of texturizing instruments such as a razor, or thinning and other texturizing shears. Blunt cut with scissors, the Bob cut occupies one end of this extreme. Too much solidity can however detract from the other valued look, namely freedom, which designates the second major system to which stylists submit in choosing the degree of control or movement they wish to introduce to the hair. The achievement of 'movement' depends on the degree to which the hair is elevated before cutting (McMurtrie, ibid.: 412–3). The Bob cut is extremely controlled because there is no elevation of the hair during the cutting process. The effect of this is to produce strict definition – but as if without any attention or effort on behalf of the wearer. Here lies the 'apparent' freedom, which accounts in part for its beguiling effect. In effect the hair achieved *both* freedom and control, but by reinventing the look of freedom. Though not spelled out by McMurtrie, the Bob cut in fact produces something more like an 'event' that both exceeds and redefines the terms within which hairstyles were previously understood and positioned [the system] – including the kind of structural semiotics deployed in the analysis of McMurtrie.

This brief exergue into history helps give some idea of the multiple and tremendously complex lines of influence that come to bear during the effort to construct the Escape Lounge. Stretching back to Antoine or Joan of Arc, the ingredients that help forge a distinctive style of loungification are more complex and varied than we might think. That the Bob cut is deserving of a history may surprise many in business and management studies, but it helps us appreciate how the contingent is made necessary, how the arbitrary becomes the rule, or how the appearance of the mundane and taken-for-granted is the product of a long history. If there is a politics to the Bob, understanding its history is an important education. It is also a history that makes us realise that Edie's Bob is a learned achievement and not merely a symbol of the commodification of the female body for the purposes of emotional labour. Indeed, the style has been popularised over the years by a number of iconic female celebrities, artists, and writers, including Amelia Earhardt, Josephine Baker, and Isadore Duncan. Here the Bob is associated for many with independence, if not even rebelliousness (Trasko 1994). At the time of its highest popularity in the 1920s those women sporting Bob cuts were considered members of the 'flappers', a contemporary term of some opprobrium used to describe the emergence of a new urban cosmopolitan group of women. Giving voice to the anxieties and prejudices of the time, journalists and novelists preoccupied with contemporary social mores were quick to note that these new urban sophisticates enjoyed a predilection for short skirts and 'listening to jazz', amongst other such foibles that marked them out as indulging a hedonistic and decadent lifestyle (Malcolmson 2013). According to some accounts flappers 'wore excessive make-up, drank hard liquor, smoked cigarettes, drove cars, generally flouted conventional social and sexual norms *and wore Bobs*' (McMurtrie 2010: 414; emphasis added).[7]

[7] One can also perhaps detect here that the term 'flapper' was used with some reverence and awe amongst certain men who may have been struggling with the challenge posed by the Bob to gender norms and gender relations. Hence, there are more connections and actors at work in making the Bob than we might have considered. This history might help explain whatever it is that makes the Bob attractive to Edie and others, but it also helps show how the Bob can become a resource within which attachments to the lounge can be cultivated.

These histories also help us appreciate the economic and commercial significance of hair. Beyond aesthetic or moral concerns there was also considerable public debate aroused at the time of the emergence of the Bob that sought to address its possible industrial and economic consequences. Some claimed, for example, that its relative simplicity would put an end to the specialist skills of the ladies hairstylist that had been built on the creation and arrangement of complex and elaborate hairstyles (Malcolmson 2013). Others took the opposite view. Some revisionist histories have argued it actually *enhanced* the economic fortunes of the French hairdressing industry with the Bob helping to expedite a transition between an older more elite industry and an emerging mass market more inclusive and democratic in tone and aspiration (Zdatny 1999, 2006).

Making Up Management

Edie was not the only one to be harnessed to the semiotic struggles of hairstyle during the making of the Escape Lounge. I am handed a DVD one day, with a warning. 'Watch this at home!' The DVD contained a film recorded for that year's airport Christmas party in which members of the Escape Lounge senior project management team had dressed up in fancy dress clothing to record a version of Band Aid's 1984 pop classic 'Do they know it's Christmas?' The participants seemed to take considerable pleasure in the display of outrageously anachronistic hairstyles and the opportunity this afforded for a certain flirtation with alternative sexualities and cross-gender transgressions. Boy George was of particular note. It was roughly the same group of managers who a couple of years later would turn up for full 'dress rehearsals' for a leaving party being organized for one of the senior executive at the airport. At this party the management pop-stars performed 'YMCA' by the Village People. What was striking was the display of camaraderie amongst these managers, most of whom had not known each other for long but who had nonetheless forged a strong team bond through the management of new commercial projects such as the Escape Lounge. Many noted that there was a 'gang-like' quality to the new team, many of whom were from outside the airport, and/or from non-traditional airport functions – marketing, projects, retail, etc.

As I pursued these finds ethnographically I became aware of the photographs hanging above the desks in Olympic House variously showing members of this team with their arms around each other, celebrating the opening of retail projects, for example, or attending parties and other public events. The display and promotion of such camaraderie was achieved in part by the willingness to participate in such apparently self-effacing if not carnival-like humiliation rituals (Rosen 1988). Their spirited performance of song and dance, and the projection of trans- and cross-gender role play it allowed, betrayed a certain confidence that appeared deliberately staged in opposition to what was portrayed as the more conservative and inhibited 'local authority' culture 'of the past' still prevalent in the airport. Engineering and operations had enjoyed the senior roles in the airport in the past but now it was retail and marketing that was in the ascendency – and hairstyling was not without its role in the politics of negotiation involved in the rise and fall of these fortunes.

This is suggestive perhaps of the possibility that we must consider hairstyling as *politics by other means*. Hence, we can say that hairstyles are not only expressions of *personal* style or aspiration, a marker of class or gender identification, but instead provides resource through which groups are forged. Hebdige (1979) has certainly shown this for punk and post-punk sub-cultures; but here at the airport, around the Bob cut or the retro 1980s exploded 'crown of thorns' sported by Boy George (Zill 2004), hairstyle becomes a way of achieving identification, of displaying the coherence and purposefulness of new groups commissioned with the responsibility to make-over the airport terminal and introduce new commercial products such as the Escape Lounge. Is it going too far to suggest that the lounge was made possible by the capacities of hairstyles to forge a stylistics of belonging that assisted in the construction and design of the lounge, or that it helped generate confidence and determination to drive through a distinctive and challenging new ambiance for the airport?

Edie is clearly not the only person to acknowledge the importance of hair, dress and personal grooming. However, what might be called 'the glamour' of the 'superficial' (Lee 2001) remains beguiling in ways that suggest it cannot be restricted to the status of an object under the control of a human actor. Hair is an active agent; it enjoys agency-like properties of its own. It is known to affect moods and behaviour, for example, and remains a subject of considerable preoccupation amongst those involved in the so-called 'make-over' culture (Weber 2009). Hence, hair must be considered something more than a symbol or representation. Particular hairstyles, for example, can even affect one's ability to get a job. According to some reports 'bad hair' can impair job performance. *Newsweek* famously reported in 2010 that in a poll of 212 corporate hiring managers 57% admitted that unattractive people find it more difficult to find work and a further 68% felt that job performance is affected by 'looks'. Slepian et al. (2015) have recently found evidence that suggests we need to grant more respect to such apparent superficialities. Their research shows that the choice of clothing can even affect one's capacity for abstract cognitive thinking. More formal clothing worn to work, for example, *enhances certain mental faculties* and can also make us feel more powerful, thereby changing the way we see the world and the way we engage with it. For Thrift (2008a) hair forms part of an emerging 'affective economy' in which the imagination is stimulated by the allure of glamour whilst helping to develop new habits and attachments to goods and services. New technologies allow hair to become more and more 'expressive' he writes, forming part of the emerging 'human-nonhuman fields of captivation' (p. 9).

One can never be sure how hair might act and this proves to be the cause of some difficulty for lounge managers. The publication of a behaviour and dress code soon after the opening of the lounge is suggestive that hair needed to be strictly policed. The code is becomes formalised as a contract to which entrants to the lounge are implicit signatories once they tick the box that seals their commitment to abide by the terms of conditions of lounging. The contract states, for example, that the airport reserves the right 'to refuse admission to any guest/person dressed in a way that might be deemed inappropriate' and that '[b]aseball caps, shorts above the knee and football shirts are not permitted, or any other item of clothing likely to cause offence to other Guests. Gentlemen's shoulders must be covered at all times'. Whilst the lounge style would appear to accommodate a number of hairstyles, the 'Mohican' or the 'Liberty Spike', whilst not explicitly proscribed by contract, is doubtless going to pose difficulties for managers in their management of what is appropriate and inappropriate.

The Unruly Materiality of Hair

At the same time hair is a recalcitrant and difficult object, not entirely under the control of the lounger or the lounge designers. The amount of time that loungers spend attending to their hair – brushing, combing, spraying, twisting, making minor adjustments etc. – suggests that this is an activity that demands a remarkable investment of time. One can only begin to appreciate the full extent of this grooming if one takes up the venerable position of the ethnographer in 'the hammock' allowing one to observe closely, and over extended periods of time, the activities of the loungers. With these facilities a world akin to those conjured by Samuel Beckett opens up to the ethnographer. However, to capture the repetitions and patterns of the loungers and their bodies as they unfold in time and space requires an extended excerpt from my field diaries (see Ehn and Lofgren 2010; Bissell 2012). In the following passage I am trying to record, rather like Perec (2010), the minute-by-minute movements of one lounger, which *in extenso* produces a text remarkably close to those of Robbe-Grillet (1958):

> 'I'm just going to get a drink', she announces. Walks off, along the polished marble effect floor tiles that mark out the path towards the bar. *Snap slap snap slap snap slap snap slap*. Flipflops. Arrives at bar. Adjusts hair, moving her hand from her left eyebrow towards her right eyebrow, her long blond hair now hooked over her right ear. She looks left, then right. Adjusts her trousers with a wriggle. 'Ok, thanks'. Clink. Glass in hand. Clink. Walks back towards high wingback chair. Sits down. Clink. Adjusts her hair, moving her hand from her left eyebrow towards her right eyebrow, her long blond hair now folded over her right ear. A few loose strands bother her and she drags these from centre forehead towards the right. She brings her thumbnail to her mouth. Bites. Returns it to her mobile phone. Looks around. Her right thumb rapidly flicks up and down. Head up, she looks around. Takes a sip from her glass. Places it back down on side table. Clink. Adjusts her hair moving her hand from slightly right of her right eyebrow towards her left eyebrow, her long blond hair now folded over her left ear. Head up, eyes flicker, left to right, right to left. Head down. Thumb rapidly flicking up and down. The down light casts a smudge of white on her left cheekbone, which spreads, consuming her nose and mouth.

I recorded these notes over a period of some 90 minutes in the Escape Lounge and page after page continues in the same vein. This young woman, of about 15 years of age, seems to be going through a repeated loop of actions and behaviour in which her hair is the central preoccupation, made available as an object of attention in part by her iPhone mirror or camera application, not to mention the surfeit of advertising and fashion magazines and the television make-over programs broadcast in the lounge. Attended to closely a pattern slowly begins to reveal itself, one best characterised as a punctuated rhythm marked by all manner of tics and twitches reflecting an ebb and flow of what appeared to be agitation and calm.

It is the hair I am principally concerned with here. Evidence of its unruliness can be found in the space devoted to hair products in the airport terminal shops, which often take up several aisles of merchandise. These products are all trying to help customers bring some order to their unruly hair. It is remarkable that those studies of hairdressing in management and organization studies (Chugh and Hancock 2009; Shortt 2012, 2015; Shortt and Warren 2012) have entirely ignored the very obvious *materiality* of hair. It grows, for example – and in all directions; it falls out, it thickens, and it thins; it changes colour; it attracts bugs and insects; soaks up sweat and other ambient smells; and in certain environments it dries out or greases up. Throughout the day one's hair is changing. With a nod to Heraclitus one might say 'you can never wear the same hair twice'. 'Sometimes when I've had it cut though it just sort of does its own thing' one respondent claims in a recent study of hairdressing salons (Holmes 2014: 98). 'It seems to have a life all of its own [Sounds of agreement from others]', she concludes (ibid.).

It is a recurring motif in the discourse of hairdressing expertise that hair is vested with a will and authority of its own. Pick up any issue of *Vogue* magazine and you will read countless articles addressing issues that invest agency in hair. 'My hair wants to be free, to grow, to play in the ocean just like the rest of me. I consider it a natural community leader: the one on top of the head' writes Ginny Jordan (2011: 42) in her startling account of what is quite clearly a politics involved in the 'journey into her body' following extended chemotherapy treatment. Hair is in one sense an object, but far from being inert it resists the efforts of its wearer to control it, and beyond this resistance it enjoys many more forms of activity that grant it an agency-like status of its own. This makes the politics of hair and the politics of the Bob cut interesting because there are now more actors at stake than simply the person who tries to 'wear' their hair. In the most simple form of politics in organization, understood as decisional and individuated activity (Dahl 1961), or more broadly as 'power in action' (Pfeffer 1981), analysis must recognize that the human individual pays heed to – or ignores them at its peril – a more extended 'ecology' of non-human actors, forces and materials.

The well-groomed lounger it seems must battle with hair and to assist in these efforts a 'Be Relax' spa and private treatment room has been made available in the Escape Lounge offering massages, manicures, pedicures and facials. Despite all this attention and pampering, however, hair grows wild: it gathers in tufts on the floor of the lounge, it gets caught in the fibres of furniture, and woven into the rugs and carpets arranged around the lounge. It is also found in air vents and air-conditioning valves. Clumps of hair collect in sink basins and half-flushed down toilets it clings to the side of the pan in streaks of black forming hairline cracks that disrupt the modernist clean lines and finish sought by the architects and designers. A whole background army of cleaners and cleaning products is required to maintain the lounge, but it is a hidden army who discretely come out at night after the last lounger has left. The airport is soon embroiled in certain 'political' problems associated with this 'ongoing repair and maintenance' (Graham and Thrift 2007). Some of the materials, textures and fibres in the lounge, for example, have never been seen before in the airport and there have been discussions about possible industrial relations repercussions between airport management and unions representing airport contract cleaners. Existing contracts specify precisely the kind of chemicals and cleaning products that will be used, but the new materials in the lounge are proving difficult.

One morning staff arrived at work to find a light discoloured stain on the reception desk. Set against the darker tone of the Cor-Ten steel used to clad the reception desk, this streaked and marbled stain – about a metre in length and 50cm wide – was evidently a disturbing presence. To the ethnographer increasingly mobilized by follicular matters, the stain seems to resemble the silhouette of Gorgon's hair. Eventually it becomes the cause of an argument between the lounge manager and the cleaner who was suspected of having caused 'the damage'. This argument was soon escalated to senior airport management, who then called a meeting with local trade union representatives. 'You wouldn't believe it', one of the project managers tells me, '... we almost had a walk-out!' Perhaps embroidered with a little exaggeration, the lounge as an object of cleaning and maintenance clearly deserves the status of a one 'mode of ordering' in an airport, and one that periodically comes into collision with others (Knox et al. 2008; cf. Mol 2002).

From this we can draw the conclusion that political consequences follow 'matter out of place' – either hair deposits where we don't expect them, or, conversely, the repercussions that might follow the over-zealous cleaning and removal of such 'dirt'. However, there is also a different kind of politics at stake here than the one we routinely diagnose in the terms of managerial factions or the mediation of wider structures of class or gender. The decision to include objects and things as actors – and moreover as actors granted something akin to intentionality – is itself of enormous political consequence (Latour 1993, 2004).[8] What causes problems for established political theory is that this turn to the object makes intentionality difficult to locate, in part because 'action' begins to be seen as something that emerges *prior* to the separation of subject and object. This designates a dimension of organization in which agency is inchoate and mercurial, but it is also a dimension of organization where surprising new alliances might be made and new hybrid-agential powers realized.

We are currently excluded from the politics that might be made out of this interstitial organization. And there are perhaps good reasons for this. To enquire into how things such as the Bob cut are *made to talk* requires a form of ethnography that is prepared to grant the pages of *Vogue* a voice, or rather to grant the possibility of a ventriloquized voice amongst object-people or actor-networks that we might call in this particular instance *hair-*

[8] Writers associated with 'speculative realism' (Harman 2010; Bryant et al. 2011; Morton 2013) have gone further and sought to remedy what they perceive to be the *lack* of sufficient agency granted to objects in Latour and versions of actor-network theory. There is an important quest for a more metaphysically grounded account of objects in this work, but it's contributions to empirical study are rather disappointing to date, though Pierides and Woodman (2012) might provide a promising start.

lounge people. Emerging in the interstices of the page and the eye (newspaper and reader) and between the divisions with which we are more familiar in the social sciences, these subject/objects, human/non-humans, structure/agents remain an unruly and unpredictable lot. In following the strands of association that lead from the carefully manicured Bob cut to clumps of unsightly hair on furniture, or the marbled streaks of staining on the oak furniture, the ethnographer begins to discover a possible politics in the making.

Political Mobilizations: The 'It' Effect, Beyond the Micro/Macro

The episode with the cleaner is revealing because it is suggestive of the possibility that certain design choices and aesthetic constructions have become deemed sufficiently coherent or distinctive (at least amongst certain groups of people) that other things are made to appear anomalous or out-of-place. It also acts as a resource through which distinctions and differences can be made, helping to form divisions between in-groups/out-groups that simultaneously stimulates the development of a whole discursive economy of judgment and reprimand. And it is here that we find a dimension of this politics in the making where by virtue of this myopic focus on the Bob cut a veritable ontology of organization normally overlooked or deemed uninteresting by political analysis is opened up. Here, we find how political capital can be made from hair!

In treating Edie's Bob cut as a centre – or a way of looking, and a focus of ethnographic conduct – the heterogeneous collection of objects, materials and relations that make up the lounge are brought into a different configuration. Such treatment helps foreground or magnify particular connectivities that traverse the familiar 'blocs' of what is called social, economic or psychological phenomena in organization, and allows us to explore potential weaknesses or vulnerabilities in their make-up. Such ethnography might develop potential avenues for change and experimentation. Similar to the affect of the cinematic close up (see Deleuze 1992), ethnography might help realize the patterns of nervous energy that accumulate around these vulnerabilities, either in efforts to *repair* – or distract attention from – their precariousness.

It will seem incredulous to some that we can trace a line of political mobilization by starting with what might seem a capricious or insignificant moment in the Escape Lounge– the appearance of the Bob cut. By tracing the networks of mediation and association that open up around the Bob cut, however, we have begun to open up a very different political landscape or 'ecology' in organization. Whilst it may appear divorced from the vast sweep of that noble sounding 'political economy', as we make our way through the threads of the Bob cut we are in fact approaching – in a tangential way – the forces and movements which become congealed in what Chia (1996) calls 'downstream organization'. It may indeed be capricious, but it opens up a different path to the accustomed map-making activities of political analysis and so renders things different, perhaps appearing a little askew or even out of kilter. Within the limitations of this chapter it is only possible to offer a preliminary sketch of this political mobilization.

Deployed ethnographically – as a lodestone or frame of reference – a preoccupation with the Bob cut allows us to adumbrate *transversal* movements that cut across any macro-micro divide, or high and low politics, to reveal surprising lines of association and preoccupation. On reaching the high offices of institutional state politics, for example, to interview the leader and chief executive officer of Manchester City Council about the airport, I am at first disappointed. My questions sought ways of approaching and understanding the politics and business of airport expansion, but the answers prove frustrating. I am discouraged at being unable to get beyond the recitation of formal policy statements and explanations that focused on committee structures and the routines of due processes, government and bureaucracy. Pushing a little further I ask about the kind of economic models and knowledge expertise that leads the council to pursue airport expansion. I am then handed a stack of books and publicity material as I struggle to work out why I had been unable to find access to what I presume must be a background of political goings-on that might help me map out and fill out the bigger picture of what is at stake organizationally in the Escape Lounge. However, as I flick through the pages of *Manchester: Shaping the City* (RIBA 2004), I am suddenly struck by the swish of a Bob cut, which leaps out of the opening cover pages.

It is perhaps this oblique movement embodied in the flick of a page that has momentarily taken me out of those disciplinary frames that encourage analysis to pursue 'the political' within the terms familiar to public policy and the institutions of formal representation. Two black suited women, both carrying large leather folio document briefcases, are caught from behind in a blur of strident animation, walking purposively – it seems – towards the glass towered atrium of the Harvey Nichols store in Manchester, a site of equally remarkable 'loungification'. It is not the questionable assumptions that might weaken the models of 'city-region growth' and economic regeneration contained in the Manchester Independent Economic Review (MIER 2009), and part authored by Edward Glaeser esteemed Professor of Economics at Harvard University, that draw my attention, but the apparently superficial glamour and stylistic continuities that help make connections back and forth between the Escape Lounge and these hallowed halls of political making.

The documents I am presented with are those that the city council distributes to businesses and potential inward investors in which lavish imagery and aesthetic design attempts to appeal to the busy executive. Here, style becomes a motif of organizing that forms part of 'The Mancunian Way' (Chlebik et al. 2002), a book included in the gift handed to me by the chief executive officer. Amidst images that recall and mirror those aspirations of the ASCENT magazine in the Escape Lounge, the visual effect of this flicker is one that offers sweeping vistas of construction and redevelopment in Manchester (the International Convention Centre, Bridgewater Hall, Hulme Arch Bridge, the City of Manchester Stadium…) where towers are soaring amidst strict horizontals and verticals and cantilevered bridges that swoop suspended over vertiginous heights. And then the Deansgate arches. Is it possible that they are Bob cuts? All aligned in standing order (see Fig. 6.1)? Late Victorian arches, not Bauhaus, as Sassoon claimed for his inspiration, but it is the formal mimesis that is suggestive of folds of organization in which we might be ensnared, a *form* of mobilization that silent in its enrolment might need to be considered of political import.

Following these threads I am led to several pages written by crime writer Cath Staincliffe (2002: 130) who in the 'telegraphic' style associated with certain practitioners of her genre writes about the emergence of

Fig. 6.1 City centre Bob cuts: sites of contemporary loungification (Photographs by author)

the now fashionable *Northern Quarter* in Manchester. In sentences short cut, neat back and sides, she writes:

> Beyond here stretches the northern territories, poor, flat lands running up to the hills of Oldham and Rochdale. The wrong side of the tracks. Northern Quarter – time as this was a sorry place; neglected, low rents, vacant lets. The warren of streets and crumbling buildings offered a whiff of opportunity to entrepreneurs, specialists, idealists, fanatics, desperadoes, collectors, revels, pioneers. Risky business. Fashionable now. The edge of town, spitting distance. Des Res. Though there's still an edge.

Not the immaculate form of the Bob, but the labyrinth of 'the warren' might be being made the central actor here, which takes us into a more cavernous and subterranean supplement to the surface appearance of control achieved by the Bob. Here, at least in the pages of this book taken from the desk of the city council chief executive officer, the state stretches into the 'wrong side of the tracks' – the 'northern territories' – where it begins to fray, immersed in a terrain of inversions and reversals that one might more easily associate with the paranoid meta-fictions of Thomas Pynchon (see Beyes 2009).

Lemm Sissay (now Chancellor of the University of Manchester), Peter Saville, and the DJ Dave Haslam are amongst some of the other former counter-culture characters who are regularly assembled and mobilised at various media events to help promote and articulate Manchester as the 'original modern' city. The alliance and/or re-appropriation of the avant-garde into spectacle that helps promote formal state and neo-liberal ambitions is an old story in critical theory (see for e.g. Frank 1997; Kellner 2003; cf. Wu 2003; Heath and Potter 2004; Boltanski and Chiapello 2005; McGuigan 2009), retold as the emergence of 'cool capitalism' and 'the rebel sell'. Many will remember however that the post-punk Manchester Music Scene (from the Buzzcocks through Ian Curtis to the 'Madchester' proliferation of 'Happy Mondays' and 'Inspiral Carpets'), with Anthony Wilson as its svengali/impressario, was anything but acceptable to formal politics and local state boosterism (Robb 2010; Middles 2011). This was a period of new hairstyles, new looks, and new political mobilisations that challenged existing institutions and practices. Largely in response to cultural movements associated with these bands, the 1994 Criminal Justice and Public Order Act was rushed through parliament in a feverish atmosphere of public anxiety. Stoked up in part by tabloid newspapers and fears of an expanding and uncontrollable 'rave-culture', these hairstyles and gangs seemed to promote subversion, liberty and license through an intoxicating mix of music, 'festivals' and new synthetic drugs. Some have gone so far as to describe this period as the emergence of an 'altered state' in the UK (Collin 1997; cf. Peace 2004).

Interestingly, this period of transition from post-punk to 'Madchester' was also a time of local Labour party transition as 'effective control was established at the centre by a younger cohort of 'new realist' politicians [Stringer, Bernstein,[9] Leese] in place of the earlier and older Labour generation' (Robson 2002: 36). Patronising the changing fashions of newly emergent pop-culture provided an important resource through which a rising cadre of politicians in Manchester sought a new image of the city and in which Manchester became an object of greater self-conscious

[9] Bernstein, the consummate politician, is clearly aware of the importance of crinicultural politics.

design and promotion mirroring the new image of 'New Labour'. This double articulation of city and politics, then, new image-politics, new image-city, marks out a space of a wider 'politics of the Bob', one that has been self-consciously fashioned and harnessed in part for the purpose of attracting investment capital to the city (Cochrane et al. 1996; Quilley 2000; Deas 2014).

It is difficult to deny that Hilary Clinton is an important mediator within these worlds of finance and political capital, and she is one of the few politicians to go public on the political importance of hair. In a seminal paper for the study of crinicultural politics Nigel Thrift (2008a: 20) quotes from Hilary Clinton's address to female students at Yale University in which she discusses the politics of hairstyling: 'The most important thing I have to say today is that hair matters', Hilary tells her audience, 'This is a life lesson my family did not teach me, Wellesley and Yale failed to instil in me: the importance of your hair. Your hair will send very important messages to those around you. It will tell you who you are and what you stand for'. As Thrift notes, this could be partly irony, or a reflection on the superficial and venal state of politics in North America. However, there can be little doubt that the power of hair is one now widely recognised by established politicians – from the Bob cut of the now Prime Minister of the UK Theresa May, to the carefully styled brand developed by Boris Johnson and described by some as 'semi-shambolic' and '[p]resented to the public like a pledge of friendliness and good-heartedness' (Berthod and Brash 2015). Joseph Roach (2007) has shown how much of Thatcher's power came from the intimidation afforded by her hair, the 'stacked, lacquered hair' that helped establish 'the principles of control, constraint and economy of force' and which 'flash through the aether' of what Roach calls the '*It-effect*', mobilizing a cult of personality through changes in fashion and appearance.[10]

However, hairstyle cannot simply be harnessed as a vehicle for political ambition – it has, as we noted earlier, a certain life, a certain agency of its own – we might perhaps have to begin to think about its possible role in

[10] David Cameron, criticized as a 'lounger' indulging in 'sofa diplomacy' (The Times, March 7th, 2014), may do well to learn some crinicultural lessons if he is to survive as leader of the current Conservative party. (This note was written in May 2016, prior to the post-Brexit change in the leadership of the UK Conservative party).

a 'parliament of things'. Latour (1993: 142–45) coined this phrase in an effort to acknowledge that contemporary politics has extended beyond mere human affairs and must now find ways of extending the franchise to the non-human and to agency that is distributed and inextricably entangled *between* humans and non-humans. A parliament of things is partly a provocation or thought experiment that seeks to challenge the arrogance of assuming an abstract human agent free of any constitutive technological or object prosthesis. This sovereignty of the human agent and its separation and division from the non-human has been identified as a major illusion of the modern settlement between the sciences and the human sciences, and to avoid this hubris we might better position the Bob cut neither as subject or object, nor human or simply non-human, but part of a metastable field composed of 'quasi objects' or 'quasi subjects'. Entangled between quasi objects and quasi subjects, primal agency or simple causality is impossible to attribute. In the processes of captivation that hold both Edie and myself in the allure of glamour, it is difficult to identify who is subject and who is object, who or what is active or passive, and what is producer and what is product. But that there is a politics here, of that there surely can be no doubt.

Conclusion

Edie is sat behind the oak panelled reception desk. She looks up as she puts down her copy of Vogue and smiles to greet you. The Bob shines jet-black casting a sheen of light that captures and tantalizes. We've seen this before, but this time, as the surface sounds of the lounge recede into the background, everything appears more pointillist, but also buzzing and blooming in confusion. Things are perhaps not so clearly defined now, they have perhaps lost a certain coherence and substantiality. Thinking with 'the Bob' makes everything connected or woven, even plaited together. Following the Bob we have seen that things are multiple and immersed in what Foucault (1980) calls 'capillary' processes that circulate from one site of instantiation to another, levelling the heights of 'state' and 'political economy' and folding them back into that which is normally considered 'low', the mundane and trivial everyday of little significance to 'Politics' (with a big P).

It is not clear who or what is in control in this fold of the high and the low: things, matters, bodies, discourse, technologies, television, magazines, the lounge manager, or even David Cameron. The once ordered and coherent surface gloss of things perhaps now appear to be made and held together 'of wire and string' (Basboll 2004). A strand of hair can be seen on the shoulder of Edie's turquoise blouse which ripples with a moiré-like effect, a scatter of dandruff, dust motes in the air… Things disintegrate and fall apart as we pull on the threads of the Bob cut to bring into play an extended 'ecology' of things and practices at work in the Escape Lounge. You might see that Edie is having a 'good hair day'; she's in control, at least for the moment. Other 'hair-lounge people' may not be so lucky. The air conditioning whirrs and rattles. Maybe hair is clogging up the inlet valve.

In an important paper de Vries (2007) recently proposed the study of what he calls 'sub-politics'. With this concept he directs our attention to scientific laboratories, materials and knowledge practices that remain 'below the radar' of political interest, but whose products very often become matters of concern in the public domain whilst simultaneously changing the nature of what it means to be 'political' or 'public' (see also Latour 2007). In this chapter we have followed only some of the practices and materials implicated in the construction of lounges, but it is helpful to see them engaged in a similar process of 'sub-politics'. The fixation on 'the Bob' offers an ethnographic experiment to test what difference the Bob might make to the practice and understanding of politics. If there is politics in a 'shopping trolley' (Cochoy 2009) or a 'teapot' (Marres 2014), in the metals of an oil pipeline (Barry 2013), or in the flight of the 'mosquito' (Mitchell 2002), then there is certainly politics in a Bob cut.

The Bob cut is but one element in this emerging phenomenon we have been calling loungification and in making it the centre of our analysis this chapter has discovered a politics that extends to the very materiality of hair. In following the rather stochastic walk that opened up as we went in pursuit of the Bob cut hairstyle we were able to explore a dimension of organization that we might identify as 'crinicultural'. At times subject, at other times object, hair becomes an unruly agent entangled in various political mobilizations. We have also used the Bob as a guide to unravel a complex weave of politics that forms around the Escape Lounge. It has also offered a way of gathering into juxtaposition a range of otherwise dispersed and heterogeneous objects, actors and materials that find expression in the lounge helping to create new subject positions and new objects and 'attachments' that link subject and object (see Hennion 2007; Latour 2013).

In terms of its form, we found certain homologies as the Bob became tangled up and at times indistinguishable from architectural and other features of the built environment. This making equivalent might seem arbitrary – or even delirious (see Lecerlce 1985) – but it is fashioned from a mode of thinking that is also being realised by the designers of the Escape Lounge (as we saw in chapter 4). Their juxtapositions and associations – in the form of tables, chairs, wallpaper, paint, and carpets – appeared to achieve a certain synthesis and coherence. However, in this chapter the analysis extracts a greater degree of discordance and dissonance in which the lounge emerges as a more unruly and even dangerous place than we might customarily think. Variously enrolled, extended, related and deployed, the occupants of the lounge might be held in webs of association that obscure, ignore or detract from the possibility of seizing other possibilities for action. However, following the processes of construction that find issue in the appearance of the apparently insignificant Bob cut helps identify strands of association that point to forces of destabilisation – albeit perhaps sporadic and episodic – that signal a more volatile and agitated 'politics' at work in organization. It is a volatility in which both the customarily designated 'high' and 'low' of politics is immersed. In this way we might begin to enter a mode of organizational analysis that deploys 'the lounge' and its 'elements' as a form of methodological experiment (see Born and Barry 2010) that might seize and amplify the much vaunted 'immanence' of forces in organization suggestive of modes of existential becoming that reach beyond current forms of organization and containment.

7

Animals and Organization: Feline Politics and the Nine Lives of 'Olly the Cat'

Critical Management Studies has recently been described as a movement that resembles 'herding cats' (Parker 2013: 175). It was perhaps not intended to say much more than the obvious, providing a casual aside that repeated a widely cited expression. However, would critical management studies know what to do if it was confronted by an actual cat? Would the discipline even take note? (Fig. 7.1).

Lounging on the front steps of Olympic House is a ginger mackerel tabby cat. She is called Olly – 'the airport cat'. Sometimes she sits on the roof of her mini-Berkshire-style townhouse, which curiously abuts the entrance to the concrete and steel glass tower of Manchester Airport Group's head office; on other occasions she appears to be on guard duties. There are periods of the day when she lies sprawled and recumbent. According to the receptionists, Olly (or Olivia)[1] had turned up at the

[1] Olly turned up at the airport as a boy (some understood Olly as a shortened pet name for Oliver) – or at least that was how people sought to relate to the cat. Once she had been diagnosed as a girl, doubts were raised about the appropriateness of her name and various suggestions were made as to how this error might be rectified, including a renaming to 'Olivia'. However, it became apparent that Olly might well serve as the cat's name, and by the silent writing of the 'y' the name has the desired advantage of retaining a gendered indistinction and beyond this a capacity for ontological 'differance' (Derrida 1982) that is so central to the story that follows.

D. O'Doherty, *Reconstructing Organization*,
DOI 10.1057/978-1-137-48922-7_7

Fig. 7.1 Olly the cat (Photograph by author)

corporate headquarters of the airport sometime in early 2007. Named after Olympic House she has become full-time resident, at first sleeping 'rough' on the marble steps, and then taking up home in what becomes colloquially known as the 'cat penthouse', purchased with funds donated by airport staff. Her presence means that those who seek admittance through the grand revolving central glass doorway must tread carefully or skirt the building perimeter to gain access via a side entrance. Night and day Olly sits there, as if a consummate lounger of organization. With this imperial grandeur she seems to offer a kind of *coda* or parodic *mise-en-scene* to the airport and this study of loungification....

The appearance of the cat comes at the end of this ethnographic study of the Escape Lounge during which we have progressively been forced to abandon the habitual categories and terms of analysis popular in management and organization studies. Not least of these casualties has been the disposal of 'the individual'. The study began with the parochial politics of personality and their very local organizational rivalries and career ambitions. However, we found this tended to encourage analytical myopia restricted to the confines of Olympic House. The ethnography began to uncover more significant features of organization to which we have to attend when one considers what is it that is *Reconstructing Organization*. The existential preoccupations of the all-too-human have therefore begun to recede from the focus of this analysis. An attempt has been made to recover things that are typically considered too obvious, or too ready-to-hand, and it was only once we entered this dimension of organization that the ethnography began to suspect important relational and transformational capacities were at work and *immanent* to this everyday. All manner of organizational and bureaucratic paraphernalia was brought into purview as we sought to attend to these everyday features of organization: Gantt charts, project paperwork, project briefs, walking practices, PowerPoint slides, office and lounge furniture, etc. (Yates 1989; Orlikowski 2007; cf. Carlile et al. 2013). And these things were often found to live a quite remarkable life. Indeed, in the last chapter our analysis was forced to consider the possibility of a materialist politics associated with *hairstyling* – and, beyond this, to contemplate the possibility that such 'crinicultural' phenomena enjoyed a certain degree of political *autonomy*!

In this final chapter a range of elements are assembled that speak of a further feature of this loungification, but standing at some askew to its dominant mode of organization. These materials emerge out of an interstice that inheres *between* the human and the animal, and which remain recalcitrant to customary methods of organization analysis. To collect these materials this chapter coins the concept 'feline politics' which when deployed analytically allows us to gather and hold together a dispersed and otherwise heterogeneous range of matters important to the vitality of organization. But, once again, things will appear to be getting out of hand.

Normally politics is kept separate from the animal, at least the animal is not typically thought to have a politics, or to embody political agency. This concept is necessary, however, precisely because organization studies remains so firmly Aristotelian in its understanding of politics. For Aristotle (Pol. 1.1253a) man is the talking animal, and it is this unique property of man that makes 'politics' possible. 'Feline politics' would seem an aberration in this respect. However, as this chapter shows, it is a concept that helps enact and explore a progressively more complex series of entanglements that emerge overtime between Olly and her ostensibly human colleagues. In so doing the chapter shows that the animal and its entanglements with the human have important political significance in our analysis of organization.

Animals are not normally considered an object of management, let alone a resource or potential ally in the management of organization. Even less are they considered an *agent* of organization. Yet, by placing the lounge at the centre of our study, analysis has begun to attend to relations that extend across an expanded ecology of matters in organization made up of what might otherwise be overlooked because of their disparate distribution, or dismissed as marginal. In this chapter human-animal entanglements at Manchester Airport provide a further example of features of organization that defy classification within the habitual dualisms of social science: culture/nature, subject/object, etc. As Haraway (2008) has argued, this suspension of habitual categories and dualisms constitutes an important lesson 'when species meet' – a lesson that we might describe as one of the 'nine lives' of Olly. One needs to discard or at least suspend many of the conceptual reifications extant within contemporary organization theory to follow the story told in this chapter.

The chapter first explores the way the cat might be understood to *mediate* organisational politics. This will not be the cause of too much offence amongst scholars in organization studies and has been considered a possibility by Ackroyd and Crowdy (1990), Hamilton (2007), and Hamilton and Taylor (2012). Beyond this though this chapter discovers a range of practices associated with what one might call a 'cult of the cat', and manifest in versions of 'Totemism', 'potlatch', 'carnival', 'resistance', etc. However, we cannot *restrict* Olly to the role of carrier or 'symbol' of wider organizational issues, a *screen* upon which (human) members of organization can project a whole set of issues. Cats have 'agency' of their own, or rather the cat-human *hybrid* produces agency – and one that is refractory and other to the logic of management control. Moreover, we will find *multiple* cats at work in Manchester: some are essentially conservative, sentimental, and saccharine – prompting analysis to consider the role of anthropomorphic projections and transferences. Others, however, open up more disruptive and challenging actions in organization. Olly invites us to consider the possibility that there are forms of politics in organization that are neither simply human, nor non-human. Hence 'feline-politics' marks a dimension of organization where a peculiar feline-inflected ontology might be at work.[2]

In the storytelling that follows all the characters and components that we have so far been able to identify as being central to the construction and management of the Escape-Lounge re-appear, but in a very different light. This reappearance reflects the fact there are multiple potential configurations of people and things. There are major and minor configurations, for example, but there are also configurations that make it extremely difficult to identify a clear distinction between that which is real or fabricated, or that which is serious and frivolous. This chapter specifically shows how difficult it is to establish whether feline politics marks a parodic subversion of the all-too-serious *human* project to construct a lounge, or whether it takes us into an 'alter-ontology' of loungification, one marked by what is being called in some recent literatures feral human-animal relations and 'multi-species becomings' (Philo and Wilbert 2000; Kirksey and Helmreich 2010; Kohn 2013; Monbiot 2014; Allen and Lavau 2015; Tsing 2015).

[2] Ethnography is also challenged by this encounter and must struggle to find a mode of narration, or storytelling, that is able to retain a certain suspension of disbelief. This allowed the author to explore the proliferation of 'voices' that sound at Manchester Airport. As one reviewer of an earlier version of this chapter noted, there are at least four voices at work in the text including the first person, the third person, the plural 'we', and the academic passive. This footnote possibly adds a fifth. The encounter with the animal triggers a period of reflexive self-questioning in which the presumed unity of the human author comes apart and begins to multiply. This remains an important methodological principle because through this multiplication one becomes more receptive to the inevitably recursive and constitutive participation of research in the enactment and performativity of particular versions of organization. 'Feline politics' attempts to provide a conceptual resource that allows the research to retain some of these multiple and inter-species 'voices' that would otherwise be precipitately separated out into nature and culture, subject and object, or man and animal – thereby losing this elusive – and perhaps, as said above, *incredulous* space, in which lively and vital organizational activities are at work.

Introducing Olly: Thinking Otherwise

October, 2009. It is a little after 8 am as I walk towards the head office of Manchester Airport Group to negotiate access for an ethnographic study of the airport. The marble steps and grand entrance appear intimidating. Bathed in glorious sunshine they seem to enact with brilliance and self-confidence a grandeur and solemnity associated with the modern corporation. A few people are milling around the entrance doors, but the day has not yet started for most of the corporate executives and senior managers. It is an unremarkable, everyday scene in which things move in and out of the doorway without apparent distinction or merit when suddenly, in front of me, only a few steps away, there appears the large, imposing, stocky figure of the group chief executive. I am a little overwhelmed, both by his role, but also by what I have heard of his approach to management, and so I hang back a little, keen to avoid a precipitous encounter. I am due to meet him in a couple of days, but today I am scheduled to see the director of group projects.

The chief executive is in his early 60s and in less than a year's time the chairman of the board of directors will announce his retirement. As he moves towards the entrance he stutters, nearly to a halt, but in making a 45-degree detour he recovers his movement to articulate a sweeping arc that skirts the perimeter of the entrance plaza where he secures access to the building in what appears to be the service door. The transfer of body weight must have been the cause of some discomfort for a man who could no longer be described as fleet of foot. As he moves out of my line of vision I notice, sprawled on the floor, a fluffed up ball of soft ginger striped hair and matter. This, as I was later to discover, was Olly the Cat. Lying on her side, with her back arched, her eyes closed and front paws stretched out in front of her, she was luxuriating in the Autumn sunshine. Described as bullish and dogmatic (O'Doherty 2016a), the chief executive officer appears to have made way for this cat. As he moves, crab-like, sideways – presumably so as not to disturb the cat – I notice his knees are stiff and wonder if he suffers from arthritis.

This was my introduction to Olly the Cat, and my first encounter with the animal in organization. Her presence was there from the beginning of the research, but I was perhaps not completely aware of this at the time, no doubt a reflection of my anxiety to secure access to what I presumed to be the corridors of power. However, a back-story began to be pieced together in which I discover that Olly had arrived on the steps of Olympic House semi-feral, underweight, riddled with fleas, and sporting a clipped or chopped, torn ear. She was limping badly, refused offers of milk, and would not allow anyone to approach. However, after a degree of trust was established between some members of the Olympic House management team, Olly was taken in and later admitted to veterinary care. Staff pooled their money to pay for expensive emergency dental work and for explorative surgery to examine possible hip replacement. The Berkshire style town house was subsequently purchased, and soon afterwards blankets and toys began to appear. She became quite a celebrity and the local BBC dispatched a camera crew to make a short film about her life. I later learn about her appointment as a 'cub-reporter' for the staff newspaper where regular columns began to appear under her name. There was also a 'philosophy corner' penned by Olly and published in the eponymously titled Manchester Airport Group quarterly group publication *MAGazine.* Here staff could read occasional 'words of wisdom', written ostensibly by Olly. The philosophy corner in the February 2010 issue asked its readers to consider the following problem: 'We were given two hands to hold, two legs to walk, two eyes to see, two ears to listen – but why only one heart?' The answer: 'Because the other was given to someone else. For us to find'.

Such wisdom was extraordinary and refreshing in the context of 6 months meticulous ethnographic study of management practices during which I had become immersed in the minutia of technical and administrative matters associated with the mundane routines of day-to-day paperwork and reporting. Shaped and informed by the aspiration to master formal systems of project management such as the ubiquitous 'PRINCE 2' methodology, management appeared obsessively fixated on what they called 'due process' and the promise of formal rationality. Olly was far from rational – as it is understood in conventional business and management – and although I could find no evidence of her in the financial accounts, or in the annual general report, Olly was clearly a significant member of this organization.

It is widely known in the social sciences and humanities that animals are 'good to think with', in an oft-quoted passage from Levi-Strauss

(1963: 89). For many, cats are not only good to *think* with (Alger and Alger 2003; Derrida 2002; Rogers 2001, 2006); in the absence of cats our very human community and civilisation itself is unthinkable and unliveable (Wasthulber 1991). With their renowned qualities for hunting and catching rodents, their early domestication and companionship made possible the construction of grain stores and the establishment of more sedentary ways of living. Beyond this, cats are often associated with spiritual and mystical dimensions of being, and in ancient Egypt were often sculpted or carved to stand guard at the gates of various temples. In certain myths, the fluctuating shape of their eyes is deemed to track the movement of the lunar calendar, and vested with seer-like status they are considered great teachers of mystery and magic offering portals of communication to the worlds of the dead and un-dead (Briggs 1980). According to some accounts, the cat could even take on the ailments and symptoms of those around it. It was these associations that perhaps help explain the worship of *Bastet*, one of the most important classical Egyptian deities, and often depicted in the form of a long, sleek and elegant cat, or with the body of a woman and the head of a cat. In the wake of this deification the cat becomes a ubiquitous feature of Egyptian art after 950 BC (Zuffi 2007). Indeed, Herodotus reports that the temple of Bastet in *Babustis* was the most grand and elaborate of all temples, richly adorned with carvings and sculptures, and notes that the annual festival for Bastet was one of the most popular and jubilant of all the holy days (Rogers 2006: 15).

Getting too close or familiar with cats is also known to have its dangers. From the 'cat familiar' in witchcraft and the occult (Durrant and Bailey 2012), to the strange intellectual and affective metamorphoses that accompanies certain academic studies of the cat, it seems we would be well advised to be wary of the cat. Kara White's (2013) 'sensory experiential methodology' and Morris Holbrook's (1998; 2008) remarkable textual experiments designed to give voice to his 'inner-cat' – in order, it seems, to better teach marketing – are perhaps a little beyond the pale for those who consider themselves the mainstream in business and management studies. However, this first ethnographic encounter with Olly is revealing, at the very least, of the *stimulation* to thought provoked by the appearance of a cat at Manchester Airport – and one that as we shall see goes to the heart of management. And I was clearly not alone in this response. However, what was striking, ethnographically, was the very incongruence of her appearance on the marble steps of Olympic House. It was this that first prompted reflections about the historical role of cats in human community and organization.

However, it was the dissolution of many of the most enduring dualisms in the applied social sciences brought about during the process of tracking 'loungification' that helped the ethnography become more attentive to phenomena like Olly that might otherwise seem marginal or aberrant. Note here how the ethnographic tale telling of Olly seems to respond to what the human and animal *shares*. As Olly is seen to limp, the ethnographer notices the stiff gait of the CEO, who walks crab-like; a certain empathy is then aroused for the CEO; there then follows a recollection that his approach to management is considered 'bullish' and 'dogmatic'; reflections on time and mortality are subsequently prompted as the ethnographer trawls the landscape for connections and associations.

Far from being a mere curiosity, these features of organizational life become increasingly significant for management as we progressively make our way in this chapter. Suggestive of a rudimentary 'thinking otherwise' as Donna Haraway (2006) shows, these 'encounters with companion species' must be developed if we are to sustain and cultivate the possible fruit of this alteration. In making progress along these lines we will have to shed the remnants of an ethnographic quest for deeper meaning. The ethnographer must also ask *how* is Olly understood by *indigenous* members of the organization. In asking these questions, of course, the ethnographer begins to participate and enact certain ways of making organization that marks a further breach of the representation/reality dualism ingrained in modern social science (Hacking 1983).

Cat Therapy and Organizational Well-Being

Responding to my increasing interest in the role and status of Olly, Bob the receptionist invites me to the back of the entrance lobby. Behind a narrow recessed corridor he shows me a small desk above which a picture of a ginger mackerel tabby cat is displayed. Sat in a field surrounded by rolling hills, there are flowers and a bird. The bird appears to have landed next to the cat and – perched on top of a strawberry plant – is offering the cat a small worm. Such a bucolic scene amidst the refuse of drab impersonal office furniture seemed odd. I was soon struck by further apparent incongruities, marginalia and ostensibly random juxtapositions of bits and pieces of discarded and found matters. On the desk there is a miniature snowman sporting a felt bucket hat and a hand-made crocheted red and white scarf, a bottle of Heinz tomato ketchup, a carafe of vinegar, and a small glass bowl filled with water and a spray of flowers. What appears to be a white plastic spoon has also been placed into the water at what must be a geometrically impossible angle. Bob turns to a large white Formica enamelled filing cabinet, which is stained and delaminating in places. He raises his eyebrows as he looks at me (was he smiling?), and then opens the doors. A cornucopia of tins and food parcels spill out from the cupboard – Whiskas 'favourites in jelly', Vitacat 12 pouch multipacks, Tesco 'premium cuts' in jelly with rabbit and game, kitty-nibbles, Go-Kat biscuits, catnip and various treats. There is also a toilet roll, black plastic bin bag liners, and a bottle of anti-bacterial spray cleaner.

It is tempting to see this attention and devotion to the cat as a surrogate resource that provides an informal means through which organisational culture is formed and expressed, a source of *mediation* that *enables* social relations to be worked and stitched together (Hamilton and Taylor 2012). The cat seemed to provide a rallying point around which otherwise neglected dimensions of collective well-being were articulated and worked through at a time when executive control and formal ownership was being taken out of the hands of the local representative district councils and placed into those of private capital.

As one member of the management team told me 'Staff respond to the cat Damian, and you can see that it helps people … people learn to be more giving and generous, it brings out the better side in a lot of us'. This would seem to confirm what has been argued in the few studies of animals conducted in management and organization studies. Hamilton and Taylor (2012), for example, show how animals help humans establish a 'common work ethos' that contributes to the development of a 'distinctive sense of common purpose and symbolic value' (Hamilton and Taylor, ibid.: 46).

At the same time as Olly was helping to generate something like a community of compassion, certain elements within airport management were concerned about low trust and morale and were devoting considerable resources into changing what senior executives understood to be 'the culture' at the airport. Operational staff would often repeat the mantra 'poor morale' and 'low motivation' to describe their experiences in recent years at the airport. During one of the regular monthly 'open forums' to which all employees were invited, one member of the airfield engineering team, becoming increasingly frustrated with his efforts to articulate to management the feelings of many 'operational staff' shouted out 'it's all broken promises'. 'You don't need pie charts on a wall or a £5 voucher' he continued, 'a lot of things are not monetary', going on to explain that his team had been involved in a major airfield snow clearance operation for which there 'had not even been a thanks'.

As management sought to address some of these problems, bringing in more and more expensive consultants and outside expertise to provide guidance, Olly seemed to motivate precisely the kind of behaviour and compassion that airport management seemed to want to design. At that time there was also an increasing emphasis on the discourse of 'authentic leadership' which began to circulate in policy pronouncements and official communications accompanied with the tag line 'You asked, we listened'.[3] Was the lack of trust in management repaired or being replaced by the emergence of trust and community that found its focus centred on Olly? In many ways it seemed as if the 'cat' provided a form of domesticity at a time when changes in management were considered to be developing a more corporate style, marked by slick communications strategy and impersonal, contract-based and performance measured targets.

The cat is also a quintessential family animal, and associations with the family are made explicit by the receptionist during our talks about Olly: 'At one time this [the airport] had all been family', Bob explains. 'When I started out as a baggage lad, you would get fathers and sons, you know'. As he is talking two colleagues join us, one of whom I am later told is taking early retirement. Bob obviously goes back a long way with his colleagues. 'Do you remember, Ron?' he says, inviting the other

[3] This is a discourse which now pervades the modern British university.

two into the conversation, 'you'd be able to look up and say 'Hey, there's Geoff's lad'. Do you remember?' They then go on to trade stories about this particularly infamous character, Geoff, who it was said used to walk around 'thinking he was really important', carrying and displaying to all the world that he was reading *The Guardian* newspaper, and 'you know, a bit above the rest of us'. With its association with family and domesticity it was possible then that the cat was helping to recover those elements of history and 'culture' that were widely perceived to have been lost in recent years, replaced by low trust and broken promises. It is also possible that a significant number of airport staff found common alliance with the cat. Arriving at the airport mangy and lame, and in general distress and poor health, staff may have projected into Olly a certain identification in ways that allowed or helped cultivate otherwise difficult and unspoken emotions.

Over time, elements of valued community seemed to be being re-built around a mascot of family and home, returning the towers of Olympic House back into the vernacular of a more domestic scaled dwelling. In this respect, the therapeutic qualities of cats have been long established.[4] However, this would all provide a rather conservative analysis and with its underlying inspiration of Freud and Durkheim the analysis unfortunately becomes consistent with some of the most regressive understandings of corporate culture in management and organisation studies (Peters and Waterman 1982; Deal and Kennedy 1982). In so doing we risk reducing the cat to a *symbol* of integration and also little more than a passive vehicle for the symbolic projections of humans, which recalls that form of analysis developed in Geertz's (1973) classic study of the cock-fight. As many have argued, however, the cat occupies a *liminal* space in the house and largely refuses the domestication of the human. In the next section we go on to consider evidence that suggests the cat might be something more than an object of succour and consolation; namely, an *active* participant in a more radical politics.

---

[4] The importance of 'companion species' for general counselling and psychology has been reported across a range of literature (see also Fick 1993; Wells et al. 1997; Wilkes 2009). Brickel's (1979) paper is particularly worthy of note in this respect showing the importance of cats in the treatment of geriatric hospital patients.

Subversion and Non-human Agency

'Olly basically divides the organization in two', the terminal operations manager tells me. There are those who love the cat, and those who think she is not appropriate for a place of work, and particularly a corporate head office with a carefully managed brand image. Olympic House is the space where senior executives of airlines, politicians, the local government chief executive officer, the leader of the council, and representatives of global investment firms, regularly meet. In having to step over and around a cat, displaying increasing signs of incontinence – complete with her gaudy paraphernalia of gifts that had begun to resemble votive offerings to some deity in a home that was increasingly taking on the appearance of an elaborate gimcrack shrine – Olly started to become the cause of considerable unease and discomfort amongst senior executives. The threat that the cat might have to leave prompted the formation of a 'cat committee' and it was only after considerable lobbying and a dramatic intervention by the Chief Executive Officer's PA, in which she confronts him by all accounts with an impassioned oratorio, that Olly was eventually allowed to stay at the airport. 'He likes the publicity that comes with the cat', one of the civil engineers tells me 'but he's shown no interest in her other than that' (Fig. 7.2).

Here we begin to detect the first stirrings of non-human agency. Note that it is Olly who is the *cause* of the division amongst different factions of management. Meanwhile as the gifts become increasingly profligate, one might be reminded that cats are widely reputed to be manipulative. But who's having who here? Can we be satisfied that the cat remains the object of human manipulations? Or, is Olly manipulating her human companions? Consider events on Christmas Day 2008 when American Airlines staff present Olly with a whole Salmon freshly caught from the upper Hudson valley. Then, a member of the airport staff makes a cushion for Olly, embroidered to read 'Olly's place', which is hung ceremonially like a crown above her 'penthouse' outside Olympic House. A pop band formed by members of the airport staff write a song about her, and a BMi baby Boeing 737 is named 'Olly Cat Baby'. Such gift giving becomes so extravagant that a call for moderation in the form of

Fig. 7.2 Olly's place (Photograph by author)

a Christmas letter is published in the December 2008 edition of *Plane Talk*. The letter explains that Olly has been 'slightly overwhelmed' by the profusion of presents and goes on to say that 'Olly asked me if he could share some of his food and bedding with his many feline and canine friends at the *Society for Abandoned Animals* who have not been as fortunate as him'. Meanwhile, a new doormat appears and for a while it sits outside Olly's kennel. Inscribed in bold letters, it reads 'The Boss'.[5]

The celebration and veneration of Olly, her placement on the steps of the marble entrance, the fact that even the chief executive officer was forced to give way, literally and metaphorically, is all suggestive of elements of subversion. Far from being simply an object of sentimental pro-

[5] The writing attempts to recover and retain astonishment at those episodes, events, and practices that rallied around Olly the Cat, but also in a way that does justice to a certain scepticism, irony, and eventually the achievement of a certain agnosticism that also can be deemed to characterize these practices. One hesitates to call these practices 'social practices' because as will become clearer, they began to make much more sense as expressions of post-human 'social' practices, or even 'inter' or 'trans'-species practices. In this way the ethnography is highly selective, even rigorously discriminatory, as it participates in the enactment of a particular form of organizational becoming. I would characterise this as a commitment to rupture and volatility that attends the emergence of undecidability.

jection or attachment, Olly might have been used as a way of exposing and ridiculing the pretensions to power of the chief executive and his corps of senior managers (cf. Stallybrass and White 1986). Capital was often made of the fact that the chief executive officer was not born with a 'golden spoon in his mouth', for example, but had made his way up from the 'school of hard knocks' (in the construction industry). Festooned with garlands of colourful cards and gifts, many airport staff clearly took great pleasure in the sight of Olly's 'penthouse'. Placed front of house on the steps of the head office, Olly's kennel might have been deployed to trigger humility or embarrassment as the executives of the airport group were metaphorically and literally 'brought down' from level 6 of the corporate glass towers to the pavement upon which had been erected improvised shelters for the homeless.

Olly may also have provided a form of protest against the perceived lack of empathy and the decline of 'the family' as increasing numbers of managers appointed to an ever more elaborate and complex corporate hierarchy put ever-more distance between management and staff. Typically, managers at Olympic House were not 'local'. University educated and mobile middle class professionals, senior management typically did not have family roots in Manchester or its environs. Despite the efforts of senior management to promote a progressive 'human relations', the general lack of trust and suspicion meant that management policies and pronouncements were often greeted with cynicism. In this respect, Olly seemed to provide a resource which reminded people that authenticity, emotional attachments, care, and nurturing, were still possible and that management were largely failing to maintain these features of organization. She brings out the 'emotions and generosity', Bob explains, 'she makes people feel good', in ways that helped mediate and subvert the ever increasing chains of command that stretched between the most senior and the most lowly of staff members at Manchester Airport.

Around this time I began to notice that Bob on reception was a little shifty as we talked about the cat. His eyes would often look over my shoulder, rapidly moving from left to right and vice-versa. If he looked in her direction, he would not cast his gaze directly at her, but to one side. The cat of course had the complete freedom of the airport campus;

she would come and go as cats are want – some of her excursions regular and apparently 'scheduled', whilst others we might imagine were more bespoke or 'chartered' in nature. I began to wonder if beyond the deference to the cat, there was some other conspiratorial relationship amongst members of the airport. It was possible that the cat was not only a *symbol* of freedom and escape, a token of protest against the pretensions and control associated with senior executives, but also a cause of its greater motivation and desire.

Olly was, in other words possibly a *secret resource*, and in Bob's wily disposition there were perhaps signs of a reticence to speak openly that made me wonder if I was being tested as to whether I could be trusted or was worthy of being initiated into what might very well be some kind of cult of Olly. Or, was this shiftiness a sign that the deference and apparent deification of the cat was itself parody? In other words, an acknowledgement that the 'secret resource' was in fact the (ironic) deification of the cat. It was the cat that done it, Guv!

These ambiguities all point to the incredible complexity of the relation between the human and animal that also draws attention to the fact that Olly could not be constructed in any consistent or singular way. The more I studied this cat, the more entangled I became in the complexity and depth of relations between the human and animal. It was an experience that slowly taught me that there was something more than merely symbolic about the cats' presence. Beyond the symbolic, let us follow the cat into a dimension of organization that is productive of an otherness and excess beyond the capacity of management to understand, control or contain.

Becoming Feline

We have seen how Olly helped stimulate all kinds of displays of emotional behaviour and attachments, many of which are the cause of discomfort and perhaps even disgust amongst some members of the community. Every day people would come and pay tribute to the cat. On the marble steps of Olympic House they would crouch down in front of her and engage in acts of stroking, rubbing, tickling, petting, nuzzling, smelling, hugging, grooming, and kissing. Both partners to these practices appeared to take pleasure, in which bodily properties were exchanged, including hair, scent, and perspiration, with the cat occasionally licking the hand and sometimes even the face of her attendant. Human and cat share a degree of intimacy here that goes far beyond routine comfort, approaching something more akin to an intensive bodily – and even what humans might call *sexual* – enjoyment (see Dekkers 2000; Beetz and Podberscek 2005). Beyond the corporeal, people would also try to find ways of talking to her, soliciting conversation and even counsel. 'How are you Olly?' many would ask; 'What are we going to do with you, hey?', or 'What do *you* think, eh, Olly?'. As I got closer to the cat it was obvious that human preoccupations extended to behaviour and even a certain moral anxiety, 'Have you been a good girl?', or even flirtatious and promiscuous, 'who's been a naughty pussy then?'

As I became more preoccupied with the cat I suddenly became aware that Olly was everywhere. Like a 'meme', cats seem to be proliferating in popular culture (Berland 2008) and for a while cats and their 'memes' appeared to be almost running wild at the airport. Displayed on greeting cards, calendars, badges and the ubiquitous 'cute-kitten' photographs, cats propagate and multiply around the desks and common areas, pinned up on office privacy screens, and displayed in digital format as screen savers. For Berland, this contemporary multi-media procreation and reproduction reflects 'the proliferation of human-cat networks in urban and electronic space' that for her is 'part of an emergent 'post-human' landscape' (Berland, ibid.: 431).

In this post-human landscape Olly increasingly takes centre stage and becomes something more than an object providing a medium and stimulus through which other activities and behaviours could be interpreted and understood. If the CEO was interpreted as walking crab-like, or his behaviour 'bullish' (see O'Doherty 2016a), it also seemed that there were people who would *prowl*, there were those who *bitched*, and some who had their *claws* out (Manchester Evening News, 26th July 2011). There were others who were involved in a 'cat and mouse' game and some identified as copycats; there were accusations of corporate 'fat cats' and in the Escape Lounge the effort to supervise commercial floor layers was described as akin to 'herding cats'.[6] At the airport there were also cats' eyes on the runway, leopard print swim suits for sale in the zone of desire, a tiger car rental, a Rampant Lion pub ('where all the deals at the airport used to be done, Damian'), and images of cats were spread as corporate livery across the fuselage of the *Cougar* Airlines fleet of Boeing 727s.

As an organizing motif, the cat also encourages analysis to make sense of a whole set of otherwise disparate phenomena, drawing associations and connections that reveal hitherto neglected dimensions through which organization is achieved – in this case human-animal relations. Inside the terminal, for example, passengers are invited to 'step inside' another cat, 'The Jaguar'. Displayed on a 40-foot plasma screen, the advert seemed to trade on its association with its animal-like prowess. We may wonder if the growl of its engine is attempting to animate something akin to those 'animal spirits' that Keynes (1936) once identified as the motivation that helps explain apparently non-rational economic decisions (to invest, consume, etc.).

Such connections and associations are sufficiently suggestive for some to characterise contemporary business and economics as a form of 'animal capital' (Shukin 2009). Elements of the cat are even appropriated for signs of rank and distinction, the stripes on the shoulder boards of the pilots and co-pilots, for example, seemed to offer a visual rhyme with the mackerel tabby stripes of Olly the cat. Everywhere one looked, there was evidence of the cat, and it dawned on me that 'organisational behaviour' and 'social relations at work' were thoroughly immersed and enmeshed within a trans-species community of human-animal transgressions and 'becomings'.

This ubiquity of the cat is also suggestive that something more than symbolism is at stake. Olly was providing a resource that helped members of organization find a mode of orientation to the wider organization that was not simply representational but was also *interventionary* and *consti-*

---

[6] If the roots of the English language and attendant conception of the world is found in a genealogy of nautical terms (Kemp and Dear 2006), there is also a case to be made that the history of the cat and our relationship to it also provides a not insignificant mode of ontological orientation. The cat therefore opens up a whole range of behaviours for identification and reflection: feline, furtive, slinky, sneaking, sneaky, stealthy – all of which have become common vernacular in the popular 'warts and all' tales of corporate life (Prashad 2002).

tutive. This agency was manifest in a number of tangible and material forms, but also in behaviours and activities. Significantly, these becomings made organization work in other ways. It was inevitable then that my own activities as an ethnographer would be understood as cat-like: snooping, undercover, covert, secretive, and sneaking. However, which way around we might like to posit cause and effect here is problematic. Was the feline ontology an (illusionary) effect of the ethnographer *getting too close to the cat* – a relationship that was helping develop language and concepts that made the world *appear* increasingly feline? Or, was this inchoate epistemology an effect and requirement of having to deal with a world that was increasingly being experienced as feline?

I was not the only one 'becoming feline'. At the risk of straying too far into *Wonderland*, consider Bob, the receptionist, who might also be considered to be increasingly assuming the form and look of the cat. Like Olly, he too is 'perched' on the front steps of Olympic House; his name Bob 'Molloy', a near anagram of Olly and – like the cat – his hair was ginger and neatly trimmed. In this relationship with the cat there appeared to be evidence of considerable visual 'mirroring' or 'rhyme' between human and animal, which is a well-observed phenomenon in pet-owner relations. In more complex terms this relation might be described as 'mise-en-abyme' or 'synecdoche-like' in structure. Beyond the immediacy of a one-to-one relation this relationship extends out to encircle wider and wider elements of the airport to include the visual rhyme played out between Olly's miniature house and Olympic House[7] in which it is strangely nested or coiled. Indeed, Bob's activities could be described as cat-like. His capacity to move silently and stealthily through the crowds of people milling in the reception whilst waiting for admission to the offices in the corporate towers could be described, for example, as almost feline. One might be engaged in a conversation when out from nowhere he would appear – a tap on the shoulder, or a quiet word in your ear.

There is also a photograph of Bob in a magazine showing him crouching over to feed the cat. He is wearing a three-quarter length ginger-

[7] Olly/Olivia, Molly, Olympic House …this forms a 'logic' of organization consistent with the way Derrida's texts work and deployed as 'applied grammatology' in Greg Ulmer's (1985) work (see also Rhodes 2001; O'Doherty 2009).

Figs. 7.3 and 7.4 Bob and Olly ©Neil Hepworth/Your Cat magazine, used with permission

brown brushed suede leather coat that matches his brown moccasin style shoes, his white chest adding to the visual mirroring of cat and man. Both he and the cat seem to mimic each other, backs arched, face down, their paws extended, one behind the other. Who might be 'following' who becomes difficult to identify (Figs. 7.3 and 7.4).

Organization in Uproar: Towards Ontological Undecidability

We might not have gone so far into 'cat ontology' as ailurophiles such as White (2013), but the evidence we have gathered is highly suggestive that there are ways of enacting the feline in organization that might be understood after Annemarie Mol (2002) as a minor 'mode-of-ordering'. It is also a *post-human* mode-of-ordering, but one in which it is not clear who is the dominant actor, or indeed whether one can even abstract a singular actor out of what remains a collective multi and trans-species network 'actant' (see Latour 1996; from Greimas 1976) – and one that we might further extend to include a far greater range of materials, entities, and living organisms (see Kirksey and Helmreich 2010; Hustak and Myers 2012; Lorimer 2016).

For Haraway (2003), the methodological challenge is to *learn something new* everyday through the development of intimate and close relations with 'companion species'. Of most significance, however, is that we also appear to learn *otherwise* with animals.[8] Earlier we saw how the ethnographer began to respond to what might formerly have been dismissed as a minutia of heterogeneous and fragmented, disconnected marginalia. A desiderata of plastic spoons, emotions, felt cotton hats, tiger stripes, snatches of conversation about family, body dispositions and movements, colours and sounds, caught the attention. Various patterns could be established by assembling and juxtaposing these elements in particular ways, in an exercise that might strike one as arbitrary, wilful, and even fantastic. However, this is precisely what we find members of organization doing, particularly as they become increasingly obsessed with Olly. It is no doubt an extension to what earlier in this study was identified as angular reasoning and the disjunctive synthesis.

We have seen that capital was made out of the cat, helping to promote the activities of the airport and acting as free publicity. In support of this interpretation, consider the front cover of the June 2010 'World Cup' special edition of the airport staff magazine 'Plane Talk' which carries a full spread colour photograph of Olly. Wearing a specially adapted 'octopus hat' designed in the colours of the St George's flag, complete with mini flags sprayed out in an elaborate fan, the headline reads 'Olly roars for England'. The creativity of the marketing and communications team seemed to know no bounds. A Christmas issue of the magazine featuring Olly, for example, depicted her wearing the antlers of a reindeer. This reflects an imagination worthy of HG Wells who gave full expression to these possibilities in his cross-species breeding novel *The Island of Dr. Moreau*. With this image readers were reminded of the 'retail offer' and special prices on selected range of products for Manchester Airport staff during the festive season. Olly was not however quite so passive an

[8] See Freccero (2011) for an example of how this thinking otherwise might develop quite terrifying results.

object for publicity and promotion. She had refused to allow her agents to dress her in a full England football T-shirt prior to the photo shoot, for example, during which several members of staff had joked that there might be a case for calling the animal protection league.

Management it seems is both troubled and in part inspired and rejuvenated by this becoming feline, but events that follow become increasingly fantastic or even incredulous and difficult to judge as to their sincerity – or rather, more precisely, the *nature of this sincerity*. The concept of feline politics is suggestive because it encourages analysis to become more receptive to this kind of phenomenon and to illuminate what might be an emerging cat-human trans-species network. With the help of this concept we are beginning to see how action and behaviour is difficult to predict and authorial agency difficult to demarcate. The chapter has also shown how we are forced to consider this world in ways beyond the all-too-human realm of the symbolic. However, the *ontological* status of this dimension of organization still remains difficult to settle and it is towards this question that the chapter now turns.

An obvious first question to ask is whether feline politics, or a feline ontology, resides only in the eye of the beholder: 'there' if you want to see it. Is it possible, however, that there is a greater sense of *shared* reality achieved in collaboration with Olly? Is this reality objective, or subjective? Is it, moreover, *cause*, or an *effect* of something other? In fact, these questions are misleading. Feline politics focuses analytical attention on phenomenon that *splits these differences* and coming before those divisions – i.e. human/animal, object/subject, etc. – 'feline politics' both generates new subject positions (and countervailing worlds of objectivity) *and exceeds these settlements as it continues to subvert and unsettle organization*. That the generation of new insights, behaviours and capacities can be attributed to this post-human network is an additional characteristic of this feline politics.

The final section of this chapter begins with the appointment of a new chief executive officer in June 2010, following which speculation about the future of Olly becomes almost pandemic. It was not clear how Olly might feature in the ambitions that the new CEO had for the group and as announcements were made that the group was investing in a major architectural and design refurbishment of the corporate head office, people began to worry about Olly's future. Some were suggesting that her days were numbered. Nevertheless, if there were machinations afoot to get rid of Olly, any initiative had to tread carefully. Olly had become quite a celebrity during her time at the airport and her number of Facebook friends was by now quite considerable, with over 2000 worldwide followers. It later transpired that clandestine investigations were being made at this time to discover the human presumed responsible for the ghost writing of the cat. Enquiries were also made to find out where her Facebook page was located, and who was responsible for its maintenance.

Deputations were then sent to the Cat Committee and a project team established to look into the possibilities of a refurbishment of Olly's kennel. Following the formation of the project team an 8-page project brief is commissioned and published on the 20th August 2010. Created by 'Vector Design Concepts', the brief summarises the main parameters of acceptability: 'It has to look like a piece of street art', the document announces, so that 'those who hate her can appreciate the art, those who love her can appreciate the new Olly house'. Also important was the clause that 'It has to be fitting to be outside the Head Office of a multi million pound business'. It seemed that her existing house was the cause of some difficulties and embarrassment because it 'gets buried in blankets that then get sprayed by foxes, other cats etc. and it then smells like we have a permanent tramp outside our building'.

In responding to some of these issues the brief proposes an outline design inspired by a set of principles and a 'philosophy' that sought to incorporate the aesthetics of flight/aviation. The design proposes a sculpture crafted from the latest acrylic materials that seems to replicate the contemporary 'glass and steel' minimalism of corporate architecture (see Dale and Burrell 2008). Here, the detailing of the design and its renderings is remarkable. The design development of the base unit, for example, reflects the accommodation and integration of a multiplicity of interacting variables. It is noted that cats will not sleep and eat in the same space, and so the designers advance a tripartite structure made up of a 'sleeping zone', a 'feeding zone' and a 'watering hole'. This is a structure that recalls the zoning of an earlier terminal retail scheme, and also that of the Escape Lounge project. The watering hole is particularly impressive. Designed to be replenished from rainwater collected from the roof, the ingenious design proposes a system based on running water – 'as cats prefer it', the brief notes – which could be achieved by 'pumping the water through a carbon filter, then up to an outlet'. Most ingenious of all, the designers note that the 'water could act', in addition, 'as a method of cooling the sleeping zone in the summer months'.

The visuals supplied with 'the brief' suggest some hybrid architectural form combining elements of Zaha Hadid's dramatic swooping cantilevers and angular projections with the organic ribbons of Anish Kapoor. In this case one might say these ribbons appear tense and coiled, as if ready to *spring* and *leap* as the eye is led from the ground up to the sky where the sculpture culminates in a dramatic replica of a Boeing 747 on take-off. Much like the creative energies of the marketing and communications department, Vector design concepts seemed to harness and extend a form of 'curiosity' that was most unusual in Olympic House, a form that might best be described as the logic of 'and' (O'Doherty 2005) – a playful and lateral movement of ideas not driven by the usual iterative and linear sequencing of the PRINCE 2-type methodologies. The result of all this is a design that realises a strange human-animal-machine hybrid, something we might perhaps describe as a cat-becoming-kennel-becoming-aircraft.

What explains these creative energies and the monstrous form of this sculpture? Perhaps we might venture the idea that it was no one actor, no one species, but rather a *multi-species becoming*, where the cat appears to form part of a complex system of inspiration and creativity. However, what was perhaps most perplexing and beguiling was the fact that the ethnography could never establish how serious it all was. For a while I felt like the unnamed narrator in Poe's System of Dr. Tarr and Professor Fether. In a tale that has been the inspiration for others in Organization Studies (Sievers 1996), it slowly dawns on the reader that the narrator has been a victim of a charade, the wardens of the hospital having been imprisoned by the patients who have assumed the role of management and who then act as hosts for the visitor/narrator. Despite considerable effort to draw out my informants, it was impossible to ascertain whether this project, with all its creaturely creativity and inspiration was genuine, fake, wishful thinking, deliberately subversive, or parodic, or even in part designed for the appetite of 'the anthropologist'. In this sense there was a considerable ontological undecidability about the project. I recalled the furtive sideways glance of Bob as he opened her food-store and looked 'towards' Olly. Were Olly and Bob in cahoots? Was there a formal 'client' that had commissioned this project brief? The paperwork would suggest there was indeed a request made somewhere for a design brief. Would it likely be denied by more senior members of the executive team? There is no doubt that should it risk subsequent embarrassment, senior managers can be expected to have prepared a counter-rationale that would allow them to deny any involvement reflecting, perhaps, a version of what Munro (1995) called 'managing by ambiguity'.

At the same time, one is compelled to ask: how sincere was this project? How serious were members of the organization involved in the project to domesticate and then re-house the cat? These questions are difficult to answer and they remain key to the emerging sense of ontological undecidability. What could not be denied was that on July 27th 2011 workers arrived at Olympic House to find that Olly's home had been removed. The night before, the Manchester Evening News ran with the headline 'Claws come out as Manchester Airport chiefs show exit door to Olly the cat', and Olly's Facebook pages later verify the truth: 'Dear Friends ... I can confirm that I am being retired by the Airport as Olympic House Security Cat. I am very saddened by the news but unfortunately I do not have a choice ...'. Despite the careful media management and behind the scenes negotiations involving the RSPCA, the outpouring of protest and grief following this news was astonishing, a reaction that shook many members of the senior management team. A selection of the posts to Olly's Facebook conveys some of this emotion, reflecting a combination of disbelief, defiance, and despair:

> 'Olly will be going nowhere, she's part of the airport and so many people love her ... They'd (sic) be up roar I'm sure ... I'll fight for it'.
>
> 'Ollie belongs at Manchester Airport. We need to keep her there. How can they do this to her. She does not harm'.
>
> 'I called into Olympic House today and I got a lump in my throat & my eyes filled up with tears'
>
> 'Oh Olly I think my heart broke in two when I walked round the corner to find no trace of u tonight ...'
>
> 'Maybe it's time for a demo outside OLYMPIC HOUSE'
>
> 'I call a strike'

> 'I keep praying for a miracle ... I still keep checking outside of Olympic House to see if you're there Olivia my gorgeous chicksi!!!

How earnest is all of this? Well, the power of Olly seemed to attain even greater heights. Soon after the Olly's retirement Bob the receptionist fell ill and had to take extended time off work for respiratory problems. After more than 35 years of service Bob was soon forced to concede that he needed to take early retirement in June 2014. Did natural processes and the usual physiological deterioration of an aging body cause this illness? Or might we even speculate that there is some 'sympathetic magic' between the cat and human?

Bob was not the only one to be 'taken in' by the cat. One of the directors for learning and development also confessed that the true motivation for his resignation was the departure of Olly: 'It was the cat, Damian'. Adding another dimension to this tone of undecidability, she told her tale in ways that would not admit the separation of 'the literal' and 'the symbolic'. It was impossible to tell if Olly was being deployed *metaphorically* – as a surrogate though which to express otherwise disavowed or clandestine criticisms of the group under the new CEO – or whether the former director meant it was *literally* the cat that forced her resignation. One is still left asking whether the cat was a projection of human sentiment, or whether she helped teach her human companions ways of thinking that helped foment discontent with emerging corporate priorities.

Conclusion

In pursuing those dimensions of organization through which loungification is being enacted and organization reconstructed we have become more sensitive to a desiderata of ethnographic 'moments', fragments and shards that would ordinarily be ignored or displaced to the margins of our analysis. At times the ethnographic descriptions have invested considerable, almost obsessive attention to the minutia of management practices and everyday mundane matters – to things without clear form or definition, the unruly, the low, the dirty, the trivial and apparently insignificant. As the hold of our customary analytical categories and divisions began to break down, we followed lines of association not depicted on formal organizational charts. Lapel badges, screen savers, shopfront signage, uniforms, plastic spoons, an abandoned stationary cupboard, bronchial infection, and a stray cat – that could easily be dismissed as just a cute company 'mascot'. Things appear more inchoate and 'germinal' (Ansell-Pearson 1999) once analysis is able to track the set of associations in which they are bound and which connects up organization – or enacts organization – in ways very different from the customary organogram in business and management studies.

In this way we have been able to trace something of the difference brought to bear on organization by Olly the Cat as he/she was constructed at Manchester Airport 2007–2011 and as Manchester Airport was (re)constructed around her. Olly the cat has prowled these pages in a multiplicity of forms: from company mascot to subversive ally, object of sentimental projection, to saccharine emotionality. A 'resource' for the generation and mediation of competing agendas and differences in organization, she was anything but marginal or insignificant. Olly was discovered to be at the centre of a complicated and lively human-animal assembly that appeared to motivate often surprising actions and behaviours as she helped stimulate management and staff into ever-greater degrees of creativity and struggle. New potentialities and new capacities were realised out of this relationality as emergent properties of 'the human' and 'the animal' were mutually learnt and acquired. That members of the airport seemed to acknowledge Olly as a fully-fledged non-human actor means she cannot be confined to a world in which only the human acts or represents, nor to a world that the ethnographer can presume to fully represent or know. In many ways, Olly remains beyond representation, resisting and deflecting our desire for consistency and the unity of a single meta-narrative. This is all suggestive of the possibility that the 'nine lives' of the cat is not just an idle metaphor.

Politics at the airport is also made *different* because of the cat. At the same time, this politics – whilst inspired by the so-called ontological turn in the social sciences – would seem to fall short of this currently fashionable term. This is because there is nothing so definitive as an ontology, or even a well-defined series of *multi*-ontologies. Our exploration of Olly's adventures has helped isolate something more like an 'ontological undecidability', which has important implications for our understanding of the politics of loungification and the politics of organization more broadly. One dimension of this undecidability has become apparent in the doubts one is forced to consider about the seriousness of the 'Olly project', if we may call it thus. What are the intentions of the various actors? Do we end up in a space of resistance and parody? Or is it a space of management by other means? This was a question to which senior management also had to confront. Difficult to call one way or another, there was however no doubt that in misreading the complexities and subtleties of the organization that had formed around Olly, management triggered reactions that could have proven catastrophic. It was interesting that management had to adopt stealth-like tactics in finding ways of removing the cat. Might it be suggested that this is another sign of becoming-cat, where we learn to see/exercise stealth in ways akin to properties associated with the feline?

Another dimension of this undecidability concerns the fact that the same mundane practices and organizational infrastructure that helped realise the Olly project were also in use on more ostensibly serious projects like the Escape Lounge. Spreadsheets, project briefs, project management methodologies, architectural drawings and designs, and other bureaucratic resources – including committees and their paperwork and other accoutrements: all formed part of the Olly project. Like characters and objects in a David Lynch film, everything forms part of at least two diverging series where realities flicker between what is sometimes referred to as the conscious and the unconscious, or from shadow into light. As we have followed Olly through the corridors of power in Manchester Airport we have discovered that it is these 'elements' through which *multiplicity* is brought into being. Available to be used in a variety of ways the same elements perform different but co-emergent realities. This made it difficult to clearly demarcate out a series of distinctive or coherent ontological multiplicities at the level of something like organization. Instead, there was undecidability at a more disaggregated level – in the very mundane materials and artefacts of routine organizational life.

In sum, feline politics has helped trace a form of 'politics by other means' in organization. As a working concept it holds together an extended repertoire of actors and agents through which new resources and new collectivities are made available for mobilisation. As we have seen these mobilisations have the capacity to challenge existing relations of power and inequality. One might, for example, now take note of the images of cats collected in the 'wildlife' books sat on the shelf in the library of the Escape Lounge. Given our efforts in this chapter to map out an infrastructure of human-animal relations at the airport one might now see this appearance of cats as part of an extend 'ecology' of organization that harbours multi-species becomings. That this exercise in feline politics has given rise to what may appear 'monstrous' forms of thinking (Thanem 2011) is perhaps not surprising. However, seeing/being with the cat helps us learn of the multiple – both major and minor – modes of *enacting* organization. As this chapter itself became progressively more entangled in these human-animal relations we were able to glimpse what might amount to embryonic and alternative forms of *transport*. These are forms of transport that do not involve jet planes and foreign holidays but brings to bear another feature of loungification and its emerging politics. That these are found latent within the airport, widely condemned as a major culprit of climate change and global warming, is perhaps even more remarkable.

8

Conclusion: Reconstructing Organization

Two students are stood facing one another on the patio of Starbucks coffee shop on the university campus located on the officially designated 'knowledge-corridor' of Manchester. They are presumably Chinese students; at least they are speaking what sounds like Mandarin. It is the distance between the two students, seemingly observed and maintained with meticulous attention during their extended interaction that might first strike an ethnographic sensibility. They are joined by a third. 'Hey, Wassup'! Salutations, fist-bumps and 'the urban' hand clasp quickly follow, before a slight withdrawal from each other marked by mock-embarrassed smiles as their bodies do what contemporary urban dictionaries define as 'the goof'. Space accommodates as they form a shifting circle marked by gesture, feint, hands, heads lolling, leaning back, and laughing. Just goofing around. 'Hanging out'. They are predominantly dressed in denims, retro-Levi styled jeans, one with a knitted slouch Beanie, another sporting a 1954 James Dean cut pair of red tab 501 jeans, frayed and cut at the bottom leg openings to reveal sandstone yellow Timberland boots. Another has a red San Francisco '49ers' baseball cap, worn backwards 'catcher fashion' as they smoke stealth-style, shuffling their feet and drawing on their cigarettes, as if in a clandestine huddle.

D. O'Doherty, *Reconstructing Organization*,
DOI 10.1057/978-1-137-48922-7_8

Organization is being reconstructed here, and whilst the traces are feint the results of this ethnographic experiment in loungification should allow us to follow the threads a little easier. At first, one might be struck by the familiarity of their postures, but also perhaps the incongruities when broken down into more elemental detail and the movement this detail helps make evident. Perhaps best described as a kind of 'hangdog', I realise I have seen these postures and movements a hundred times before, as doubtless they have too, in a experience that reflects another example of Strathern's (1999) ethnographic moments.

Marcel Mauss (1973) recounts a similar episode. Confined to a hospital bed in New York, Mauss is inspired to consider where he had previously seen examples of the very distinctive way in which his nurses were walking. In a 'kind of revelation' he realised that it was in contemporary Hollywood film, which was promoting what he called an 'American walking fashion'. It didn't take long before this walk was adopted on the streets of Paris.

The television series *Friends* has a lot to answer for in the case of our Starbucks episode (Sadler and Haskins 2005), but it is a fashion I have come to understand to be an important component in this phenomenon of loungification that we have been attempting to study and navigate in this ethnography. The airport is perhaps the site in which loungification currently finds its clearest expression, but there are also signs of its formulation in the high streets of our cities in the UK where banks, shops, schools and universities are slowly being *loungified*. After Foucault (1977: 228) we might be tempted to ask whether it is any wonder these days that airport lounges resemble factories, schools, barracks, hospitals, which all resemble lounges.

But this reconstruction of organization is taking place in a dimension of organization still unfamiliar to most working within the discipline. 'Is it real?' the discipline asks. What we have followed is perhaps a zone of organization somewhere between the real and the non-real, a space of *realization* in which organization emerges to try and separate out the real from the un-real, a distinction that perhaps can only be learned by trying to make real. One sense of this 'making real' might be grasped from the reported discrepancy between the occupancy rates and commercial viability of 'Media City' in Manchester[1] circulating in various media. Reading this material would leave one in little doubt about the success of the lounge. Indeed, the Media City website presents a 'collection' of lounges that betrays an unremitting confidence in the capacity of the lounge to stimulate business activity. It certainly keeps a whole lot of marketers, website designers, and actors employed. Here we find people dressed in business suits, variously lounging, attending presentations and 'networking events', talking on mobile phones, and huddling around tables in break-out rooms. Apparently in earnest discussion about important business matters, some recline in leather sofas, or sit at desks making use of the digital facilities in the 'post production club'. 'It's a digital space for like-minded creative people and food lovers' reads the website, 'with opportunities for private hire and deal-making privacy'.

When following these traces of loungification we are reminded that the boundaries of the airport are flexible and expanding, reaching into the heart of the old terrestrial cities. Reconfiguring social practices and relations in ways that suggest we are all living 'life in the air' (Gottdiener 2001) – increasingly spending time preparing or recovering from the latest flight, or standing in a queue 'waiting for a bag search and pat down' (Fuller and Harley 2004: 48). Part shopping-centre and part prison, the airport is at the centre of profound changes in the way organization is being reconstructed. It changes the way we navigate and see the world. For some it is the centre of a 'topology of relations continuously folding and unfolding in and out of a multitude of dimensions' in 'a modulation that shapes the earth' and 'build[s] new worlds' (Fuller and Harley, ibid.: 108). Indeed, there are some who have taken permanent refuge 'airside' in the airport, which might eliminate any inconsistencies that reflect the legacy of pre-airport lives in cities and their environs. Perhaps we will learn to see these people as the first citizens of a new emerging post-national space for which existing nation state arrangements do not know what to do with. The case of Mehran Kerami Nasseri who lived for nearly 20 years in Paris Charles de Gaulle is perhaps only the most

[1] Media city in Manchester remains a contentious political issue, the press coverage of which paints a picture that rivals the intrigue and drama of the HBO television series, The Wire.

famous case of this apparent trend for 'termination' (Mehran and Donkin 2005). There are many others, one of whom might very well be this airport ethnographer.

The Business of Airport Growth: Beyond the Social

The growth of loungification might well be connected to this challenge of adapting to life lived in the permanent suspension of a queue. Yet while we queue, there is also danger at the borders. Given the carbon costs associated with air travel some see the expansion of airports and air-travel as short sighted and even apocalyptic (Bows and Anderson 2007; Bows et al. 2008). Yet, whilst there is big business in air-travel, airports will continue to expand. The argument that UK airports should not retreat from the international stage whilst no alternative and holistic model for a sustainable post-carbon economy exists to show how people will continue to enjoy the kind of lifestyle they have come to expect as their right also persists as powerful rhetoric. Expansion will happen anyway, it is claimed, with or without the UK,[2] and the industry can best exercise influence in the development of low carbon technological solutions by continuing to participate on the international stage of aviation. Hence, if the industry claims best to represent the needs of travellers, whilst also championing the mitigation effects of enlightened UK aviation expansion, we need to understand why people travel and why they desire international flights if we want to explore ways of reducing the desire for air travel. What is the promise and allure of airports and air-travel? More basic than this: what is happening to us at the airport? On the other hand, what elements of an alternative future might be evident at the airport?

---

[2]An argument that forms part of the recent evidence compiled by the UK Davies Airports Commission. Ostensibly commissioned in response to pressures articulated by many in the industry to develop a 3rd runway at Heathrow Airport, the formal remit of the Davies Commission was to consider whether the UK needs further aviation expansion, and if so how the country can best accommodate this. Despite the publication of the final report with its recommendation that Heathrow be expanded (July 2015), no political decision has yet been made (September 2016), reflecting the impassioned nature of the public controversy that also threatens electoral consequences and internal party political wrangling for the Conservative party.

Loungification is one attempt to answer these questions, an answer made possible by the development of an experimental form of ethnography committed to the recovery of immanence in organization (Deleuze 2001). The intricacy of the descriptions that come out of this ethnography contrasts markedly with most efforts to understand the desire for air-travel in which it is variously seen an expression of personal identity and/or the disciplinary effects of structural norms (Randles and Mander 2009; Hibbert et al. 2013; Griggs and Howarth 2014; Young et al. 2014). Yet, few of these studies understand how the *business* of making consumers and products works in practice, and they show little appreciation of the problem of organization. Many understand that choices and tastes are historical and contingent, which become either embedded psychologically in existential identity attachments or structurally consolidated in social norms and 'hegemonic' discourse that is deemed to serve the interests of capital and prevailing political settlements. However, this deference to a landscape of modern sociology, where things like society, context, political economy, structure and agency still preside, inhibits the reach of the explanation in these studies.

Much of this sociological repertoire certainly finds its limits when trying to understand loungification. Here there is no 'Social', and following the practices which help develop and extend this way of being in the world leads to nothing that would reassure us that something like a 'wider context' exists to determine or restrain and shape such activities. Nor are these activities 'social' *as such*, and the activities we have explored in this book might better be characterised as post-social (Knorr-Cetina 1997), involving cats, talking chairs, Wii machines, data doppelgangers, and crinicultural struggles. Indeed, assuming there is such a thing as 'context' or 'the social' precisely helps to maintain a modern sociological illusion that works to discipline and confine the possibilities for change (Bauman 1989). Ethnography is able to discover that members of organization are not quite so disciplined by modern social theory and social sciences as those who profess expertise in the academy. However, it takes a commitment to ethnography in order to tease out the empirical subtleties and nuances of this practical deconstruction of modern social science.

Ethnography in Business and Management Studies: Seeing the World Anew

Prospects for ethnography remain in a state of high uncertainty in the business school. Despite the recent upsurge of interest in management and Organization Studies (Kostera 2007; Neyland 2008; Ybema et al. 2009; Czarniawska 2012; Garsten and Nyqvist 2013),[3] ethnography runs against the grain of many prevailing assumptions about studying business. This reflects a wider problem within the discipline of Management and Organization Studies, which faces a difficult and uncertain future itself. In part, the difficulty of Organization Studies arises because of its location in the contemporary Business School. As noted by many, some of the most conservative assumptions about business continue to be generated in the business school serving to promote and maintain a mainstream that restricts and inhibits what can be said and done (Khurana 2007; Muff et al. 2013; Steyaert et al. 2016). This is ironic because even the most superficial survey of the business world would suggest that it is far from the sober world depicted in the MBA syllabus. It is surely beyond an open 'secret' these days that guns, drugs and pornography – if they don't quite make the world go around – remain the most profitable businesses in the world. Only those prepared to sacrifice the institutional comforts of the academy seem willing to think and speak of how much of contemporary business relies on 'excess, play and pataphysics' (Rehn 2013). It is the patience of ethnography, however, that is perhaps best able to tease out the intricate ways in which the familiar is being rendered strange (and vice-versa) by contemporary management and organization.

At one time it was airports that promised to see the world anew. Gateways to the future, part of the infrastructural building of twentieth century nation states, they opened out into a jet-set age of international if not post-national modes of being, complete with all the hopes and ambitions for modern utopia (Pascoe 2001). Yet, if utopia is a non-place, then so too is the airport (Augé 1995). So close to dystopia, the contemporary airport has become a space of extraordinary passions and

[3] Including the launch of two new journals in 2012, the *Journal of Organizational Ethnography* and the *Journal of Business Anthropology*.

contradictions. Indeed, we must beware making declarative statements about what an airport 'is'. As Koolhaas (2002) has shown, the airport remains a 'Bermuda triangle' for concepts. However, at least in some respects we might see the airport as an on-going experiment, a construction site to a future that fewer and fewer people seem to have faith or commitment.

In addition to these futures, the airport deposits around it the ruins of an older industrial heritage. Bleached white car parks soaked in sodium light extending out far beyond the horizon, windswept corridors of hotels and logistics centres, warehouses and concrete flyovers, the airport seems a bleak and soulless place, a 'junkspace' of disorientation and deconstruction (Koolhaas, ibid.). Its montage of spaces and different temporalities is perhaps only the most superficial of the disorientating effects of the airport. Yet, it is this very *flattening* of the landscape that is revealing. Not simply destructive, this flattening is also generative of new and unexpected forms of being.[4] Loungification is perhaps one of these forms of being, and despite its apparently innocuous and benign pleasures we have seen how the rise of this phenomenon poses a tremendous challenge to business and management.

Critical Management Studies

Critical Management Studies has been the most vociferous and arguably the most successful in its challenge to the mainstream world of business, advancing a form of organization analysis that acknowledges the inevitable political assumptions and consequences of all forms of theory and method. However, it now provides a series of its own master tropes that practitioners have become increasingly adept at moving around like ready-made formulas to summarily explain what is wrong with contemporary business and management: emancipation, neo-liberal capitalism, globalization, power and inequality, poverty, discrimination, suffering, oppression, etc. These are big sounding words that give its users a sense of

[4] Tsing (2014) has recently turned towards the exploration of emerging life forms in what she calls 'blasted landscapes'.

purpose and moral righteousness. And there is certainly enough violence, poverty, and suffering in the world to feel indignation and to seek to want to hold someone or something accountable.[5] However, it finds its limits when confronted with something like 'loungification' to which it would probably settle on the label 'decadence', 'subjugation', or 'pretension' as a critique.

Such judgements and an increasingly mechanistic application of *a priori* analytical categories, which often duplicate the categories of those they castigate as mainstream, mean that empirical enquiry conducted under the supervision of critical management studies offers little surprise for researchers. Moreover, in the prosecution of the current critical agenda students learn or grasp little of what might be *new* in organization.[6] Hence, for a variety of reasons what has recently been called the 'event' of organization gets missed (Bohm 2006; Papadopoulos 2010; Beyes and Steyaert 2013). To seize the evidential traces of this 'event' demands the sacrifice of utopian and 'strong' politics and a capacity to dwell in unknowingness. Such ignorance motivates empirical enquiry to a radical immanence where one can explore the ever-finer lines of connection and association that hold us in organization.

Efforts to promote reflexivity, de-naturalisation and anti- or critical performativity (Fournier and Grey 2000; Spicer et al. 2009, 2016; Alvesson and Spicer 2012; Cabantous et al. 2016), and a recent interest in developing a 'more mature politics' (Grey 2005),[7] are promising, but it seems that strong politics and strong theory inevitably inhibit the messy and agonisingly slow work of empirical enquiry. In this enquiry we have been unable to find either an author or culprit upon which to hang responsibility for loungification, and this poses problems to the critically motivated. More recent post-humanist extensions to the mainstream of critical management studies do much to extend its ontological complexity

[5] Occasional pieces wrangle with self-loathing as critical scholars work out their own implication in what they see as the corruptions of the salaried and professional middle classes benefiting from corporate managed pension funds and promoting multinational publishing and media companies (Wray-Bliss 2002; Bell and King 2010; Harvie et al. 2012).

[6] On the other hand see the important paper by Pullen and Rhodes (2010) on 'neophilia' in organization studies.

[7] Which is not without its own moralizing and disciplinary tone.

showing the entanglements of human and non-human which problematize simplistic desire for emancipation. Even here though, and in what amounts nevertheless to a serious adjunct to current critical management studies, the desire to ask '*who* controls collective self-transformation' (Papadopolous 2010) would appear to resume a battle of humanist proportions, even if the aspiration is for *post-humanist* emancipation.

Throughout this study we have been confronted with what we called earlier the 'post-social' (Knorr-Cetina, 1997) nature of loungification where objects appear to enjoy something resembling what the humanist tradition calls agency. In this study of the lounge we have not found any simple 'determinism' by objects and matters, which is the fear of many in critical studies[8] when analysis seeks to acknowledge the possibility that objects, technologies or 'the technical' enjoy a certain degree of difference and autonomy. Granting this difference and autonomy, however, calls for an extension of our cognitive faculties to realise possibilities that may lie beyond the capacity for collective 'ideal speech' in human relations. In an attempt to nurture this extension, this study sought to pursue with some obstinacy this conceptual and practical ethnographic experiment in loungification.

This was a concept initially launched by means of a modest inflection or deflection of the term 'lounge', which for some might recall Heidegger's enigmatic notion of a *Verwindung*.[9] Giving rise to a different mode of engaging with organization, loungification provides no judgment or moral high ground. Indeed, only if we can suspend this desire for judgment and moralising is it possible to explore the creative opportunities available in our own analytical entanglement in and *enactment* of organization (O'Doherty 2015; cf. Mol 2002). There is a kind of *submission*

[8] Perhaps also keen to avoid accusations of returning to a form of structure or structural determinism.

[9] In the Stambaugh translation (2002) of the passage in *Identität und Differenz* (1957: 15) this is rendered 'Such a transformation [Verwindung] of the frame [Ge-Stells] into the event of appropriation [Ereignis], by virtue of that event, would bring the appropriate recovery – appropriate, hence never to be produced by man alone – of the world of technology from its dominance back to servitude in the realm by which man reaches more truly into the event of appropriation' (Heidegger 2002:37). However, *Verwindung* is better appreciated when placed in its full range of cognate and etymological associations in German, which can be rendered as: winding, twisting, twisting out, like a coil.

in this method, which resists the imposition of an entirely abstracted and etic terminology whose full meaning and implication is known only to an elite community of academics.[10] And there can be no doubt we have entered some pretty peculiar thinking, at least peculiar from the perspective of a business school. As the study progressed we have had to contend with 'MAG men' and talking chairs, various existential data doubles and doppelgangers, angular reasoning, and disjunctive synthesis, but also disorderly convulsions and scattered attention, criniculturalpolitics, and feline becomings. Does this not amount to the construction of an equally abstracted theoretical armature? However, designed for the purposes of intervention and a certain enactment of organization, their 'political' capacity is one that works to recover immanence. Can we draw a plane of immanence specific to the airport? If so, I think loungification does some of this work, but its concepts and theories must soon be cast to one side as we shift the focus of our ethnographic attention from airports to other sites of business and management as starting points for ethnographic enquiry.

Airports and the Realm of the Fantastic

We should, however, not be surprised by the proliferation of such fantastical creatures in the airport. This is, after all, a privileged site of *extra-terrestrial* transformations, of the transmutation of the earth-bound into the realm of air where 'dreams of flight' and a 'poetics of wings' finds expression (Bachelard 1988; Pascoe 2001; Schaberg 2012, 2015). The airport terminal is part depository and part generator of these fantasies,

[10] It took this ethnographer about 12 months of full time fieldwork to shed the baggage of theoretical concepts and an overarching explanatory framework inherited from theoretical academic work conducted over 15 years of scholarship prior to entering the airport. Only once this emptying out had been achieved was I able to make progress empirically and ethnographically, allowing the people, the spaces and materials of the ethnography to guide me in my quest for understanding. The etymology of this term *under-standing* is telling because we might liken the practice of organization analysis developed in this study to practices of study implied by an emerging *post*-foundational discourse, in which learning proceeds when it acknowledges there is nothing to stand on, or rather it proceeds only when it can practically participate in the ongoing making of *something*. One might follow here Mark Taylor's (1995) notion of *inter-standing* that Cooper was fond of citing (Cooper 1997: 698; 1998: 129–143; 2001).

and if one thinks business and management the preserve of the sober and rational, then we would be forced to think again by the seriousness with which management prosecutes its business at the airport with concepts such as 'Manchester Experience' or 'the Manchester vibe'. Even this seems relatively tame in contrast to the spirit of shamanic metamorphosis which has been recently conjured in the terminal at Vancouver International where two huge native Indian totem poles and a sculpture of the 'Spirit of Haida Gwaii' invite passengers to stroll and lounge. Yet following the managers working on the design and construction of the Escape Lounge provides the conditions in which creatures equally as fantastic as 'the raven' or the 'mouse woman' depicted in the Haida Gwai sculpture come into being. For our managers the talk was of things like 'the market' and 'the business', 'shareholder value', 'alpha territory' people, 'suburban mindsets' and 'soccer mums and dads', all fantastic in themselves, but also formed out of practices and debates that are worthy of the same reverence and awe we usually reserve for traditional anthropological study. The investment of time to extract and identity 512 discrete stages of a project through which projects like the Escape should be 'charted', for example, led to debates of ever finer gradations in scholarship and subtlety amongst members of MAG projects. Folly in many respects, this desire for total representation was simultaneously an exercise in infinite regress and proliferation, the apparent absurdity of which draws comparisons to Kafka, who for some is the most astute 'theorist' of management (Warner 2007; Munro and Huber 2012; McCabe 2015). Yet, the defamiliarisation of the everyday achieved in this study of the Escape Lounge has not been forged by any contrary frivolity inspired by irony, but rather has been realised by way of an experimental approach to ethnography.[11]

This study began with an experiential lesson that showed how despite being immersed theoretically in prevailing 'poststructural' theory, when it came to making progress in understanding how organization worked at

[11] In an early finding I discovered that my interlocutors were more effective ethnographers than I (see chapter 2). A paper in progress works out some of the implications of putting concepts into circulation amongst those to whom the concepts were in part deployed in an effort to understand them. In many ways this reflexivity and enactment is a logical procedure in any ethnography, in which questions, phrasings and lines of enquiry emerge out of the often-tense relationships one forms with so-called 'informants'.

Manchester Airport Group I could not escape a more basic default position that prioritised people, identities and roles. Here, whatever might be understood, or explained theoretically, *experientially* it still made sense to think of organization as something bounded and confined by the immediate space of an employer and a workplace. However, these experiences typically *severed* relations between what might be divided as local practices from 'the bigger picture', context, or political economy, to which the critical school still defer when looking to locate what they call the 'forces' and 'relations of production' and to explain more local instantiations of production and reproduction. Wedded to such preoccupations also encourages the quest for a deep or hidden truth. In what remains a quite tautological discourse, the critical school is quick to rationalise any ignorance or denial of this truth. Typically their default explanation will evoke concepts such as 'subjugation' or an appeal to various other strategies of displacement and obfuscation to which non-critical members of organization are presumed vulnerable.

All this meant that I was unable to see the significance of what was opening up around me during the Escape Lounge project. Specifically, this was a vast chain of connections being practically crafted, instantiated, created and modified in ways that transgressed any divide between the macro and micro (Callon and Latour 1981; Latour 2005a). Early in the project, the term 'MAG men' was coined in an effort to suspend judgment and to follow the work of translating and connecting performed by my informants. This proved helpful in finding a way to retain local specificity without succumbing to an off-the-shelf conceptual category that could explain it away in terms of an all encompassing and domesticating macro context or an all conquering historical dialectic. 'MAG men' helped take the study beyond a preoccupation with the domestic career machinations and organizational politics and towards a greater consideration of reflexively enacted practices – practices in which I was increasingly implicated as an ethnographer. This concept also helped build *empathy* for a form of life for which critical studies are more often contemptuous. The work of building concepts is reflexively achieved and efficacious and if it is a truism that every way of looking at organization is a way of *not* looking, then we need to add that there is no looking *without acting and enacting*.

Organizational Movement: Loungification Beyond the Micro/Macro

Whilst studying how managers treat paperwork it became obvious that what I was studying was in no sense confined to *local* micro practices. In fact I was watching the effects of Microsoft Office and Google search engines, PowerPoint, CAD/CAM design software, Prince2 methodology, building construction practices, national legal 'frameworks', and even nation state formation in the form of such things as security practices, passports, and Department for Transport inspections and guidance documents. The macro was intertwined with the micro, the local in the global, in what some have sought to characterise as 'the glocal' (Czarniawska 2004a).

In turn, there appeared to be nothing more substantial or foundational to all this than on-going practices and thin trails of paper, sometimes found on office desks, but normally stored as word docs or pdfs on hard drives and server space. Without their continued reference, use, and circulation, they would disappear. In tracing back some of the explicit terms of the JCT (the Joint Council Tribunal) 'design and build contract', for example – used for the contracting of the construction of the lounge – we would find nothing more than paper in circulation. This takes the form of emerging case law verdicts published in specialist trade magazines, for example, but all of which was subject to interpretation, revision and amendment. Since Wittgenstein we know that routines and rule following are far from a passive transmission realised by 'cultural dopes'. Similarly, law is clearly not a legal *framework*, but more of a practice.

If the 'local' is always implicated in the 'global' – then loungification maps out a unique configuration in its interstice, and one through which we can trace emerging organizational patterns implicated in what Latour (2005a) calls a 'reassembly of the social'. Existing between a whole series of prevailing analytical and categorical divisions in Organization Studies, loungification is easy to miss. Its 'movement' or pattern of organization remains inaccessible to Management and Organization Studies because it does not observe the boundaries in which the subject has sought to establish its academic and disciplinary distinction. Typically, Organization Studies remains preoccupied with discrete work practices confined within an employment organization.[12] In making claims to this unique object of study, the subject can perhaps justify a disciplinary originality that is not simply derivative of the work done in departments of social science (Parker 2000a, Rowlinson and Hassard 2011). However, we unnecessarily restrict the study of organization if we see it as subordinate to a place of work, an employer organization, an economic form, or any of the ways in which organization gets domesticated in ways that are familiar to business and management. More fruitful is to consider organization as something *beyond* any instantiation in a business or a managed organization.[13]

In following the patterns of organization in the interstices of formal analytical categories we soon realise that we must also allow for the *dissolution* of our customary boundaries that demarcate materials, technologies, practices, and people, so that we can begin to tackle processes and movements taking place at a more basic pre-divided realm whose phenomena is marked by greater ontological confusion. When we engage with organization in this dimension we find that the typified categories of division and definition in the social sciences consistently fail to achieve much purchase. In part this is because organization is so messy in this state – inchoate, nascent, and experimental. This extends to the very notion of 'a social', still routinely deployed as a description of something *inside of which* organization is located. By contrast, Loungification marks a 'movement' *across* or *through* this divide between 'social context' and what is presumed more micro content (text, as opposed to context). Around this movement their gathers (partly) new actors, new capacities and energies, new products and services. If it becomes any more popular we might be justified in the claim that out of this organization there is emerging new *ways of being-in-the-world*. In other words, 'the social' is always a convenient reification that detracts from the processes and events in which 'the social' is always beginning anew.

In this regard it is helpful to recall that the airport is often thought of as a space of endings and new beginnings (Schaberg 2012) and – as we

[12] This was seen to be one of the limitations of current thinking in the promising turn to the empirical study of materialities and 'practice' in organization analysis that follows 'practice-theory' (Nicolini 2012; Carlile et al. 2013; cf. Gad and Jensen 2014).

[13] In other words, we might be better to reverse our normal assumptions and work with the idea that business is made *out of* organization, or a cutting of its network (Strathern 1996).

shall see – in this dimension of organization we are certainly compelled to always begin anew.

An Ontological Turn

In following the recent 'ontological turn' in the social sciences we have been able to identify and study these movements in more extended dimensions of organization. Our study of loungification has helped extract those relations that make organization *reality making*, and treating it as anything less seems to diminish the scope of our engagement with organization. The ethnographer is necessarily implicated in this and as we have followed the emergence of new expertise in lounge management, original ways of inhabiting space, novel ways of relating to people and things, and emergent new social and existential struggles, we have also had to contend with the possibility that this ethnography is implicated in making this ontologically more credible.

This has implications for one of the key concepts in the critical school, namely 'power', which is normally mobilised to indicate how the on-going reproduction of business and capital maintains social elites and 'structured' inequality. However, as this study sought to follow and understand the rise of new sources of expertise, career, and power, being forged out of loungification, a far more *relational* view of power began to emerge. Incipient forms of management were new because – in part – there was strictly no subject (a lounger) or object (a lounge) prior to the opening of the lounge and around which management could enjoy established expertise. New objects and new subjects are mutually constitutive and management is also partly their outcome, rather than originator or agent. Without a stable subject/object relation management will necessarily be surprised by what comes out of this co-emergence of lounge and lounger.

As management is slowly reconstructed around the lounge it is forced to grapple with a bewildering array of new materials, capacities, energies and knowledge. Management rapidly finds itself out of its depth when confronted with this heterogeneity and we noted that things have a nasty habit of 'coming out of the woodwork' during the course of a project. Moreover, one outcome of this, namely the 'lounger', remains always unfinished and unpredictable and as we saw potentially dangerous, which was something recognised in older studies of the rise of the hotel 'lounger' (Hayner 1928).[14] New dress codes, contracts and 'behavioural' policies came into existence soon after the opening of the Escape Lounge, all of which is suggestive of the unanticipated and unprecedented mutations that follow the birth of a new subject.

By attending to a more extended ontology of organization we were also able to identify that the dangers of the lounge do not simply lie with human agents, or the unintended consequences of action. Instead it is the new, unknown and unknowable hybrids, or man-machine assemblages, that are becoming dangerous in their activism and animation: talking chairs, sofa disease, compulsive lounging, or something that members of the airport referred to as 'airport brain', etc. It is difficult to say to whom we might attribute cause or intentionality to these outcomes, and hence its *danger* – in part because it makes remedial action difficult to focus or target. In attributing some of the cause of this behaviour to the lounge itself we avoid a blame or judgemental position of critique that extends the scope for the politicisation of the lounge.

However slight or marginal these new 'forms' of behaviour and management, to grasp phenomenon in a state in which our normal assumptions of causation and cause-effect, subject/object, macro/micro, structure/agent etc. are in suspense, requires its own contingent and disposable 'site-specific' concepts. Such concepts seem even more urgent when we cannot even rely on simple economic calculations of price to get a fix on what is happening during the purchase of materials during the construction of the lounge. In these conditions it seemed that there were no laws of demand and supply; indeed the separation of demand and supply seemed a dubious assumption, and certainly there was little evidence of the operation of a hidden hand or Walrasian auctioneer serving to spontaneously derive a market price for lounge entrance (Callon 1998). Perhaps it is the fear of economics and/or 'envy' (i.e. Pfeffer 1993) that has discouraged Organization Studies from a study of the practices and practical technicalities of economic theory, which is remarkable because it takes an astonishing amount of organization to establish a market 'rate'

[14] As a new form of travel it recalls those contemporary studies of the impact of the railway and rail travel on subjectivities and social relations (Schivelbusch 1980).

for a good or service (Callon and Muniesa 2005; Muniesa 2007; Çalişkan 2010). If demand and supply cannot be separated in practice, drawing a clear line between client and contractor proved equally difficult. There was not even an apriori business case to help guide practices. We discovered how the 'business case' was dependent on 'the market' – i.e. what would an airport customer want of an airport lounge and what would they be willing to pay. To acquire this information required some budget. And those working at the airport were also well aware of the *performative* effect of their enquiries. During the bid to purchase Gatwick airport, for example, Manchester management discovered that merely making a telephone call to solicit the price had an effect on the offer price.

It is more readily understandable how all of this confusion of boundaries and distinctions contributes to the outbreak of 'disorderly convulsions' – which remains a phenomenon rarely observed in studies of management and organization. This study of the lounge found that management is not a technical abstraction, as mainstream and critical management studies seem to concur. It makes more sense to think of management as a practice in a perpetual crisis of identity. Not because of any underlying existential anxiety and its theoretical metanarratives (Watson 1994; Knights and Willmott 1999), but by virtue of its organizational position, sitting somewhere between the ideals of abstraction and the entanglements of practice. Roles, responsibilities, and positions, as depicted in the ideal typical organogram of reporting lines and governance structure, are partly suspended, and all subject to intricate trials and tests during the process of a project (Muniesa and Lindhardt 2011). Who has authority, what the objectives are, and what the respective responsibilities might be in management are all being enquired, tested and worked out amongst multiple combatants, some human, some non-human. The sheer unpredictability of all this and its shifting balance of power – in which the ethnographer must also tread with care – can be understood to be largely responsible for the disorderly convulsion we witnessed during the management of the construction of the lounge.

Most of the time management does not of course convulse, at least not visibly or in any evidentially obvious way! Instead, the most successful of managers working in conditions of such uncertainty exercise something like a form of 'scattered attention' that allows them to retain a degree of scepticism and even agnosticism about information and data. This repose provides the conditions in which management is able to advance a project by way of 'angularity' – the capacity to take apparent deviations and digressions through translation and association, and sometimes even transgressions, often unprecedented and incalculable in nature. This helps us understand how strange hybrid phenomena – part object/part subject, confusions of the animate/inanimate, the human/ and non-human – emerge as a form of 'disjunctive synthesis'.[15] Only such incredulous phenomena it seems are adequate to the challenge of multiple, competing and often incompatible pressures which arise during a project. The 'Manchester vibe' or the 'Manchester experience' was one such phenomenon and we tracked the way in which a kind of agreement was reached between the different parties to a project around this object. At the same time we noted this agreement was achieved in part by what appeared to be a collective and judicious deferral to silence (cf. Mol 2002; Moreira 2006).

Studying these practices, one realises that it is not only the human who has voice. At times, voice is *invested* or projected into objects in ways that reflect a kind of anthropomorphism; but there were also voices that transpired which seemed to speak a language not entirely familiar – at least not familiar to all the participants. It might be better to say that voice and thinking emerged out of a socio-technical assemblage in the form of *loungification-thoughts* or *loungified-thinking*. If the 'mosquito can speak' of political economy, as Mitchell (2002) finds, then what of BRATA – the tool of imaginization deployed during early design conception? This seemed to give rise to ideas that were not typical of management at the airport and it seems reasonable to conclude from this that bodies and minds were being taken into alternative ways of being during the lounge design. This should not be surprising. In part this was the very ambition the project team intended for the 'Escape lounge'. This is where we first got a glimpse of something that called out for a

[15] Inspired by Deleuze and Guattari of course, disjunctive synthesis is used here in a completely different way. Whilst it is not a subject who synthesises in the disjunctive synthesis, but instead the subject who emerges out of disjunctive synthesis, for Deleuze and Guattari (1983) the disjunctive synthesis is coined to explain the historical emergence of what they call the barbaric, imperial society in which the states *overcodes* the flux of desire.

concept that could keep our attention focused on what was happening between all our customary analytical categories. *Who* or *what* was thinking? Was management in part created and caused by the lounge? Were their specific features of management practice that might best be attributed to the lounge? Remember there were no customers for this product, and hence our analysis needed something to capture what was processual and emergent, open ended in nature. It is this which in part explains why loungification was forged and deployed as an active form of ethnographic practice and exploration, a practical experiment in some ways that allowed us to navigate the world of airports in a different way, somewhat angular to the customary ways in which organization is traversed and treated in empirical enquiry.

The Politics of Loungification

What of the politics of the loungification? And what does politics add to our understanding of organization more generally? On one level, loungification is but one mode of ordering an airport (Knox et al. 2008). But within this mode there are also multiplicities immanent to and at play in the Escape lounge which cannot be so easily confined to the neat identification of a 'mode'. The zoning of the lounge, for example, designed to accommodate different needs of business, leisure, families, children, etc. is indicative of the way that different *types* of loungers – or sub-loungers – are brought into being. We have followed some of the tensions and antagonisms that emerge between these different sub-modalities of ordering in the lounge. One repercussion of this fractious multiplicity is that alongside emotional and aesthetic lounge-hostess skills, there is also a need for lounge managers to train staff to think in terms of 'crowd management'. Dress codes, behavioural policies, exclusion policies, strict policing of the free food, and particularly the free drink, was suggestive that the invitation to Escape produced behaviour that was not always deemed appropriate. Judgemental and moralistic responses amongst lounge staff were not untypical, but finding ways of evading this practice as an ethnographer allowed this analysis to raise questions about the dangers and seductions associated with these new spaces without casting judgement as to what is good and bad, excessive, indulgent, aspirational, nouveau-riche, snobbery, or what have you. In a move similar to the dictum not to blame the victim (albeit without the judgement of victim), we were able to see the lounge as a complex socio-technical assemblage in which agency was distributed, multiplied and confused across human and non-human entities. Lounging clearly does not come easily to many people. Does it have its dangers? The profusion of materials from advertising, legal contracts, magazines, and the 'coaching' offered by the lounge hostesses, worked in part to shape and discipline the emerging lounger, of course, but this was never entirely successful.

There is another politics to this loungification, and this refers to the proliferation of lounges that is transforming our high streets, workplaces, banks, and universities. Even the presumed apex of British political power was found to bear traces of this loungification. However, of most significance for the advance of a new politicisation of Organization Studies is the discovery that power was being generated *through* the lounge. In many ways, power is not *apriori*. Tracing this requires the methods of an ethnographer, who can move transversally across different domains and expertise. 'Vertical' understandings of power, in what Foucault (1980) might call the legacy of a prevailing sovereign and juridical view of power, can only see the congealment or crystallisation of inherited power. When its 'organization' becomes evident, the politics comes late, too late. In order to understand emerging tensions and changes, research has to find a way of sticking to the 'surface' of social practices where new passions and energies are being created[16] but not yet inscribed into existing categories and institutions of politics for their articulation. Here Organization Studies acquires another important contribution to understanding the politics of loungification, leaving traditional departments of political science to map the constitutional and bureaucratic procedures of power.

[16] Working with the resources of Stoic thinking, Deleuze writes in the 'Fifteenth series of Singularities' that 'everything happens at the surface' and drawing on the structure of crystals as an illustration of the way he wants to develop his thinking on material formations more widely (and later social formations) adds 'which develops only on the edges' (Deleuze 1990: 103). Formations and organization happens laterally, there is no underlying foundation (genetics, laws, dialectics) or structure that pre-determines, shapes or influences their development.

Politics as it is understood in Organization Studies is still preoccupied with charting the contours of freedom and constraint (or structure and agency in modern sociological terms) as this finds expression in terms of class, gender, ethnicity, etc. In contrast to this Kantian and Lockean inheritance, following the practices invested in the Escape Lounge encourages analysis to explore a space *prior* to or *tangential* to this division. If there is no subject, there is no object, and constraints in the form of contract stipulations and behavioural rules all come after 'the event' – the effects of which are still traceable in the always-surprising twists and turns in behaviour and subject formation. Current organization analysis would find it difficult to track the coming-into-being of new subject positions such as 'the lounger' – in part because 'the lounger' is simultaneously co-emergent with its object, namely the lounge.

Evidence of this co-emergence is difficult because it is only found dispersed in a vast and heterogeneous range of objects, artefacts and practices, and the connections that might reveal patterns that form a recognisable figure cannot be found through the rote application of established concepts. Hence, loungification will not register in most Organization Studies because – for at least during the period of its formation – it does not appear in the form of habitual analytical social science dualisms such as structure or agency. In these dimensions of organization where loungification is most active, politics is not something contextual or 'higher' but in a process of being reanimated through the intimacy and immanence of organizational practice. Insofar as politics is about power and the generation and allocation of resources, then clearly something political is happening in loungification where new techniques of calculation brings with it new divisions, new knowledges, new centres of expertise, new forms of management, and new social imaginaries (cf. de Vries 2007; Latour 2007).

With this in mind this study of the lounge has experimented with the possibility of an emerging 'crinicultural politics', which maps an interesting line of assembly around new knowledge practices, bodies and materialities. In some respects this politics of hair in organizations is easy to grasp. Goffman's (1961) study of total institutions, for example, showed the importance of shaving as a ritual of initiation into a new role – when joining the army, for example, or being admitted onto a psychiatric ward. When the Beatles stepped off PanAm flight 101 at JFK airport in February 1964, it was their 'mop-tops' that attracted as much 'Beatlemania' as the songs, and there can be little doubt of a politics at play here where the reorganization of tastes and consumer habits brings with it new social groups and new 'political' interests.

Hair forms an important part of the loungification of society, in part it serves as a focus for the tension of the public/private division which is being transformed and turned inside out by the proliferation of lounges (Warner 2002). Again, mapping this network crosses all kinds of micro/macro and other such allied dualisms and divisions, and takes us into the institutions of 'high' government in ways that analytically slice them open in ways otherwise not possible. In this process this transversal movement helps render analysis more sensitive to process and movements in which the slightest tremor or disturbance might register and stand out as worthy of further explortion. We noted that for Hilary Clinton, hair-styling was one of the most important ingredients of success in politics. Like discussions about the weather, such preoccupations seem to form a kind of 'social' background of low-level noise, but through the machinations of the crinicultural there can be little doubt that we are being targeted and judged, allied with some groups, whilst being opposed to others.[17] If silently organized by the crinicultural, matters also gets out of hand as we discovered the active, agency-like properties of hair. For some it can produce existential renewal, new outlooks on life, and even new identities. How much political support someone like Boris Johnson is able to muster on its basis is perhaps an indication of the power of this crinicultural.

As yet we have been unable to identify a distinctive 'lounge style'; the lounge it seems can accommodate all kinds of hairstyle. As management begins to adopt more 'relaxed' dress codes and alternative hairstyling, we might have cause to wonder about the direction of causality. Is the lounge as outcome of management, or is management, rather, being 'made over' in the image of the lounge? Further evidence of this was suggested in the results that followed the close observation and study of management in its 'walking practices', which caused us to consider something like a lounge effect. With the proliferation of new lounges and 'break out'

[17] What revolutionary group today could not afford to think about such things as part of its media branding campaign?

spaces management is surely now being 'lounged', if not fully taking up the role of 'management loungers' – a category that probably only exists in that fabled 'next 5 minutes' conjured by science fiction writer J G Ballard.[18] However, in his design of Google's new London head office, Lee Penson is certainly taking seriously the possibility that management might be more fully lounged in a design that features 3 lounge spaces and 'sunken snugs, comfort, fun, comfy slippers, squishy carpets, cushions, [and] daybeds …' (quoted in Morley 2012).

As we followed these lines of association marking out a distinctive socio-technical assemblage of lounging, we made increasing use of 'the lounge' as an experiment in ways of thinking. Placing it at the centre of our analysis, in which we might have ended up seeing or *thinking like a lounge* (cf. Scott 1998), the ethnography became increasingly attentive to the possibility that chairs might embody a certain agency and that something like a 'crinicultural' politics could vest a degree of autonomy in the political agency of hair.

We also began to take more seriously the presence of the airport cat – Olly – who seemed to flagrantly exhibit her uninhibited lounging across the campus of the airport. In learning about the agency of objects and materials, we also became more receptive to the idea that this non-human animal was also helping to forge a peculiar feline 'political agency' in organization. Whilst the lounge was intended to develop 'wow factors', to astonish whilst also calming its occupants, and to bring something of the home (a lounge) into a public space, the cat seemed to be at the centre of a way of making organization that was spontaneously encouraging many of these qualities. Intentionality and agency was difficult to identify here. Feline practices, as we might call them, made the organization ontologically more complex, seeming to 'double' and re-use the same objects, techniques, materials and practices that helped construct the lounge. Hence, we might say a project was being doubled, creating two semi-autonomous realms of activity, two 'modes of ordering' (cf. Mol 2002) through which strange correspondences and interferences played themselves out. It was tempting to see the 'cat project' as a parody or

---

[18] Ballard, J G (1991). *The Next five minutes: literature and history*. BBC for the Open University, [London].

mimicry of management, but the ethnography also allowed the research to consider the possibility that it was precisely its undecidability (serious/non-serious) that was most significant, a quality maintained by levels of complexity and subtlety that refused simple definition.

As yet business and management *studies* will no doubt recognise none of this as relevant. Of the business created on the basis that lounging might be encouraged, there can be no doubt. Business studies will remain principally a parasitic practice and an embodiment of necrophilia if it finds no way of taking seriously what is happening on what we have called the 'surface' of organization (Deleuze 1990). This is an unstable and fissile space for which we have as yet developed few techniques for its study in organization analysis. But it is here where *reconstructing organization* is happening. How do we take our students into this space? What business futures might be made possible by the experience of this space, where animals and objects claim their stake in a wider 'parliament of things' that many now deem essential for our survival in the era of the 'Anthropocene'? To continue dividing Organization Studies into 'constructivist' and 'realist' paradigms (O'Doherty and Willmott 2001) will only serve to distract us from the stakes of this debate, and in this modest contribution to a now well established ontological turn in the social sciences, we can see that Organization Studies can do more.

As the lights are turned off in the Escape Lounge and the last jet plane rotates into take-off on runway 05/23 at Manchester, we might contemplate further experiments in ethnographic study in these borderland spaces where there are surely other forms of nascent organization that will expand our understanding of future possibilities. Whether we want to *lounge* in this future must remain an open question.

Ethnography at a Critical Distance: A Postscript to Loungification

Fabian Muniesa

Critique and ethnography: both sound complicated enough when taken separately, but it is in their intertwining where the most remarkable tensions appear. And this is probably truer when critique and ethnography are both plunged in the medium of business – that network of certainties and anxieties in which the proper understanding of the organization of economic conduct fall quite naturally under the jurisdiction of the proverbial business school. Is the ethnographic examination of business conducive to objections, scruples or concerns? Or is it rather something that would stand in the way of incisive debunking? Elaborating a critique of business reality certainly means producing first a realistic account of it. But the denunciation of the limits and operations of managerialism, capitalism or neoliberalism (to name a few standard critical targets) can also find in the qualitative realism of such an account a sort of a distraction, if not a diversion.

This old discussion, known well to the readers that have found their way to these pages, is full of paradoxes. Some are very practical, other are more intellectual. What does it mean to cultivate an interest for ethnographic research inside a business school? What is the purpose? Is it to contribute to the process of business or is it to put it to an alternative Are we inside

D. O'Doherty, *Reconstructing Organization*,
DOI 10.1057/978-1-137-48922-7

it, outside it or alongside? What kind of distance do we put between us and the process of business? And who is this 'we' I am referring to? Is it 'us' ethnographers, 'us' business scholars, 'us' critics of capitalism, or advocates of it? Those questions are practical insofar as they into academic tags, mundane alliances and hostilities, and research budgets. And those questions are sometimes paradoxical insofar as they into impossibilities and disorientations. One would be, for example, the alleged impossibility of being several things at once; another the confusion caused by the act of critically contributing to capitalism's best fuel, which is precisely self-critique, as convincingly argued by authors such as Luc Boltanski or, before him, by Herbert Marcuse.

The intellectual paradoxes of the interplay between the ethnographic and the critical are perhaps best encapsulated by the problem of what has been rightly termed 'critical distance'. Critique, it is said, means taking a step aside, considering something from an angle that provides some room for intellectual manoeuvre. But then with this move the object of critique becomes smaller, more distant. The details are blurred, and, we are told, we end up being critical about something that in fact wears the traits of fantasy. "That is not global capitalism! That is just an accountant working on an Excel sheet! You've been mystified by your critical distance! You are watching your own pebble glasses!" Against critical distance, some would claim, what we need is 'critical proximity'. That would be, for example, the position of Bruno Latour, who emphatically considers 'critical distance' as one of, if not the prime hallucinatory syndrome of modern thought. Others, like Luc Boltanski, would explicitly develop the idea of a sociological examination of critique, that is, an empirical inquiry into mundane critical capacities, as opposed to an authoritative academic use thereof. These and comparable lineaments lead to a praise for entanglement with the object of inquiry, or even, more extremely, an attachment to it – an idea articulated by Antoine Hennion, for example. One common enemy, of course, for all these approaches would be the king sociologist speaking from his overhead position, sitting in his elevated critical plane: a persona that often materializes in the form of Pierre Bourdieu.

From a methodological perspective, this war is fought with explicit reference to a pragmatist tradition in philosophy, to the crafts of ethnographic description, to the moral repertoire of consent and collaboration, to reflexivity and to the critique of scientism. In order to become intelligent, in short, critique needs to dissolve into its object. Fine! What is wrong with that? Well, it depends of course on the point of view, as a pragmatist would have it. And the truth is that the paradox is inescapable. There are surely interesting things that you may miss if you only rely on politeness to get them. And, as anyone with hyperopia will tell you, looking at something at a distance might be the only way to actually see it. If ethnography is to produce more than a candid account of things, it seems that it needs more than ethnography: a theory, some would say, or at least an intellectual take, a point of comparison, a concern that is external to the concerns that govern whatever it is that is going on in the site of investigation. In order to develop his extraordinary critique of modernity, Bruno Latour himself had to step outside modernity itself, despite proximity. And, in order for his critique to remain intelligent, he certainly had to take the pain of not dissolving it into modernity. But, more centrally, as many critics have pointed out, consent and collaboration can turn into endorsement and collaborationism. What kind of critical proximity can the infamous 'embedded anthropologist' develop? And what about capitalism proper? Is not the accountant working on an Excel sheet something else than just an accountant working on an Excel sheet? And, in order to realise that, should we not examine the Excel sheet from a viewpoint slightly different from that of the accountant? Is not intelligence, after all, about changing positions? And is not intelligence what we are paid for, ultimately?

But then, again, the question needs to be asked: how wise is it to be intelligent, after all?

Some might find these questions silly, but they surely populate our scholarly world, and also, perhaps more irresponsibly, the minds of our students. Something should be certainly done about that, and there are of course plenty of resources to do so: to be found for example in current debates on critical performativity and, more largely, on critical and post-critical management studies, also on governmentality and on financialization, and on the challenges ethnographic proximity proper. But one can find also extremely valuable resources in ethnographic accounts proper, and there exists a remark that Damian O'Doherty offers in his ethnography of Manchester Airport that certainly deserves attention here. In the chapter devoted to the airport's premium hospitality facility known as the Escape Lounge, the ethnographer indicates the following, almost in passing: "it took time to become an acceptable critic".

What is happening here? The ethnographer has been sitting there for months, interacting with staff and guests, participating in assignments such as the administration of consumer satisfaction questionnaires. The ethnographer has also explored other related sites, such as the back-office, but also more largely the distant sites from which this place is controlled, or attempted at being controlled. This includes the offices in which decisions are made as to whether or not this service should be developed, the bureaus in which the lounge's business model is elaborated and discussed, the industry conferences in which its overall impact on the airport's own business model is examined, the market research companies in which the customer orientation of the lounge is designed, and so forth. For sure, this research aims at making sense of a compound of sites, devices, persons, flows and practices that determine, to quite a very large extent, this pervasive rendering of the atmosphere of economic modernity that the author quite appropriately calls 'loungification'. But what is loungification? We do not know exactly, as of yet. But we surely recognize the traits of a transformation of economic conduct that goes hand in hand with a transformation of anthropological disposition: comfort in estrangement, mastery of personal profile, the killing of time, the imperative of value creation, the realisation of revenue, etc.

The ethnographer is aware of the fact that on can see quite easily in loungification a sort of a cultural syndrome. And he is utterly right about that. And that is precisely why he could claim loungification as a critical concept, that is, as an intellectual vehicle that allows delineating critical distance. "I have been there in the lounge, plunged into this atmosphere, contributing to it in order to better grasp it. But now I am safely back, ready to analyse, ready to ruminate, ready to criticize". And here is where the trouble starts. What happened? "Too quick," the ethnographer thought.

The critical way, I want to suggest, is the way that can start from just a look at the lounge. We do not need ethnography in order to see how this reality operates. Loungification is clearly an instance of, you name it: neoliberal governmentality, for sure! The traveller is transformed into a client, and the client is transformed into an entrepreneur of her waiting time. Waiting time is accordingly transformed into an asset, and the lounge is therefore entirely controlled by the template of value proposition and value creation, that is, of capital. This inescapably goes hand in hand with the ultimate bundle of business crafts: customization, commodification, privatisation, modelisation, capitalization, financialization. Manchester Airport buys into a solution to economic problems that fosters a new array of problematizations. And this is not all what there is. The person itself is transformed, because in order to thrive the passenger herself, now a 'customer', has to let herself conform to the persona of the lounger. We become the prototypes of the new atmosphere of capitalism: self-trained into profile management, fully aware of our sense of preferences, ready to surrender our behaviour to the data complex that makes life easier, irreducibly confined into a miniaturization of society, a space in which public existence is rendered exclusively through an earplug.

What we need is not ethnography. What we need is Foucault, Deleuze, Sloterdijk, Adorno, Marx, Leibniz and Spinoza. And Samuel Beckett, to that matter. Loungification just needs the right references in order to surpass the processes of mcdonaldisation, disneyfication, nudgification, googlification, moneyfication, queueification and goldmansachsisation that describe our world's emerging condition. But here comes the trouble, a trouble shared both by the ethnographer and the reader. The trouble is with easiness. The trouble is with comfort and swiftness in the critical position. The ethnographer is struggling with loungification, but he is also concerned, perhaps even more strongly, with the loungification of critique. Critique distilled from the user-friendly bibliometric desktop, uttered from the well-equipped rhetoric lounger.

What does it mean to write that "it took time to become an acceptable critic"? And what does it mean to write it precisely from the Escape Lounge at Manchester Airport? What problem is the ethnographer trying to solve? Perhaps a problem of attitude: attitude in writing, in part, but certainly first and foremost a problem of critical attitude within the lounge. This is where this remark comes in. But what do we mean by 'acceptable critic'? Acceptable to whom? And about what? One first interpretation is about the moral etiquette of ethnography vis-à-vis participants. The ethnographer is certainly preoccupied with the ethics of feedback, with this being both a question of respect towards participants in the field, and a question of data robustness. For critique to be acceptable, it needs first to comply with the consent and confirmation of the people that should arguably be more affected by it. The ethnographer's remark comes in a moment of the narrative in which the lounge workers are depicted as co-workers with whom the ethnographer exchanges regularly on the vagaries of routine work. In order to be robust, the critique needs to be spelled out, submitted, or, in other words, made explicit in terms that can be acknowledged or at least recognized by the persons that live the critical reality first-hand.

But there is perhaps more to it than that. Aiming at a state of acceptable critique can also be read as a move that parallels the take that Boltanski suggested against Bourdieu. Critique is a mundane capacity. It is not the stuff that we researchers invent but the stuff that social reality is made of and that we ought to study. Every ethnography, we could claim, is an ethnography of critique insofar as its empirical matter is made of justifications, objections, interpretations and demonstrations. That is what we collect from fieldwork, after all: critique. The clerk at the lounge is a critic, and so are the marketing designer, the airport manager or the traveller passing by. The ethnographer is recording critical styles, examining their composition. His capacity to tell the acceptable from the intolerable or the fulfilling from the alienating depends on the quality of the records. Taking the time to become an acceptable critic might mean, then, doing a properly scientific job: that is, learning the critical codes that make up the situation as something socially interpretable by and for participants. To put it in the terms of Harold Garfinkel: becoming an acceptable critic can mean something like meeting the requirements of unique adequacy.

But there exist other possible interpretations. Perhaps the ethnographer is only aiming at becoming an acceptable critic to himself, in his own eyes. The burden here is on the side of exigency. The postulate would be the following: if critique is to be truthful, then it is required that it shall be difficult. Is it really true that the Escape Lounge epitomizes the atmosphere of capitalism? Is it really true that it constitutes a vehicle for neoliberal subjectification? Is it really true that what it offers as substance and content wears the marks of void and alienation? Is it not a place that I can just enjoy while still preserving my multifarious integrity? The acceptable critique is just the critique that remains attentive to the perils of critical hallucination. It is not that critical hallucination is to be banned: on the contrary, its demanding character should be acknowledged at face value. Do note here that the economic atmosphere epitomised by the lounge inherits heavily, both in spirit and execution, from the ornamental tradition invented by Salvador Dalí, who had previously developed (perhaps in order to cope with its own aftermarth) the doctrine of the paranoid-critical method as a truly critical vehicle, but one that would explicitly care for its hallucinatory key to understanding. The ethnographer in Manchester Airport is in this respect perhaps facing a task comparable to the one famously faced by Carlos Castaneda in his ethnography of psychedelic shamanism.

The notion of acceptable critic contained in the ethnographer's remark thus oscillates between several interpretations, from research diplomacy to intellectual commitment to precaution in the face of overdose. But let us now focus on two elements of this maxim that we neglected so far: "it took time" and "to become".

"It took time": time is indeed amongst the most challenging mysteries of ethnography. It is the problem that remains more incomprehensible for the non-ethnographer. Why such a length? Why months? Why years? Should not a couple of interviews do? Or perhaps ten or twenty, augmented with a couple of so-called observations, but no more? Time is also the thing that, alas, we do not have in our mutating scholarly world. Only anthropologists dare to do what others see as a blatant insult: the out-of-the-office email disclaimer that says that the person is in fact busy with work instead of just holidays. That is a treasure that should be protected by all means. "It took time to become an acceptable critic": this remark introduces a crucial temporal dimension indeed. The productive sense of 'critical distance' is perhaps not only about spatial distance, it is about temporal distance too. Accounts need to decant in order to preserve the sediment. If one wants to figure the exact opposite of this, that would be perhaps the sense of urgency and performance that governs streamlined management consultancy today, or the sense of quasi-immediate delivery that characterizes laboratory or computer-based science.

And this leads us to the "to become". The measuring instrument that the ethnographer uses in his particular blend of science is himself. It is clear from the account of the Escape Lounge at Manchester Airport that only time can serve the process of realization that the critical ethnographer requires. Taking time is what the patient student requires in order to achieve learning. It is also what the learned scholar needs in other to avoid a triumphant theoretical denouement. But taking time, as odd as this may sound, is also simultaneously a form of resistance. Luc Boltanski and Eve Chiapello suggested this point in *The New Spirit of Capitalism*, where they identify an emerging critical repertoire that sees in slow motion the response to the excesses of capitalism (whatever this means). The ethnographer takes time here precisely in order to prevent critique from being loungified, that is, a critique whose main fuel would be the killing of time.

In the section titled "Being there: anthropology and the scene of writing" of his masterful *Works and Lives: The Anthropologist as Author*, Clifford Geertz writes the following:

> "The ability of anthropologists to get us to take what they say seriously has less to do with either a factual look or an air of conceptual elegance than it has with their capacity to convince us that what they say is a result of their having penetrated (or, if you prefer, been penetrated by) another form of life, of having, one way or another, truly "been there.""

This is of course, as Geertz indicates in the essay, a matter of writing tricks, such as the skilful use of quotation marks. But it is also a key to the time it takes to become an acceptable critic. Acceptable critique is the result not only of having penetrated, but also more importantly (Geertz suggests) of having been penetrated by the object of inquiry. I am sure that, writing as he was about writing, Geertz was utterly aware of the potentials of that metaphor of penetration. If we read "it took time to become an acceptable critic" through this metaphor, then we obtain yet another useful insight for our interpretation: we realize that critical ethnography is or can be an interpenetration, with all that this entails in terms of trials, equivoques, malaises, confidences, discoveries and negotiations.

Perhaps after all, the key to critical distance, or to critical time, is not a 'yes' or a 'no', but precisely an ethnographic appraisal of distance: what is the distance that needs to be travelled, what is the time that needs to be taken in order to produce an acceptable critique. Can the answer to this question be provided ethnographically? Can critical distance be described ethnographically? Can the ethnographer sitting at the lounge provide an ethnographic account of the critical position he finds himself occupying *there*? I suggest that this is the intriguing achievement that ethnographic time produced in and about the Escape Lounge at Manchester Airport.

References

Ackroyd, S., & Crowdy, P. A. (1990). Can culture be managed? Working with "raw" material: The case of the English slaughtermen. *Personnel Review, 19*(5), 3–13.

Adams, C. (2006). PowerPoint, habits of mind, and classroom culture. *Journal of Curriculum Studies, 38*(4), 389–411.

Adler, P. S. (2009). *The Oxford handbook of sociology and organization studies: Classical foundations*. Oxford: Oxford University Press.

Adler, P. S., Du Gay, P., Morgan, G., & Reed, M. (Eds.). (2014). *Oxford Handbook of sociology, social theory and organization studies: Contemporary currents*. Oxford: Oxford University Press.

Agamben, G. (2004). *The open: Man and animal*. Stanford: Stanford University Press.

Al-Amoudi, I., & Willmott, H. (2011). Where constructionism and critical realism converge: Interrogating the domain of epistemological relativism. *Organization Studies, 32*(1), 27–46.

Alcadipani, R., & Hassard, J. (2010). Actor-network theory, organizations and critique: Towards a politics of organizing. *Organization, 17*(4), 419–435.

Alcadipani, R., & Hodgson, D. (2009). By any means necessary? Ethnographic access, ethics and the critical researcher. *TAMARA: Journal of Critical Postmodern Organization Science, 7*(3/4), 127–146.

D. O'Doherty, *Reconstructing Organization*,
DOI 10.1057/978-1-137-48922-7

Alger, J., & Alger, S. (2003). *Cat culture: The social world of a cat shelter* (Vol. 36). Philadelphia: Temple University Press.

Allen, J., & Lavau, S. (2015). 'Just-in-time' disease: Biosecurity, poultry and power. *Journal of Cultural Economy, 8*(3), 342–360.

Alvesson, M. (2002). *Understanding organizational culture*. London: Sage.

Alvesson, M., & Willmott, H. (Eds.). (2003). *Studying management critically*. London: Sage.

Alvesson, M. (2013). *The triumph of emptiness: Consumption, higher education, and work organization*. Oxford: Oxford University Press.

Alvesson, M., & Sköldberg, K. (2000). *Reflexive methodology. New vistas for qualitative research*. London: Sage.

Alvesson, M., & Spicer, A. (2012). Critical leadership studies: The case for critical performativity. *Human Relations, 65*(3), 367–390.

Alvesson, M., & Willmott, H. (Eds.). (1992). *Critical management studies*. London: Sage.

Alvesson, M., & Willmott, H. (1996). *Making sense of management: A critical introduction*. London: Sage Publications.

Alvesson, M., Kärreman, D., Sturdy, A., & Handley, K. (2009a). Unpacking the client (s): Constructions, positions and client–consultant dynamics. *Scandinavian Journal of Management, 25*(3), 253–263.

Alvesson, M., Bridgman, T., & Willmott, H. (Eds.). (2009b). *The Oxford handbook of critical management studies*. Oxford/New York: Oxford University Press.

Andriopoulos, C., & Lewis, M. W. (2009). Exploitation-exploration tensions and organizational ambidexterity: Managing paradoxes of innovation. *Organization Science, 20*(4), 696–717.

Ansell-Pearson, K. (1999). *Germinal life: The difference and repetition of Deleuze*. London: Routledge.

Appadurai, A. (Ed.). (1986). *The Social life of things: Commodities in cultural perspective*. Cambridge: Cambridge University Press.

Araujo, L. (2007). Markets, market-making and marketing. *Marketing Theory, 7*(3), 211–226.

Araujo, L., Finch, J., & Kjellberg, H. (2010). *Reconnecting marketing to markets*. Oxford: Oxford University Press.

Aristotle. (1988). *Aristotle, the politics*. In S. Everson (Ed.), Cambridge: Cambridge University Press.

Ariztia, T. (2015). Unpacking insight: How consumers are qualified by advertising agencies. *Journal of Consumer Culture, 15*(2), 143–162.

Arnould, E. J., & Cayla, J. (2015). Consumer fetish: Commercial ethnography and the sovereign consumer. *Organization Studies, 36*(10), 1361–1386.

Ashmore, M. (1989). *The reflexive thesis: Wrighting sociology of scientific knowledge*. Chicago: University of Chicago Press.

Augé, M. (1995). *Non-places: Introduction to an anthropology of supermodernity*. London: Verso.

Auslander, L. (1996). *Taste and power: Furnishing modern France*. Berkeley: University of California Press.

Bachelard, G. (1988). *Air and dreams: An essay on the imagination of movement*. Dallas: Dallas Institute Publications, Dallas Institute of Humanities and Culture.

Bailey, J. R., & Clegg, S. R. (2008). *International encyclopedia of organization studies* (Vol. 4). London: Sage.

Bain, P., & Taylor, P. (2000). Entrapped by the 'electronic panopticon'? Worker resistance in the call centre. *New Technology, Work and Employment, 15*(1), 2–18.

Baldry, C. (1999). Space-the final frontier. *Sociology, 33*(3), 535–553.

Ball, K. (2010). Workplace surveillance: An overview. *Labor History, 51*(1), 87–106.

Ballard, J G (1991). *The Next five minutes: Literature and history*. London: BBC for the Open University.

Barry, K. (2007). *Femininity in flight: A history of flight attendants*. Durham: Duke University Press.

Barry, A. (2013). *Material politics: Disputes along the pipeline*. Oxford: Wiley-Blackwell.

Basboll, T. (2004). The organization of wire and string: Notes on an attempt to follow the Ben Marcus. *Ephemera, 4*(4), 347–352.

Bateson, G. (1972). *Steps to an ecology of mind: Collected essays in anthropology, psychiatry, evolution, and epistemology*. San Francisco: University of Chicago Press.

Baum, J. A. C. (Ed.). (2002). *The Blackwell companion to organizations*. Oxford: Blackwell Publishers.

Bauman, Z. (1989). *Legislators and interpreters: On modernity, post-modernity, and intellectuals*. Cambridge: Polity Press.

Beardsworth, R. (1996). *Derrida & the political*. London: Routledge.

Beetz, A. M., & Podberscek, A. L. (2005). *Bestiality and Zoophilia: Sexual relations with animals*. West Lafayette: Purdue University Press.

Bell, E., & King, D. (2010). The elephant in the room: Critical management studies conferences as a site of body pedagogics. *Management Learning, 41*, 429–442.

Benjamin, W. (1978). *Reflections: Essays, aphorisms, autobiographical writings*. New York: Harcourt Brace Jovanovich.

Bennett, J. (2010). *Vibrant matter: A political ecology of things*. Durham: Duke University Press.

Bennis, W. G., & O'Toole, J. (2005). How business schools lost their way. *Harvard Business Review, 83*(5), 96–104.

Bentley, C. (2009). *PRINCE2: A practical handbook*. Oxford: Butterworth-Heinemann.

Berland, J. (2008). Cat and mouse. *Cultural Studies, 22*, 431–454.

Berthod, J. & Brash, A. (2015) Cut Boris Johnson's Hair, *ElectoAesthetics Blog*. http://electoaesthetics.blogspot.co.uk/2015/04/cut-boris-johnsons-hair.html. Accessed 12 Jan 2016.

Beyes, T. (2009). An aesthetics of displacement: Thomas Pynchon's symptomatology of organization. *Journal of Organizational Change Management, 22*(4), 421–436.

Beyes, T., & Steyaert, C. (2012). Spacing organization: Non-representational theory and performing organizational space. *Organization, 19*(1), 45–61.

Beyes, T., & Steyaert, C. (2013). Strangely familiar: The uncanny and unsiting organizational analysis. *Organization Studies, 34*(10), 1445–1465.

Bijker, W. E., Hughes, T. P., & Pinch, T. J. (2012). *The social construction of technological systems: New directions in the sociology and history of technology*. Cambridge, MA: MIT Press.

Bissell, D. (2012). Agitating the powers of habit: Towards a volatile politics of thought. *Theory & Event, 15*(1).

Bittner, E. (1965). The concept of organization. *Social Research, 32*(3), 239–255.

Blaser, M. (2010). *Storytelling: Globalization from the Chaco and beyond*. Durham: Duke University Press.

Boddy, D. (2008). *Management: An introduction*. Harlow: Pearson Education.

Boden, D. (1994). *The business of talk: Organizations in action*. Oxford: Blackwell.

Boggs, C. (2000). *The end of politics: Corporate power and the decline of the public sphere*. New York: Guilford Press.

Böhm, S. (2006). *Repositioning organization theory: Impossibilities and strategies*. Houndmills: Palgrave Macmillan.

Boltanski, L., & Chiapello, E. (2005). *The new spirit of capitalism*. London: Verso.

Bolton, S. C. (2000). Emotion here, emotion there, emotional organisations everywhere. *Critical Perspectives on Accounting, 11*(2), 155–171.

Bolton, S. C. (2009). Getting to the heart of the emotional labour process: A reply to Brook. *Work, Employment & Society, 23*(3), 549–560.

Bolton, S. C., & Boyd, C. (2003). Trolley dolly or skilled emotion manager? Moving on from Hochschild's managed heart. *Work, Employment & Society, 17*(2), 289–308.

Borgerson, J. (2003). Animal. In C. Jones & D. P. O'Doherty (Eds.), *Manifestos for the business school of tomorrow*. Finland: Dvalin Press.

Born, G., & Barry, A. (2010). Art-science. *Journal of Cultural Economy., 3*, 103–119.

Boswijk, A., Peelen, E., Olthof, S., & Beddow, C. (2012). *Economy of experiences*. Amsterdam: European Centre for the Experience and Transformation Economy.

Bourdieu, P. (1973). The Berber house. In M. Douglas (Ed.), *Rules and meanings: The anthropology of everyday knowledge*. London/New York: Routledge.

Bows, A., & Anderson, K. L. (2007). Policy clash: Can projected aviation growth be reconciled with the UK government's 60% carbon-reduction target? *Transport Policy, 14*(2), 103–110.

Bows, A., Anderson, K., & Upham, P. (2008). *Aviation and climate change: Lessons for European Policy*. Hoboken: Taylor & Francis.

Brewis, J., & Wray-Bliss, E. (2008). Re-searching ethics: Towards a more reflexive critical management studies. *Organization Studies, 29*, 1521–1540.

Brickel, C. M. (1979). The therapeutic roles of cat mascots with a hospital-based geriatric population: A staff survey. *The Gerontologist, 19*(4), 368–372.

Briggs, K. (1980). *Nine lives: The folklore of cats*. New York: Pantheon Books.

Brook, P. (2009). In critical defence of 'emotional labour' refuting Bolton's critique of Hochschild's concept. *Work, employment & society, 23*(3), 531–548.

Brown, J. S., & Duguid, P. (2002). *The social life of information*. Boston: Harvard Business School Press.

Bruni, A (2006) Access as trajectory: Entering the field in organizational ethnography. *EGOS Colloquium*, 6–8 July, Bergen.

Bryant, L., Srnicek, N., & Harman, G. (Eds.). (2011). *The speculative turn: Continental materialism and realism*. Victoria: re. press.

Bryman, A. (2004). *The Disneyization of society*. London: Sage.

Bryman, A., & Bell, E. (2015). *Business research methods*. Oxford: Oxford University Press.

Burawoy, M. (1979). *Manufacturing consent: Changes in the labor process under monopoly capitalism*. Chicago: University of Chicago Press.

Burawoy, M. (1985). *Politics of production: Factory regimes under capitalism and socialism*. London: Verso.

Burawoy, M., Blum, J. A., George, S., Gille, Z., & Thayer, M. (2000). *Global ethnography: Forces, connections, and imaginations in a postmodern world*. Berkeley: University of California Press.

Burrell, G. (1997). *Pandemonium: Towards a retro-organization theory*. London: Sage Publications.

Burrell, G. (2003). The future of organization theory. In C. Knudsen & H. Tsoukas (Eds.), *The Oxford handbook of organization theory*. Oxford: Oxford University Press.

Burrell, G. (2013). *Styles of organizing: The will to form*. Oxford: Oxford University Press.

Burrell, G., & Dale, K. (2003). Building better worlds?: Architecture and critical management studies. In Alvesson, M. & Willmott, H. (Eds.), *Studying management critically*. London: Sage.

Burrell, G., & Morgan, G. (1979). *Sociological paradigms and organisational analysis: Elements of the sociology of corporate life*. London: Heinemann.

Burrows, R., & Gane, N. (2006). Geodemographics, software and class. *Sociology, 40*(5), 793–812.

Cabantous, L., Gond, J. P., Harding, N., & Learmonth, M. (2016). Critical essay: Reconsidering critical performativity. *Human Relations, 69*(2), 197–213.

Çalışkan, K. (2010). *Market threads: How cotton farmers and traders create a global commodity*. Princeton: Princeton University Press.

Callaghan, G., & Thompson, P. (2002). 'We recruit attitude': The selection and shaping of routine call centre labour. *Journal of Management Studies, 39*(2), 233–254.

Callon, M. (1998). *The laws of the markets*. Oxford: Blackwell Publishers/Sociological Review.

Callon, M. (2009). Elaborating the notion of performativity. *Le libellio d'AEGIS, 5*(1), 18–29.

Callon, M., & Latour, B. (1981). Unscrewing the big Leviathan. In A. Cicourel & K. Knorr Cetina (Eds.), *Advances in social theory and methodology*. Boston: Routledge & Kegan Paul.

Callon, M., & Law, J. (2005). On qualculation, agency, and otherness. *Environment and Planning D: Society and Space, 23*(5), 717–733.

Callon, M., & Muniesa, F. (2005). Economic markets as calculative collective devices. *Organization Studies, 26*(8), 1229–1250.

Callon, M., Millo, Y., & Muniesa, F. (2007). *Market devices*. Malden: Blackwell.

Calori, R. (2002). Essai: Real time/real space research: Connecting action and reflection in organization studies. *Organization Studies, 23*(6), 877–883.

Carat. (2011). *Escape Lounge: Summary of findings*. Presentation to Manchester Airport Group, September, 2011.

Carlile, P., Nicolini, D., Langley, A., & Tsoukas, H. (2013). *How matter matters: Objects, artifacts, and materiality in organization studies*. Oxford: Oxford University Press.

Carr, A. N., & Hancock, P. (Eds.) (2006). Space and time in organizations. Special edition of the *Journal of Organizational Change Management, 19*(5), 545–557.

Carroll, P. (2006). *Science, culture, and modern state formation*. Berkeley: University of California Press.

Carveth, R., & South, J. B. (2010). *Mad men and philosophy: Nothing is as it seems*. Hoboken: Wiley.

Case, P. (1999). Organizational studies in space: Stanislaw Lem and the writing of social science fiction. *Organization, 6*(4), 649–671.

Casey, C. (1995). *Work, self, and society: After industrialism*. London: Routledge.

Castells, M. (1996). *The rise of the network society*. Malden: Blackwell Publishers.

Cederström, C., & Fleming, P. (2012). *Dead man working*. Winchester: Zero Books.

Cederström, C., & Spicer, A. (2014). Discourse of the real kind: A post-foundational approach to organizational discourse analysis. *Organization, 21*(2), 178–205.

Cederström, C., & Spicer, A. (2015). *The wellness syndrome*. Cambridge: Polity.

Chappell, D. (2003). *Understanding JCT standard building contracts*. Abingdon: Routledge.

Charvat, J. (2003). *Project management methodologies: Selecting, implementing, and supporting methodologies, and processes for projects*. New York: Wiley.

Chia, R. C. H. (1996). *Organizational analysis as deconstructive practice*. Berlin: Walter de Gruyter.

Chia, R. (1999). A 'rhizomic' model of organizational change and transformation: Perspective from a metaphysics of change. *British Journal of Management, 10*(3), 209–227.

Chia, R., & Holt, R. (2006). Strategy as practical coping: A Heideggerian perspective. *Organization Studies, 27*(5), 635–655.

Chlebik, J., Grant, L., Herrmann, P., & Price, J. (2002). *The Mancunian way: Manchester*. Manchester: Clinamen.

Chugh, S., & Hancock, P. (2009). Networks of aestheticization: The architecture, artefacts and embodiment of hairdressing salons. *Work, Employment & Society, 23*(3), 460–476.

Civil Aviation Authority. (2009). *The through airport passenger experience: An assessment of the passenger experience and airport operations at Heathrow, Gatwick, Stansted and Manchester airports*. London: CAA.

Clark, T., & Mangham, I. (2004). Stripping to the undercoat: A review and reflections on a piece of organization theatre. *Organization Studies, 25*(5), 841–851.

Clegg, S. R. (2006). Why is organization theory so ignorant? The neglect of total institutions. *Journal of Management Inquiry, 15*(4), 426–430.

Clegg, S., & Kornberger, M. (Eds.). (2006). *Space, organizations and management theory*. Oslo: Liber.

Clegg, S., Hardy, C., & Nord, W. R. (1996). *Handbook of organization studies*. London: Sage Publications.

Clifford, J., & Marcus, G. E. (Eds.). (1986). *Writing culture: The poetics and politics of ethnography*. Berkeley: University of California Press.

Cochoy, F. (2007). A brief theory of the 'captation' of publics: Understanding the market with Little Red Riding Hood. *Theory, Culture & Society, 24*, 203–223.

Cochoy, F. (2008). Calculation, qualculation, calqulation: Shopping cart arithmetic, equipped cognition and the clustered consumer. *Marketing Theory, 8*(1), 15–44.

Cochoy, F. (2009). Driving a shopping cart from STS to business, and the other way round: On the introduction of shopping carts in American Grocery stores (1936–1959). *Organization, 16*(1), 31–55.

Cochrane, A., Peck, J., & Tickell, A. (1996). Manchester plays games: Exploring the local politics of globalisation. *Urban Studies, 33*(8), 1319–1336.

Coleman, S., & Von Hellermann, P. (Eds.). (2012). *Multi-sited ethnography: Problems and possibilities in the translocation of research methods*. New York: Routledge.

Collin, M. (1997). *Altered state, the story of ecstasy culture and acid house*. London: Serpent's Tail.

Collins, H. (2004). *Gravity's shadow: The search for gravitational waves*. Chicago: University of Chicago Press.

Collinson, D. L. (1992). *Managing the shopfloor: Subjectivity, masculinity, and workplace culture*. Berlin: W. de Gruyter.

Cook, S. (2008). *Customer service skills in your organisation*. Wimbledon: Chartered Institute of Personnel & Development.

Cooper, R. (1992). Formal organization as representation: Remote control, displacement and abbreviation. In M. Reed & M. Hughes (Eds.), *Rethinking organization: New directions in organization theory and analysis* (pp. 254–272). London: Sage.

Cooper, R. (1997). Millenium notes for social theory. *The Sociological Review, 45*(4), 690.

Cooper, R. (1998). Assemblage notes. In R. Chia (Ed.), *Organized worlds: Explorations in technology and organization with Robert Cooper*. London: Routledge.

Cooper, R. (2006). Making present: Autopoiesis as human production. *Organization, 13*(1), 59–81.

Cooper, R. (2007). Organs of process: Rethinking human organization. *Organization Studies, 28*(10), 1547–1573.

Cooper, R., & Fox, S. (1990). The 'texture'of organizing. *Journal of Management Studies, 27*(6), 575–582.

Corbusier, L. (1935). *Aircraft*. London: Trefoil.

Corman, L. (2011). Impossible subjects: The figure of the animal in Paulo Freire's "pedagogy of the oppressed". *Canadian Journal of Environmental Education, 16*, 29–45.

Costas, J. (2013). Problematizing mobility: A metaphor of stickiness, non-places and the kinetic elite. *Organization Studies, 34*(10), 1467–1485.

Costas, J., & Grey, C. (2014). Bringing secrecy into the open: Towards a theorization of the social processes of organizational secrecy. *Organization Studies, 35*(10), 1423–1447.

Cova, B., Pace, S., & Skålén, P. (2015). Marketing with working consumers: The case of a carmaker and its brand community. *Organization, 22*(5), 682–701.

Cox, C., & Widdows, L. (2005). *Hair and fashion*. London: Victoria & Albert Museum.

Crainer, S., & Dearlove, D. (2004). *Financial times handbook of management*. Harlow: Financial Times/Prentice Hall.

Crozier, M. (1964). *The bureaucratic phenomenon*. Chicago: University of Chicago Press.

Csikszentmihalyi, M. (1990). *Flow: The psychology of optimal experience*. New York: Harper & Row.

Cunliffe, A. L. (2003). Reflexive inquiry in organizational research: Questions and possibilities. *Human Relations, 56*(8), 983–1003.

Cunliffe, A. L. (2008). *Organization theory*. London: Sage.

Curtin, M. (1987). *Propriety and position: A study of Victorian manners*. New York: Garland.

Czarniawska, B. (2004a). On time, space, and action nets. *Organization, 11*(6), 773–791.
Czarniawska, B. (2004b). *A tale of three cities: On the glocalization of city management* (p. 161). Oxford: Oxford University Press.
Czarniawska, B. (2012). Organization theory meets anthropology: A story of an encounter. *Journal of Business Anthropology, 1*(1), 118–140.
Czarniawska, B., & Mazza, C. (2003). Consulting as a liminal space. *Human relations, 56*(3), 267–290.
Czarniawska-Joerges, B. (1998). *A narrative approach in organization studies.* Thousand Oaks: Sage Publications.
Dahl, R. A. (1961). *Who governs?: Democracy and power in an American city.* New Haven: Yale University Press.
Dai, C. X., & Wells, W. G. (2004). An exploration of project management office features and their relationship to project performance. *International Journal of Project Management, 22*(7), 523–532.
Dale, K., & Burrell, G. (2008). *The spaces of organisation and the organisation of space.* Basingstoke: Palgrave Macmillan.
Dale, K., & Latham, Y. (2015). Ethics and entangled embodiment: Bodies-materialities-organization. *Organization, 22*(2), 166–182.
Dalton, M. (1959). *Men who manage: Fusions of feeling and theory in administration.* New York: Wiley.
Darlington, R. (1995). Restructuring and workplace unionism at Manchester Airport. *British Journal of Industrial Relations, 33*(1), 93–115.
de la Cadena, M. (2010). Indigenous cosmopolitics in the Andes: Conceptual reflections beyond "politics". *Cultural Anthropology, 25*(2), 334–370.
de la Cadena, M. (2015). *Earth beings: Ecologies of practice across Andean worlds.* Durham: Duke University Press.
de Rond, M. (2008). *The last amateurs: To hell and back with Cambridge Boat Race crew.* Thriplow: Icon.
de Vries, G. (2007). What is political in sub-politics? *Social Studies of Science, 37*(5), 781–809.
Deal, T. E., & Kennedy, A. A. (1982). *Corporate cultures: The rites and rituals of corporate life.* Reading: Addison-Wesley Pub. Co.
Deas, I. (2014). The search for territorial fixes in subnational governance: City-regions and the disputed emergence of post-political consensus in Manchester, England. *Urban Studies, 51*, 2285–2314.
Dekkers, M. (2000). *Dearest pet: On bestiality.* London: Verso.
Deleuze, G. (1988). *Bergsonism.* New York: Zone Books.

Deleuzc, G. (1990). *The logic of sense*. London: Athlone Press.
Deleuze, G. (1992). *Cinema 1: The movement-image*. London: Athlone Press.
Deleuze, G. (2001). *Pure immanence: Essays on a life* (trans: Boyman, A.). New York: Zone Books.
Deleuze, G., & Guattari, F. (1983). *Anti-Oedipus: Capitalism and schizophrenia*. Minneapolis: University of Minnesota Press.
Deleuze, G., & Guattari, F. (1987). *A thousand plateaus: Capitalism and schizophrenia*. Minneapolis: University of Minnesota Press.
Department for Transport. (2008). *Improving the air passenger experience: An analysis of end-to-end journeys with a focus on Manchester*. London: Department for Transport.
Derrida, J. (1982). *Margins of philosophy*. Chicago: University of Chicago Press.
Derrida, J. (1992). Force of law: The mystical foundation of authority. In D. Cornell, M. Rosenfeld, & D. Carlson (Eds.), *Deconstruction and the possibility of justice*. New York: Routledge.
Derrida, J. (1994). Spectres of marx. *New Left Review, 205*, 31–58.
Derrida, J. (1996a). *Archive fever: A Freudian impression*. Chicago: University of Chicago Press.
Derrida, J. (1996b). Remarks on deconstruction and pragmatism. In C. Mouffe (Ed.), *Deconstruction and pragmatism: Simon Critchley, Jacques Derrida, Ernesto Laclau & Richard Rorty*. London: Routledge.
Derrida, J. (2002). The animal that therefore I am (more to follow). *Critical Inquiry, 28*, 369–418.
Dery, D. (1998). "Papereality" and learning in Bureaucratic organizations. *Administration and Society, 29*(6), 677–689.
Descola, P. (2013). *Beyond nature and culture*. Chicago/London: University of Chicago Press.
Doganis, R. (1992). *The airport business*. Abingdon: Routledge.
Doganis, R. (2005). *The Airline business*. Abingdon: Routledge.
Donaldson, L. (1985). *In defence of organization theory. A reply to the critics*. Cambridge: Cambridge University Press.
Dong, A. A. S. (2008). *The language of design: Theory and computation*. London: Springer Science & Business Media.
Dopson, S. (2005). The diffusion of medical innovations: Can figurational sociology contribute? *Organization Studies, 26*(8), 1125–1144.
Drori, I., & Ellis, S. (2011). Conflict and power games in a multinational corporation: Sensegiving as a strategy of preservation. *European Management Review, 8*, 1–16.

Durrant, J., & Bailey, M. D. (2012). *Historical dictionary of witchcraft*. Lanham: Scarecrow Press.
du Gay, P. (1996). *Consumption and identity at work*. London: Sage.
du Gay, P. (2000). *In praise of bureaucracy: Weber-organization-ethics*. London: Sage.
Edgerton, G. R. (Ed.). (2011). *Mad men: Dream come true TV*. London: IB Tauris.
Egan, J. (1998). *Rethinking construction, construction task force report for department of the environment, transport and the regions*. London: HMSO.
Egan, P., Cruikshank, R., Cruikshank, G., & Hotten, J. C. (1869). esq. and his elegant friend Corinthian Tom Day and night scenes of Jerry Hawthorn. In *Life in London, or, The day and night scenes of Jerry Hawthorn, esq. and his elegant friend Corinthian Tom*. London: Chatto and Windus.
Ehrenzweig, A. (1967). *The hidden order of art: A study in the psychology of artistic imagination*. Berkeley: University of California Press.
Ekman, S. (2014). Is the high-involvement worker precarious or opportunistic? Hierarchical ambiguities in late capitalism. *Organization, 21*(2), 141–158.
Engwall, L., & Zamagni, V. (1998). *Management education in historical perspective*. Manchester: Manchester University Press.
Experian. (2009). *Mosaic United Kingdom: The consumer classification of the United Kingdom*. Nottingham/Ediburgh/London: Experian.
Ezzamel, M., & Willmott, H. (2014). Registering 'the ethical' in organization theory formation: Towards the disclosure of an 'invisible force'. *Organization Studies, 35*(7), 1013–1039.
Farthing, R. (2010). The politics of youthful antipolitics: Representing the "issue" of youth participation in politics. *Journal of Youth Studies, 13*(2), 181–195.
Featherstone, M. (1991). *Postmodernism and consumer culture*. London: Sage.
Feldman, S. P. (1988). Secrecy, information, and politics: An essay on organizational decision making. *Human Relations, 41*(1), 73–90.
Feldman, M. S., & Orlikowski, W. J. (2011). Theorizing practice and practicing theory. *Organization Science, 22*(5), 1240–1253.
Fick, K. M. (1993). The influence of an animal on social interactions of nursing home residents in a group setting. *American Journal of Occupational Therapy, 47*(6), 529–534.
Fleetwood, S. (2005). Ontology in organization and management studies: A critical realist perspective. *Organization, 12*(2), 197–222.
Fleetwood, S., & Ackroyd, S. (2004). *Critical realist applications in organisation and management studies*. London: Routledge.

Fleming, P. (2009). *Authenticity and the cultural politics of work: New forms of informal control.* Oxford: Oxford University Press.

Fleming, P. (2010). You are where you are not: Lacan and ideology in contemporary workplaces. In C. Hoedemaekers & C. Cederström (Eds.), *Lacan and organization*. London: Mayfly.

Fleming, P., & Banerjee, S. B. (2016). When performativity fails: Implications for critical management studies. *Human Relations, 69*, 257–276.

Fleming, P., & Spicer, A. (2002). Workers' playtime?: Unravelling the paradox of covert resistance in organizations. In S. Clegg (Ed.), *Management and organization paradoxes*. Amsterdam: John Benjamins.

Fleming, P., & Spicer, A. (2003). Working at a cynical distance: Implications for power, subjectivity and resistance. *Organization, 10*(1), 157–179.

Fleming, P., & Spicer, A. (2005). How objects believe for us: Applications in organizational analysis. *Culture and Organization, 11*(3), 181–193.

Fletcher, D., & Watson, T. (2007). Voice, silence and the business of construction: Loud and quiet voices in the construction of personal, organizational and social realities. *Organization, 14*(2), 155–174.

Fontenelle, I. A. (2015). Organisations as producers of consumers. *Organization, 22*(5), 644–660.

Foucault, M. (1971a). Nietzsche, genealogy, history. In D. F. Bouchard (Ed.), *Michel Foucault: Language, counter-memory, practice: Selected essays and interviews*. Ithaca: Cornell University Press.

Foucault, M. (1971b). *The order of things: An archaeology of the human sciences.* New York: Pantheon Books.

Foucault, M. (1977). *Discipline and punish: The birth of the prison.* London: Allen Lane.

Foucault, M. (1980). In C. Gordon (Ed.), *Power/Knowledge: Selected writings and other interviews 1972–1977*. New York: Pantheon.

Foucault, M. (2003). *"Society must be defended": Lectures at the Collège de France, 1975–1976*. London: Allen Lane.

Foucault, M. (2008). *The birth of biopolitics: Lectures at the Collège de France, 1978–1979*. Basingstoke: Palgrave Macmillan.

Foucault, M. (2009). *Security, territory, population: Lectures at the Collège de France*. Basingstoke: Palgrave Macmillan.

Fourcade, M. (2011). Cents and sensibility: Economic valuation and the nature of "nature". *American Journal of Sociology, 116*(6), 1721–1777.

Fournier, V., & Grey, C. (2000). At the critical moment: Conditions and prospects for critical management studies. *Human relations, 53*(1), 7–32.

Francis, G., Humphreys, I., & Fry, J. (2002). The benchmarking of airport performance. *Journal of Air Transport Management, 8*(4), 239–247.

Frank, T. (1997). *The conquest of cool: Business culture, counterculture, and the rise of hip consumerism*. Chicago: University of Chicago Press.

Freathy, P. (2004). The commercialisation of European airports: Successful strategies in a decade of turbulence? *Journal of Air Transport Management, 10*(3), 191–197.

Freccero, C. (2011). Carnivorous virility; or, becoming-dog. *Social Text, 29*(1 106), 177–195.

French, R., & Grey, C. (Eds.). (1996). *Rethinking management education*. London: Sage.

Frost, P. J., Moore, L. F., Louis, M. R., Lundberg, C. C., & Martin, J. (1985). *Organization culture*. Beverly Hills: Sage.

Fuller, G., & Harley, R. (2004). *Aviopolis: A book about airports*. London: Black Dog Pub.

Furlong, A., & Cartmel, F. (2012). Social change and political engagement among young people: Generation and the 2009/2010 British Election Survey. *Parliamentary Affairs, 65*(1), 13–28.

Gabriel, Y. (1995). The unmanaged organization: Stories, fantasies and subjectivity. *Organization Studies, 16*(3), 477–501.

Gabriel, Y. (2005). Glass cages and glass palaces: Images of organization in image-conscious times. *Organization, 12*(1), 9–27.

Gabriel, Y., & Lang, T. (1995). *The unmanageable consumer: Contemporary consumption and its fragmentations*. London: Sage Publications.

Gabriel, Y., & Lang, T. (2006). *The unmanageable consumer* (2nd ed.). London: Sage.

Gad, C., & Jensen, C. B. (2014). The promises of practice. *The Sociological Review, 62*(4), 698–718.

Gagliardi, P. (1990). *Symbols and artifacts: Views of the corporate landscape*. Berlin: W. de Gruyter.

Garfinkel, H. (1967). *Studies in ethnomethodology*. Englewood Cliff: Prentice-Hall.

Garsten, C. (1999). Betwixt and between: Temporary employees as liminal subjects in flexible organizations. *Organization Studies, 20*(4), 601–617.

Garsten, C., & Nyqvist, A. (2013). *Organisational anthropology: Doing ethnography in and among complex organisations*. London: Pluto Press.

Geertz, C. (1973). *The interpretation of cultures: Selected essays*. New York: Basic Books.

Gennep, A. (1909). *Les rites de passage: Étude systématique des rites de la porte et du seuil, de l'hospitalité de l'adoption*. Paris: E. Nourry.

Giddens, A. (1976). *New rules of sociological method: A positive critique of interpretative sociologies*. New York: Basic Books.

Giddens, A. (1979). *Central problems in social theory: Action, structure, and contradiction in social analysis*. Berkeley: University of California Press.

Giddens, A. (1982). *Sociology, a brief but critical introduction*. New York: Harcourt Brace Jovanovich.

Gleick, J. (1987). *Chaos: Making a new science*. New York: Viking.

Glynos, J., Klimecki, R., & Willmott, H. (2012). Cooling out the marks: The ideology and politics of the financial crisis. *Journal of Cultural Economy, 5*(3), 297–320.

Glynos, J., Klimecki, R., & Willmott, H. (2015). Logics in policy and practice: A critical nodal analysis of the UK banking reform process. *Critical Policy Studies, 9*(4), 393–415.

Goffman, E. (1961). *Asylums: Essays on the social situation of mental patients and other inmates*. Garden City: Anchor Books.

Goleman, D. (1995). *Emotional intelligence*. New York: Bantam Books.

Gond J. P., Cabantous L., Harding, N., & Learmonth, M. (2015). What do we mean by performativity in organizational and management theory? The uses and abuses of performativity. *International Journal of Management Reviews*. doi: 10.1111/ijmr.12074.

González-Santos, S., & Dimond, R. (2015). Medical and scientific conferences as sites of sociological interest: A review of the field. *Sociology Compass, 9*(3), 235–245.

Gottdiener, M. (2001). *Life in the air: The new culture of air travel*. Lanham: Rowman & Littlefield.

Graham, A. (2013). *Managing Airports 4th edition: An international perspective*. Abingdon: Routledge.

Graham, S., & Thrift, N. (2007). Out of order. *Theory, Culture & Society, 24*(3), 1–25.

Granter, E., McCann, L., & Boyle, M. (2015). Extreme work/normal work: Intensification, storytelling and hypermediation in the (re) construction of 'the new normal'. *Organization, 22*(4), 443–456.

Greenwood, R., Oliver, C., Sahlin-Andersson, K., & Suddaby, R. (Eds.). (2012). *Institutional theory in organization studies* (Vol. 4). London: Sage.

Greimas, A. (1976). *Sémiotique et sciences sociales*. Paris: Éditions du Seuil.

Grey, C. (1994). Career as a project of the self and labour process discipline. *Sociology, 28*(2), 479–497.

Grey, C. (2004). Reinventing business schools: The contribution of critical management education. *Academy of Management Learning & Education, 3*(2), 178–186.
Grey, C. (2005). Critical management studies: Towards a more mature politics. In D. Howcroft & E. M. Trauth (Eds.), *Handbook of critical information systems research: Theory and application*. Cheltenham: Edward Elgar.
Griggs, S., & Howarth, D. R. (2014). *The politics of airport expansion in the United Kingdom: Hegemony, policy and the rhetoric of 'sustainable aviation.* Manchester: Manchester University Press.
Grint, K., & Woolgar, S. (2013). *The machine at work: Technology, work and organization*. Oxford: Wiley.
Gross, D., Shortle, J. F., Thompson, J. M., & Harris, C. (2008). *Fundamentals of queueing theory*. Hoboken: Wiley.
Guldi, J. (2012). The history of walking and the digital turn: Stride and lounge in London, 1808–1851. *The Journal of Modern History, 84*(1), 116–144.
Hacking, I. (1983). *Representing and intervening: Introductory topics in the philosophy of natural science*. Cambridge: Cambridge University Press.
Hacking, I. (2002). *Historical ontology*. Cambridge, MA: Harvard University Press.
Halford, S., & Leonard, P. (2006). Place, space and time: Contextualizing workplace subjectivities. *Organization Studies, 27*(5), 657–676.
Halpern, N., & Graham, A. (2013). *Airport marketing*. Abingdon: Routledge.
Hamilton, L. (2007). Muck and magic: Cultural transformations in the world of farm animal veterinary surgeons. *Ethnography, 8*(4), 485–501.
Hamilton, L., & Taylor, N. (2012). Ethnography in evolution: Adapting to the animal "other" in organizations. *Journal of Organizational Ethnography, 1*(1), 43–51.
Hancock, P., & Tyler, M. (2007). Un/doing gender and the aesthetics of organizational performance. *Gender Work and Organization, 14*(6), 512–533.
Haraway, D. J. (1989). *Primate visions: Gender, race, and nature in the world of modern science*. New York: Routledge.
Haraway, D. J. (2003). *The companion species manifesto: Dogs, people, and significant otherness*. Chicago: Prickly Paradigm Press.
Haraway, D. (2006). Encounters with companion species: Entangling dogs, baboons, philosophers, and biologists. *Configurations, 14*(1), 97–114.
Haraway, D. J. (2008). *When species meet*. Minneapolis: University of Minnesota Press.
Harman, G. (2010). *Towards speculative realism: Essays and lectures*. Ropley: Zero Books.

Harris, R., Sleight, P., & Webber, R. (2005). *Geodemographics, GIS and neighbourhood targeting.* West Sussex: Wiley.

Harvie, D., Lightfoot, G., Lilley, S., & Weir, K. (2012). What are we to do with feral publishers? *Organization, 19*(6), 905–914.

Hassard, J., & Parker, M. (Eds.). (1993). *Postmodernism and organizations.* London: Sage.

Hatch, M. J. (2012). *Organization theory: Modern, symbolic, and postmodern perspectives.* Oxford: Oxford University Press.

Hatch, M., & Yanow, D. (2008). Methodology by metaphor: Ways of seeing in painting and research. *Organization Studies, 29*(1), 23–44.

Hayner, N. S. (1928). Hotel life and personality. *American Journal of Sociology, 33*, 784–795.

Heath, J., & Potter, A. (2004). *The rebel sell: Why the culture can't be jammed.* Toronto: HarperCollins.

Hebdige, D. (1979). *Subculture: The meaning of style.* New York: Methuen.

Heidegger, M. (1957). *Identität und Differenz.* Pfullingen: G. Neske.

Heidegger, M. (1962). *Being and time.* Oxford: Blackwell.

Heidegger, M. (2002). *Identity and difference.* Chicago: University of Chicago Press.

Heider, J. (1985). *The Tao of leadership.* Atlanta: Humanics New Age.

Helgesson, C. F., & Kjellberg, H. (2013). Introduction: Values and valuations in market practice. *Journal of Cultural Economy, 6*(4), 361–369.

Hennion, A. (2007). Those things that hold us together: Taste and sociology. *Cultural Sociology, 1*(1), 97–114.

Hernes, T. (2008). *Understanding organization as process: Theory for a tangled world.* London: Routledge.

Hertz, R., & Imber, J. B. (1995). *Studying elites using qualitative methods.* Thousand Oaks: Sage Publications.

Hibbert, J. F., Dickinson, J. E., Gössling, S., & Curtin, S. (2013). Identity and tourism mobility: An exploration of the attitude–behaviour gap. *Journal of Sustainable Tourism, 21*(7), 999–1016.

Hill, G. M. (2014). *The complete project management office handbook.* Boca Raton: CRC Press.

Hochschild, A. R. (1983). *The managed heart: The commercialism of human feeling.* Berkeley: University of California Press.

Hodgson, D. (2002). "Know your customer": Marketing, governmentality and the "new consumer" of financial services. *Management Decision, 40*(4), 318–328.

Hoffmeyer, J. (2008). *Biosemiotics: An examination into the signs of life and the life of signs.* Scranton: University of Scranton Press.

Hofstede, G. H. (1991). *Cultures and organizations: Software of the mind.* London: McGraw-Hill.

Hoholm, T., & Araujo, L. (2011). Studying innovation processes in real-time: The promises and challenges of ethnography. *Industrial Marketing Management, 40*(6), 933–939.

Holbraad, M., Pedersen, M. A., & Viveiros de Castro, E. (2014). The politics of ontology: Anthropological positions. *Cultural Anthropology Online*, 13 January. www.culanth.org/fieldsights/462-the-politics-of-ontology-anthropological-positions

Holbrook, M. B. (1998). The katatche of catology in research on marketing: Breakfast at Tiffany's stereography, subjective personal introspection, and cat. *Irish Marketing Review, 11*(2), 29.

Holbrook, M. B. (2008). Pets and people: Companions in commerce? *Journal of Business Research, 61*(5), 546–552.

Holmes, H. (2014). Chameleon hair: How hair's materiality affects its fashionability. *Critical Studies in Fashion & Beauty, 5*(1), 95–110.

Hoskin, K. (1995). The viewing self and the world we view: Beyond the perspectival illusion. *Organization, 2*(1), 141–162.

Hoskin, K. W., & Macve, R. H. (1986). Accounting and the examination: A genealogy of disciplinary power. *Accounting, Organizations and Society, 11*(2), 105–136.

Huault, I., Perret, V., & Spicer, A. (2014). Beyond macro-and micro-emancipation: Rethinking emancipation in organization studies. *Organization, 21*(1), 22–49.

Hull, M. S. (2012). *Government of paper: The materiality of bureaucracy in urban Pakistan*. Berkeley: University of California Press.

Hustak, C., & Myers, N. (2012). Involutionary momentum: Affective ecologies and the sciences of plant/insect encounters. *Differences*, 23(3), 74–118.

Hutchins, E. (1995). *Cognition in the wild.* Cambridge: MIT Press.

Jackall, R. (1988). *Moral mazes: The world of corporate managers.* New York: Oxford University Press.

Jameson, F. (1990). *Late marxism: Adorno, or, the persistence of the dialectic.* London: Verso.

Jarzabkowski, P., & Seidl, D. (2008). The role of meetings in the social practice of strategy. *Organization Studies, 29*(11), 1391–1426.

Jobs, S. (1989). The entrepreneur of the decade. An interview by George Gendron and Bo Burlingham, *Inc.* http://www.inc.com/magazine/19890401/5602.html

Jones, G., McLean, C., & Quattrone, P. (2004). Spacing and timing. *Organization, 11*(6), 723–741.

Jordan, G. (2011). *Clear cut: One woman's journey of life and in the body.* New York: Lantern Books.

Kaplan, S. (2011). Strategy and PowerPoint: An inquiry into the epistemic culture and machinery of strategy making. *Organization Science, 22*(2), 320–346.

Kasarda, J. D., & Lindsay, G. (2011). *Aerotropolis: The way we'll live next.* Houndsmills: Macmillan.

Kellner, D. (2003). *Media spectacle.* London: Routledge.

Kemp, P., & Dear, I. (2006). *The Oxford companion to ships and the sea: Over 2600 entries.* Oxford: Oxford University Press.

Kenny, K., & Fotaki, M. (2015). From gendered organizations to compassionate borderspaces: Reading corporeal ethics with Bracha Ettinger. *Organization, 22*(2), 183–199.

Keynes, J. M. (1936). *The general theory of employment interest and money.* London: Macmillan.

Khurana, R. (2007). *From higher aims to hired hands: The social transformation of American business schools and the unfulfilled promise of management as a profession.* Princeton: Princeton University Press.

Kim, W. C., & Mauborgne, R. (2005). *Blue ocean strategy.* Boston: Harvard Business School Press.

Kirksey, S., & Helmreich, S. (2010). The emergence of multispecies ethnography. *Cultural Anthropology, 25*(4), 545–576.

Kittler, F. A. (1999). *Gramophone, film, typewriter.* Stanford: Stanford University Press.

Klein, M. (1959). *Envy and gratitude: A study of unconscious sources.* London: Tavistock.

Knights, D. (1990). Subjectivity, power and the labour process. In D. Knights & H. Willmott (Eds.), *Labour process theory* (pp. 297–335). Basingstoke: Macmillan.

Knights, D. (2008). Myopic rhetorics: Reflecting epistemologically and ethically on the demand for relevance in organizational and management research. *Academy of Management Learning & Education, 7*(4), 537–552.

Knights, D., & Murray, F. (1994). *Managers divided: Organisation politics and information technology management.* Chichester: Wiley.

Knights, D., & Willmott, H. (1989). Power and subjectivity at work: From degradation to subjugation in social relations. *Sociology, 23*(4), 535–558.

Knights, D., & Willmott, H. (1999). *Management lives: Power and identity in work organizations*. London: Sage.

Knorr, C. K. (1997). Sociality with objects: Social relations in postsocial knowledge societies. *Theory, Culture & Society, 14*(4), 1.

Knox, H., O'Doherty, D. P., Vurdubakis, T., & Westrup, C. (2008). Enacting Airports: Space, movement and modes of ordering. *Organization, 15*(6), 869–888.

Knox, H., O'Doherty, D. P., Vurdubakis, T., & Westrup, C. (2010). The devil and customer relationship management: Informational capitalism and the performativity of the sign. *Journal of Cultural Economy, 3*(3), 339–359.

Knox, H., O'Doherty, D. P., Westrup, C., & Vurdubakis, T. (2015). Something happened: Spectres of organization/disorganization at the airport. *Human Relations, 68*(6), 1001–1020.

Knudsen, C. (2003). Pluralism, scientific progress, and the structure of organization theory. In H. Tousakas & C. Knudsen (Eds.), *The Oxford handbook of organization theory*. Oxford: Oxford University Press.

Kohn, E. (2013). *How forests think: Toward an anthropology beyond the human*. Berkeley: University of California Press.

Kondo, D. K. (1990). *Crafting selves: Power, gender, and discourses of identity in a Japanese workplace*. Chicago: University of Chicago Press.

Koolhaas, R. (2002). Junkspace. *October, 1*(100), 175–190.

Korczynski, M. (2003). Communities of coping: Collective emotional labour in service work. *Organization, 10*(1), 55–79.

Kornberger, M., & Clegg, S. R. (2004). Bringing space back in: Organizing the generative building. *Organization Studies, 25*(7), 1095–1114.

Kostera, M. (2007). *Organisational ethnography: Methods and inspirations*. Lund: Studentlitteratur.

Kracauer, S. (1999). The hotel lobby. *Postcolonial Studies, 2*(3), 289–297.

Kritzman, L. D. (1988). *Foucault: Politics, philosophy, culture: Interviews and other writings, 1977–1984*. New York: Routledge.

Laclau, E. (1990). *New reflections on the revolution of our time*. London: Verso.

Laclau, E., & Mouffe, C. (1985). *Hegemony and socialist strategy: Towards a radical democratic politics*. London: Verso.

Laing, R. D. (1967). *The divided self: An existential study in sanity and madness*. Harmondsworth: Penguin Books.

Land, C., Loren, S., & Metelmann, J. (2014). Rogue logics: Organization in the grey zone. *Organization Studies, 35*(2), 233–253.

Langdon, D. (2007). *Spon's architects' and builders' price*. Abingdon: Taylor Francis.

Latham, M. (1994). *Constructing the team: Joint review of procurement and contractual arrangements in the United Kingdom construction industry: Final report*. London: HMSO.

Latour, B. (1993). *We have never been modern*. Cambridge: Mass. Harvard University Press.

Latour, B. (1996). On actor-network theory: A few clarifications. *Soziale welt, 47*, 369–381.

Latour, B. (1999). On recalling ANT. In J. Law & J. Hassard (Eds.), *Actor network and after*. Oxford: Blackwell.

Latour, B. (2004). Why has critique run out of steam? From matters of fact to matters of concern. *Critical Inquiry, 30*(2), 225–248.

Latour, B. (2005a). *Reassembling the social: An introduction to actor-network-theory*. Oxford: Oxford University Press.

Latour, B. (2005b). 'Thou shall not freeze frame', or, how not to misunderstand the science and religion debate. In J. Proctor (Ed.), *Science, religion and the human experience* (pp. 27–48). New York: Oxford University Press.

Latour, B. (2007). Turning around politics: A note on Gerard de Vries' paper. *Social Studies of Science, 37*(5), 811–820.

Latour, B. (2013). *An inquiry into modes of existence: An anthropology of the moderns*. Cambridge, MA: Harvard University Press.

Latour, B., & Stengers, I. (2016). The sphinx of the work, forward to Etienne Souriau, *The different modes of existence* (trans: Beranek, E., & Howles, T.). Minneapolis: Univocal Publishing.

Latour, B., & Woolgar, S. (1979). *Laboratory life: The social construction of scientific facts*. Beverly Hills: Sage Publications.

Latour, B., & Yaneva, A. (2008). Give me a gun and I will make all buildings move: An ANT's view of architecture. In U. Staub & R. Geiser (Eds.), *Explorations in architecture: Teaching, design, research* (pp. 80–89). Basel/Boston: Birkhauser verlag ag.

Law, J. (1994). *Organizing modernity: Social ordering and social theory*. Oxford: Blackwell.

Law, J. (2004). *After method: Mess in social science research*. London: Routledge.

Law, J., & Benschop, R. (1997). Resisting pictures: Representation, distribution and ontological politics. *The Sociological Review, 45*(S1), 158–182.

Leach, E. R. (1964). *Anthropological aspects of language: Animal categories and verbal abuse*. Cambridge, MA: MIT Press.

Lecercle, J.-J. (1985). *Philosophy through the looking-glass: Language, nonsense, desire*. La Salle: Open Court.

Lee, N. (2001). Becoming mass: Glamour, authority and human presence. *The Sociological Review, 49*(S2), 174–188.

Lessig, L. (2004). *Free culture: How big media uses technology and the law to lock down culture and control creativity*. New York: Penguin Press.

Lévi-Strauss, C. (1963). *Totemism*. Boston: Beacon Press.

Lewis, M. W. (2000). Exploring paradox: Toward a more comprehensive guide. *Academy of Management Review, 25*(4), 760–776.

Linstead, S., & Höpfl, H. (2000). *The aesthetics of organization*. London: Sage.

Linstead, S., & Thanem, T. (2007). Multiplicity, virtuality and organization: The contribution of Gilles Deleuze. *Organization Studies, 28*(10), 1483–1501.

Linstead, S., Grafton, S. R., & Jeffcutt, P. (1996). *Understanding management*. London: Sage Publications.

Lofgren, O., & Ehn, B. (2010). *The secret world of doing nothing*. Berkeley: University of California Press.

Lok, J., & Willmott, H. (2014). Identities and identifications in organizations: Dynamics of antipathy, deadlock, and alliance. *Journal of Management Inquiry, 23*(3), 215–230.

Lomnitz, L. (1983). The scientific meeting: An anthropologist's point of view. *4S Review, 1*(2), 2–7.

Lorimer, J. (2016). Gut buddies: Multispecies studies and the microbiome. *Environmental Humanities, 8*(1), 57–76.

Lury, C., & Marres, N. (2015). Notes on objectual valuation. In M. Kornberger, L. Justesen, A. K. Madsen, & J. Mouritsen (Eds.), *Making things valuable*. Oxford: Oxford University Press.

Lyon, D. (2001). *Surveillance society: Monitoring everyday life*. Buckingham: Open University.

MacKenzie, D. A. (2006). *An engine, not a camera: How financial models shape markets*. Cambridge, MA: MIT Press.

MacKenzie, D. A., & Wajcman, J. (1985). *The social shaping of technology: How the refrigerator got its hum*. Milton Keynes: Open University Press.

MacKenzie, D. A., Muniesa, F., & Siu, L. (2007). *Do economists make markets?: On the performativity of economics*. Princeton: Princeton University Press.

Malafouris, L. (2013). *How things shape the mind: A theory of material engagement*. Cambridge, MA: The MIT Press.

Malcolmson, P. (2013). *Me and my hair: A social history*. Luton: Andrews UK.

Mangham, I. L., & Overington, M. A. (1987). *Organizations as theatre: A social psychology of dramatic appearances*. Chichester/New York: Wiley.

March, J. G. (2007). The study of organizations and organizing since 1945. *Organization Studies, 28*(1), 9–19.

Marcus, G. E. (1995). Ethnography in/of the world system: The emergence of multi sited ethnography. *Annual Review of Anthropology, 24*, 95–117.

Marcus, G. E. (2007). Ethnography two decades after writing culture: From the experimental to the baroque. *Anthropological Quarterly, 80*(4), 1127–1145.

Marres, N. (2014). The environmental teapot and other loaded household objects. In P. Harvey, E. C. Casella, G. Evans, H. Knox, C. McLean, E. B. Silva, N. Thoburn, & K. Woodward (Eds.), *Objects and materials: A Routledge companion*. London: Routledge.

Marres, N., & Lezaun, J. (2011). Materials and devices of the public: An introduction. *Economy and Society, 40*(4), 489–509.

Marx, K. (1954). *Capital: A critique of political economy*. London: Lawrence & Wishart.

Maurer, B. (2005). *Mutual life, limited: Islamic banking, alternative currencies, lateral reason*. Princeton: Princeton University Press.

Mauss, M. (1973). Techniques of the body. *Economy and Society, 2*(1), 70–88.

Mayo, E. (1945). *The social problems of an industrial civilization*. Boston: Division of Research, Graduate School of Business Administration, Harvard University.

McCabe, D. (2015). The Tyranny of distance: Kafka and the problem of distance in bureaucratic organizations. *Organization, 22*(1), 58–77.

McFall, L. (2009). Devices and desires: How useful is the 'new' new economic sociology for understanding market attachment? *Sociology Compass, 3*(2), 267–282.

McGuigan, J. (2009). *Cool capitalism*. London: Pluto Press.

McMurtrie, R. J. (2010). Bobbing for power: An exploration into the modality of hair. *Visual Communication, 9*(4), 399–424.

McRobbie, A. (2004). Notes on 'what not to wear' and post-feminist symbolic violence. *The Sociological Review, 52*, 97–109.

Mears, M. (2009). *Leadership elements: A guide to building trust*. New York: iUniverse.

Meek, J. (2015). The shock of the pretty: Mad men. *London Review of Books, 37*(7), 29–32.

Mehan, H., & Wood, H. (1975). *The reality of ethnomethodology*. New York: Wiley.

Mehran, A., & Donkin, A. (2005). *The terminal man*. Leicester: Ulverscroft.

Mensendieck, B. M. (1954). *Look better, feel better*. New York: Harper.

Meredith, J. R., & Mantel, S. J. (2011). *Project management: A managerial approach*. Hoboken: Wiley.

Middles, M. (2011). *Factory: The story of the record label*. London: Random House.

MIER (Manchester Independent Economic Review). (2009). *Understanding labour markets, skills and talent: Final report of project 5*. Manchester: MIER.

Miller, B. (2012) Is it leadership or an organization's culture that drives success?. MBA thesis, Manchester Business School, University of Manchester.

Miller, P., & Rose, N. (1997). Mobilizing the consumer: Assembling the subject of consumption. *Theory, Culture & Society, 14*(1), 1.

Miller, P., & Rose, N. (2008). *Governing the present: Administering economic, social and personal life*. Cambridge: Polity.

Mintzberg, H. (1973). *The nature of managerial work*. New York: Harper & Row.

Mintzberg, H. (2004). *Developing managers not MBAs: A hard look at the soft practice of managing and management development*. London: Prentice Hall.

Mitchell, T. (1991). The limits of the state: Beyond statist approaches and their critics. *The American Political Science Review, 85*, 77–96.

Mitchell, T. (2002). *Rule of experts: Egypt, techno-politics, modernity*. Berkeley: University of California Press.

Mitchell, T. (2008). Rethinking economy. *Geoforum, 39*(3), 1116–1121.

Mol, A. (1999). Ontological politics. A word and some questions. *The Sociological Review, 47*(S1), 74–89.

Mol, A. (2002). *The body multiple: Ontology in medical practice*. Durham: Duke University Press.

Mol, A. (2008). *The logic of care: Health and the problem of patient choice*. London: Routledge.

Monbiot, G. (2014). *Feral: Rewilding the land, the sea, and human life*. Chicago: University of Chicago Press.

Morand, D. A. (1995). The role of behavioural formality and informality in the enactment of bureaucratic versus organic organizations. *Academy of Management Review, 20*(4), 831–872.

Moreira, T. (2006). Heterogeneity and coordination of blood pressure in neurosurgery. *Social Studies of Science, 36*(1), 69–97.

Morgan, G. (1986). *Images of organization*. Beverly Hills: Sage Publications.

Morgan, G. (1993). *Imaginization: The art of creative management*. Newbury Park: Sage.

Morley, S. (2012). An office for human beings, worldarchitecturenews.com, 1 August 2012, last accessed 30 Oct 2013.

Morton, T. (2013). *Hyperobjects: Philosophy and ecology after the end of the world.* Minneapolis: University of Minnesota Press.

Muff, K., Dyllick, T., Drewell, M., North, J., Shrivastava, P., & Haertle, J. (2013). *Management education for the world: A vision for business schools serving people and planet.* Cheltenham: Edward Elgar.

Mullins, L. J., & Christy, G. (2013). *Management and organisational behaviour.* Harlow: Pearson.

Muniesa, F. (2007). Market technologies and the pragmatics of prices. *Economy and Society, 36*(3), 377–395.

Muniesa, F. (2014). *The provoked economy: Economic reality and the performative turn.* Abingdon: Routledge.

Muniesa, F., & Linhardt, D. (2011). Trials of explicitness in the implementation of public management reform. *Critical Perspectives on Accounting, 22*(6), 550–566.

Muniesa, F., & Trébuchet-Breitwiller, A.-S. (2010). Becoming a measuring instrument. *Journal of Cultural Economy, 3*(3), 321–337.

Munro, R. (1995). Managing by ambiguity: An archaeology of the social in the absence of management accounting. *Critical Perspectives on Accounting, 6*(5), 433–482.

Munro, I., & Huber, C. (2012). Kafka's mythology: Organization, bureaucracy and the limits of sensemaking. *Human Relations, 65*(4), 523–543.

Murphy, D. (2005). Boxing. In C. Jones & D. O'Doherty (Eds.), *Manifestos for the business school of tomorrow.* Turku: Dvalin Books.

Museum, D. (2009). *Fifty chairs that changed the world.* London: Conran Octopus.

Nader, L. (1972). Up the anthropologist – Perspectives gained from studying up. In D. Hymes (Ed.), *Reinventing anthropology.* New York: Pantheon Books.

Nancy, J. L. (2007). *Listening.* New York: Fordham University Press.

Nayek, A., & Beckett, A. (2008). Infantilized adults or confident consumers? Enterprise discourse in the UK retail banking industry. *Organization, 15*(3), 407–425.

Newton, R. (2006). *Project management step by step: The proven, practical guide to running a successful project, every time.* Harlow: Pearson/Prentice Hall Business.

Neyland, D. (2008). *Organizational ethnography.* London: Sage.

Nickson, D., & Korczynski, M. (2009). Editorial: Aesthetic labour, emotional labour and masculinity. *Gender, Work & Organization, 16*(3), 291–299.

Nicolini, D. (2012). *Practice theory, work, and organization: An introduction*. Oxford: Oxford University Press.

Noon, M., & Delbridge, R. (1993). News from behind my hand: Gossip in organizations. *Organization Studies, 14*(1), 23–36.

O'Doherty, D. P. (2002). *Subjugation and labour process deconstruction: The problematic status of order/disorder in the labour process*. Doctoral dissertation, University of Manchester: UMIST.

O'Doherty, D.P. (2005). David Knights and Hugh Willmott: The subjugation of identity and... and... and organization-to-come... *The Sociological Review, 53*(s1), 148–162.

O'Doherty, D. P. (2007). The question of theoretical excess: Folly and fall in theorizing organization. *Organization, 14*(6), 837–867.

O'Doherty, D. P. (2008). The blur sensation: Shadows of the future. *Organization, 15*(4), 535–561.

O'Doherty, D. P. (2009). Retrieving the missing subject in labour process analysis. In M. Alvesson, T. Bridgman, & H. Willmott (Eds.), *The Oxford handbook of critical management studies*. Oxford: Oxford University Press.

O'Doherty, D. (2015). Missing connexions: The politics of airport expansion in the United Kingdom. *Organization, 22*(3), 418–431.

O'Doherty, D. P. (2016a). Manners, taste, and etiquette: New practices of 'politesse' in business and management. In C. Steyaert, T. Beyes, & M. Parker (Eds.), *The Routledge companion to reinventing management education*. Abingdon: Routledge.

O'Doherty, D. P. (2016b). Feline politics in organization: The nine lives of Olly the cat. *Organization Online First*. doi:10.1177/1350508416629450.

O'Doherty, D. P., & Willmott, H. (2001). Debating labour process theory: The issue of subjectivity and the relevance of poststructuralism. *Sociology, 35*(2), 457–476.

O'Doherty, D. P., de Cock, C., Rehn, A., & Ashcraft, K. L. (2013). New sites/sights: Exploring the white spaces of organization. *Organization Studies, 34*(10), 1427–1444.

OGC (Office of Government Commerce). (2009). *Managing successful projects with PRINCE2*. London: The Stationery Office.

Orlikowski, W. J. (2007). Sociomaterial practices: Exploring technology at work. *Organization Studies, 28*(9), 1435–1448.

Papadopoulos, D. (2010). Insurgent posthumanism, *Ephemera, 10*(2), 134–151

Parker, M. (2000a). The sociology of organizations and the organization of sociology: Some reflections on the making of a division of labour. *The Sociological Review, 48*(1), 124–146.

Parker, M. (2000b). *Organizational culture and identity: Unity and division at work*. London: Sage.

Parker, M. (2002). *Against management: Organization in the age of managerialism*. Oxford: Polity.

Parker, M. (2010). The sclerosis of criticism: A handbook of critical management studies? *Critical Policy Studies, 4*(3), 297–302.

Parker, M. (2013). What is to be done? CMS as a Political Party, in Malin, V. Murphy, J. & Siltaoja, M. (Eds.), *Getting Things Done: Dialogues in Critical Management Studies*. Bingley, Bradford: Emerald, 165–181.

Pascoe, D. (2001). *Airspaces*. London: Reaktion Books.

Passoth, J. H., & Rowland, N. (2010). Actor-network state. *International Sociology, 25*(6), 818–841.

Peace, D. (2004). *GB84*. London: Faber and Faber.

Penttinen, E. (2007). *Globalization, prostitution and sex trafficking: Corporeal politics*. Abingdon: Routledge.

Perec, G. (2010). *An attempt at exhausting a place in Paris*. Adelaide: Wakefield Press.

Peters, T. J. (1994). *Thriving on chaos: Handbook for a management revolution*. New York: Knopf.

Peters, T. J., & Waterman, R. H. (1982). *In search of excellence: Lessons from America's best-run companies*. New York: Harper & Row.

Petroski, H. (1992). *The evolution of useful things: How everyday artifacts—From forks and pins to paperclips and zippers—Came to be as they are*. New York: Alfred A. Knopf.

Pfeffer, J. (1981). *Power in organizations*. Marshfield: Pitman.

Pfeffer, J. (1993). Barriers to the advance of organizational science: Paradigm development as a dependent variable. *The Academy of Management Review, 18*(4), 599–620.

Pfeffer, J. (2009). Renaissance and renewal in management studies: Relevance regained. *European Management Review, 6*(3), 141–148.

Pfeffer, J., & Fong, C. T. (2002). The end of business schools? Less success than meets the eye. *Academy of Management Learning & Education, 1*(1), 78–95.

Pfeffer, J., & Fong, C. T. (2004). The business school 'business': Some lessons from the US experience. *Journal of Management Studies, 41*(8), 1501–1520.

Philo, C., & Wilbert, C. (2000). *Animal spaces, beastly places: Critical geographies*. London: Routledge.

Phillips, S. (2010). Toward a research practice: Frederick Kiesler's design-correlation laboratory. *Grey Room, 38*, 90–120.

Pickering, A. (1995). *The mangle of practice: Time, agency, and science*. Chicago: University of Chicago Press.

Pierides, D., & Woodman, D. (2012). Object-oriented sociology and organizing in the face of emergency: Bruno Latour, Graham Harman and the material turn. *The British Journal of Sociology., 63*, 662–679.

Pine, B. J., & Gilmore, J. H. (1999). *The experience economy: Work is theatre & every business a stage*. Boston: Harvard Business Press.

Pirsig, R. M. (1974). *Zen and the art of motorcycle maintenance: An inquiry into values*. New York: Morrow.

Pollner, M. (1987). *Mundane reason: Reality in everyday and sociological discourse*. Cambridge [Cambridgeshire]: Cambridge University Press.

Power, M. (1997). *The audit society: Rituals of verification*. Oxford: Oxford University Press.

Prasad, A. (2013). Historicity and multi-sited ethnography: Fieldwork in the age of postmodernism and globalization. In *Academy of management proceedings* (Vol. 2013, No. 1, p. 15231). St. Louis: Academy of Management.

Prashad, V. (2002). *Fat cats & running dogs: The Enron stage of capitalism*. London: Zed.

Pullen, A., & Rhodes, C. (2014). Corporeal ethics and the politics of resistance in organizations. *Organization, 21*(6), 782–796.

Quattrone, P. (2015). Governing social orders, unfolding rationality, and Jesuit accounting practices: A procedural approach to institutional logics. *Administrative Science Quarterly, 60*(3), 411–445.

Quilley, S. (2000). Manchester first: From municipal socialism to the entrepreneurial city. *International Journal of Urban and Regional Research, 24*(3), 601–615.

Randles, S., & Mander, S. (2009). Aviation, consumption and the climate change debate: 'Are you going to tell me off for flying?'. *Technology Analysis & Strategic Management, 21*(1), 93–113.

Reed, M. (1997). In praise of duality and dualism: Rethinking agency and structure in organizational analysis. *Organization Studies, 18*(1), 21–42.

Reedy, P., & Learmonth, M. (2009). Other possibilities? The contribution to management education of alternative organizations. *Management Learning, 40*(3), 241–258.

Rehn, A. (2013). *Dangerous ideas: When provocative thinking is your most valuable asset*. Cork: BookBaby.

Rhodes, C. (2001). *Writing organization:(Re)presentation and control in narratives at work (vol. 7)*. Amsterdam: John Benjamins Publishing.

Rhodes, C., & Pullen, A. (2010). Editorial: Neophilia and organization. *Culture and Organization, 16*(1), 1–6.

RIBA (Royal Institute of British Architects). (2004). *Manchester: Shaping the city*. London: RIBA Enterprises.

Riles, A. (2001). *The network inside out.* Ann Arbor: University of Michigan Press.

Riles, A. (2011). *Collateral knowledge: Legal reasoning in the global financial markets*. Chicago: University of Chicago Press.

Ringler, W. A. (1979). "Beware the cat" and the beginnings of English fiction. *Novel: A Forum on Fiction, 12*(2), 113–126.

Ritzer, G. (1993). *The McDonaldization of society: An investigation into the changing nature of contemporary social life*. London: Sage.

Roach, J. R. (2007). *It*. Ann Arbor: University of Michigan Press.

Robb, J. (2010). *The north will rise again: Manchester music city 1976–1996.* London: Aurum.

Robbe-Grillet, A. (1958). The Voyeur (trans: Howard, R.). New York: Grove Press.

Robinson, T. (2006). *Connemara: Listening to the wind.* Dublin: Penguin Ireland.

Robson, K. (1992). Accounting numbers as "inscription": Action at a distance and the development of accounting. *Accounting, Organizations and Society, 17*(7), 685–708.

Robson, B. (2002) Mancunian ways: The politics of regeneration. In J. Peck,& K. Ward (Eds.), *City of revolution: Restructuring Manchester.* Manchester: Manchester University Press.

Rodrigues, S. B., & Collinson, D. L. (1995). 'Having fun'?: Humour as resistance in Brazil. *Organization Studies, 16*(5), 739.

Roethlisberger, F. J., & Dickson, W. J. (1939). *Management and the worker.* Cambridge, MA: Harvard University Press.

Rogelberg, S. G., Scott, C., & Kello, J. (2007). The science and fiction of meetings. *MIT Sloan Management Review, 48*(2), 18.

Rogers, K. M. (2001). *The cat and the human imagination: Feline images from Bast to Garfield.* Ann Arbor: University of Michigan Press.

Rogers, K. M. (2006). *Cat.* London: Reaktion Books.

Rosen, M. (1988). You asked for it: Christmas at the bosses expense. *Journal of Management Studies, 25*(5), 463–480.

Rosen, M. (2000). *Turning words, spinning worlds: Chapters in organizational ethnography.* Amsterdam: Harwood Academic Publishers.

Rosenthal, P., & Peccei, R. (2007). 'The work you want, the help you need': Constructing the customer in jobcentre plus. *Organization, 14*(2), 201–223.

Rosler, M. (1998). *In the place of the public: Observations of a frequent flier.* Ostfildern-Ruit: Cantz.

Rowlinson, M., & Hassard, J. (2011). How come the critters came to be teaching in business schools? Contradictions in the institutionalization of critical management studies. *Organization, 18*(5), 673–689.

Rubin, R. S., & Dierdorff, E. C. (2009). How relevant is the MBA? Assessing the alignment of required curricula and required managerial competencies. *Academy of Management Learning & Education, 8*(2), 208–224.

Sacks, H. (1992). *Lectures on conversation.* 2 vols. Edited by Gail Jefferson with introductions by Emanuel A. Schegloff. Oxford: Blackwell.

Sadler, W., & Haskins, E. (2005). Metonymy and the metropolis: Television show settings and the image of New York City. *Journal of Communication Inquiry, 29*(3), 195–216.

Samuelson, P. A., & Nordhaus, W. D. (1998). *Economics.* Boston: Irwin/McGraw-Hill.

Sandberg, J., & Tsoukas, H. (2016). Practice theory: What it is, its philosophical base, and what it offers organization studies. In R. Mir, H. Willmott, & M. Greenwood (Eds.), *The Routledge companion to philosophy in organization studies.* Abingdon: Routledge.

Savage, M. (2013). The 'social life of methods': A critical introduction. *Theory, Culture & Society, 30*(4), 3–21.

Savage, M., & Burrows, R. (2007). The coming crisis of empirical sociology. *Sociology, 41*(5), 885–899.

Sayed, M. E. E., Harold, L., & Volville, F. (1997). Why is a third of your time wasted in meetings? *Journal of Management Development, 16*(9), 672.

Scarry, E. (1985). *The body in pain: The making and unmaking of the world.* New York: Oxford University Press.

Schaberg, C. (2012). *The textual life of airports: Reading the culture of flight.* London: Continuum.

Schaberg, C. (2015). *The end of airports.* New York: Bloomsbury.

Schatzki, T. (2006). On organizations as they happen. *Organization Studies, 27*(12), 1863–1873.

Schivelbusch, W. (1980). *The railway journey: Trains and travel in the 19th century.* Oxford: Blackwell.

Schmitt, B. (2000). *Experiential marketing: To get customers to relate to your brand.* New York: Free.

Schön, D. A. (1983). *The reflective practitioner: How professionals think in action.* New York: Basic Books.

Schwartzman, H. B. (1989). *The meeting: Gatherings in organizations and communities.* New York: Plenum Press.

Scott, J. C. (1998). *Seeing like a state: How certain schemes to improve the human condition have failed.* New Haven: Yale University Press.

Serres, M. (1982). *The parasite.* Baltimore: John Hopkins University.

Shortt, H. (2012). Identityscapes of a hair salon: Work identities and the value of visual methods. *Sociological Research Online, 17*(2), 22.

Shortt, H. (2015). Liminality, space and the importance of 'transitory dwelling places' at work. *Human Relations, 68*(4), 633–658.

Shortt, H., & Warren, S. (2012). Fringe benefits: Valuing the visual in narratives of hairdressers' identities at work. *Visual Studies, 27*(1), 18–34.

Shukin, N. (2009). *Animal capital: Rendering life in biopolitical times.* Minneapolis: University of Minnesota Press.

Sievers, B. (1996). 'Accounting for the Caprices of Madness. Narrative Fiction as a Means of Organizational Transcendence'. *Arbeitspapiere des Fachbereichs Wirtschaftswissenschaft der Bergischen Universität Wuppertal,* (176).

Skålén, P. (2009). Service marketing and subjectivity: The shaping of customer-oriented employees. *Journal of Marketing Management, 25*(7–8), 795–809.

Skeggs, B. (2005). The making of class and gender through visualizing moral subject formation. *Sociology, 39*(5), 965–982.

Slepian, M. L., Ferber, S. N., Gold, J. M., & Rutchick, A. M. (2015, January 01). The cognitive consequences of formal clothing. *Social Psychological and Personality Science, 6*(6), 661–668.

Sloterdijk, P. (1988). *Critique of cynical reason.* London: Verso.

Sloterdijk, P. (2014). *In the world interior of capital: For a philosophical theory of globalization.* Cambridge, UK: Polity Press.

Smith, W. K., & Lewis, M. W. (2011). Toward a theory of paradox: A dynamic equilibrium model of organizing. *Academy of Management Review, 36*(2), 381–403.

Sosteric, M. (1996). Subjectivity and the labour process: A case study in the restaurant industry. *Work Employment & Society, 10*(2), 297–318.

Souriau, E. (1943). *Les différents modes d'existence.* Paris: Presses Universitaires de France.

Spicer, A., & Böhm, S. (2007). Moving management: Theorizing struggles against the hegemony of management. *Organization Studies, 28*(11), 1667–1698.

Spicer, A., Alvesson, M., & Kärreman, D. (2009). Critical performativity: The unfinished business of critical management studies. *Human Relations, 62*(4), 537–560.

Spicer, A., Alvesson, M., & Kärreman, D. (2016). Extending critical performativity. *Human Relations, 69*(2), 225–249.

Staincliffe, C. (2002). Northern Quarter. In Chlebik, J. et al pp.130–139

Stallybrass, P., & White, A. (1986). *The poetics and politics of transgression*. London: Methuen.

Stark, D., & Paravel, V. (2008). PowerPoint in public. *Theory, Culture and Society, 25*(5), 30–55.

Stengers, I. (2010). *Cosmopolitics vol. I.*. Minneapolis: University of Minnesota Press.

Stengers, I. (2011). *Cosmopolitics vol. 2.*. Minneapolis: University of Minnesota Press.

Steyaert, C., Beyes, T., & Parker, M. (2016)(Eds.). *The Routledge companion to reinventing management education*. Abingdon: Routledge.

Stoddart, S. F. (2011). *Analyzing Mad men: Critical essays on the television series*. Jefferson: McFarland & Company.

Strathern, M. (1988). *The gender of the gift: Problems with women and problems with society in Melanesia*. Berkley: University of California Press.

Strathern, M. (1991). *Partial connections*. Savage: Rowman & Littlefield Publishers.

Strathern, M. (1996). Cutting the network. *Journal of the Royal Anthropological Institute, 2*, 517–535.

Strathern, M. (1999). *Property, substance, and effect: Anthropological essays on persons and things*. London: Athlone Press.

Strati, A. (1999). *Organization and aesthetics*. London: Sage.

Sturdy, A. (1998). Customer care in a consumer society: Smiling and sometimes meaning it? *Organization, 5*(1), 27–53.

Sturdy, A., & Wright, C. (2011). The active client: The boundary-spanning roles of internal consultants as gatekeepers, brokers and partners of their external counterparts. *Management Learning, 42*(5), 485–503.

Sturdy, A., Grugulis, I., & Willmott, H. (Eds.). (2001). *Customer service: Empowerment and entrapment*. Houndmills/Basingstoke: Palgrave Macmillan.

Taylor, M. (1995). Rhizomic fields of interstanding. *Tekhnema, 2*, 24–36.

Taylor, P. J. (2004). *World city network: A global urban analysis*. London: Routledge.

Taylor, P., & Bain, P. (1999). 'An assembly line in the head': Work and employee relations in the call centre. *Industrial Relations Journal, 30*(2), 101–117.

Taylor, S., & Spicer, A. (2007). Time for space: A narrative review of research on organizational spaces. *International Journal of Management Reviews, 9*(4), 325–346.

ten Bos, R. (2000). *Fashion and utopia in management thinking.* Amsterdam: John Benjamins Pub.

Thanem, T. (2011). *The monstrous organization.* Cheltenham/Gloucester: Edward Elgar.

Thompson, P. (1983). *The nature of work: An introduction to debates on the labour process.* London: Macmillan.

Thompson, M., & Willmott, H. (2015). The social potency of affect: Identification and power in the immanent structuring of practice. *Human Relations, 68*, 1–24.

Thrift, N. (1999). The place of complexity. *Theory, Culture & Society, 16*(3), 31–69.

Thrift, N. (2008a). The material practices of glamour. *Journal of Cultural Economy, 1*(1), 9–23.

Thrift, N. J. (2008b). *Non-representational theory: Space, politics, affect.* London: Routledge.

Townley, B. (1994). *Reframing human resource management: Power, ethics and the subject at work.* London: Sage.

Trasko, M. (1994). *Daring do's: A history of extraordinary hair.* Paris: Flammarion.

Trentmann, F. (2006). *The making of the consumer: Knowledge, power and identity in the modern world.* Oxford: Berg.

Tsing, A. L. (2014). Blasted landscapes (and the gentle arts of mushroom picking). In E. Kirksey (Ed.), *The multispecies salon.* Durham: Duke University Press.

Tsing, A. L. (2015). *The mushroom at the end of the world: On the possibility of life in capitalist ruins.* Princeton: Princeton University Press.

Tsoukas, H. (2005). *Complex knowledge: Studies in organizational epistemology.* New York: Oxford University Press.

Tsoukas, H., & Knudsen, C. (2003). *The Oxford handbook of organization theory.* Oxford: Oxford University Press.

Tufte, E. R. (2003). *The cognitive style of PowerPoint.* Cheshire: Graphics Press.

Turner, V. W. (1969). *The ritual process: Structure and anti-structure.* London: Routledge & Kegan Paul.

Tyler, M., & Cohen, L. (2010). Spaces that matter: Gender performativity and organizational space. *Organization Studies, 31*(2), 175–198.

Tyler, M., & Hancock, P. (2001). Flight attendants and the management of gendered organizational bodies. *Explorations in Sociology, 59*, 25–34.

Ulmer, G. L. (1985). *Applied grammatology: Post(e)-pedagogy From Jacques Derrida to Joseph Beuys*. Baltimore: Johns Hopkins University Press.

van Gils, W., & Kraaykamp, G. (2008). The emergence of dual-earner couples. *International Sociology, 23*(3), 345–366.

van Maanen, J. (1988). *Tales of the field: On writing ethnography*. Chicago: University of Chicago Press.

van Maanen, J. (2011). Ethnography as work: Some rules of engagement. *Journal of Management Studies, 48*(1), 218–234.

Van Marrewijk, A., & Yanow, D. (2010). *Organizational spaces: Rematerializing the workaday world*. Cheltenham: Edward Elgar Publishing.

Verran, H. (2001). *Science and an African logic*. Chicago: University of Chicago Press.

Viveiros de Castro, E. V. (1992). *From the enemy's point of view: Humanity and divinity in an Amazonian society*. Chicago: University of Chicago Press.

Viveiros de Castro, E. V. (1998). Cosmological deixis and Amerindian perspectivism. *Journal of the Royal Anthropological Institute, 4*(2), 469–488.

Warhurst, C., Nickson, D., Witz, A., & Cullen, A. M. (2000). Aesthetic labour in interactive service work: Some case study evidence from the new Glasgow. *Service Industries Journal, 20*, 1–18.

Warner, M. (2002). *Publics and counterpublics*. New York: Zone Books.

Warner, M. (2007). Kafka, Weber and organization theory. *Human Relations, 60*(7), 1019–1038.

Wasthulber, J. (1991). History of domestic cats and cat breeds. In N. C. Pedersen (Ed.), *Feline husbandry* (pp. 1–59). Goleta: Am. Vet. Publ.

Watson, T. (1994). *In search of management: Culture, chaos and control in managerial*. London: Routledge.

Watson, T. J. (2011). Ethnography, reality, and truth: The vital need for studies of 'how things work 'in organizations and management. *Journal of Management Studies, 48*(1), 202–217.

Webber, R. (2009). Response to 'the coming crisis of empirical sociology': An outline of the research potential of administrative and transactional data. *Sociology, 43*(1), 169–178.

Weber, B. R. (2009). *Makeover TV: Selfhood, citizenship, and celebrity*. Durham: Duke University Press.

Weick, K. (1985). Chaos & Cosmos: Sense & nonsense in electronic contexts. *Organisational Dynamics, 14*(2), 50–64.

Weick, K. E. (1993). The collapse of Sensemaking in organizations: The Mann Gulch disaster. *Administrative Science Quarterly, 38*(4), 628–652.

Weick, K. E., & Roberts, K. H. (1993). Collective mind in organizations: Heedful interrelating on flight decks. *Administrative Science Quarterly, 38*(3), 357–381.

Weiner, M. (1981). *English culture and the decline of the industrial spirit, 1850–1980*. Cambridge: Cambridge University Press.

Wells, E. S., Rosen, L. W., & Walshaw, S. (1997). Use of feral cats in psychotherapy. *Anthrozoos: A Multidisciplinary Journal of The Interactions of People & Animals, 10*(2–3), 2–3.

Westwood, R. I., & Rhodes, C. (2007). *Humour, work, and organization*. London: Routledge.

White, D. A. (1996). 'It's working beautifully!' Philosophical reflections on aesthetics and organization theory. *Organization, 3*(2), 195–208.

White, K. (2013). And say the cat responded? Getting closer to the Feline Gaze. *Society & animals, 21*(1), 93–104.

Whittle, A., & Spicer, A. (2008). Is actor network theory critique? *Organization Studies, 29*(4), 611–629.

Whittle, A., Mueller, F., Lenney, P., & Gilchrist, A. (2014). Interest-talk as access-talk: How interests are displayed, made and down-played in management research. *British Journal of Management, 25*(3), 607–628.

Wieder, D. L. (1974). *Language and social reality: The case of telling the convict code*. The Hague: Mouton.

Wilkes, J. K. (2009). *The role of companion animals in counseling and psychology: Discovering their use in the therapeutic process*. Springfield: Charles C Thomas Publisher.

Williams, C. (2003). Sky service: The demands of emotional labour in the airline industry. *Gender, Work & Organization, 10*(5), 513–550.

Willmott, H. (1990). Subjectivity and the dialectics of praxis: Opening up the core of labour process analysis. In D. Knights & H. Willmott (Eds.), *Labour process theory* (pp. 336–378). Basingstoke: Macmillan.

Willmott, H. (1993a). Strength is ignorance; slavery is freedom: Managing culture in modern organizations. *Journal of Management Studies, 30*(4), 515–552.

Willmott, H. (1993b). Breaking the paradigm mentality. *Organization Studies, 14*(5), 681–719.

Willmott, H. (2005). Theorizing contemporary control: Some post-structuralist responses to some critical realist questions. *Organization, 12*(5), 747–780.

Willmott, H. (2015). Why institutional theory cannot be critical. *Journal of Management Inquiry, 24*(1), 105–111.

Wilson, J. F. (1992). *The Manchester experiment: A history of Manchester Business School, 1965–1990*. London: Chapman.

Wittel, A. (2001). Toward a network sociality. *Theory, culture & society, 18*(6), 51–76.

Witz, A., Warhurst, C., & Nickson, D. (2003). The labour of aesthetics and the aesthetics of organization. *Organization, 10*(1), 33–54.

Witzel, M., & Warner, M. (Eds.). (2013). *The Oxford handbook of management theorists*. Oxford: Oxford University Press.

Wolkowitz, C. (2006). *Bodies at work*. London: Sage.

Wood, D., & Beck, R. J. (1994). *Home rules*. Baltimore: Johns Hopkins University Press.

Woolgar, S. (1991). The turn to technology in social studies of science. *Science, Technology & Human Values, 16*(1), 20–50.

Wray-Bliss, E. (2002). Abstract ethics, embodied ethics: The strange marriage of Foucault and positivism in labour process theory. *Organization, 9*(1), 5–39.

Wu, F. (2003). Transitional cities. *Environment and Planning A, 35*(8), 1331–1338.

Yaneva, A. (2005). Scaling up and down. *Social Studies of Science, 35*(6), 867–894.

Yaneva, A. (2009). *The making of a building: A pragmatist approach to architecture*. Oxford: Peter Lang.

Yanow, D. (2009). Organizational ethnography and methodological angst: Myths and challenges in the field. *Qualitative Research in Organizations and Management: An International Journal, 4*(2), 186–199.

Yates, J. (1989). *Control through communication the rise of system in American management*. Baltimore: Johns Hopkins University Press.

Yates, J., & Orlikowski, W. (2007). The PowerPoint presentation and its corollaries: How genres shape communicative action in organizations, In M. Zachry, & C. Thralls (Eds.), *Communicative practices in workplaces and the professions* (pp. 67–92) Amityville: Baywood.

Ybema, S., Yanow, D., Wels, H., & Kamsteeg, F. H. (2008). *Organizational ethnography: Studying the complexity of everyday life*. London: Sage Publications.

Ybema, S., Yanow, D., Wels, H., & Kamsteeg, F. H. (2009). *Organizational Ethnography: Studying the Complexity of Everyday Life*. London: Sage Publications.

Young, S. B., & Wells, A. (2011). *Airport planning and management*. New York: McGraw-Hill.

Young, M., Higham, J. E., & Reis, A. C. (2014). 'Up in the air': A conceptual critique of flying addiction. *Annals of Tourism Research, 49*, 51–64.
Zdatny, S. (Ed.). (1999). *Hairstyles and fashion: A hairdresser's history of Paris, 1910–1920*. Oxford/New York: Bloomsbury Academic.
Zdatny, S. (2006). *Fashion, work, and politics in modern France*. Abingdon: Palgrave Macmillan.
Zill, D. (2004). *Boy George & culture club*. Berlin: Schwarzkopf und Schwarzkopf.
Zizek, S. (1989). *The sublime object of ideology*. London: Verso.
Zuffi, S. (2007). *The cat in art*. New York: Abrams.
Zwick, D., & Denegri, K. J. (2009). Manufacturing customers. *Journal of Consumer Culture, 9*(2), 221–247.

Legal Cases

Jarvis, J., & Sons -v- Westminster Corporation. (1978). 7 BLR 64 HL.
Mariner International Hotels Ltd v Atlas Ltd. (2007). 10 HKCFAR 246.
Neville, H. W. (Sunblest) Ltd -v-William Press and Son Ltd. (1981). 20 BLR 78

Index

D. O'Doherty, *Reconstructing Organization*,
DOI 10.1057/978-1-137-48922-7

W

Y

Z

MIX
Papier aus verantwortungsvollen Quellen
Paper from responsible sources
FSC® C105338

Printed by Books on Demand, Germany